Jazz Pedagogy
The Jazz Educator's Handbook and Resource Guide

by J. Richard Dunscomb and Dr. Willie L. Hill, Jr.

Stream or download the video & audio content for this book.
To access, visit: **alfred.com/redeem**

Enter this code:

00-0582B-62678351

Project Manager: **Pete BarenBregge**
Production Coordinator: **Hank Fields**
Art Design and Layout: **Nancy Rehm** and **Carmen Fortunato**
Video/Graphics Coordinator: **Karl Bork**
Copy Editor: **Nadine DeMarco**
Editorial Consultant: **Julia Fraser**
Editorial Assistant: **Marcia Dunscomb**

Video Authoring and Production:
Dave Olive
2nd Camera and DVD Authoring:
Ed Favara
Vertical Hold, Inc
3004 West Aquilla
Tampa, FL 33629
813-251-5931

alfred.com

ISBN-10: 0-7579-9125-4
ISBN-13: 978-0-7579-9125-7

Jazz Timeline Photos Courtesy of Michael Ochs Archives

Jazz Pedagogy
The Jazz Educator's Handbook and Resource Guide

by J. Richard Dunscomb and Dr. Willie L. Hill, Jr.

PREFACE

ABOUT THE AUTHORS

ABOUT THE AUTHORS

J. Richard Dunscomb is recognized nationally and internationally as one of the leading experts in the field of jazz music and jazz education. He is active as a clinician, author, guest conductor, adjudicator, and consultant. Mr. Dunscomb created and designed the jazz program at Florida International University, where he served as professor of music and director of jazz studies.

Mr. Dunscomb has been recognized with many honors and awards throughout his career. He was elected to the International Association for Jazz Education (IAJE) Hall of Fame in 1992. He was awarded the prestigious Medal of Honor by the Midwest International Band and Orchestra clinic in 1999. He has served as president of the 8,000-member IAJE and is currently the international coordinator for the organization. He is active as a guest conductor with numerous all-state and honors jazz bands throughout the U.S. and abroad. He is on the board of directors for the Midwest Clinic, an annual event with more than 12,000 worldwide participants. Mr. Dunscomb has more than 200 publications to date.

Dr. Willie L. Hill, Jr., is director of the fine arts center at the University of Massachusetts–Amherst and is a professor in music education. He received a B.S. degree from Grambling State University and earned M.M. and Ph.D. degrees from the University of Colorado–Boulder. He is currently the president of the National Association for Music Education (MENC), past-president of the International Association for Jazz Education (IAJE), a member of the writing team for MENC's Vision 2020, and a member of the national board of directors for Young Audiences, Inc.

Dr. Hill was a professor in music education and the assistant dean of the College of Music at the University of Colorado–Boulder for 11 years and director of education for the Thelonious Monk Institute. Prior to his tenure at the University of Colorado, Dr. Hill taught instrumental music and was music supervisor for 20 years in the Denver Public Schools.

As a professional musician, he has performed with Liza Minnelli, Lena Horne, Lou Rawls, Ben Vereen, Lola Falana, Johnny Mathis, Sammy Davis Jr., Dizzy Gillespie, and many others. He is co-author of *Learning to Sight-Read Jazz, Rock, Latin, and Classical Styles* (Ardsley House Publications) and the author of *The Instrumental History of Jazz* (N2K, Inc.) and *Approaching the Standards* (Belwin Jazz/Alfred Publishing Co.). Dr. Hill is listed in the first edition of *Who's Who Among Black Americans* and *Who's Who Among International Musicians*.

Acknowledgments

I thank my wife, Marcia Dunscomb; my friend and editor, Pete BarenBregge; Bob Dingley; Jose Diaz; Jerry Tolson; Shelly Berg; Julia Fraser; Mike Orta; Nicky Orta; Lindsey Blair; Remy Taveras; Ignacio Berroa; Gary Campbell; Bill McFarlin; Bob Mintzer; and Chris Dorsey. Thanks also to the graduate students in the 2001 FIU Jazz Pedagogy class for their research assistance: Carlos Averhoff, Victor Payano, Sakiko Kikucki, Fabricio Monteagudo, and Michael Kaplan.

J. Richard Dunscomb
Tyrone, Georgia
July 2002

I thank my wife, Beverly Hill; Pete BarenBregge; Bob Dingley; Julie Fifield; Fred Tillis; June Hinckley; Shelly Berg; Julia Fraser; Marcia Dunscomb; Jose Diaz; Arthur Dawkins; Chris Vadala; Bob Montgomery; Pete Olstead; Alan Kaplan; Jennifer Shelton-Barnes; Steve Kirkland; Dave Detwiler; and Kim McCord.

Dr. Willie L. Hill, Jr.
Amherst, Massachusetts
July 2002

PREFACE

Yes, you can teach jazz! *Jazz Pedagogy: The Jazz Educator's Handbook and Resource Guide* (with video) will assist you in creating and maintaining a rewarding jazz program. It is an ideal textbook for university courses in jazz pedagogy as well as an important resource for all jazz educators, novice or experienced.

Learning about jazz music and how to teach it is just as essential to music educators as learning and teaching baroque, classical, romantic, and contemporary music styles. Yet a lack of understanding about jazz has left many music educators ill equipped to teach it successfully and has even caused some of them to avoid the music itself.

Barriers to jazz education need not exist. Desire, interest, and patience are among the most necessary requirements to becoming a successful jazz educator. Jazz music developed into an art form that was passed down aurally, either in person or by recordings, through many generations. The vital steps of jazz teaching—listening, singing, and then playing—are incorporated throughout this publication and blend well with current educational philosophies.

This book begins with the very first steps to building an outstanding jazz program and then gradually expands into more advanced topics. You will find realistic approaches to such challenging topics as scheduling, budgeting, rehearsal techniques, swing and Latin styles, selecting music, the jazz ensemble, the jazz combo, the role of each instrument, how the rhythm section works, improvisation, technology, vocal jazz, festivals, adjudication, and tours. The extensive Resource Guide section provides significant jazz reference information and uses the Internet as an ongoing reference tool that provides Web site listings. The innovative online media provides audio/video demonstrations of rehearsal techniques and jazz concepts with middle school, high school, and university jazz ensembles; an in-depth video on how to teach jazz improvisation; selected videos on how to understand and improve the rhythm section; and a series of excerpted jazz arrangements to use as models for jazz concepts and styles.

This publication draws upon our more than 60 years of teaching at the public school and university levels plus our collective performing and administrative experience. The text has been further enhanced with the input of other leading experts in the field of jazz education. Jazz education is an exciting and rewarding profession. Enjoy the process, and help jazz music live through your students!

J. Richard Dunscomb   Dr. Willie L. Hill, Jr.

Chapter 1

WHY MUSIC EDUCATION? WHY JAZZ EDUCATION?

by Dr. Willie L. Hill, Jr.

Music has played such an important role in my life. It has taught me how to live, respect others, laugh, experience beauty through different sets of eyes and ears, and have an endearing love for humanity. Most important, however, music has filled my life with incredible sounds and emotions connected with those sounds, experiences that transcended words. Music has communicated with me like nothing else in my life. It was early on when I felt that music had the power to connect me to history, tradition, and my heritage. I knew that studying and experiencing an art form such as music would give me insight into my own culture and the cultures of others. Thus, it would help me be more appreciative of what the world has to offer, as well as help me become more sensitive to cultural issues. In short, I felt it would enable me to experience humanity at its best. I'm convinced that it turned on my senses and emotions and helped me reach into the depths of my soul so that I could experience inner peace and tranquility.

MUSIC EDUCATION

My experiences with music were not happenstance. I did not just suddenly listen to music with great understanding. I was taught to listen to and make music. My music teacher fueled my desire to hear more, play more, learn more. The more I learned, the more I heard and the more I understood. I wanted to share those types of experiences with others, just as my music teacher shared his passion for music with me. I decided to make music education my career.

How many special teachers do you remember from your elementary, middle, or high school days? If music is a significant part of your life today, most likely your general music, vocal, orchestra, or band teacher was a big factor in making that happen.

The thing I remember most about my band teacher was his love of music. He knew the power of music to open up our minds and spirits in his classroom—the sense of pride that it gave each of us when we finally mastered a rhythm or a difficult passage on our instruments. Most important, he knew the fun, pleasure, and enjoyment we experienced each day in that special room—the band room. He knew we would do better in school because his class made school a more exciting and worthwhile place to spend our time. He knew that belonging to the band meant we "belonged" in school, that our connection with school was a positive one. We didn't have time for getting into trouble or doing drugs. We were too busy making music before, during, and after school. Music was his passion, so it was our passion.

I'm not sure if my music teacher was even concerned that music enhanced the skills needed to learn math, science, English, and other academic subjects. However, I am convinced that he knew it would help us stay focused, concentrate, and work as a team to make the music sound great. We need more sensitive and passionate teachers like him in our classrooms to serve as role models for the students of today and tomorrow.

National Standards for Music Education

My music teacher did more than inspire us, however. He taught us the basics of performing, reading music, playing a varied repertoire, understanding theory fundamentals, and listening with understanding and discrimination. As music educators today, we have that same responsibility to teach the basics, to ensure that our students receive the highest quality musical experiences that the school curriculum can offer. Those experiences have to include high expectations presented in an educational arena that is optimal for the learner and taught by qualified teachers. We have an advantage that my music teacher did not. We have a roadmap that outlines the basics of a high-quality experience in music, the National Standards for Music Education. The National Standards for Music Education can guide us toward the goal for which all quality music programs should strive, the comprehensive development of music knowledge and skills within our students.

The National Standards show school principals, teachers, parents, students, and other concerned citizens what every child should know and be able to do in music by the end of his or her fourth-, eighth-, and twelfth-grade years of studying music. Fortunately, most school districts throughout the United States that offer instrumental, general, and vocal music opportunities for their students have some variation of these standards in place. The results of having a common vision of what the basics of quality music instruction should include have proven to be most effective. This is especially true when the musical experiences have been sequentially taught by a qualified music educator, someone who has been trained to deliver and assess content based upon the National Standards for Music Education as presented by MENC (The National Association for Music Education). Those nine voluntary content standards written by a blue-ribbon Music Task Force of MENC and adopted in March 1994 are:

1. Singing, alone and with others, a varied repertoire of music.

2. Performing on instruments, alone and with others, a varied repertoire of music.

3. Improvising melodies, variations, and accompaniment.

4. Composing and arranging music within specified guidelines.

5. Reading and notating music.

6. Listening to, analyzing, and describing music.

7. Evaluating music and music performances.

8. Understanding relationships between music, the other arts, and disciplines outside the arts.

9. Understanding music in relation to history and culture.

Why Is Teaching Music Important?

You may ask, "Why is it so important that music be taught well and comprehensively?" After all, lots of people who have not had the benefit of a music education enjoy music. Music is interwoven throughout the fabric of our society. Just turn on the radio or television, go see a movie, walk into a mall or department store, or go to a football or basketball game. Can you imagine a world without music at these events? Think about videos, symphony halls, dance halls, church services, patriotic ceremonies, and so on—all without music? What about the many jobs that have been created as a result of music? Can you possibly conceive of the impact on tourism? Anything that is this pervasive, this influential, should and must be taught—and taught well so that its impact is considered intellectually as well as emotionally.

Music is a part of almost everyone's life on this planet and has always played a role in all cultures throughout mankind. Besides being significant for its ancillary values, it is significant for its *historical* and *aesthetic* values as an art form. Therefore, it should be a part of the basic curriculum for every child and serve as a core experience in all students' lives. In *Vision 2020: The Housewright Symposium on the Future of Music Education,* music educators said this: "Whenever and wherever humans have existed, music has existed also. Since music occurs only when people choose to create and share it, and since they always have done so and no doubt always will, music clearly must have important value for people." (Madsen, p. 219)

Because music is so important, it is vital that we are clear and vocal about the necessity of its inclusion in a complete educational experience for our young people. There are times when music educators need more tangible ammunition than the intrinsic value that arguments about aesthetics might offer. Although it can be quite a daunting task to convince principals, school board members, and even parents that music is a worthwhile subject to be seriously studied along with math, science, English, and other academic subjects in this climate of tight budgets, it must be done. Let's examine the research relating to the benefits of a music education.

Research Results

Within the past five to ten years, there has been an abundance of data supporting the benefits of a well-structured, meaningful music education for all students. The research is very clear about the important role music can play in the lives of young people. However, as we share this information with others, we must always keep in mind that music is an art form that can stand on its own merit—not only for its ancillary benefits. Music should be taught and experienced for the beauty and joy that it brings to our daily lives.

In a publication published by VH1 called *Save the Music*, researchers showed that a very strong relationship exists between a student's success in academic achievement (reading, math, SAT scores, and so on), social development skills (self-esteem, self-discipline, ability to work with others, and so on), and their participation in strong music education programs (Music Education = Brain Power, 2000). MENC states that "the study of music helps students achieve success in school, develop intelligence, success in society, and success in life." (The Benefits of the Study of Music, 2000)

Let's examine additional research findings. Is this just happenstance?
- Research studies in two Ohio school districts measure total creativity scores four times higher for elementary students in fine arts programs, such as music, than for students who were not involved in the fine arts programs. (Murfee, 1996)
- Research shows that students who are involved in music achieve higher in reading and math. (Hamann & Walker, 1995)
- Statistics show that high school music students have higher grade point averages than non-music students in the same school. In Southern California, the overall grade point average for music students was 3.59, and for non-music students the grade point average was 2.91. (Horne, 1981)

Engaging students in music-making has proven to have an incredibly positive impact on students' social, emotional, spiritual, and academic success in life. All one has to do is look at the research pointing to higher test scores, lower dropout rates, lower gang-related involvement, and fewer drug and alcohol abuse cases of students participating in music classes and those who are not involved in the study of music—the correlations are astonishing. Looking at the statistics alone behooves parents to support music in the classroom by encouraging their children's participation and by encouraging decision-makers in school districts to offer music to all students, because every child deserves a high-quality, well-rounded education.

Communication

As music educators, we know why music is important, but we need to be able to tell our colleagues, administrators, community leaders, and students a clear, precise, compelling, and passionate story about the important role music and the other arts play in the lives of our students and communities. Communicating the importance of music will assist us in these ways:
- Facilitate the recruitment and retention of qualified teachers.
- Promote greater parental involvement and awareness; promote greater community involvement and awareness.
- Increase the possibilities for significant partnership and alliance building in our quest for excellence in schools.

Benefits of Music Study

Here are discussion points for you to use when talking with school board members, principals, parents, students, and others in your respective communities about your program:
- Music has the power to awaken a child's imagination. It can help make the learning experience more meaningful, interesting, and fulfilling.

- Music helps to ensure that students develop a richer and deeper appreciation for what the world has to offer.
- Music offers students a variety of ways to express themselves and communicate with others throughout the world.
- Music helps develop self-discipline, self-control, and cooperation through teamwork. Music students constantly strive for excellence. Every note must be near perfect if the performance is going to be successful.
- Music supports diversity and tolerance in our students. They learn about different cultures, traditions, and their heritage through the history of music.
- Music contributes to students becoming well-rounded, open-minded, passionate, and creative thinkers in the workplace.
- Music promotes better study habits in our students.
- Music is just plain ol' fun!

JAZZ EDUCATION

I have made it clear that music education includes teaching about culture. The National Standards also address the importance of including diverse genres and making cultural connections as a part of a total music education program. Many believe that America's most significant and original contribution to the world of music is jazz. Although it is important that music programs include the music of many cultures in their selection process, it is essential that we also include the music of our own culture—and that music, in my mind, is jazz.

Jazz education is about teaching students skills in the art of improvisation, helping them acquire knowledge in the jazz idiom (history, theory, arranging, composition, and so on), and leading them to understand the fusion of cultures and music traditions that made and continue to make jazz a reflection of the diversity in America. Early players like Buddy Bolden and Louis Armstrong and later ones like Dizzy Gillespie and Thelonious Monk were primarily self-taught. They learned tunes "trial by fire"—at nightclubs and jam sessions; it was on-the-job training and working with great mentors. Others like Johnny Dodds and Jimmie Noone (in the 1920s) and those from a later generation—Miles Davis, Cannonball Adderley, and John Coltrane—were formally trained in grade schools, in military service organizations, by private teachers, and at universities.

Can Jazz Be Taught?

One question that has been batted around for many years is "Can jazz be taught?" *You bet!*

Excellent examples of younger lions and lionesses today who have gone through public schools/colleges/universities and made their marks in jazz history are Wynton and Branford Marsalis, Joshua Redman, Terrence Blanchard, Kenny Garrett, Roy Hargrove, Geri Allen, Regina Carter, Diane Reeves, Diana Krall, Christian McBride, Ryan Kisor, Jeff "Tain" Watts, Jim Snidero, Danilo Perez, and many others. Of course, these individuals had wonderful mentors, excellent teachers, incredible drive, and a strong love for the music.

As a fledgling music educator some thirty years ago, I remember being asked by my principal to develop a jazz education program at my junior high school. Wow, what an opportunity! The orchestra and concert band programs were very strong, but the jazz program was weak. One big problem, even though I was excited about the opportunity, was that I had very limited expertise in working with small or large jazz ensembles. I felt the need to get busy learning the hows, whys, whats, whens, whos, and wheres 〜 to jazz education.

 music educators, I had no formal experience in learning about jazz in high school or at the 'aved the tenor saxophone in small combos (garage bands) throughout high school and demic classes or performance experiences were offered at my small college in 〜g those days.

entrating on developing my own musicianship in the jazz idiom.

I began playing in a variety of small jazz combos and dance bands. I joined the Musicians Union to play as many gigs as possible and to meet and hear other jazz artists. I visited many classrooms of colleagues who were successful jazz educators. I attended conferences that were jazz-oriented and joined the National Association of Jazz Educators (NAJE), now the International Association for Jazz Education (IAJE). I took classes in jazz pedagogy, theory, history, and performance. I felt the need to develop the knowledge, skill, and confidence to teach this art form that I had grown to love so dearly— jazz. I knew that I had to develop my aural skills and build a personal jazz vocabulary if I was to become an effective jazz educator. By going through this process, I would have a better chance at articulating these concepts to my students. It worked!

Congressional Recognition for Jazz

In 1987, Representative John Conyers Jr. of Michigan was able to persuade the House of Representatives to pass a resolution designating jazz "a rare and valuable national American treasure." Representative Conyers brought to the attention of those in attendance that jazz artists were very effective individuals in "bringing disparate groups of people and countries together." Before this resolution, Congress had never expressed its appreciation of those talented artists who had championed this unique American art form. It was made evident that jazz musicians had always served as ambassadors to enhance this country's image since the beginning of the Cold War and were even sanctioned by the State Department. So, Congressman Conyers felt it was time to give proper recognition to jazz.

House Congressional Resolution 57 states:

Whereas jazz has achieved preeminence throughout the world as an indigenous American music and art form, bringing to this country and the world a uniquely American musical synthesis and culture through the African-American experience, and--

(1) Makes evident to the world an outstanding artistic model of individual expression and democratic cooperation within the creative process, thus fulfilling the highest ideals and aspirations of our republic,

(2) Is a unifying force, bridging cultural, religious, ethnic, and age differences in our diverse society,

(3) Is a true music of the people, finding its inspiration in the cultures and most personal experiences of the diverse peoples that constitute our Nation,

(4) Has evolved into a multifaceted art form which continues to give birth to and to nurture new stylistic idioms and cultural fusions,

(5) Has had a historic, pervasive, and continuing influence on other genres of music both here and abroad,

(6) Has become a true international language adopted by musicians around the world as a music best able to express contemporary realities from a personal perspective, and

(7) Has provided a creative paradigm broadly influential on other contemporary art forms, including dance, literature, theater, film, and the visual arts;

Whereas this great American musical art form has not yet been properly recognized nor accorded the institutional status commensurate with its value and importance;

Whereas it is important for the youth of America to recognize and understand jazz as a significant part of their cultural and intellectual heritage;

Whereas there exists no effective national infrastructure to support and preserve jazz;

Whereas documentation and archival support required by such a great art form has yet to be systematically applied to the jazz field;

Whereas it is in the best interest of the national welfare and all of our citizens to preserve and celebrate this unique art form;

Whereas the continuing development of new technologies and avenues of communication offer formidable possibilities as well as challenges to artists and audiences;

Whereas recent research has proven the positive cognitive impact of jazz education and appreciation on childhood development;

Whereas there is an increasing emphasis on public-private partnerships at the cutting edge of support for cultural institutions and the arts; and

Whereas the last decade has seen the passing of all but a few of the artists who made definitive contributions in the development of traditional jazz, swing era jazz, and modern jazz: Now, therefore be it

Resolved by the House of Representatives (the Senate concurring), That it is the sense of the Congress that jazz is hereby designated as a rare and valuable national American treasure to which we should devote our attention, support, and resources to make certain it is preserved, understood, and promulgated. (http://thomas.loc.gov/cgi-bin/query/z?c105:H.CON.RES.57:)

In passing this resolution, the U.S. government gave a stamp of approval to the significant role jazz has played in this country's history. Jazz is a valuable and worthwhile art form that students at all levels of instruction should have the opportunity to study in public schools and at the college/university level. It is a valid musical art form and it deserves support. It is music that originated in this country from the African, Latin, European, brass bands, and ragtime experience. Today, look at the impact jazz has on television, commercials, movies, CDs, synthesizers, and the Internet—all having a tremendous impact on the lives of people throughout the world.

Studying Jazz Is Important

Researchers, performers, teachers, and students are studying jazz at every level of the curriculum—elementary through college/university. The inclusion of jazz study at all levels has had a tremendous impact on expanding the musical horizons of students who are exposed to and immersed in this music's history, organizational forms, and diverse styles and genres. Students have the opportunity to develop strong musicianship by being responsible for that 1st alto, 2nd tenor, drum, or bass part. This is a challenging musical experience young people don't get in their regular band or orchestra classes—it enhances the whole notion of being responsible individuals. Also, it helps them become better all-around players.

Some music educators believe that jazz classes embody the perfect environment in which to teach all of the National Standards for Music Education. Students have to become keen listeners as well as good readers; they have to have excellent performance skills, good rhythmic sense, and great intonation; and they must be able to improvise and play in a variety of styles. Playing in small jazz combos as well as larger jazz ensembles can help build a student's self-confidence and self-esteem and promote teamwork.

Think about when your students perform at the top of their form at a concert or jazz festival. Or how about when one of your students or your ensemble is singled out for an award or certificate for outstanding performance. Obviously students and programs that get recognition are tailor-made advocacy and public relations vehicles, but more important than public accolades is the kind of learning that is embodied in creating jazz. Pride in performance is amplified in the jazz experience because of its very nature—small group teamwork, individual responsibility, reliance upon others, and individual responsiveness to the whole group.

The Essence of Jazz? Improvisation!

If you were to ask me what is the essence of jazz as a musical genre, I would have to say it is improvisation. In the National Standards for Music Education, improvisation is Content Standard Three described as "Improvising melodies, variations, and accompaniment." Remember Mozart and Bach? Improvisation was one of their most valued abilities. In Bach's time there were contests to see who was the most creative improviser. This is not a new concept in music-making, but it is a skill area in which many musicians today feel less than competent. Somewhere along the line in the process of promoting music literacy, we stopped teaching improvisation. In many programs, it is the single most neglected area of music instruction.

I believe that all music students, not just those in jazz programs, need to have some ability to improvise, but it is a must for jazz programs. Perhaps we simply need to think differently about improvisation. Instead of seeing it as something formidable, just think of it as a means to create, to come up with new ideas, or as a way to express oneself without the benefit of written notes. Listen to small children sing and play instruments; they improvise naturally. We can help our students regain that same musical freedom they felt early in life.

The exciting thing about improvisation is that everyone can do it; everyone has imaginative powers and creative talents to make music extemporaneously. We must realize that everyone does not yet have our need to be "right." They are interested and excited about learning to improvise and to be musically creative. For others, creativity may take time to awaken and may have to be nurtured by a variety of enlightening factors. Just as speakers need to have a verbal vocabulary to be able to speak extemporaneously, musicians need a musical vocabulary to be able to improvise. Building that vocabulary can go a long way in giving them the confidence and the skills they need to be successful improvisers. They also need musical models to emulate, to give them musical ideas, and to give them a sense of how improvisation is done. Listening to recordings, attending concerts, and hearing you improvise all can contribute to building that musical vocabulary.

Teaching young people to improvise is an art, but it is also a process, just as teaching them to read music is a process. By teaching the basics, offering a safe environment in which they can experiment, and providing listening models to stimulate their creativity, you will lay the groundwork for developing that ability. It may take work on your part to feel comfortable with your own improvisational skills, but the pay-off with your students will be immeasurable.

Our Future

We as jazz and music educators must be concerned with the training and nurturing of our future jazz artists and audiences. Some of our students may go on to become performers, a talented few may be composers or arrangers, and many will continue to play in small groups, community organizations, church orchestras, or wherever. We always hope that those we teach will continue to be lifelong music-makers. Whether or not they keep up their performance abilities, however, we know they will in some way be music consumers in their adult lives. We must emphasize that they all can and should support jazz as an art form by attending live concerts, buying recordings, and encouraging its place in their communities.

The future of jazz in this country depends upon having educated and supportive audiences. Jazz traditions have always grown out of our diversity, and they will continue to do so. Jazz has the power to be a cultural binding force, but for some it is an acquired taste. Helping our young people acquire a taste for jazz, an understanding of its complexity, and an appreciation of its traditions is vital to our future. If we don't do it, who will?

Jazz!

America's Original Art Form

by Marcia F. Dunscomb

By the time of the big band era (1930s–1945), jazz was the most popular music in America. Jazz was the music played on the radio, the top-selling recordings, the music played on jukeboxes, and the music of the 1930s version of music videos: "soundies" played on machines called panorams. America was in love with big bands.

Often called swing bands, hundreds of big bands were touring the country playing one-nighters in ballrooms where a thousand or more people had come to listen and dance to the infectious beat of the music. The public knew the bandleaders, the sidemen, and the singers by name and by their sound. Just as avid major-league sports fans know when a player is traded, the public knew when an important sideman moved from one band to another. Some bands played in a style that was "hot" (more syncopation, improvisation, and swinging eighth notes) while others played "sweet." Some bands were more about entertainment than music, but each band had an identifiable sound and style.

Origins of Jazz

But where did jazz come from? How did this music get its start? When the Civil War ended and slavery was abolished, the southern United States was rich with many types of music. The city of New Orleans, one of the most important cities in the evolution of jazz, housed one of the first opera houses in the United States as well as two symphony orchestras. Military installations in and around New Orleans had brass marching bands. The many social clubs had their own band to march in parades as well as to perform at the lodge for dancing and entertainment. Houses of prostitution, legal in New Orleans at this time, hired piano players to entertain the guests in the parlor. Music was an important part of all religious services and in all aspects of life.

The Piano, the Voice, and Small Ensembles

Elements from all of these sources blended in the melting pot that would become jazz. The music began to develop into jazz in three areas: solo piano music, vocal music, and small instrumental ensembles.

After the abolishment of slavery, the classically trained Creole musicians in New Orleans began to perform with the self-taught musicians who were descendants of slaves. Self-taught boogie-woogie pianists influenced classically trained ragtime piano players. The emotionally charged singers, singing of the strife of everyday life, influenced all who heard them. Instrumentalists began to imitate the sound of the voice and its ability to bend the pitch.

Solo Piano Music

Highly syncopated "ragtime" was usually composed piano music in rondo form with even eighth notes. Before there was any recorded music, Scott Joplin's ragtime compositions were best-sellers in sheet music and piano roll formats. Boogie-woogie was improvised piano music in 12-bar blues form with swinging eighth notes. Art Tatum, James P. Johnson, and others blended elements from ragtime and boogie-woogie into a new style called stride. From ragtime, stride borrowed the "root-chord" left hand and syncopation. From boogie-woogie, stride borrowed swinging eighth notes, improvisation, and emotion.

Vocalists—Blues Singers

African-Americans working in the cotton and sugar cane fields would sing to ease the pain and boredom of their task, incorporating African traditions such as falsetto and call-and-response. As slaves they had been forced to attend the protestant worship services of the plantation owners where they learned gospel and spiritual songs. The earliest vocalists working as entertainers were often unaccompanied or self-accompanied on the banjo (an African instrument) or guitar. Later they began to be accompanied by small combos (combination of instruments). Sixteen-bar forms evolved into the new musical form, the 12-bar blues.

Early Instrumental Ensembles

Marching bands and brass bands were an important part of life at the turn of the twentieth century. Parades were held for many occasions, including funerals. After a parade, a brass band would go to their lodge and play for dancing.

The instrumentation of the marching band was the instrumentation of the early combos: The cornet, clarinet and trombone played the melody while the snare drum, tuba (brass bass), and banjo provided the rhythm section. As the groups began to perform more in club settings than in parades, the instrumentation changed. The tuba was replaced by the string bass, the piano was added, the guitar replaced the banjo, and the snare drum began to build into the drum set with bass drum and cymbals.

The style of the early instrumental combo was with even eighth notes and a two-beat bass pattern. The cornet, the loudest instrument prior to electronic amplification, usually played the melody. The clarinet wove a countermelody as the trombone emphasized the chord changes with its characteristic smears. Performances featured collective improvisation with each performer contributing to the ensemble.

It was not until Louis Armstrong, with his amazing abilities, that a soloist began to be featured. The "root-chord" of the stride pianists caused the beat emphasis to shift from the first and third beats to the second and fourth.

Employment Opportunities

As employment opportunities in the northern states attracted African-Americans to cities such as Detroit, Chicago, and New York, the music followed them. Riverboats traveling the Mississippi carried the music to other cities, such as St. Louis and Kansas City. The Volstead Act (Prohibition) prompted the closing of many places of employment in New Orleans, causing musicians to leave the city. Clubs operated by members of organized crime, serving alcohol during Prohibition, became a source of employment for jazz musicians. Many of these clubs, called speakeasies, were located in Chicago and New York City. When Congress repealed the Volstead Act, making alcohol legal again, the public wanted to dance to the music they had been dancing to in the speakeasies, so ballrooms began to be built throughout the country.

Evolution From Combos to Big Bands

The music was still acoustic, but playing in the larger ballrooms required more sound volume. The only way to add more volume to an acoustic group was to add more musicians. The combo with one each cornet (or trumpet), clarinet, and trombone plus rhythm section began to grow into an ensemble with horn *sections* (trumpet section, clarinet/saxophone section, trombone section) plus rhythm section. Because a saxophone is louder than a clarinet, it was used with or in place of the clarinets.

There was no written music for the early jazz instrumental combo because a combo of six musicians can improvise successfully. A jazz orchestra with ten to twenty musicians needs arrangements to get the best sound, so the arranger became an important member of the orchestra. One of the first important arrangers was Fletcher Henderson, who wrote first for his own ensemble (a who's who of jazz musicians) and later provided arrangements for Benny Goodman's orchestra.

Big Band's Golden Era Ends

Many historians disagree about the causes of the end of the big band era, but it was most likely a combination of many events. Musically, there was little opportunity to improvise when playing big band charts and jazz musicians wanted more musical freedom. America's involvement in World War II resulted in many musicians enlisting in the military or being drafted. With resources such as gasoline and automobile production diverted to the war effort, keeping big bands touring became impossible. Other factors such as a musicians' strike and recording ban only added to the problem.

New Styles Emerge

Small groups began to perform a new style, which became known as bebop, that featured much more improvisation, unfamiliar melodies, fast tempos, and use of extreme ranges of the instruments. Musicians who played bebop successfully had to have complete command of their instruments and many new musical ideas. Not all musicians wanted to play bebop, so other styles began to emerge, such as cool jazz. Many of the jazz clubs on the East Coast focused on the intense bebop style, while on the West Coast, the jazz clubs centered on the more relaxed cool jazz style. Of course, there were notable exceptions to this generalization.

Another generalization is that classical music is the composer's art while jazz belongs to the performer. Because each musician brings new ideas to the music and each performance contains fresh energy and musical ideas, jazz is always evolving, always blending one style with another, always remaining new.

Bebop's Influences

After bebop was introduced, it influenced every jazz style that followed. Journalists dubbed one style as hard bop with variations known as straight-ahead or mainstream. This style included elements of bebop blended with gospel, soul, blues, and more. The result was a return to the emotional music of earlier times.

Other musicians experimented with mixing elements of jazz with elements of rock 'n' roll or R&B, resulting in jazz-rock fusion. Still other musicians wanted freedom from forms, chord changes, meters, and so on, and began to play free jazz. Latin rhythms from Brazil, Cuba, Puerto Rico, and the Caribbean are blended with elements of bebop to create the style known generally as Latin jazz or more specifically by the individual style, such as Afro-Cuban jazz. Musicians from all over the world are performing jazz and blending musical elements from their respective countries.

The Future of Jazz

The final chapter will never be written. Because the heart of jazz is based on today's musicians bringing new ideas and energy to the music, it will always be evolving. Jazz of the past will always be important, while jazz of the future is waiting for today's musicians to show us the way.

JAZZ HISTORY TIMELINE

by Dr. Willie L. Hill, Jr.

(See pages 16–27)

RAGTIME

1897:
Storyville opens
in New Orleans

1901:
Victrola introduced

1903:
First powered airplane flight
by the Wright brothers

1906:
First radio broadcast

1912:
Titanic sinks

1914:
WWI begins
Panama Canal opens

1915:
First transconti-nental
telephone call

1896

Important cities in the ragtime period:
Kansas City, Chicago

Characteristics

- Highly syncopated
- Ragged time feel
- Written music
- Strict tempo
- Form and harmony important
- Performed on piano

Composer
Scott Joplin
1868–1917

The Entertainer

Maple Leaf Rag

Musicians

Eubie Blake
1883–1983
W. C. Handy
1873–1958
Scott Joplin
1868–1917
Joseph Lamb
1887–1960
James Scott
1886–1938
Tom Turpin
1873–1922

EARLY JAZZ

1917:
First jazz recording by
Original Dixieland Jazz Band

1918:
WWI ends

1919:
Prohibition of alcohol

1920:
First radio station
KDKA, Pittsburgh

1925:
Charleston dance craze

1927:
Sound for
motion pictures

1929:
Stock market crash,
Great Depression begins

1917   1929

Important cities in early jazz:
New Orleans, Chicago, New York

Characteristics

- Roots: blues, ragtime, and
  brass band literature
- Combo style of performance
- Collective improvisation
  (polyphonic)
- Two-beat feel
- Musicians had specific roles
  in ensemble

Composer
Louis Armstrong
1901–1971

Struttin' With Some Barbeque

West End Blues

Musicians & Bands

Louis Armstrong
1901–1971
Sidney Bechet
1897–1959
Bix Beiderbecke
1903–1931
Fletcher Henderson
1898–1952
Jimmie Lunceford
1902–1947
Jelly Roll Morton
1890–1941
King Oliver
1885–1938
Kid Ory
1886–1973

The Creole Jazz Band
The Hot Five
The Hot Seven
Original Dixieland
Jazz Band
Red Hot Peppers

Jelly Roll Morton
1890–1941

Bix Beiderbecke
1903–1931

SWING

1933:
FDR, President

1935:
Benny Goodman
"Let's Dance" radio program

1935:
Gershwin's
Porgy and Bess opens

1936:
Jesse Owens wins four
gold medals at Berlin Olympics

1939:
Germany invades Poland, WWII begins

1930

Important cities in the swing era:
Kansas City, Chicago, New York

Characteristics

- Large ensembles
- Swinging eighth notes
- Solo improvisation
- Written arrangements
- Steady rhythmic pulse
- Riffs and shout choruses
- Full saxophone section

Composer
Duke Ellington
1899–1974
Mood Indigo
It Don't Mean a Thing
(If It Ain't Got That Swing)

Musicians

Harry "Sweets" Edison
1915–1999
Duke Ellington
1899–1974
Coleman Hawkins
1904–1960
Fletcher Henderson
1898–1952
Earl Hines
1903–1983
Art Tatum
1909–1956
Thomas "Fats" Waller
1904–1943
Mary Lou Williams
1910–1981
Lester Young
1909–1959

Thomas "Fats" Waller
1904–1943

SWING

| 1940: Great Depression ends | 1941: Attack on Pearl Harbor | 1941: Penicillin first used to treat humans | 1944: D. Day at Normandy | 1944: Glenn Miller vanishes over English Channel | 1945: Atomic bomb, WWII ends |

1941   1945

Band Leaders
Count Basie
Cab Calloway
Tommy Dorsey
Billie Eckstine
Duke Ellington
Benny Goodman
Lionel Hampton
Fletcher Henderson
Harry James
Andy Kirk
Jimmie Lunceford
Jay McShann
Glenn Miller
Benny Moten
Don Redman
Artie Shaw
Chick Webb
Paul Whiteman

Compositions
Air Mail Special
I'm Getting Sentimental Over You
Jumpin' at the Woodside
King Porter Stomp
Mood Indigo
Moten Swing
One O'Clock Jump
Satin Doll
Shiny Stockings
Sing, Sing, Sing
Stompin' at the Savoy
Take the "A" Train
The Stampede
Wrappin' It Up

Glenn Miller
1904–1944

Count Basie
1904–1984

Vocalists
Blues, Swing, and Beyond

Louis Armstrong
Ernie Andrews
Tony Bennett
Ray Charles
June Christie
Nat King Cole
Ella Fitzgerald
Eddie Jefferson
Johnny Hartman
Billie Holiday
Shirley Horn
Peggy Lee
Carmen McCrae
Mark Murphy
Frank Sinatra
Bessie Smith
Sarah Vaughan
Dinah Washington
Joe Williams

BEBOP

1945: Charlie Parker collaborates with Dizzy
Gillespie to perform what would become bebop

1947: Parker records
Scrapple From the Apple

1949:
Birdland opens

1945   1949

Important cities in the bebop era:
New York

Characteristics

- Fast-paced tempos
- Small combos
- Complex harmonies, melodies, and rhythms
- Riffs and improvisation
- Unison lines
- Clipped phrase endings
- Greater use of dissonance
- Listening (not for dancing)
- Performed in small clubs
- Head charts

Composer
Charlie "Bird" Parker
1920–1955

Anthropology

Confirmation

Ornithology

Musicians

Dizzy Gillespie
1917–1993
Dexter Gordon
1923–1990
J. J. Johnson
1924–2001
Thelonious Monk
1917–1982
Charlie Parker
1920–1955
Oscar Peterson
b. 1925
Bud Powell
1924–1966
Max Roach
b. 1925

Dizzy Gillespie
1917–1993

COOL JAZZ

1949: Miles Davis/Gil Evans
Birth of the Cool

1949

Important cities in the cool jazz era:
Los Angeles

Characteristics

- Lighter and softer sounds
- Shorter improvisations
- Slow to fast tempos
- Little vibrato
- Simpler melodies and rhythms
- Greater use of arrangements
- Use of classical instruments
  (flute, clarinet, bass clarinet, French horn)

Composer
Dave Brubeck
b. 1920

Blue Rondo à la Turk

Take Five

Musicians

Chet Baker
1929–1988
Dave Brubeck
b. 1920
Miles Davis
1926–1991
Paul Desmond
1924–1977
Bill Evans
1929–1980
Stan Getz
1927–1991
Gerry Mulligan
1927–1996
Shorty Rogers
b. 1924
Bud Shank
b. 1926

1954: School segregation outlawed by the U. S. Supreme Court

1955: Montgomery bus boycott

1955: Bird dies.

1955

Important Groups

Dizzy Gillespie Sextet
Dexter Gordon Quartet
Thelonious Monk Trio
Charlie Parker Quintet
Charlie Parker and Dizzy Gillespie Quintet
Oscar Peterson Trio
Bud Powell Trio
Max Roach/Clifford Brown Quintet

Compositions

Afternoon in Paris

Billie's Bounce

Criss Cross

Donna Lee

Evidence

Groovin' High

In Walked Bud

Ko-Ko

Manteca

A Night in Tunisia

Now's the Time

Parisian Thoroughfare

'Round Midnight

Shaw Nuff

COOL JAZZ

1950–1953: Korean War

1950: Beat era begins

1950: USSR and China sign a 30-year pact

1952: First electric guitar by Les Paul

1955: Art Blakey & The Jazz Messengers

1955

Important Groups

Chet Baker Quartet
Dave Brubeck Quartet
Gerry Mulligan Quartet
Miles Davis Nonet
Modern Jazz Quartet

Compositions

All Blues

Bernie's Tune

Boplicity

Con Alma

Coup de Gras

Django

Move

So What

Subconscious Lee

Walkin' Shoes

Miles Davis
1926–1991

HARD BOP

1957: Little Rock, Arkansas race riots; Russians launch Sputnik

1958: U.S. launches Explorer; Jet airline service begins

1962: U.S. astronaut John Glenn orbits the earth

1956   1968

Important cities in the hard bop era:
New York, Philadelphia, Detroit, San Francisco

Characteristics

- Tightly arranged tunes
- Tenor sax, trumpet, piano, bass, and drums
- Hard-driving rhythms
- Emotional emphasis
- Original forms
- Funk, soul, blues, and gospel-derived
- Latin elements often employed

Composer
John Coltrane
1928–1967

Blue Train

Giant Steps

Musicians

Cannonball Adderley
1928–1975
Art Blakey
1919–1991
Clifford Brown
1930–1956
John Coltrane
1928–1967
Miles Davis
1926–1991
Joe Henderson
b. 1937
Freddie Hubbard
b. 1938
Charles Mingus
1922–1979
Sonny Rollins
b. 1930
Horace Silver
b. 1928
McCoy Tyner
b. 1938

Sonny Rollins
b. 1930

Clifford Brown
1930–1956

FREE JAZZ

1960:
Sit-ins against segregation begin

1963: March on Washington D.C.; President Kennedy assassinated

1964: Civil Rights Act of 1964 prohibits job discrimination on the basis of sex, color, race, national origin, and religion

1964:
Coltrane records *A Love Supreme*

1968: Dr. Martin Luther King Jr. assassinated; Robert Kennedy assassinated

1960   1968

Important cities in the free jazz era:
Los Angeles, New York

Characteristics

- Acoustic
- Experimentation with new textures and tonal colors
- Free, collective improvisation
- Few predetermined harmonies
- Unusual instrumentation (double quartet)
- Steady tempo is not an issue
- Sketchy ensemble arrangements
- Visual effects

Composer
Ornette Coleman
b. 1930

Free Jazz

Lonely Woman

Musicians and Groups

Albert Ayler
1936–1970
Lester Bowie
b. 1941
Anthony Braxton
b. 1945
Don Cherry
b. 1936
Ornette Coleman
b. 1930
Eric Dolphy
1928–1964
Sun Ra
1914–1993
Cecil Taylor
b. 1929
Art Ensemble of Chicago
World Saxophone Quartet

FUSION

1969: U.S. troops
withdraw from Vietnam

1969: Miles Davis ushers in
fusion era with *Bitches Brew*

1971:
Louis Armstrong dies

1972:
Watergate scandal

1974: Duke Ellington dies,
President Nixon resigns

1969   1979

Important cities in the fusion era:
Los Angeles, San Francisco, New York

Characteristics

- Synthesizer effects
- Electronic keyboard
- Electric bass
- Steady rhythm
- Straight eighth notes
- Rock beats
- Intricate unison melodies
- Vamp section
- Modal harmonies

Composer
Herbie Hancock
b. 1933

Cantaloupe Island

Dolphin Dance

Watermelon Man

Musicians and Groups

Gary Burton
b. 1943
Chick Corea
b. 1941
Miles Davis
1926–1991
Keith Jarrett
b. 1945
Pat Metheny
b. 1954
Wayne Shorter
b. 1933
Joe Zawinul
b. 1932

The Brecker Brothers
Headhunters
Jeff Lorber Group
The Mahavishnu
Orchestra
The Pat Metheny Group
Return to Forever
Steps Ahead
Weather Report
The Yellowjackets

Wayne Shorter
b. 1933

Chick Corea
b. 1941

A New Generation
of Big Band Leaders

Toshiko Akiyoshi
Louis Bellson
Don Ellis
Maynard Ferguson
Bob Florence
Woody Herman
Bill Holman
Thad Jones
Mel Lewis
Stan Kenton
Rob McConnell
Sammy Nestico
Buddy Rich
Doc Severinsen
Bill Watrous
Patrick Williams

SMOOTH JAZZ/CONTEMPORARY

1982: Musical Instrument Digital Interface (MIDI) and polyphonic keyboards introduced

1984: Macintosh computer introduced

1980

Important cities in smooth jazz:
Los Angeles, New York

Characteristics

- Smooth, easy-listening sounds
- Electric keyboard and bass
- Small groups
- Blues, jazz, gospel, R&B, pop, and
  rock-influenced
- Hip-hop and rap-influenced grooves
- Arranged compositions
- Commercial approach
- Less space for improvisation

Grover Washington Jr.
1943–1999

MAINSTREAM/ECLECTIC

1981: U.S. Space Shuttle Columbia launched; IBM sells first personal computer; former Beatles member John Lennon assassinated

1983: Cell phones introduced

1986: Space Shuttle Challenger explodes

1987: Bill Gates first computer billionaire; President Reagan introduces trillion-dollar budget

1980

Important cities in mainstream and eclectic:
New York, Los Angeles, Washington D.C., San Francisco

Characteristics

- Small groups
- Arranged compositions
- Diverse musical styles
- Reinterpretations of standards
- Space for improvisation
- Slow to fast tempos

Composer
Wynton Marsalis
b. 1961

"Work Song" from
Blood on the Fields

1991: Gulf War   1991: President Bill Clinton sworn into office   1993: Terrorists attack World Trade Center   1997: Mars Pathfinder lands   1998: Frank Sinatra dies

1990   1999

Musicians and Groups

George Benson
b. 1943
The Crusaders
Dave Grusin
b. 1934
Kenny G
b. 1959
Hiroshima
Bob James
b. 1939
Earl Klugh
b. 1954
The Rippingtons
Joe Sample
b. 1939
David Sanborn
b. 1945
Spyro Gyra
George Winston
b. 1949

Crusaders
Hiroshima
The Rippingtons
Spyro Gyra

Emerging Smooth Jazz Musicians

Gato Barbieri
Chris Botti
Rick Braun
Brian Culbertson
Richard Elliott
Boney James
Dave Koz
Eric Marienthal
Keiko Matsui
Richard Smith

MAINSTREAM/ECLECTIC

1990: Berlin Wall comes down; Nelson Mandela released from South African prison; Manuel Noriega surrenders to U.S.   1992: Los Angeles riots; World Wide Web available for home use   1995: Oklahoma City federal building bombed   1998: Jonesboro, Arkansas school shootings   1999: Columbine, Colorado school shootings

1990   1999

Mainstream Artists

Geri Allen
b. 1957
Jane Ira Bloom
b. 1955
Michael Brecker
b. 1949
Randy Brecker
b. 1945
Kenny Garrett
b. 1960
Dave Liebman
b. 1946
Joe Lovano
b. 1952
Branford Marsalis
b. 1960
Greg Osby
b. 1960
Ernie Watts
b. 1945

Jump Swing Bands

Atomic Fireballs
Big Bad Voodoo Daddy
Cherry Poppin' Daddies
Royal Crown Revue
Brian Setzer Orchestra
Squirrel Nut Zippers

Jump Swing Characteristics

• Hard rock rhythm section

• Swinging horn lines

• Drums prominent

• Small to medium-sized horn section

• Often with vocalist

• Danceable and accessible

LATIN JAZZ

2000
2001

Important cities in Latin jazz:
Miami, Los Angeles, New York

Characteristics

- Latin jazz also called Afro-Cuban jazz
- Emphasis on percussion and Cuban
  instruments
- Danceable and accessible
- Latin jazz, Afro-Cuban, Brazilian,
  and New York salsa are most
  familiar types

Musicians and Groups

Mario Bauza
1911–1993
Luiz Bonfá
1922-2001
Paquito D'Rivera
b. 1948
Dizzy Gillespie
1917–1993
Machito (Frank Grillo)
1912–1984
Tito Puente
1923-2000
Arturo Sandoval
b. 1949
Mongo Santamaria
b. 1922
Cal Tjader
1925–1982
Chuco Valdez
b. 1941

Buena Vista Social Club
Irakere

2000: Portable MP3 players

2001: President George W. Bush
sworn into office

2001: Hijackers fly airplanes into
World Trade Center and Pentagon;
U.S. begins war against terrorism

MAINSTREAM/ECLECTIC

2000
2001

Important cities in mainstream and eclectic:
New York, Los Angeles, Washington D.C., San Francisco

Musicians

Terrance Blanchard
b. 1962
Roy Hargrove
b. 1970
Delfayo Marsalis
b. 1965
Brad Mehldau
b. 1970
Nicholas Payton
b. 1973
Chris Potter
b. 1971
Joshua Redman
b. 1961
Renee Rosnes
b. 1962
Jacky Terrasson
b. 1966
Jeff 'Tain Watts
b. 1960

Joshua Redman
b. 1961

Vocalists/Vocal Groups

Carmen Bradford
Dee Dee Bridgewater
Harry Connick Jr.
Kurt Elling
Nnenna Freelon
Al Jarreau
Diana Krall
Abbey Lincoln
Kevin Mahogany
Manhattan Transfer
Jane Monheit
Barbara Morrison
New York Voices
Dianne Reeves
Vanesa Rubin
Singers Unlimited
Tierney Sutton
Cassandra Wilson
Nancy Wilson

Today

Musicians	Compositions
Laurindo Almeida 1917–1995	*Corcovado*
Charlie Byrd 1925–1999	*Dance the Bossa Nova*
João Gilberto b. 1931	*Desafinado*
Antonio Carlos Jobim 1927–1994	*The Girl From Ipanema*
Eddie Palmieri b. 1936	*Groovin' High*
Astor Piazzolla 1921–1992	*How Insensitive*
Gonzalo Rubalcaba b. 1963	*Manha de Carnaval*
David Sanchez b. 1968	*Manteca*
Pancho Sanchez b. 1951	*Meditation*
	One Note Samba
	Oye Como Va
	Para los Rumberos
	Samba de Orfeu
	Triste
	Wave

MAINSTREAM/ECLECTIC

Today

**A New Generation
of Big Band Leaders and Big
Bands**

BBC Big Band
John Clayton
Diva
Jon Faddis
John Fedchock
Gordon Goodwin
Tom Kubis
Maiden Voyage
Frank Mantooth
Wynton Marsalis
Bob Mintzer
NDR Big Band (Hamburg)
Kim Richmond
Maria Schneider
Bill Warfield
WDR Big Band (Cologne)

Chapter 3

THE IMPORTANCE OF LISTENING
A KEY TO SUCCESSFUL JAZZ EDUCATION

by J. Richard Dunscomb

It is virtually impossible to teach or perform jazz music without having listened to it. It would be like a young basketball player trying to play without watching those who know how, or like trying to speak a foreign language without hearing the language spoken.

LISTEN, LISTEN, LISTEN

As with any language, music is learned through a process of hearing it first, followed by practicing and perfecting your "speaking" and communication skills. Similarly, learning the jazz language is most successfully accomplished by first immersing yourself in listening to the music. Directors or students that fail to understand the importance of this step are swimming upstream against a strong current.

Developing Aural Skills

Playing jazz by reading strictly what is indicated on the printed music will result in very square, non-jazz sounding music. On the other hand, consistent listening to jazz recordings will illuminate how to interpret the written notes correctly and bring the music to life. This is the aural process jazz musicians have used successfully throughout jazz history.

To develop aural skills means to listen productively—to absorb and learn; to hear and identify a phrase, note, riff, pattern, or musical idea and be able to sing it; and going a step further, to find that aural example on your own instrument (or the piano) and then practice it and digest it. Jazz improvisers generally play without music, and their ultimate goal is to play what they hear with their jazz vocabulary.

Jazz Vocabulary

The jazz vocabulary is derived from songs, melodies, rhythms, harmonies, scales, chords, patterns, modes, sequences, riffs, quotes, snippets, chord progressions,

---

Classic Recordings

Listening to classic recordings by jazz masters will help you set evaluation standards for your ensemble. Esteemed jazz artist-educator Shelly Berg offers this list of recordings as a great place to start:

- Miles Davis – *Kind of Blue, Seven Steps to Heaven*
- Count Basie – *Basie Straight Ahead, April in Paris*
- Charlie Parker – *Yardbird Suite*
- Chick Corea – *Light as a Feather*
- Dexter Gordon – *Go*
- Wayne Shorter – *Speak No Evil, JuJu*
- Art Blakey – *Art Blakey and the Jazz Messengers*
- Thad Jones – *Solid State*
- Oscar Peterson – *The Trio*
- Weather Report – *Heavy Weather*
- Duke Ellington – *The London Concerts*
- Ella Fitzgerald – (anything by this master)
- Bill Evans – *Bill Evans and Tony Bennett*
- John Coltrane – *John Coltrane and Johnny Hartman, Giant Steps*

---

and so on. Just as the impromptu speaker mentally organizes and regurgitates internalized information (knowledge and experience), jazz musicians should strive to be able to bring forth musical information that has been stored and digested and adapt it into a musical setting, arrangement, tempo, key, style, or chord progression.

Where to Start

Listening to big band recordings is probably the most accessible place to begin. You can focus easily on the sound, balance, instrumentation, articulation, and styles that will be present when you work with your jazz ensemble.

After you begin to understand the jazz language through big band recordings, expand your listening to small group recordings. The small group or combo ensemble will help you focus intently on interpretation, phrasing, expression, concept, style, articulation, and balance—all the ingredients of jazz. At first, some small group recordings may seem abstract because they will almost always include more improvisation. Dig deep into the music and have fun!

Repeated Listening

Listening to an individual selection not once, not twice, but many, many times is necessary to gain the proper perspective on style as well as each player's role.

Begin this process by selecting one jazz recording to use as a model for your students. Listen to it many times. Each time you listen, determine a specific component to which you want to draw their attention.

By listening in this fashion, you will develop an ear for communicating the sound you want your band to produce. Your ensemble may not be able to replicate the sound in the beginning. However, as long as you have the desired sound in your ear and you play the recording for your students and talk about it, they will understand the musical role model that you are all striving to imitate.

Working together as a team toward a common goal is essential. If your ensemble can apply what they've learned with your listening model to the performance of a few great bars of music, they will set a musical standard that they relate to and recognize as the goal.

Listening Model

Set aside time in rehearsal to listen to jazz recordings. This can be daily, weekly, or bi-weekly depending on your schedule. Listen for characteristic jazz concepts such as:
- Style—what style of jazz is the chart? Swing, shuffle, Latin (samba, bossa nova), and so on.
- Form—identify the form: 12-bar blues, 32-bar AABA, 16-bar AB, and so on.
- Balance/blend—identify the sound of balanced playing within each section and between sections, winds, and rhythm.
- Sound—identify the jazz sound of each instrument and notice the difference from a traditional classical type of sound or tone.
- Instrumentation—identify the instruments and the textures created by the various combinations of instruments in the arrangement.
- Tempo.
- Feel—what is the feel of the chart, even or swing eighths, laid-back, relaxed, pushed forward on top of the beat (slightly ahead of the center of the beat), and so on.
- Jazz nuances—the articulations, bends, scoops, phrasing, tone, licks, sequences, texture of the sections, and so on. Where do they occur—ask students to find specific nuances, identify, and mimic.
- Arrangement—the outline of the musical structure, intro, head, and so on, and identify who plays in each section and what is being played.
- Identify recurring motifs, riffs, patterns, sequences, and harmonic variations.
- Melody—sing the melody and then identify where it is being played and by what instrument(s). Have all the students do the same, especially the rhythm section.
- Solo sections—harmony, extensions, structure of the chord changes, and the characteristic style of the soloists.

- Individual sections—the role of each section and the key players and lead players.
- Rhythm section—hear the overall section and then listen for just one instrument at a time—piano, bass, drums, guitar (if present)—and how each instrument contributes to the total rhythmic feel, harmonic texture, and overall time.

In the Music Room

Post a listening guide in the music room and update it regularly with suggestions and reviews from magazines such as *Down Beat, Jazziz, Jazz Times, Jazz Educators Journal,* and *Billboard.* Here are some realistic listening goals for your students:

- As students enter the room prior to each rehearsal, have a professional jazz recording playing. This sets the tone for the musical standard you hope to achieve and opens the door for the serious music making that will follow.
- Create a library for students to check out recordings, and encourage them to buy their own jazz CDs.
- Make regular listening assignments for your students, and encourage them to focus their listening habits.

LISTENING IN REHEARSALS

The jazz sounds of individual instruments, tones, timbres, mouthpieces, reeds, and so on, are fully discussed in Chapter 17. This section will concentrate on how to achieve the characteristic big band sound with your ensemble.

1. The unique sound of a jazz ensemble results greatly from the fact that there is only one player to a part. Therefore, doubling parts will produce an unbalanced and uncharacteristic sound. At no time should lead parts be doubled. If you make a decision to double parts in rehearsals so that more students can participate in the program, remember that it is not acceptable to do so in performance. Rotate your multiple players instead.

2. Identify who has the melody and be sure everyone can hear it.

3. When the entire jazz ensemble is playing, the two outside voices should be heard—the lead trumpet and the bari sax. These two parts should be distinguishable, not dominant.

4. Pay particular attention to balance within sections by having lower parts play up to the lead player's volume to support the blend but not overpower the lead line.

5. Use proper jazz articulations with all instruments.

6. Unison lines can always be played softer than lines that are harmonized, and players should never use vibrato when playing unison or unison octave lines. Having the lower octave play stronger than the upper octave strengthens unison octave lines.

7. Fast passages are always played more accurately when played lightly.

8. Bring out moving lines.

9. Think and play in four-bar phrases whenever possible.

10. Play all dynamic levels. Exaggerate dynamics.

11. Understand the texture of the scombination of instruments that are used often in jazz charts. When the tenors and trombones are playing the same line, have the trombones play slightly on top of the sound. When altos and trumpets are playing the same line, have trumpets play slightly on top of the sound. This will help tuning as well as balance and give more energy to the unison sound.

12. Ascending phrases have subtle crescendos. Descending phrases have subtle decrescendos. Phrases that ascend and descend should follow the same subtleties.

13. When using mutes, players should use plenty of air support to produce the desired musical texture or color.

14. Understand the proper balance within the rhythm section, as well as the tone quality that is appropriate for the style. Continually keep the rhythm section aware of the balance with the wind sections.

15. The rhythm section should automatically play softer on two sections: the head and the solo.

SUCCESS STORIES

In Chapter 4, five band directors discuss their success stories in detail. It is interesting to view the importance of listening from the perspective of those directors in the following excerpts:

Edison Middle School (Champaign, Illinois), Sam Hankins, Director

Listening. We do not have a jazz library, but I am working on one. During jazz band sectional rehearsals at least half the time is spent working on listening and improvisation and the rest of the time spent working on the music. I believe listening—whether it's to classical or jazz music—is very important to my success. I have the students listen to at least one or two jazz artists on their particular instrument. I do play the recording of the jazz tunes that we are working on for the ensemble. I do have the students sing a lot to work on the articulation and the style of the piece.

Washington Middle School (Seattle, Washington), Robert Knatt, Director

Listening. Every Friday is listening day. We listen to jazz standards because that is what we play. I believe listening to music by greats such as Miles Davis, Thelonius Monk, Sonny Rollins, and Dizzy Gillespie is the best way to get a young player to understand how his or her part is to be played and the function of that part within the group. Discussing balance, blend, intonation, phrasing, articulation, and, most of all, listening leads to understanding the parts well enough to ensure good listening habits. I pick recordings that correspond stylistically to the charts we are playing, and some are the same as the original versions. To help students hear the subtleties of the music, we use technology in the classroom regularly to listen to original and more recent recordings of this great music. This way, students can hear what they are trying to emulate and can adjust their playing accordingly.

MacArthur High School (Decatur, Illinois), Jim Culbertson, Director

Listening. I insist that my students listen to all of the music they play at MacArthur, whether it is a concert band selection or a Basie recording of a jazz chart. They listen for interpretation and style. They also sight-read a lot of new music to improve reading skills. I believe that jazz phrasing can't be learned from a book. The number of directors who do not have a jazz library astounds me! Directors need to be exposing students (and themselves) to big bands, traditional jazz greats in combo settings, and some current pop/jazz fusion groups. Without such exposure, the students will not grow to enjoy the music, and chances are quite good that they will never perform it in the style it was intended.

Los Alamitos High School (Los Alamitos, California), Chuck Wackerman, Director

Listening. We have a library of jazz CDs and software that students can check out and take home. In class we listen to various recordings of pieces we are preparing. We also have a listening lab in our school that the students can use.

MacArthur High School (Houston, Texas), Jose Diaz, Director

Listening. To learn about this style of music, as with any style, listening is a must. MacArthur does not have a listening library (budget doesn't allow for it), so I encourage students to share recordings with each other and listen to the one jazz radio station in Houston. I also share my personal jazz recording library with them. I ask my students to listen to as many forms of jazz styles as they possibly can, as well as to other forms of music. The jazz world is changing so much with our advanced technology (mainly the Internet) that music indigenous to cultures around the world is making an impact on the development of jazz.

DIRECTOR'S CHECKLIST FOR LISTENING

Simply put, if you don't hear it, you won't be able to teach it!

• Prioritize time for jazz listening. Think jazz vocabulary and aural skills!

• Use the demo recording included with many published arrangements.

• Make tape copies of these demo recordings for the students (for educational purposes only and not for any other use).

• Set realistic and attainable listening goals for yourself and for your students.

• Have a recording playing when students arrive in class. Set the standard and the mind for jazz.

• Identify a model or example recording to study and analyze. Listen repeatedly.

• Create a library for students to check out recordings and encourage them to purchase/ exchange their own jazz CDs.

• Post a suggested jazz listening list and update it regularly. Assign listening homework for extra credit.

• As often as possible, listen to live musical performances. It is sometimes difficult to perceive dynamics of great jazz artists when listening to recordings. Live performances provide overall reception that is auditory as well as visual; this adds considerably to listening experiences.

• Early listening techniques may include identifying the melody. Attempt to sing along. If melodies are too complicated, as many are on an initial listening, try to identify with another aspect (for example, rhythm or dynamics) that may be of interest or accessible to the students.

• Seek recommendations for listening to live or recorded music from respected mature musicians.

• Listen with the goal of being able to identify some musical aspects such as riff, rhythm, melody, harmony, style, tempo, instrumentation, feel, nuances, solos, key players, and the rhythm section.

Chapter 4

GOALS AND SUCCESS STORIES

by J. Richard Dunscomb

A successful jazz program, like a house, should be built on a solid foundation. The program must have a secure base, such as the feel that is created by a great rhythm section. It must exhibit creative design, much like the mood inspired by superbly improvised solos. And the program must feel comfortable, which is achieved by maintaining a well-rehearsed jazz ensemble. This chapter will examine the elements needed for a successful jazz program in your school and view some success stories to see how they are built.

Establish Goals

Jazz is not a mystery, only another style of music, and you know many other styles of music already—baroque, classical, romantic, and so on. Just as you have studied and prepared various musical styles and forms thus far in your career, learning how to teach jazz is simply another step in that same direction. It will require study, effort, and time on your part, but the goal of being a successful jazz educator is attainable.

First Steps

Survey the current situation in your school and determine the best steps to ensure a good start. Begin with one jazz performance group. Concentrate on making that one a quality experience that enhances student learning, and your program will be off to a great start.

Expand Your Horizons

Be honest about your own strengths and weaknesses. Do you have jazz experience? Can you improvise? Do you have well-trained music students? If you are unfamiliar with jazz, do not be intimidated—get involved and learn! There are many resources now available to use in building a jazz program. The purpose of this book is to provide a template from which a successful jazz program can be built. An enormous Resource Guide is included at the end of this book to further assist you. The included video also provides invaluable reference.

If you have the desire and interest to build a jazz program, you can succeed. It has been our experience that if you present students with the opportunity to play jazz, many will have the desire and motivation to work hard. Jazz music embodies limitless boundaries for self-expression, an attraction for good students in any situation. It is your responsibility to provide a positive jazz environment for them.

Focus on Listening

The single most important step to educating yourself about jazz is to devote time to listening to jazz. Make this a priority!
- Listening is essential to learning the jazz language and aural skills.
- Listening to the jazz masters will inspire both you and your students.
- Jazz with its aural tradition has had its timbres, inflections, articulations, and rhythms transmitted from one generation to the next largely through recordings and live performances.
- Listen repeatedly. It will set the proper standard of excellence for you to measure the accomplishments in your program.

- Have a recording playing when students arrive in class. It focuses the mind and sets the standard.
- Create a library for students to check out recordings, and encourage them to buy/exchange their own jazz CDs.
- Establish regular listening assignments with realistic and attainable goals.
- Read Chapter 3 for more details about listening.

Join the International Association for Jazz Education

Joining the International Association for Jazz Education (IAJE) is a must for all serious jazz educators. With a mission to ensure the continued growth and development of jazz through education and outreach, IAJE serves 8,000 members in 40 countries. A voluntary non-profit organization, IAJE initiates programs that nurture the understanding and appreciation of jazz and its heritage, provides leadership to educators regarding curriculum and performance, and assists teachers, students, and artists with information and resources. The IAJE Annual Conference, held each January, is acknowledged as the largest annual gathering of the global jazz community. The *Jazz Educators Journal,* the official magazine of IAJE, is published six times a year. See Chapter 19 for details.

Write a Mission Statement and a Philosophy Statement

Creating a mission statement and a philosophy statement may seem like a university classroom assignment. However, doing so for any program, regardless of level, will help you succinctly spell out statements that you may use to further justify your program. Samples of each statement follow:

Jazz Program Mission Statement

The mission of the [insert your school name] jazz program is to provide excellence in academic and professional career preparation for the challenges facing today's musician. Our mission is fulfilled by combining the study of classical and jazz music with strong emphasis on quality musicianship in solo, combo, and big band settings. Additionally, the program provides a supportive environment for the study and teaching of jazz music. The jazz education program at [insert your school name] represents the contexts and challenges encountered by contemporary musicians.

Jazz Program Philosophy Statement

A contemporary music education must relate the traditional to the new. To be an educated musician today requires both a breadth of knowledge and specialized skills including an informed creativity and capacity for musical growth. Today, education must be a catalyst for continued learning and the ability to relate self to society and to a profession filled with change and new challenges. All of the teachers in the program support this philosophy and serve as role models in their highly successful careers.

SET THREE-YEAR GOALS

Set a series of realistic three-year goals that will outline a map for the future. Following are examples of such goals for a high school jazz program. Tailor them to fit your teaching situation.

First Year
- Prepare a detailed budget for the program.
- Develop musical skills so the students can read, play all major and minor scales by memory, and have a sense of musical tuning.
- Create a jazz music library containing books, videos, CD recordings, improvisation materials, fake books, small ensemble charts, and big band charts.
- Start working with duos, trios, quartets, and small ensembles with any combination of instruments leading toward the formation of a big band.

- Schedule periodic in-school recitals for soloists, duos, trios, quartets, and small ensembles, incorporating percussion instruments, bass, piano, and guitar into these ensembles. Invite parents to attend.
- Take students to festivals and/or live jazz performances as observers.
- Develop rehearsal techniques that will include discipline, musicianship, and the individual responsibilities of the students. Work toward identifying section leaders.
- Present classic jazz recordings in class and encourage the students to create their own discography and library of the most important jazz masters.

Second Year
- Continue to develop musicianship through solid rehearsal techniques.
- Set up an audition process for the students at the beginning of each semester.
- Organize section rehearsals.
- Incorporate jazz listening, improvisation, and theory into rehearsals.
- Continue to take students to live jazz performances, or provide information resources.
- Recruit outside jazz "experts" for seminars and clinics.
- Identify qualified teachers on each instrument and encourage the students to take private lessons.
- Continue building the jazz library.
- If prepared, take the performing group to a jazz festival in a "for comments only" category.
- Present periodic concerts in a school setting for the community.

Third Year
- Incorporate different styles of music in the ensemble's repertoire.
- Continue to develop musicianship through solid rehearsal techniques.
- Continue having "experts" come in, and create specific clinics with them.
- Continue building the jazz library and identify new needs.
- Produce an annual event featuring the performing groups in the program.
- Stimulate and provide participation in educationally based jazz festivals.
- Present public concerts periodically both in school and in the community.
- Consider an interschool jazz concert or festival.

SUCCESS STORIES

What Works and Why

It is important to see how successful programs work. We asked several leading leading public school jazz educators, whose programs have been noted as being successful over a period of many years, to tell us their secrets.

What works and how do these directors make it work? The following stories are all told in the words of the director. Use these success stories as models. Look for the similarities that are present in many of the programs. Those are key elements you will want to include in yours. Although no two outstanding programs are exactly alike, be assured that quality is at the core of each program.

Directors were provided with the following format:

- **Name of your school and your name:** Include the enrollment of your school; the make-up gradewise; how many in the band program; when, how often, and for how long your groups meet; what the groups and classes are, and so on.

- **Philosophy:** State your philosophy and goals.

- **Auditions:** What is your audition policy (if you have auditions)?

- **Listening:** What do you do about listening to jazz with the students? Does your program have a jazz CD library? What do they listen to? How important is this to your success?

- **Improvisation:** How, when, and where do you teach improvisation to your students?

- **Concerts and Competitions:** State your feelings about concerts and competitions as they relate to you and your program.

- **Additional Comments:** Anything else you would like to include that does not fall into the categories above.

Success Story #1

Edison Middle School (Champaign, Illinois), Sam Hankins, Director

Enrollment in school: 670 students in grades 6–8.

Number of students in music program: 102

This is a typical middle school, not a performing arts magnet

Two jazz bands:

    6th, 7th, and 8th grade concert bands meet for 40 minutes every day

    Jazz Band 1 meets Monday and Friday after school for one hour

    Sax sectional—Tuesday after school for one hour

    Brass sectional—Wednesday after school for one hour

    Rhythm sectional—Thursday after school for one hour

    Jazz Band 2—same schedule but different days for full jazz band (this group is directed
       by the school orchestra director)

Philosophy. The Edison Middle School band program is an active program dedicated to giving students the opportunity to grow musically, socially, and academically. Through musical performance, students learn how to work together to achieve common goals and develop group discipline and respect for fellow students. Students learn to focus on goals and achievements that are more than personal as well as develop self-discipline. Through study of harmony, scales, rhythms, and so on, students develop skills that will allow them to truly understand and appreciate the foundation of music as well as the aesthetics.

At Edison there is a sixth, a seventh, and an eighth-grade concert band. Students play a variety of music from classical to jazz and popular literature. Emphasis is placed on the development of fundamental skills related to posture, breathing, singing, embouchure, rhythm, and etudes, as well as the skills needed to perform band literature designed for the middle school band. Daily practice is a must, and private instruction is strongly encouraged.

Auditions.

1. The director assigns each student a chair in the various sections of the band according to the student's ability and/or the musical needs of the ensemble.
2. A student who wishes to move up in his or her section may challenge the person directly ahead of him or her.
3. A player must accept the challenge or lose the chair.
4. Challenges are over music in the folder and/or additional music selected by the director.
5. Challenges are conducted and recorded on tape during the class period. Challenges are not held within one month prior to a performance.
6. When one player beats another player two consecutive times with at least two weeks between the challenges, there are no more challenges between those players until the beginning of the next quarter.

Listening. We do not have a jazz library, but I am working on one. During jazz band sectional rehearsals, at least half the time is spent working on listening and improvisation and the rest of the time spent working on the music. I believe listening—whether it's to classical or jazz music—is very important to my success. I have the students listen to at least one or two jazz artists on their particular instrument. I do play recordings of the jazz tunes that we are working on for the ensemble. I do have the students sing a lot to work on the articulation and the style of the piece.

Improvisation. As mentioned above, at least half of each sectional rehearsal is spent listening and improvising.

Concerts and Competitions. Concerts are one part of the Edison band program. I feel that the students have the need to show what they have learned over a two- or three-month period. Concerts are goals that give instant gratification when things fall into place. I am for competitions, but I know they can be all-consuming. I do not let them become the most important things in our program. When we compete at a contest, we are competing against ourselves or some other school. It gives the students pride within themselves to work harder and to succeed together. Comments from judges at competitions help me a lot personally, too. They help me look at certain things in the score, bring out certain parts in the music, or better my conducting skills.

Additional Comments. The bottom line is to make music that touches someone out in the audience in either a concert or competition.

Success Story #2

Washington Middle School (Seattle, Washington), Robert Knatt, Director
Enrollment in school: 1,035 students in grades 6–8
Number of students in music program: 489

This is a typical middle school, not a performing arts magnet school. Students meet daily for 55 minutes in all music classes from September to June. The class offerings are as follows:

1st Period Beg. Instruments	1st Period Beg. Strings
2nd Period Sr. Jazz Band	2nd Period PREP
3rd Period Beg. Concert Band	3rd Period Gen. Music
4th Period Jr. Concert Band	4th Period Jr. Orchestra
5th Period PREP	5th Period Choir
6th Period Sr. Concert Band	6th Period Sr. Orchestra

Additionally, the Parks and Recreations Department funds an after-school program that gives us the opportunity to offer Beginning and Jr. Jazz Band classes three days a week. We presently have the following (from October through June):
Mondays - Beg. Jazz Band (2:30–4:30)
Tuesdays - Jr. Jazz Band I (2:30–4:30)
Thursdays - Jr. Jazz Band II (2:30–4:30)

Philosophy. Washington Middle School is located in the Central District of Seattle, with an ethnically and academically diverse student population. For the last six years, our music program has earned top awards at a variety of festivals, including sweepstakes three times at the Lionel Hampton Jazz Festival, the only middle school band to win sweepstakes. I believe we have been successful because I create student excitement for learning, use innovative teaching methods, and help students appreciate the importance and value of every individual in the group, all of which have a continued impact on students through time.

Student Excitement for Learning. Probably the most important ingredient for making exceptional music is creating an excitement in students about what they are doing. Given the ethnic and academic diversity of our school, it is important to engage the interest of students of all backgrounds. I try to create excitement by introducing the students to challenging music usually reserved for high school bands. I let the students know that if they are able to master the music, we will perform it; if not, we will not. Likewise, at the beginning of the year, students form combo groups and are given time to work on the music independently. Those groups who have reached a high performance level are invited to perform at Jazz Night; those who have not reached this level do not perform.

I have found that by setting the standards high and letting students show me what they can do, they become highly motivated for self-learning. Because of this, students tend to make exceptional learning progress throughout the year, both individually and as a group, as evidenced by the fact that year after year.

Innovative Methods in Teaching. It is highly unusual for a middle school to be playing high school or college charts. Thus, probably the most innovative teaching method I employ is to enrich the prescribed curriculum with exceptionally advanced material. Often, this includes classic jazz standards that are out of print or are exact transcriptions from actual performances decades ago. This way, students are exposed to "the real thing." To help students hear the subtleties of the music, we use technology in the classroom regularly to listen to original and more recent recordings of this great music. This way, students can hear what they are trying to emulate and can adjust their playing accordingly. I also rely heavily on collaborative learning and problem-solving strategies in my teaching. Rather than spoon-feeding the students, I give them guidance but expect them to learn on their own. For example, at the beginning of the year, I teach students how to tell when their instruments are out of tune with each other. In no time, the students are responsible for tuning the entire band, even at performances. This approach seems to be working because our bands are consistently rated highly for intonation. Likewise, sections of the band often work together independently, with more advanced students helping less advanced ones master their parts. Probably the most enhanced teaching technique I use, however, is simply setting high standards and teaching them not to settle for less. If students do not master a part in the music, they keep working individually or as a group until they do. I believe strongly that if the standards are high, if students are given the tools to learn, and if students are excited about learning, young people can achieve at very high levels.

Appreciation for the Importance and Value of Every Individual. As any bandleader knows, the quality of a musical group's performance depends entirely on every single member of the group. Every musician has a role, and without that role the group as a whole suffers. The music students in our program learn this from day one. They understand that festivals are not about winning; they are about setting standards and seeing how close we can come to them. But if we win, we win as a group; if we lose, we lose as a group. Every musician is critical to our success as a whole. And by the end of the year, the bonds of friendship are strong throughout the entire band.

Continued Impact on Students Over Time. Previous students and their parents tell me that participation in Washington Middle School's music program has a profound impact on their lives. Many students go on to establish exceptional musical careers; others simply play for fun as adults. Our program helps give students options musically. But more important, according to past students, participation in our music program has a continued impact over time. By experiencing the excitement of learning, the commitment to high standards, the value of hard work, the importance of every individual in a community, the rewards of community participation, and other important "non-musical" concepts, students acquire critical skills for successful daily living. I am proud to be a part of Washington Middle School's educational and musical community and, even more important, to be a part of these young people's lives.

Auditions. Incoming sixth-graders have to audition to determine proper class placement. Students must prepare a piece, play scales, and bring music books they studied from during the year for purposes of sight-reading. Auditions occur from May to July. Sr. Jazz Band auditions start in July and end in August. Because most of the students are current Washington Middle School students, I have some idea of their playing ability, so the summer rehearsals are primarily to determine adaptability and understanding of jazz concepts.

Listening. Every Friday is listening day. We listen to jazz standards because that is what we play. I believe listening to music by greats such as Miles Davis, Thelonius Monk, Sonny Rollins, and Dizzy Gillespie is the best way to get a young player to understand how his or her part is to be played and the function of that part within the group. Discussing balance, blend, intonation, phrasing, articulation, and, most of all, listening leads to practicing parts well enough to ensure listening. I pick recordings that correspond stylistically to the charts we are playing, and some are the same as the original versions. To help students hear the subtleties of the music, we use technology in the classroom regularly to listen to original and more recent recordings of this great music. This way, students can hear what they are trying to emulate and can adjust their playing accordingly.

Improvisation. We are extremely fortunate to have approximately 52% of all music students taking private lessons with area professional musicians, either during the school day or outside of school, which is the basis for our students' learning basic fundamentals of improvisation. We use Dr. Willie Hill's *Approaching the Standards,* Bill Holcombe's *24 Jazz Etudes,* and Jim Snidero's *Jazz Conceptions,* as well as the Jamey Aebersold studies. We strive to work daily during class on improvisational techniques with a monitoring and adjusting approach, but the only way to become proficient in improvisation is to listen to great players.

Concerts and Competitions. Washington Middle School's music program has consistently won top awards at virtually every festival entered. Participating in these festivals and studying jazz legends also teaches students they are a part of a larger community of musicians who can impact the direction of music worldwide, thus promoting citizenship in a global village. Also, because of our record, roughly half of all Washington Middle School students are involved in the music program. This helps create a strong sense of school pride, belonging, and academic commitment. (Students are not allowed to participate if their grades are low.) Together, these factors help improve student retention because students feel successful and connected to others. Competitions are not about winning but rather about setting standards and seeing how close we can come to them. Additionally, the most important components at the festivals we attend are the clinics with professional musicians and their feedback. How could you not be excited attending a clinic with Ray Brown, Lou Rawls, or Bill Watrous?

Success Story #3

MacArthur High School (Decatur, Illinois), Jim Culbertson, Director
Enrollment in school: 1,200 students grades 9–12
Students in the band program: 140
This is a typical high school, not a performing arts school
The band program includes:
  Symphonic/Marching/Pep Band depending on the season of the year
  9th-grade band
  2 music theory classes
  2 jazz combos
  5th and 6th-grade bands in two elementary schools.
  Jazz Band 1 rehearses one hour, three to four times a week, after school (late
    October through May)
  Jazz Band 2 (freshmen and sophomores) rehearses 40 minutes, two times a
    week (during the winter)
  Combos meet as needed

Philosophy. My philosophy is firmly entrenched in wanting all aspects of the band program to do well, with concert band at the core of the program. We set the same goals for jazz band as concert band. The students learn basic musical skills as well as the discipline of good rehearsals. We believe in providing real big-band jazz literature for our groups. Music that is challenging but will not take all semester to learn is the norm.

Since jazz band does not rehearse on school time, we carefully choose when to hold rehearsals. It is important to check to see when other school groups are meeting and pick a time that avoids conflicts.

Auditions. We do have auditions for jazz band and provide the students with the printed music and tapes ahead of time. I do not have time in my full day to run sectional rehearsals, so my students do. I expect my older and more experienced students to become "mentors" to the younger ones.

Listening. I insist that my students listen to all of the music they play at MacArthur, whether it is a concert band selection or a Basie recording of a jazz chart. They listen for interpretation and style. They also sight-read a lot of new music to improve reading skills. I believe that jazz phrasing can't be learned from a book. The number of directors who do not have a jazz listening library astounds me! Directors need to be exposing students (and themselves) to big bands, traditional jazz greats in combo settings, and some current pop/jazz fusion groups. Without such exposure, the students will not grow to enjoy the music, and chances are quite good that they will never perform it in the style it was intended.

Improvisation. All students start with music that has written-out solos. I believe the initial step has to be one that is met with success in this important area. As they gain confidence, they are encouraged to transcribe recordings of the great jazz players. This is accomplished using a half-speed tape deck, which slows the tempo and drops the pitch an octave.

Concerts and Competitions. Separate performances for concert and jazz bands are spaced two to three weeks apart so it is not too demanding on parents. This concept works fine; attendance is great for concert band and usually a "sell-out" for the jazz band concerts. I believe in the spirit of competition and think it is a great incentive for students. Keeping things in perspective and not overemphasizing winning are keys to success in this area. The real competition is with the music, not other bands.

Success Story #4
Los Alamitos High School (Los Alamitos, California), Chuck Wackerman, Director
Enrollment in school: 2,500 students grades 9–12
Students in the jazz program: 45
This is a typical high school, not a performing arts high school
The jazz program consists of two jazz bands:
    Jazz Band 1 – meets every day for 50 minutes during 0 period
    Jazz Band 2 – meets every day for 50 minutes during 2nd period

Philosophy. My goal is to have my students develop an appreciation for jazz. I do this by exposing them to all styles of jazz including contemporary. I believe it is very important to develop the improvisational skills as well as their ensemble playing.

Auditions. We do have auditions. The students are given an audition packet including a required piece to play and written-out scales including all major scales, blues scales, and minor scales—both harmonic and melodic.

Listening. We have a library of jazz CDs and software that students can check out and take home. In class we listen to various recordings of pieces we are preparing. We also have a listening lab in our school that the students can use.

Improvisation. Working on improvisation is included three days a week during rehearsals using the John Rinaldo book. We also record the rhythm section for soloists to work with at home. Having these recordings allows improvisation by the students to be carried on outside the school rehearsal. Using major and minor scales for warm-up each day helps the students know their scales. Over a couple of weeks they will play all of the scales, not just a few.

Concerts and Competitions. We participate in six festivals a year. They are quite important to our program. We learn a lot and value the feedback from judges. In addition, the opportunity to interact with clinicians is valuable and inspiring to our students.

Additional Comments. I believe strongly in commissioning arrangements for our jazz ensemble. These charts are a big key to our success. We also have professional guest artists and bands at our school. This is another valuable part of our students' exposure to jazz music at its top level.

Success Story #5

MacArthur High School (Houston, Texas), Jose Diaz, Director
Enrollment in school: 2,750 students grades 9–12
This is a typical high school, not a performing arts school
The band program has 144 students in Marching Band, Symphonic Band, Concert Band, and Jazz Ensemble

MacArthur High School has a *block schedule* that allows four classes to meet every day for 90 minutes. The jazz ensemble does meet every day for 90 minutes and after school when necessary. Although each of the ensembles meets daily, the block scheduling allows for only one jazz ensemble class to meet. Because of this block scheduling, it is very difficult to keep students in the jazz ensemble classes because of other class conflicts. These conflicts affect enrollment in the jazz ensemble as well as in the other band classes. The block scheduling we have is called *accelerated block,* meaning that each session (semester) students can take four credits, or classes. Those credits were designed to be two core and two elective credits. In many cases, students take four core classes and therefore are not available for electives like band or jazz ensemble. This creates many challenges, and the school is in the process of looking at alternative scheduling.

Philosophy. Music is an integral aspect of every individual's life—either directly or indirectly—and music education should provide a healthy, well-rounded program that reflects the diversity of our country's multicultural society. This philosophy is reflected throughout the entire instrumental music program at MacArthur High School.

Auditions. We have open enrollment. Students are allowed to perform when they attain a certain standard. We have auditions for placement in all of the ensembles except jazz. In the jazz ensemble, I place the students on parts.

Listening. To learn about this style of music, as with any style, listening is a must. MacArthur does not have a listening library (budget doesn't allow for it), so I encourage students to share recordings with each other and listen to the one jazz radio station in Houston. I also share my personal jazz recording library with them. I ask my students to listen to as many forms of jazz styles as they possibly can, as well as to other forms of music. The jazz world is changing so much with our advanced technology (mainly the Internet) that music indigenous to cultures around the world is making an impact in the development of jazz.

Improvisation. I teach improvisation during my jazz ensemble rehearsal; this is not the ideal situation, but because of block scheduling, it is one that I have to contend with. I also encourage students to transcribe solos even if it's just a couple of measures. Any experience that students have from going through this process is a tremendous learning situation. Aside from using some of the great improvisation methods available, I invite some of the talented musicians in the Houston area to present a clinic on improvisation.

Concerts and Competitions. I concentrate on performing more concerts and learning as much literature as possible rather than entering competitions. I used to compete with my program often early in my career and we did extremely well—we won virtually every competition we entered. I, however, was not satisfied with the knowledge students were gaining through this competition-driven program. I found myself teaching only the tunes we were going to compete with and very little else. I strongly believe that teaching students about music is about learning and sharing the art form. In general, my students have a better understanding of and more love for the music because the program is more performance-oriented.

Summary

It is almost a given that there are success stories in your area. Do not hesitate to call upon your fellow directors for assistance. Although they may be more experienced in the jazz area, you could provide your expertise in return. Working together creates a healthy environment for jazz education and provides a good example for your students.

DIRECTOR'S CHECKLIST FOR BUILDING YOUR JAZZ PROGRAM

- Evaluate your strengths and weaknesses for teaching jazz. This should be ongoing as you continue to grow.

- Do not be intimidated by jazz—jump on board and learn!

- Create jazz listening as a priority for yourself and your students.

- Encourage your students to buy selected CDs.

- Create a three-year set of goals—follow them and adjust them as necessary.

- Join IAJE.

- Find the commonalities in the success stories.

- Establish your own philosophy, audition plan, improvisation plan, and feeling on competitions.

- Work together with directors in your area, sharing your teaching talents to help each other.

CONQUERING SCHEDULING CHALLENGES

by J. Richard Dunscomb

Congratulations! Making the decision to augment your music program with jazz instruction is an exciting opportunity for your students. Naturally you will need to examine how the addition of a jazz combo or jazz ensemble will impact class scheduling at your school.

As with most of life's successes, things do not happen by accident. Careful planning, awareness, and overall knowledge are necessary tools for building an excellent jazz program. Chapter 1 provides preliminary information and justification that you will want to review when it comes time to meet with your school administration.

ANTICIPATE CHANGE

Class schedules, class lengths, and the number of class periods differ greatly from one school to the next. However, one thing that is similar from school to school is this: things do change! Every music educator should be prepared to deal creatively with changes in class scheduling, period lengths, and administration—both short-term and long-term. Plan ahead and anticipate.

One of the biggest scheduling challenges for music educators in recent years has been block scheduling. The following article provides excellent insight into the pros and cons of block scheduling and modified block scheduling and offers realistic and specific ways to address the issue if it becomes a topic of conversation in your school district. In addition, refer to "Goals and Success Stories" in Chapter 4.

BLOCK SCHEDULING

The following three-part series appeared in Director Magazine *(1996–97), a publication of* United Musical Instruments, Inc. Reprinted *courtesy of United Musical Instruments, Inc.,* unitedmusical.com.

Jazz Trends in Schools

Based on a survey of jazz ensemble directors and administrators in public high schools and middle schools in California, Florida, Georgia, Illinois, Massachusetts, New York, Texas, and Virginia, the following trends emerged:

Average number of jazz ensemble rehearsals per week:

High school: 3
Middle school: 2

Percentage of jazz ensemble rehearsals held during the school day:

30% during school
35% before school
25% after school

Source: Warner Bros. Publications, 2001

PART I

BUILDING BLOCKS—MAKING MUSIC FIT
INTO BLOCK SCHEDULES

High school music educators across the United States are tuning up to save their programs in the face of a powerful educational trend that cuts the number of courses students can choose each semester. Block scheduling, touted by some academics as America's response to more intense schooling in Europe and Asia, divides the school day into fewer longer periods.

Under the traditional schedule of six to eight class periods per day, students typically take core English, history, math, and science courses. With the class hours left over, students choose elective courses such as band, chorus, art, and foreign language. With a block schedule, however, the class day is usually divided into four longer class periods. Overall, students may have fewer choices and less flexible schedules.

The trend is not without its critics. Still, many educators tout the model as providing the sort of back-to-basics education essential in our competitive economy.

The repercussions for high school music programs are significant. In some small schools, scheduling conflicts are threatening to wipe out music programs entirely. In large schools that offer many courses, music students tend to thrive in environments that offer longer rehearsal time and more credit.

A Tale of Two Schools

At Montezuma Cortez High School, in a small town in Southwestern Colorado, veteran band director Gary Hall has seen his music program flounder since block scheduling was implemented three years ago.

"Four years ago, we had a vibrant band program of 125 students," says Hall. "We had a concert band, a marching band, and two full jazz bands, and we offered a variety of music courses, including music theory and three sections of guitar and piano." Today, according to Hall, the Montezuma Cortez school band has only 104 members in the first semester and fewer than 60 participants in the second. Moreover, the school now offers only two music courses, a combined marching band/concert band period, and a course in music theory. Says Hall, "We've had to cancel our jazz band entirely." In addition, he has had a difficult time convincing talented junior and senior musicians to stick with the program because of the seemingly insurmountable scheduling conflicts. Hall has also found that the erratic enrollment in the second semester has caused a drop in the quality of music his band can play and that the layoff hurts re-enrollment for the next term. "My top trumpet player dropped out of the band in the second semester of last year," says Hall. "He promised he'd be back, but he's not." In addition, Hall has found that younger students are having trouble concentrating in the long 90-minute teaching blocks.

In marked contrast to Hall's experience, Andy Nelson, associate band director at Blaine High School in Minneapolis, has seen his band program swell from 160 members to 260 out of an enrollment of 2,800 since his school corporation instituted block scheduling three years ago.

"We have not lost any kids because of the four-period day," Nelson says. "The administration sat down with us to create a schedule that works well for everybody."

"In effect," continues Nelson, "the students are getting eight choices for classes per year, and two of these choices are going to be band." Nelson believes he has found a solution to the problem of attrition. He simply does not allow students who have dropped out after a semester to return to the band.

Nelson explains further that their program was designed to offer a modified block schedule, whereby freshmen and sophomores can take music plus another course in the same block on alternate days. Nelson has found that this schedule makes music courses more accessible to younger students. The top-level concert band at Blaine enjoys 85-minute rehearsals every day. The student performers receive honors credit. Nelson conducts early morning practices for a thriving jazz ensemble.

Indeed, the experience of these two schools is very different under block scheduling. But, according to the findings of two recent studies, these two schools seem to reflect accurately some common trends throughout the country. Researchers in Kentucky and Colorado found that band directors from small schools, offering fewer courses, reported having more scheduling difficulties than directors at large schools where many sections of a course are offered at different times of the day.

In addition, researchers have found that music programs have fared worse under a strict four-block system than under a modified block schedule that allows students to take two courses in one block, either in split classes or on alternate days.

Coping With Change

As block scheduling continues to gain adherents, many band directors are entering the debate with mixed feelings and some uncertainty.

"The English teachers tell me block scheduling will work out fine," says Rich Hahn, music instructor at Forest Lake High School in Forest Lake, Minnesota. "But our school offers 30 courses during only one time slot. I'm afraid our program is going to take a hit if kids start having to make hard choices." According to Hahn, his school is slated to vote this year on whether to implement block scheduling.

Gary Stith isn't too concerned about block scheduling. Stith is a music instructor for a suburban Buffalo, New York school district that is currently phasing in block scheduling. "Our music program has quite a reputation," he says. "There are so many ways these schedules can be adapted."

At J.P. Taravella High School in Coral Springs, Florida, band director Mark Humphreys reports that his faculty has voted down block scheduling four times in the past couple of years, despite pressure from the superintendent to implement it. "Our strong sentiment is that block scheduling will decimate our music program," says Humphreys. "We don't want to change our school, and people are worried. But too many music teachers tend to just keep their heads in the band room."

Helping band directors and school administrators cope with the looming changes is Edward Lisk, a music education consultant from Oswego, New York. Lisk leads seminars to instruct music educators on how to present the benefits of their programs in the current atmosphere of educational reform. He believes it is only a mater of time before all schools move to block scheduling. "I've spoken in 35 states," says Lisk. "Everywhere, educators are dealing with the same issues, using the same terms. Music educators need to move forward and be proactive if they are to keep their music programs as part of the school day."

Promote Real Value

To maintain strong music programs under block scheduling, Lisk tells band directors to actively promote the academic value of music programs. "Too often," he says, "the administrators and others outside of our discipline look at us as entertainers. They don't perceive music as a language or an academic discipline."

With cost-conscious administrators, Lisk believes band directors must also tout the practical values of their programs. One aim of Lisk's seminars is to enable music educators to fight with the kind of facts a school board can understand, such as dollars invested and students enrolled.

According to John Benham, president of Music in World Cultures, Inc., effective economic arguments can be made to support band programs. Benham has worked for 14 years with parents' groups to save school music programs.

"It costs more to hire teachers for several small classes than to hire one band director to teach a large group of students," says Benham. "I'll sit down with administrators and show them, dollar for dollar, that keeping their music program makes smart fiscal sense."

Shaping New Programs

Edward Lisk believes that universities, the music industry, and professional associations are going to need to work cooperatively to develop innovative new music courses that can be recognized as core subjects.

Dr. Andrew Dabczynski, supervisor of fine arts for the Waterford School District in Waterford, Michigan, agrees. "We have to consider whether the sole purpose of a music program is to meet with students daily and prepare them to perform a concert or whether we should strive for comprehensive musicianship. That way, on those occasions when not everyone can meet together, children can learn composition, basic instrument skills, music history, or maybe even music criticism."

Dabczynski also believes teachers will need to be much more flexible. "I think we've been trained to be myopic," he says. "But we are moving into the age of the generalist. Teachers are going to need to be open to teaching new courses and implementing new educational initiatives."

Bill Gora, of the Appalachian State University School of Music in Boone, North Carolina, cautions directors not to rest on their laurels. "Initially," he says, "parents may be supportive because you have established a great program. But in four years, you'll have new kids and new parents who will be wondering, 'What right do you have to take 25 percent of my child's education?' You have to keep proving yourself."

So it appears that, as block scheduling becomes a reality in school districts across the country, the major challenge for music educators will lie in their ability to promote continually the genuine value of music education to students, parents, and administrators.

"Playing a music instrument is a form of communication and a language of expression and of emotion," Edward Lisk reminds us. "It is a vital part of a child's education. When they talk about Shakespeare, we must remind them of Beethoven."

Block Scheduling Pros and Cons

Pros

- With a four-period day, band students enjoy more rehearsal time in longer class periods.
- Students receive more academic credit for band and music courses.
- Band has full academic standing. It is not just an elective.
- With a modified block schedule, students may benefit from longer rehearsals on alternate days rather than shorter daily rehearsals.

Cons

- Band students who have scheduling conflicts with a four-period day may drop out of band.
- Schools may have to group music and band courses together and cut back the number of music offerings because of scheduling difficulties.
- Students may take band for only one semester out of the year, which may lead to erratic instrument representation in a school's band.
- With modified block schedules, when students are absent, they miss a lot of instruction time, which can be a problem when a band is preparing for a concert.

15 Steps You Can Take to Prepare for Block Scheduling

William Gora

1. Know the money side of your band program. Find out how much of your school's budget is being spent on your music program. Also, ask band parents how much money they invest annually in music lessons and instruments. When administrators realize the private investment parents are making in music, they may value your program more highly.
2. Know your program. Find out the enrollment figures for your music program. Also, track the academic performance of your band students (standardized test scores, class ranking, GPAs). This can be helpful information to bring to faculty discussions.
3. Tout the academic value, not the trophies. Band programs successfully teach key educational skills such as decision-making and logical thinking. Do not let the total focus of your program revolve around performance opportunities; otherwise, people will perceive your purpose as strictly entertainment. (See no. 9)

Dr. William A. Gora is the director of bands at Appalachian State University, Boone, North Carolina. Dr. Gora writes extensively and conducts seminars on school reform issues.

4. Take a close look at the block scheduling proposal for your school. Don't immediately assume it will hurt your program. Although strict block schedules could have a negative impact on music programs, a modified block schedule may offer some advantages, such as longer rehearsals and more choices. (See no. 12)

5. Have your wish list ready. With change comes the opportunity to enhance your program and, possibly, to get your wishes. Go for it. Maybe you can work into the program a new class you've always wanted.

6. Be actively involved from the beginning. Thinking that everything will take care of itself means you'll have to take what's given to you. (See no. 11)

7. Keep focused on the kids. This is a student issue, not an adult issue. As best you can, ask others to articulate the benefits for students from suggested changes, not the benefits for adults, teachers, and administrators. Keep asking, "Will this change help the kids?"

Dr. John Benham is a national consultant, speaker, and author and the president of Music in World Cultures, a program to advance music literacy in Third World countries. Dr. Benham has helped music teachers and parent groups throughout the United States and Canada save and restore school music programs in the face of budget reductions.

Edward Lisk

8. Stay on top of recent developments in education. Read educational journals to find out what's happening around the country with block scheduling. Recommended sources are *Educational Leadership* and *Phi Delta Kappan*. (Ask your administrator if your school subscribes to these publications, because most do. If not, these journals are often readily available in university libraries.

9. Learn to communicate the academic benefits of your band program. A great resource for getting up to speed is the publication *Spin Offs: The Extra Musical Advantage of a Band Education* from your local UMI dealer. (See no. 3)

10. Speak out. Make it a long-term goal to take advantage of opportunities to present the academic value of bands to adult audiences, be it parent groups, community leaders, or civic associations.

Dr. Edward L. Lisk is a well-known seminar leader and author on rehearsal technique and former director of bands for highly acclaimed Oswego High School, Oswego, New York. He is past president of the National Band Association.

Dean Christopher

11. Make sure you are on the block scheduling implementation committee. (See no. 6)

12. Accept the challenge in ways that will allow you to address and correct problems that the regimentation of the past wouldn't allow. (See no. 4)

13. Give enough time to planning so that when school ends in the spring, everyone knows what they're getting into the next fall.

14. To alleviate course conflicts, schedule single-offering classes first, not only music but also physics, expository work, and so on—whatever subject that may meet at the same time as other courses offered at more than one time period.

15. Pace rehearsals with an 85-minute rehearsal in mind. Each rehearsal plan will be different, depending on the individual.

M. Dean Christopher received a bachelor of music education from Western Michigan University and did his graduate work at Western Michigan and Wayne State. He has been an adjudicator at every Michigan Competing Bands State Final since 1978 (except 1992) and every Michigan Color Guard

Circuit Final since 1993. He is also band director at West Ottawa High School, Holland, Michigan, and plays trumpet professionally.

PART II

BETTER AND BETTER

A Michigan Band Director Critiques the New Block System in His School

M. Dean Christopher, band director at West Ottawa High School, Holland, Michigan, feels that the block scheduling his school initiated last fall is getting "better and better." Christopher, who is also a K–12 music coordinator for West Ottawa Public Schools, is in his twenty-fourth year as a high school band director, for the past six years at West Ottawa. Although it is too early to fully evaluate, he thinks the new scheduling is working, and most faculty agree. Christopher lists these pluses:

Pluses

1. Students are more on task, more focused, and approach class more refreshed. Tuesday through Friday they have only four courses each day, and each day is different.
2. Because of the longer sessions, block scheduling provides the flexibility to get more done per class period and to meet the specific needs of students.
3. In the past, scheduling has been the main reason for losing band students after their freshman year because of the competition for their time. Students can now choose from seven courses rather than six, as before, a plus for electives. Music classes are bigger because of this option.
4. Two seminar blocks a week are used for assemblies, pep rallies, student council, make-up work, remedials, special projects—anything above and beyond the regular school day. Classes are uninterrupted.

Minuses

1. Block scheduling in high school is not compatible with non-block middle schools for teachers with middle-school responsibilities. [Christopher was relieved of his work with sixth-grade band. The school district hired another instructor for that band, who also assists Christopher.]
2. The school added a seventh course, a seminar, and expanded passing time and lunch periods, resulting in 58 fewer minutes of class time per week. [However, by using part of the seminar time, Christopher actually has the same class time as before. Band meets in assigned groups during the marching season and then splits into symphony and concert bands during the regular class period plus half the lunch hour.]
3. By not meeting every day, some continuity is lost. Some classes don't meet from Thursday until Monday, a long time between rehearsals.

Apprehensions Groundless

Some apprehensions regarding the new schedule proved groundless: whether students would be able to adapt to the change or to keep up if they didn't have the same class each day; if they would remember where they were supposed to be on a given day; and whether fatigue would be a factor with longer classes. Not only have there been few such problems, but also the students, especially incoming freshmen, really like the new schedule.

The eight-block schedule at West Ottawa High School is in effect on Tuesday through Friday (Monday has seven 40- to 45-minute periods), with only four classes each day. There's an 89-minute first hour and 84-minute third, fifth, and seventh hours Tuesday and Thursday. Wednesday and Friday, there's an 89-minute second hour and 84-minute fourth, seminar, sixth, and eight hours. There are two 40-minute lunch periods.

Other faculty have 24 students (six pupils each, from ninth through twelfth grades) assigned to them for seminar. Although not assigned students, Christopher works with an average of 30 students on solos, ensembles, sections, and whatever else is needed during each semester. West Ottawa High School has 1,600 students, 100 of whom are in freshman band, 112 in high school/marching band (56 each concert and symphonic), and 74 in two jazz classes—one a "zero-hour" (6:55 a.m.) session that meets daily (additional to block). There are also 36 students in freshman orchestra, 46 in high school orchestra, and 180 in three choirs, with which he assists.

Performance-Oriented

West Ottawa bands are very performance-oriented—with pep, jazz, marching, solos, ensembles, concerts, parades, and so on—averaging one performance every three-and-a-half school days. "Because of this high performance level and participation in competition events, music is highly accountable, perhaps more so than the academics," says Christopher. He is, however, adamantly opposed to a "getting-ready-to-perform" rote teaching method. He does not repeat performance selections; and he's big on sight-reading, which he feels is important in achieving his goal of turning out "total musicians." At this point, he believes West Ottawa's block scheduling can help him achieve these goals. In summing up, Dean Christopher says: "Capitalize on the advantages of block scheduling for your situation. By planning ahead, you can minimize the negatives." He offers the following suggestions.

M. Dean Christopher: Eight Ways to Make Block Work

1. Make sure you are on the block scheduling implementation committee.
2. Accept the challenge as an opportunity to expand in ways that will allow you to address and correct problems that the regimentation of the past wouldn't allow.
3. Communicate your goals. Expect to compromise. Be open-minded.
4. Give enough time to planning so that when school ends in the spring everyone knows what to expect the next fall.
5. First schedule those classes that are offered at only one time period, whatever the subject— music, physics, expository work, and so on—so that they do not conflict with each other.
6. If responsible for middle-school classes, hire additional instructors if needed.
7. Make sure students are fully informed well in advance.
8. Pace rehearsals. Each rehearsal plan will be different, depending on the instructor. [Christopher, for example, does more read-throughs at the end of his rehearsal periods.]

PART III

DO WHAT IS RIGHT FOR YOUR SCHOOL

**Jon Milleman: "Be involved in the change from the beginning.
Don't let the change happen to you. Make it happen with you."**

Jon Milleman prepared this article for Director *as the third in a series examining block scheduling and its effect on band students and their directors. Milleman has been director of the Angola (Indiana) High School band program since 1993. Previously, he was the director of bands at Central Noble Community Schools (Albion, Indiana) from 1989 to 1993. He holds a bachelor of music education degree from Western Michigan University and is currently pursuing a master's degree in secondary administration from Indiana University in Fort Wayne, Indiana.*

Our high school has approximately 850 students in predominantly rural northwest Indiana. The level of trust between the school and the community is high. Our band booster organization is strong and growing.

The band program at Angola offers concert band, jazz band, marching band, pep band, winter color guard, solo and ensemble participation, and a small number of private lessons. Enrollment in band requires participation in marching band, concert band, and pep band. Lessons, solo and ensemble, jazz band, and winter guard are optional.

Planning the Four-by-Four Schedule

Since 1992, our staff and students have gone through an extensive examination of possible alternate schedules that would help lower the daily number of students per teacher, lessen the stress on the teacher and the student, and enhance student learning. Additionally, we wanted to preserve our strength as a band program as well as maintain our requirements for participation in concert and marching band. I was consulted through every step of the process. The philosophy in dealing with music was "Let's not try to fix something that is not broken."

Planning the schedule also included the use of research by consultants Joseph Carroll and Robert Lynn Canady. Dr. Canady opened the eyes of our staff to the enormous possibilities of alternate schedules. One of the important points of his discussions was the need to tailor a schedule to the unique characteristics of your school. Use the research, learn from other schools, but ultimately do what is right for your situation.

Our Old Schedule

Previously we were on a seven-period day. Students in band took band plus six other classes or band plus five classes and a study period. Jazz band met in the morning outside of the school day for no credit.

Our New Schedule

Our new band schedule uses the full 90-minute block of time for the first nine weeks as full band rehearsal. This is during the marching band season when there is typically a great deal more rehearsal time required.

During marching band, we rehearse before school Monday and Wednesday mornings beginning at 7 a.m. On the weeks of ISSMA Regional and State Finals, we rehearse Monday, Tuesday, and Wednesday mornings at 7 a.m. We dismiss the students from the morning rehearsal at 9:30 a.m. This gives us a two-and-a-half-hour rehearsal on these mornings. Of course we still see the students for 90 minutes Tuesday, Thursday, and Friday. (We met 80 minutes on these days, factoring transit time and equipment concerns). We also held rehearsals Thursday evenings (one night per week) to allow our staff to rehearse with the entire band.

Band students receive one full credit for the first nine weeks. In the four-by-four schedule, a nine-week grading period is the same as a semester in the old schedule. During the second, third, and fourth nine weeks, the band splits the first 90-minute block between concert band and jazz band. For the first 45 minutes of the block, the band meets in concert band. At the end of the 45 minutes, the students in jazz band move to another rehearsal space (the stage in our case) and rehearse for the second 45 minutes. Those students who are not in jazz band go to seminar.

Seminar is much like a traditional study hall except it has the feature of being supervised by a classroom teacher. There are classroom teachers supervising seminars during each block. For the student, this means that there is tutoring available in each subject from a classroom teacher (not necessarily the teacher they have in a given subject, but a teacher in each subject is available).

We also allow the winter color guard members to stay during the second 45 minutes. They work on cleaning their equipment and go over parts of their show. These students are required to log their practice time, and the captains must sign the practice log to verify that the work was completed.

Also, because we are in a team teaching situation in all bands, my assistant director uses the second 45 minutes to coach solo and ensemble students and work with various sections of the concert band on upcoming concert or contest music. We accomplish this individualized coaching by publishing a seminar schedule at least a week in advance. This notice gives the students the opportunity to plan ahead. They will know in advance the days that they are expected to stay for the full 90 minutes. During the week of concerts, we typically have the full band stay for the entire 90 minutes. Students must come to my office before band starts to sign out of seminar. We then take the list of students to the seminar supervisor so she will know who will be attending.

One reason that this plan is attractive to band students is they are able to have 45 minutes of study time daily (something my students say is better than the long 90-minute study period). Then the students are able to fill up on the remaining three blocks with classes, allowing them to take their requirements as well as electives.

I counsel my freshmen to take physical education during the first nine weeks along with another low-homework class. This greatly reduces the stress of dealing with the transition into high school along with the busy marching band schedule. Our guidance department counsels all students to balance the low-homework classes with the high-homework classes.

Remember, since nine weeks is the same as a semester, the old traditional semester classes meet for only nine weeks. Therefore, students are able to take two classes during the same block of time within the same semester. I have freshmen in band who are enrolled in seven other classes.

Sample Band Student Schedule Under Block System

Students are given credit and a grade for band. They receive a half credit each for the second, third, and fourth nine weeks unless they are in jazz band, in which case they receive one credit for each nine weeks. Students in jazz band receive four credits, and non-jazz band students receive two-and-a-half credits.

The choir schedule is essentially the same. However, the choir meets in a different block of time. Choir could be scheduled during the same block for some schools to assist students who wish to do both. Because we share teachers with the middle school, this is very difficult.

At this point, we are very pleased with the flexibility of the schedule. We are able to require a full year of participation without disrupting the students' diploma track or Advanced Placement track schedule. Students have morning rehearsals, which require less outside rehearsal time. (We actually gained about one-and-a-half hours more rehearsal time in marching band).

I do caution, however, that we are currently in the first semester of this schedule. I do not anticipate any problems that we will not be able to address. I feel confident that the lines of communication are open among the band, the committee, and the administration.

OLD SCHEDULE

Period 1	Period 2	Period 3	Period 4	Period 5	Period 6	Period 7
Band	Class or study hall	Class or study hall	Class or study hall	Class or study hall	Class or study hall	Class or study hall

NEW SCHEDULE
FIRST NINE WEEKS

Period 1	Period 2	Period 3	Period 4
Band 90 minutes	Class 90 minutes	Class 90 minutes	Class 90 minutes

SECOND, THIRD, AND FOURTH NINE WEEKS

Period 1	Period 2	Period 3	Period 4
Band, seminar, or jazz ensemble 45 minutes	Class	Class	Class

TYPICAL WEEKLY REHEARSAL SCHEDULE

Time	Monday	Tuesday	Wednesday	Thursday	Friday
First 45 minutes	Full concert band, full jazz band rehearsal	Full concert band, jazz band saxes and rhythm	Full concert band, full jazz band rehearsal	Full concert band, jazz band brass and rhythm	Full concert band, full jazz band rehearsal
Second 45 minutes	Solos and ensembles w/assistant director	Concert and brass ensembles w/assistant director	Solos and ensembles w/assistant director	Concert and brass ensembles w/assistant director	Solos and ensembles w/assistant director

SAMPLE BAND STUDENT SCHEDULE UNDER BLOCK SYSTEM

First Semester	First Semester	Second Semester
First nine weeks	Second nine weeks	
Band 90 minutes	Band 45 minutes, seminar or jazz band 45 minutes	Band 45 minutes, seminar or jazz band 45 minutes
P.E. English Computer App.	P.E. English Basic Art	Science Math Foreign language

Why It Is Working

- The administration made a conscious effort to protect our success as a band program.
- The scheduling committee communicated with the band director throughout the entire process.
- Angola High School researched and studied other schedules for three years before implementing.
- The administration agreed to preserve the current policy requiring a full year of participation in band.
- We informed band parents about the new schedule in advance.
- We have an eighth-grade information night each year before scheduling. Our parent organization is strong and they ask questions throughout.
- We are able to offer jazz band for credit and meet every day.
- The use of the second 45 minutes during concert band makes solo and ensemble coaching available during the school day, eliminating some of the after-school scheduling conflicts.
- Private lessons can be taught during the second 45 minutes.
- Instructional videos and special guests can be brought in during the entire 90 minutes.

Do

- Ask questions about the reasoning in each scheduling decision.
- Keep your parents informed about the process.
- Keep your students informed about the process.
- Make sure that you can live with the amount of rehearsal time that you will have in the new schedule.

Don't

- Assume anything that you want is understood.
- Appear inflexible.
- Let the situation happen to you. Be proactive.
- Trust someone to convey your message or concerns. Do it yourself.
- Misinform your students throughout the process.
- Make enemies.
- Take sides in the discussions. Do what is best for the band students.

Summary

The above article illustrates a few examples of how directors have adapted to scheduling challenges in their districts. Every school district is different! The MENC Web site (www.menc.org) contains many interesting links to music and arts advocacy groups and articles on a variety of music education topics including scheduling, research studies on the benefits of music education, and much more. They also offer an extensive selection of publications and toolkits to assist educators and administrators. Contact MENC: The National Association for Music Education, 1806 Robert Fulton Drive, Reston, VA 20191-4348. The International Association for Jazz Education (IAJE) is also a great resource: P.O. Box 724, Manhattan, KS 66505, (785) 776-8766 (www.iaje.org).

DIRECTOR'S CHECKLIST FOR SCHEDULING

- Anticipate scheduling challenges and solve them with awareness, knowledge, and creativity.

- Compare and share solutions with colleagues.

- Develop teamwork and strong relationships with colleagues from all subject areas and the administrator in charge of scheduling.

- Sectionals, rehearsals, student conductors, and performances are all critical areas that may challenge you. Expect changes and anticipate solutions.

- Communicate, educate, and solidify awareness with administrators, your students, and their parents.

Chapter 6

BUDGET

WHAT YOU NEED AND HOW TO GET IT

by J. Richard Dunscomb

Did you ever think, *If only I had the money, I could . . . with my jazz groups?* The most important step in gaining that financial resource is to ask for it based upon solid educational reasons.

BUDGET PHILOSOPHY

Your budget should clearly reflect your philosophy and long-range goals. Pre-planning your budget is another important and necessary step in laying a successful foundation for your jazz program. It is much easier to convince your principal or department chair that your budget requests are necessary if they are solidly tied into your three-year goals.

If you are a first-year teacher or new to the position, recognize that in the first year of your program you will probably enjoy a "honeymoon period," so take advantage of this time to ask for all you need. Keep in mind that initiating and continuing jazz programs, compared to the cost of operating most other music programs, is relatively inexpensive.

Research

Do some research into the purchasing policies of your school or school district. Discover how the budget works in your area from the person who will be responsible for approving your budget. An operating budget might include line items for music, instruments, equipment, textbooks, audio-visual, library needs, guest artists or consultants, repairs/maintenance of the foregoing, and so on. Or it may be that you are allocated a specific amount for your budget. Either way, you will need to be specific when setting up your budget.

When submitting your budget, you should plan on requesting 10–15% above your minimum budgetary needs. Most administrators pare down budget requests, so expect to have that happen to you.

Budget Emphasis

If you have a strong emphasis on any particular area of your program, the budget should reflect it. For example, if you have a $2,000 budget, do you spend it all on music or do you set aside some for guest artists? Although there is almost never enough money for all you want and need for your program, it is important that you spend all you are allocated. Any money left in the budget at the end of the year will be an indication that you didn't need it, and as a result you probably will be allotted less in the next budget.

Create an Inventory List

If you are inheriting a program that has instruments, music, and the like, create an inventory list. Divide the list into specific areas. Begin by determining the condition of each item, which will provide you with an overall look at the status of your physical property. Repairing and maintaining your inventory can save you much aggravation in the future. Taking inventory will also give you a clearer picture where new monies will best be spent.

Internet Research and Your Local Music Dealer

When you need to gather information on purchasing items, the Internet is a great resource tool. Many of the current Internet sites that provide reliable information are listed in this book's Resource Guide. Even though using the Internet is quick and easy, don't neglect your local music dealers when making a decision on where to purchase. Music retailers sell and lease instruments, provide instrument repair service, stock essential instrument accessories, and offer solutions to many challenges. Many have traveling representatives who will personally service your school. Not only are they experienced with the school purchase order and billing procedures, but also they can support music advocacy programs and are strong allies in the community. These services and benefits are not readily available on the Internet. Although prices from local retailers may appear to be slightly higher than those on the Internet (but not always), the difference in service to you and your program may be significant.

Bids and Purchase Orders

Most schools require bids when purchasing items over $500. In any case, you need to provide your purchasing agent with the following information:
- A complete description of the item, including brand and model numbers.
- Cost per item.
- Name of the vendor, including address, fax, phone, and name of your contact person.

Remember

Contact, get to know, and support your local music dealer. They will offer service you won't often receive from a Web-based wholesale merchant. Most dealers will be able to provide their school customers with some discounts.

INSTRUMENTS AND OTHER CAPITAL PURCHASES

Most schools have a separate budget for purchasing capital items. Musical instruments usually fall into that category

Assuming students in your school own or rent their own alto/tenor saxophone, trumpet, trombone, guitar, bass, and drum set, the following list shows additional instruments that most schools traditionally purchase for their programs. Remember that instruments are available in various levels of quality—from student-line instruments up to professional instruments—so prices will vary with the quality of the instrument. You can also lease instruments from some leading instrument manufacturers. Additional information is available for each wind and rhythm section instrument in their appropriate chapters.

Minimum-Level Funding

Here are some of the basics you will need at the minimum level:
- Music (refer to Chapter 15)
- Baritone sax with low A
- Bass trombone
- Piano (if not currently available and in good repair) or electronic keyboard with amplifier
- Guitar amp
- Bass amp
- Drum set with cymbals
- Jazz CDs, DVDs/videos (refer to the Resource Guide)
- Sound system
- Repairs/maintenance
- IAJE membership for the director

- Computer workstation:
  Hardware suggestions:
    - Computers connected to General MIDI keyboards with powered speakers or headphones
    - Computers that are Internet capable, with General MIDI sound generation (internal sound card for Windows; QuickTime Musical Instruments for MacOS) connected to powered speakers or headphones
    - Computers that are Internet capable, with powered speakers or headphones
    - Printer for computers
  Software suggestions:
    - Web browser software such as Netscape Communicator or Internet Explorer
    - Morton Subotnick's Making More Music software
    - Notation software such as Music Time or Print Music
    - Accompaniment software such as Band-in-a-Box or Visual Arranger
    - Sequencing software such as Musicshop or Cakewalk Home Studio
    - Spreadsheet software such as AppleWorks, Microsoft Works, or Microsoft Excel
    - Word processing software such as AppleWorks, Microsoft Word, or WordPerfect
    - Basic Internet access and Hyperstudio software
  Hardware/software combinations:
    - www.soundtree.com offers a MIDI Educator Bundle, which includes computer, synthesizer, speakers, sequencing software, notation software, Soundtree Learning Bundle (MiBac Music Lessons, Band-in-a-Box, and Musical Hearing), Warner Bros. Publications' *Tech Start* book series, MOTU FastLane USB MIDI interface, damper pedal, cables and connectors, and set-up guide.

Mid-Level Funding

As the program moves to the next financial level, here are suggestions for purchases:
- Music (refer to Chapter 15)
- Tenor sax
- Acoustic bass with pickup or microphone
- Latin percussion—two conga drums with stands and hand percussion
- Timbales
- Vibes
- Guest artists
- Synthesizer and amp
- Computer workstation:
  Hardware suggestions:
    - Computers that are Internet capable, with video-in capability connected to powered speakers
    - Computers that are Internet capable, with microphone, connected to General MIDI keyboards with powered speakers or headphones
    - Computers that are Internet capable, with CD-ROM or DVD-ROM player connected to powered speakers or headphones
    - Cassette tape recorder
  Software suggestions:
    - Multimedia authoring software such as HyperStudio, PowerPoint, or AppleWorks
    - Computers with General MIDI sound generation (internal sound card for Windows; QuickTime Musical Instruments for MacOS) connected to powered speakers or headphones
    - Computer music workstation: minimum-level equipment plus upgraded computer with Finale music-writing software and additional jazz improvisation software

Advanced-Level Funding

The next level will require the following purchases to round out the complete program (in addition to the above):

- Music (refer to Chapter 15)
- Jazz music software
- Computers for the rehearsal room
- Guest artists
- Flugelhorns
- Sound system complete with microphones, speakers, monitors, etc.
- Soprano sax
- Special mutes for brass (bucket, Harmon, etc.)
- School membership or individual student memberships in IAJE
- Music folders (hardbound)
- Music composed and/or arranged specifically for your jazz ensemble
- Stand fronts for the band
- Lights for music stands
- Travel cases for the large instruments (cost varies with size of case)
- Travel cases for music folders
- Computer workstation:

  Hardware suggestions:
  - Advanced high-end computer with ability to record digital audio and video
  - DVD and digital audio sequencer
  - Computer display projector
  - CD-ROM burner
  - Mixer
  - Sampler

  Software suggestions:
  - Web page authoring software, such as Netscape Composer or Microsoft FrontPage Express
  - Notation software, such as Finale or Sibelius
  - Sequencing software with digital audio, such as Cakewalk Home Studio, Metro 5, or Micrologic
  - Page layout software, such as Quark, Pagemaker, Appleworks, or Microsoft Word
  - Video teleconferencing software, such as CU-See-Me or Netmeeting
  - Video editing software, such as Premier or Avid Cinema

DIRECTOR'S CHECKLIST FOR BUDGET

- Create a budget for your program.

- Be sure that your philosophy and long-range goals are reflected in the budget.

- Know the purchasing policies of your school and/or district.

- Make an accurate inventory of any items already on hand and keep it updated.

- Use the funding levels as examples to create a step-wise plan for your program needs.

- Make long-range (three years or more) budget plans.

- Incorporate technology in teaching whenever possible—both for group and individual needs—using CDs, videos, software, etc.

- Check the specific instrument chapters for additional information.

Music Books, CDs, Videos, and Jazz Software

Music, books, CDs, videos, and jazz software are essential items for every program. Chapter 15, "Selecting Music for Your Ensemble," will help you know what music to purchase. Although purchasing music is necessary, sometimes many other items are overlooked or not given high priority.

Teaching jazz to students can be put into high gear if they have materials to work with independently while not under your supervision. There is a world of materials available that will fill these additional audio/visual resource needs and help you have educated students at the same time. You will quickly discover those students who have initiative and interest in becoming better jazz musicians by opening this opportunity to them. Students can and will improve skills in improvisation, listening, theory, arranging, jazz nuances, and sophisticated techniques on how to play their instrument. Below are but a few of the suggested areas.

MUSICAL INSTRUMENTS/EQUIPMENT MANUFACTURERS

www.boosey.com

www.calicchio.com

www.daddario.com

www.edwards-instruments.com

www.gleblanc.com

www.guildguitars.com

www.jupitermusic.com

www.kanstul.com

www.kyddbass.com

www.ludwig-drums.com

www.pearldrum.com

www.rayburn.com

www.remodrums.com

www.ricoreeds.com

www.rolandUS.com

www.sabianltd.com

www.samashmusic.com

www.selmer.com

www.steinway.com

www.thomastik-infeld.com

www.unitedmusical.com

www.usahorn.com

www.vandoren.com

www.vicfirth.com

www.wwandbw.com

www.yahama.com

www.yahama.com/band

www.yahamadrums.com

www.zildjian.com

MUSIC PUBLISHERS/DISTRIBUTORS

www.advancemusic.com

www.alfred.com

www.arts.unco.edu/UNCJazz

www.barnhouse.com

www.fjhmusic.com

www.halleonard.com

www.jazzatlincolncenter.org

www.jazzbooks.com

www.jfraser.com

www.jwpepper.com

www.kendormusic.com

www.kjos.com

www.marinamusic.com

www.melbay.com

www.otterdist.com

www.ottermusicsales.com

www.oup.co.uk.com

www.pendersmusic.com

www.scarecrowpress.com

www.seabreezejazz.com

www.secondfloormusic.com

www.shermusic.com

www.sierramusic.com

www.walrusmusic.com

www.warnerbrospublications.com

www.wwandbw.com

www.yahama.com

MUSIC SOFTWARE

www.ars-nova.com/practica

www.cakewalk.com

www.cdromshop.com

www.childrenseducationalsoftware.com

www.codamusic.com

www.halycom.com

www.jumpmusic.com

www.jwpepper.com

www.mcc.ac.uk

www.mccormicksnet.com/smartscr

www.midisoft.com

www.motu.com

www.musicalsoftware.com

www.musicians.about.com

www.musitek.com

www.noteworthy.com

www.opcode.com

www.pendersmusic.com

www.pgmusic.com

www.playjazz.com

www.pyware.com

www.rising.com.au/auralia

www.sfoundry.com

www.sibelius.com

www.soundquest.com

www.soundtree.com

www.soundtrek.com

www.sseyo.com

www.voicecrystal.com

www.votetra.com

www.wildcat.com

www.windmusicplus.com

www.wwandbw.com

New software programs are being produced at a rapid rate. Some that are available as of this printing include:

Allegro 2000 (from Finale) **www.codamusic.com**
> This software contains full MIDI features and everything you need to compose, play back, and print your own music.

Amadeus al Fine **www.pyware.com**
> A hardware box that converts "microphone input" of any wind instrument into standard MIDI file data. Also can track student performances plus keeps records of grades and progress.

Auralia **www.rising.com.au/auralia**
> A computer-based aural training course for beginning to advanced music students. Its testing features make preparation of exams and quizzes easy. For Windows only.

Band-in-a-Box **www.pgmusic.com**
> Type in the chords to any song and select from 75 styles, and Band-in-the-Box does the rest. It can automatically generate a complete professional-quality arrangement of bass, drums, piano, guitar, and strings.

Cakewalk Home Studio **www.cakewalk.com**
> Play along with more than 30 song files. Easily record new music with an instrument or vocals. Supports up to four tracks of digital audio along with MIDI. A scaled-down version of Cakewalk Professional.

Cakewalk Professional www.cakewalk.com

A powerful MIDI and digital audio software application that allows you to produce music and sound projects quickly and affordably. It provides many of Cakewalk's advanced technologies, with a focus on the needs of the commercial project studio.

Fanfare www.cdromshop.com

A comprehensive music theory program designed to help a musician master aural perception, rhythm, and theory skills through a progression of a number of topics designed to help with all of the hard-to-learn areas of music theory.

Finale www.codamusic.com

The #1 choice of music notation software used by publishers and music educators who want publisher-quality notation that's easy to use.

Intonation Trainer www.codamusic.com

Teaches woodwind and brass students how to listen for and eliminate intonation beats. Students learn which notes on their instrument are out of tune and to anticipate pitch problems and how to solve them.

Metro (by Cakewalk) www.cakewalk.com

For Mac users only, this is software based on sophisticated MIDI and digital audio recording software.

MidiScan www.musitek.com

Designed to quickly and accurately convert printed sheet music into multi-track MIDI files. Also enables users to capture and play back complex musical arrangements in minutes.

Music Administrator www.pyware.com

A fully interactive data-gathering program designed specifically for the music educator. You can produce comprehensive statistical, financial, and student data reports pre-designed in the system or design your own.

Music Office System www.pyware.com

Records can be displayed in a list style or in individual windows with navigator buttons that traverse from one record to another.

Overture www.cakewalk.com

For complete orchestral arrangements, lead sheets, individual cues, or simple notation examples.

Practica Musica www.ars-nova.com/practica

Music theory and ear-training software includes customizable learning activities that meet a wide variety of needs.

Print Music! 2000Opus (from Finale) www.codamusic.com

Provides a way to create, play, and print music from scratch or from any MIDI file.

Score Writer www.cakewalk.com

For band arrangements, lead sheets, solo parts, or simple notation examples.

Sibelius www.sibelius.com

Designed for composing, arranging, teaching, playing, and publishing music of every kind to the highest professional standards.

SmartScore www.mccormicksnet.com/smartscr

Has fully integrated music scoring, MIDI sequencing, and music scanning with advanced recognition technology.

Please refer to the Resource Guide Index.

Chapter 7

THE JAZZ CONCEPT—SWING

by J. Richard Dunscomb

Here are some questions for the jazz educator:
- Can you get the band to swing?
- Can you demonstrate the jazz concept?
- Can you explain jazz improvisation?
- Can you explain the jazz feel?
- Can you teach jazz?

Here is the answer to all of these questions: Yes, you can! Jazz is not another language—it is another musical genre that can be learned and taught. Check out these logical steps toward understanding jazz in a swing style.

SWING-STYLE BASICS

Understanding jazz music, conceptually, and being able to pass it on to the students is perhaps the most important aspect of making the jazz ensemble sound like a professional big band. This chapter deals specifically with playing in the swing style. Although many of the concepts discussed will apply to all styles, the swing style should be considered first, because: 1) it represents the essence and core of jazz music, and 2) it is the most foreign to your students. Certainly, the ability to swing will be the most important step young musicians take toward understanding jazz. There are a number of essential tasks that add up to your ability to teach the swing concept. These include but are certainly not limited to the following:
- Listen, repeatedly, to professional jazz recordings to identify and begin to understand jazz style.
- Identify the jazz sound, both in that of the entire ensemble and in developing an understanding of individual players' roles in the styles. The rhythm section is particularly important in this regard.
- Identify the steady beat or time and know how to make it work.
- Understand the swing eighth-note concept.
- Identify characteristic jazz nuances, shapes, and musical language.
- Understand proper jazz articulation.
- Be able to sing confidently with jazz syllables, connecting visual and aural skills.
- Learn to phrase in a jazz style.

It Comes Down to Listening

Listening to professional jazz recordings is an absolute must for you and your students because it is essential to learning the language of jazz. Listening steeps the inexperienced students in the jazz concept and when done creatively expands the knowledge of even the most experienced educators. You must develop aural skills to a high degree because jazz style, concept, and articulation are nearly impossible to notate exactly. When you play the music precisely as notated on the page, it results in very "square," non-jazz sounding music. On the other hand, the comprehension of style gained through listening to jazz can allow the written notes to come alive. This is the process that jazz musicians have used successfully throughout the years, and it is explored further in Chapter 3.

Repeated Listening

Repeated listening is a must for all and is certainly a key to understanding jazz style as well as each player's role. Listening to an individual selection not once, not twice, but many, many times is necessary to gain the proper perspective. Every time you listen, you should determine specific things to listen for and to. For instance, consider the element of style. What style is the chart? Is it swing, shuffle, rock, pop, Latin (samba, bossa nova, cha-cha-cha, mambo, Afro-Cuban), waltz, or another style?

Play Recordings at Rehearsals

Each rehearsal should begin with a professional jazz recording playing as the students enter the room. This sets the tone for the musical standard you will work with your students to achieve and opens the door for them to enter into the serious music making that will follow.

STEADY PULSE

Steady time is crucial to invoking a jazz feel. A steady pulsation of the beat is the foundation of jazz. Exceptions are rare and mostly exhibited in rubato ballads. Underscore the importance of "time" to your students. While listening to professional jazz recordings, you may hear some slight fluctuation of the tempo, but generally great bands have great time. Many directors use electronic devices, like Dr. Beat, which is a metronome that can be run through an amplifier to create a steady pulse (also known as a click track). You can set the pulse either on every beat or on beats 2 and 4. Although there are many variations on how to use a pulsating time reference for the students, this author's preference is a hand-held metronome with an audible click and flashing light. Although the metronome is effective as an aid in kicking off the tune, it is even more effective to demonstrate where the time groove or tempo has fluctuated during various sections of the chart.

The Count-Off

The standard way to count off a tune verbally in four is "1-click, 2-click, 1-2-3-4." In rehearsal, the click can be the metronome or fingers snapping, while in performance it will be your fingers snapping. You can help students focus on this issue of steady time by having them take turns counting off a tune.

Time-Keeping

Generally the bassist and drummer are the timekeepers of the jazz ensemble. That assertion, however, does not mean that just one or two individuals are totally responsible for time. Time-keeping is essential for every member of the ensemble. Jazz educator Shelly Berg uses an analogy of a large piece of metal, weighing five hundred pounds, hanging over the entire ensemble. It would be nearly impossible for one person alone to lift the metal slab. But if the entire ensemble were to work together, lifting the metal would be quite easy. Using this analogy or a similar one, you can explain to your ensemble that the time is the responsibility of everyone and quite effortless when we all think, feel, and work together.

Occasionally having the wind sections play in rehearsal without the rhythm section will allow these players to develop a sense of time on their own. Many charts have written passages with this kind of playing. Until the winds in your ensemble can establish steady time on their own, a simple tap on each quarter note by the drummer on a closed hi-hat or snare drum will help. Try this exercise with individual sections as well.

Students seem to have great difficulty staying with the music during rests. In any genre of music, paying close attention to the pulse is essential for a proper entrance following a rest. In addition, that mindfulness will show respect and interest for what is being played by the rest of the ensemble during that rest. Quite simply, in jazz we should not have any rests, just space that some of the players do not actually play in, and yet they are still making music! Remember, without steady time, a jazz feel cannot be achieved.

SWING: THE MAIN INGREDIENT

Recognizing the swing eighth notes in jazz and imparting to the students how to play them are the most critical steps toward the realization of authentic jazz style. First of all, a line of eighth notes in a swing style is played with a triplet subdivision—with lengths approximating the 12/8 feel as notated in Example 1. This is the traditional (and easiest) written way of explaining swing eighths. In other words, two eighth notes are played with the first note longer than the second—not even and rigid but relaxed and bouncy. As always, listening to jazz is the best way to internalize the true swing eighth feel. Later in this chapter we recommend teaching swing eighths in the context of a chart, listening to the professionals play them first. Written notes can only approximate the true feel, which is gained through listening and repetition.

Jazz is an aural tradition, and variations in swing feel occur at different tempos. Although the triplet feel is more pronounced at a slow tempo, it is less apparent at a medium tempo. When the music is fast or very fast, the swing feel will disappear and for all practical purposes the eighth notes will become even.

Jazz Syllables

Jazz syllables are used throughout the examples of this text, and mastering them is important to the success of helping your students attain the characteristic jazz feel. Jazz syllables (or scat syllables) refer to phonetic sounds that imitate those made by wind players in the jazz idiom.

Example 1

Swing or Shuffle?

Some publishers in the past would notate "dotted eighth–sixteenth note" to mean swing eighths. However, this is no longer the case. So, if you see a dotted eighth–sixteenth figure in recently published jazz ensemble music, it should be played as written and will affect what is referred to as the shuffle style.

Example 2

Eighth Rests

Eighth rests in jazz are treated the same way as eighth notes—with a swing style. Therefore, if an eighth rest is written on the downbeat, it will be equal to the first two-thirds of the beat. This analysis may seem academic, but it is critical in order to grasp the swing eighth concept. Example 3 shows how the rests are written and how they are actually played.

Example 3

Quarter Notes

Quarter notes in jazz style, unless otherwise marked as legato, are normally played short (detached). Successive quarter notes in jazz elicit a strong tendency to rush. The expression "to hold back" is often used in referring to a tutti section with successive quarter notes. In these passages, advise your students to relax and not to rush or be too rigid with the time. This concept provides a perfect example for learning through listening and imitating. Example 4 depicts the quarter-note style. Notice in the example that for jazz style the accents appear on beats 2 and 4, rather than the "1 and 3" stress, which would typify classical style. It is important to help your students achieve this accentuation of quarter notes because most of the pop music they hear also heavily emphasizes beats 1 and 3. Spend time experimenting with a metronome, setting the click on 1 and 3, then 2 and 4. Hear the difference. Sing jazz examples with both click patterns and see which feels better and more like jazz. Also try different tempos and see how the feel becomes more even and smooth as the tempo increases.

Example 4

Eighth Notes

The most efficient way to teach swing eighths is to do so in the context of a chart. The chart we have selected is "Just Friends," as arranged by Joe Jackson. On the video, which is discussed further in Chapter 22, you will notice that the band is playing in what is referred to as the Basie style. "Just Friends" is a jazz standard tune, and this arrangement is a big band educational lesson for understanding and teaching the jazz swing style. Although the chart is not difficult to absorb, it contains many of the essential elements of jazz concepts. The excerpt begins with the rhythm section, and next it moves through a soft ensemble section for full band (listen to the soft jazz articulations that begin each series of notes). It concludes with a full band "shout chorus" where, although the energy and volume increase, the articulations remain consistent. Notice the way the notes are articulated throughout. You will hear that they are not all tongued, and certainly not tongued in a classical style. The vocal syllables are included for reference. Listen now to the recording of "Just Friends" on the online media.

Example 5

IDENTIFYING JAZZ NUANCES

Now listen again to the recording of "Just Friends" and begin to identify each of the following: swing style, jazz nuances, shapes, and musical language.

- This recorded example features a superb rhythm section sound in the swing style. The players all know their roles well. The passage from measures 65 to 88 (Example 5) demonstrates the characteristic rhythm section sound and blend for this particular style. The pianist solos in the sparse Basie style. The bass player lays down the walking feel of four quarter notes in each measure. The guitar player is playing steady quarter notes, too, in the Freddie Green style. The drummer knows his or her role: stay simple and make everyone else sound good.
- The full ensemble enters at measure 88, and their playing, in essence, is a clinic on executing smoothly in a jazz style and using phrase-ending eighth notes correctly.
- The phrasing in this section is in two-measure increments. Even with the short quarter note in measure 97, the phrase continues. Although phrase marks are not included on this chart, they are implied, and you can count on a great deal of jazz music to be organized in two- or four-measure phrases. Be prepared to mark phrases to help students interpret more thoroughly.
- The shout chorus starts with the notes leading into measure 109. Listen to the clarity and unity of the ensemble. The increase in dynamics is very effective, particularly contrasting the very soft section that preceded it.

• For the shout chorus, the rhythm section now assumes a different role. In particular, listen to the drummer using backbeats (heavy accents on beats 2 and 4) and to the simple but effective drum fills that set up the band entrances (these are called set-ups).
• Notice the typical Count Basie ending in the piano.
• Finally, observe again the way the notes are articulated throughout, which is not at all in a classical style. This is detailed in the next segment.

SING AND PLAY JAZZ ARTICULATION

Proper jazz articulation is essential to all successful jazz ensembles, and without it, jazz never gains its character. Being able to sing using jazz syllables and teach your ensemble to sing is a key to your group's successful performance of the jazz style. There are many variations on jazz scat syllables. Therefore, please consider the syllables used in these examples as some of the phonetic possibilities. It is important to be consistent in establishing a set of jazz syllables that you and the students will use regularly when singing their parts.

As you will have ascertained after hearing the arrangement of "Just Friends," the performance produces nuances, shapes, and musical language in a compelling, smooth feel. This is in large part due to the jazz articulations as executed by the musicians.

Do Not Be Intimidated!

Do not be intimidated by the jazz concept of articulation! Most classically trained musicians have spent many years learning and perfecting traditional phrasing and articulation. To expand, adapt, and vary the concepts for the jazz style is a skill acquired only by listening to and imitating accomplished jazz masters. Singing the jazz articulations is absolutely essential to the learning process since it demands the tongue be used to attack and release the vocal scat syllables exactly as they are executed on the wind instruments. Please, do not be bashful about singing along with jazz recordings. And, once again, do not be intimidated by jazz articulations or concepts. As a trained musician, you have developed superb ears sensitive to nuances, and you can easily learn the jazz style through imitation.

To articulate in a jazz style, the "ta," "tu," or "tut" beginning articulation used by the concert band brass player is replaced with a "doo" or "dah" tongue in the jazz ensemble. This change places the tongue lower in the mouth and creates a smoother articulation and phrase. Saxophone players can use the same approach with a softer attack similar to that of brass players.

Eighth-Note Lines

In the swing style, eighth-note lines are characteristically played *legato* unless otherwise marked, and typically these feature offbeat breath accents. Of course, the line may be interrupted with syncopation, shorter notes, harder accents, and many other common idiomatic jazz nuances; however, as you introduce swing eighth notes to an inexperienced band, your first priority is to achieve a smooth feel. The last eighth note in the run will be emphasized (or accented) and played shorter than the others. Most students will readily adapt to this tonguing style when they learn to sing the lines, so instruct your students to sing using jazz syllables. Notice in the trumpet part in Example 6 how syllables are used under each note. Remember, typical jazz syllables begin with soft sounds such as "doo" or "dah." Always be ready to sing to the ensemble, because it communicates articulation, accents, dynamics, and feeling. In other words, you need to bring the jazz concept to life for the students.

Phrase Beginnings and Endings

Jazz lines typically end with emphasis, but even then they employ the soft beginning sound with a harder ending. The line of notes below combines these beginning and ending sounds. Sing it yourself and you will see that it swings and will be easily taught to students. It is important to have all students sing it. Brass players will use the same tongue placement to sing scat syllables as to play their instruments, and for reed players the concept is quite easily transferred to their tonguing. Also have the members of the rhythm section sing scat syllables because they, too, will learn these concepts of style. Singing during jazz rehearsals occurs at all levels: middle school, high school, university, and professional. Singing is not only a proven technique for working on jazz concepts, but it is a "chops saver" as well.

Example 6

Example 7 shows the accent on the final note of the phrase. In this case, it is also appropriate to put a space before articulating the final note. Doing so will give more energy to that last syncopated note. This stylistic device is unique to jazz and therefore an important part of the jazz concept.

Example 7

Licks, lines, and phrases are consistently played differently from the way they are written. The eminent jazz educator Dr. David Baker has termed patterns and licks that are continually shared by virtually all of the great players, whether improvising or playing charts, as "the language of jazz." The repetitive nature of jazz patterns and licks will occur regularly in the jazz charts you play. Since this is such an integral part of making the music sound correct, please impress upon your students the significance of proper interpretation and execution. As you check out the following examples, remember that the focus is on the swing style. Remember, making a point of emphasis with an accent is enhanced when the line preceding it is played softer. Typical jazz lines often include predominant eighth-note motion mixed with triplets, as demonstrated in Example 8.

Example 8

Another idiomatic occurrence in jazz is the repeated jazz lick. Repeated licks almost always have the same feel and emphasis. In the example below, the line is stated, repeated, and followed by variations. The interpretation shown here is the typical way it would be played by a professional jazz musician.

Example 9

A catalog of jazz articulations, as published by IAJE, is shown on the next page. Although most are self-explanatory, a few require further clarification, which follows the chart. These articulation devices are also shown in the context of a typical jazz arrangement. Even though these articulations are primarily for wind instruments, rhythm section players should try to imitate them on their instruments as well.

THE STANDARDIZATION OF JAZZ ENSEMBLE ARTICULATIONS

International Association for Jazz Education

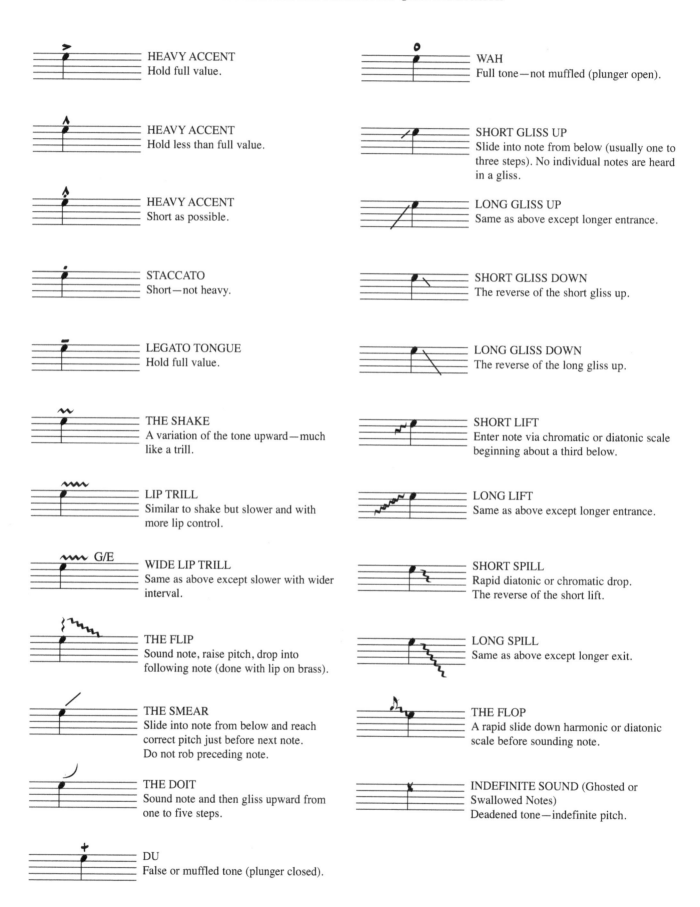

HEAVY ACCENT
Hold full value.

HEAVY ACCENT
Hold less than full value.

HEAVY ACCENT
Short as possible.

STACCATO
Short—not heavy.

LEGATO TONGUE
Hold full value.

THE SHAKE
A variation of the tone upward—much like a trill.

LIP TRILL
Similar to shake but slower and with more lip control.

WIDE LIP TRILL
Same as above except slower with wider interval.

THE FLIP
Sound note, raise pitch, drop into following note (done with lip on brass).

THE SMEAR
Slide into note from below and reach correct pitch just before next note. Do not rob preceding note.

THE DOIT
Sound note and then gliss upward from one to five steps.

DU
False or muffled tone (plunger closed).

WAH
Full tone—not muffled (plunger open).

SHORT GLISS UP
Slide into note from below (usually one to three steps). No individual notes are heard in a gliss.

LONG GLISS UP
Same as above except longer entrance.

SHORT GLISS DOWN
The reverse of the short gliss up.

LONG GLISS DOWN
The reverse of the long gliss up.

SHORT LIFT
Enter note via chromatic or diatonic scale beginning about a third below.

LONG LIFT
Same as above except longer entrance.

SHORT SPILL
Rapid diatonic or chromatic drop. The reverse of the short lift.

LONG SPILL
Same as above except longer exit.

THE FLOP
A rapid slide down harmonic or diatonic scale before sounding note.

INDEFINITE SOUND (Ghosted or Swallowed Notes)
Deadened tone—indefinite pitch.

Sometimes familiar markings from classical music appear in a jazz chart without an accompanying explanation of their special meaning. In the case of a mordant (or as it is called in jazz, a turn), it is important to know how jazz playing differs from classical interpretation, as in Example 11.

Example 11

Mordants

In jazz, mordants are often used to frame the chord tones. In these instances, rather than being played as four sixteenth notes, the mordant is commonly executed as a sixteenth-note triplet followed by an eighth note, as shown in Example 12. Remember that most idiomatic jazz licks were originally sung and then imitated by the instrumentalists; therefore, many of the figures are approximately notated.

Example 12

Quick Turns

A quick turn is quite effective and used often. It is, in essence, a flip above the first note and into the second note. As with many of the articulations, the quick turn can best be understood when seen in the context of a chart, as shown below.

Example 13 (Quick Turn)

Falls

Falls (or spills), as in Example 14, are quite common in jazz charts. Falls are played in various lengths, determined by the musical context in which they are found and considering what follows each fall. In full ensemble passages, no one should fall longer than the lead trumpet or lead section player. For a long fall, it is a good idea to mark a release at the end of a fall. Falls can be indefinite in sound, chromatic, or diatonic. However they are played, falls require lots of air to be effective. Be absolutely certain to establish the pitch or tonality of the note before the fall.

Example 14 (Fall)

Doo-Wah

Brass players encounter doo-wah figures at all stages of their development. The most common performance errors involve not making enough difference in sound between the two notes. For correct execution, the plunger is closed (or almost closed) on the "+" and open (or almost open) on the o. Experiment with the sounds until both can be heard clearly. All players must use the same technique for the sections to achieve an effective doo-wah sound.

Example 15 (Doo-Wah)

Ghosted Notes

Ghosted, or swallowed, notes are used to emphasize the notes around them. These notes are played with little sound, to produce a tone much softer than usual (or a dead tone). A half-valve sound on a trumpet is somewhat analogous to the sound of a ghosted note. Example 16 is a typical depiction of ghosted notes in a jazz chart.

Example 16 (Ghosted)

PHRASING IN THE SWING STYLE

Phrasing in a jazz style is essential to musical performance. In a style of music that has evolved primarily though the aural (as opposed to written) tradition, many elements are implied, not necessary written. A jazz musician looks at a line of notes and knows how to make a phrase out of them. Although not all publishers have adopted the practice of marking phrases in jazz, many are beginning to do so.

Characteristic Phrasing

Phrasing in jazz music follows the musical line in much the same manner as classical music. Typically, peaks of phrases are emphasized. Of course, interpretation is an individual art, and as long as it is done within the context of the jazz concept, there are probably no "wrong" ways, although some interpretations are hipper than others! Look at Example 17 to examine phrasing as we have discussed it here. First the line is notated as it might appear on a chart and then as a jazz performer might play it. Although the phrase below ends with descending notes, the final eighth note is still short and emphasized.

Example 17

Releases

A sure giveaway for an "amateur" group is its failure to use proper releases. It is standard in jazz that long notes tied into eighth notes use the eighth note as the release. Whole notes are released on beat 1 of the next bar, half notes end on the third beat after the attack, and so on. Example 18 shows marking "—4" to indicate the beat where the release is made. Paying attention to this detail gives a jazz band the same power and impact on note endings as it has on note beginnings.

Example 18

Phrase Marks

The classical slur mark is quite often used as a phrase mark in jazz; therefore, in the example below, the music is not always slurred throughout. As in Example 19, the music may have interruptions and yet still be part of the phrase.

Example 19

Rhythmic Figures

Since many rhythms in jazz are not played as written, knowing the standard jazz interpretations of these figures is essential. One of the most often-written, and therefore misplayed, figures is eighth note, quarter note, eighth note. The traditional, classical interpretation of this is, of course, short, long, short. At a slow or medium tempo, with the triplet subdivision of eighth notes, the jazz interpretation of the same rhythmic pattern is long, short, short (or doo, dit, daht). The caution is to feel the triplet so as not to rush into the second and third notes.

Example 20

PUTTING IT ALL TOGETHER

Putting it all together now becomes the true test. Once the component parts are understood, putting jazz lines and phrases together becomes fun. An interesting way to challenge the students is by preparing a series of jazz examples on a single note. Once they are able to execute this (and that will be quite soon), they can move on to examples with moving notes. Try rehearsing a number of charts that contain similar lines, licks, and phrases. Check out Examples 21 and 22 for interpreting the written lines.

Example 21

Example 22

Watch the Video for Hands-On Jazz Concepts

Now would be a good time to watch the video showing the rehearsals of the Hammocks Middle School Jazz Band with Dr. Willie Hill, Miami Northwestern High School Jazz Band with J. Richard Dunscomb, and Florida International University Jazz Band with Bob Mintzer.

Create a List of Musical Rules for Your Jazz Students

The authors believe that having a consistent approach to interpreting jazz rhythms and articulations is important. Here is the way one of today's leading jazz educators, Jerry Tolson, does it. Professor Tolson is a jazz pianist who teaches at the University of Louisville and at the Jamey Aebersold Summer Workshop.

TOLSON'S JAZZ COMMANDMENTS—THE JAZZER'S DOZEN

Guidelines for Proper Swing Style and Articulation

JAZZ BILL OF RIGHTS:
ALL EIGHTH NOTES ARE NOT CREATED EQUAL

1. Any quarter note or eighth note followed by a rest is played (or sung) short. If not followed by a rest, then they are played long unless the following rules apply.
2. Quarter notes that occur on the downbeats of 1 or 3 are usually played long.
3. Quarter notes that occur on the downbeats of 2 and 4 are usually played short.
4. Quarter notes (or the equivalent thereof) that occur on an upbeat between two eighth notes (or rests) are played short.
5. All upbeat entrances after a rest should be anticipated with an accent.
6. A succession (three or more) of quarter notes (or equivalent) on consecutive upbeats is usually played long.
7. Two eighth notes followed by a rest are articulated with the syllables *doo-dot*.
8. In a line of eighth notes, accent the highest note and any wide leap changes of direction, and ghost (swallow) the lowest note.
9. Triplet eighth notes are usually articulated by slurring the first two and tonguing the last one.
10. Any note longer than a dotted quarter note moves dynamically up or down and is played long.
11. Dynamics in a line of eighth notes usually follow the direction of the line.
12. All three notes of a quarter-note triplet are played long.

Be creative! Now that you have all the necessary basic components of the jazz concept, be creative. Not all published jazz charts will be marked as clearly as the ones we have used as examples in this chapter. Many times you will have to add the markings, articulations, and shadings and make decisions about interpretations. Do it! To continue to grow and gain expertise in this area is essential. The way to accomplish this and most other jazz nuances is through continued listening.

DIRECTOR'S CHECKLIST FOR THE JAZZ CONCEPT—SWING

• Be sure you and your band listen to professional jazz recordings.

• Listen repeatedly to understand jazz style and to develop an understanding of individual players' roles in the styles, especially the rhythm section.

• Understand and identify the steady beat or time, and know how to make it work.

• Understand the swing eighth-note concept.

• Identify the jazz nuances, shapes, and musical language.

• Understand proper jazz articulation.

• Be sure you and your band can sing confidently with jazz syllables, connecting visual and aural skills.

• Teach your ensemble to phrase in a jazz style.

THE JAZZ CONCEPT— LATIN JAZZ

by J. Richard Dunscomb and Jose Diaz

The term *Latin jazz* is used broadly to describe the fusion of Afro-Cuban, Brazilian, and other Latin-American music with jazz. Latin jazz has been popular for more than 60 years and continues to evolve. Therefore, it is essential for all jazz educators to understand it and to learn how to teach it, just as with swing, bebop, funk, and so on.

Traditional Latin-American music is comprised of many rhythms such as son, cha-cha-cha, rumba, guaguanco, bomba, samba, bossa nova, and merengue. This chapter provides a practical overview of such styles and their application in the fused Latin jazz idiom, with a focus on styles encountered frequently in jazz ensemble charts.

First covered are styles with historical roots in Cuba; second are styles with their roots in Brazil. The Resource Guide lists a broad selection of books, recordings, and videos that will enable you to delve further into specific styles.

When you begin to discover and distinguish between the many forms of Latin jazz, you and your groups will be able to create more accurate and meaningful performances.

IT'S IN THE RHYTHM

Although melodic and harmonic aspects are significant in Latin American music, they are quite often secondary to the primary characteristic, the rhythm.

Traditionally, all Latin rhythms were handed down from one generation to the next by singing and playing. Therefore, the importance of hearing and feeling the rhythms through verbal interpretations is critical. This process is different from the process by which most Western musicians learn music, for example, by reading notes and rhythms. Today, learning Latin rhythms can be accomplished by listening to the music both in live performances and on recordings.

Common Pitfalls

The term *Latin groove* appears on a number of jazz charts and lead sheets and is a vague and sweeping generality at best. Unfortunately many jazz musicians interpret the term *Latin groove* to mean play with an even eighth-note feel, with the bass and drums playing a two-beat quasi-bossa nova pattern (sometimes mistakenly called samba) or a quasi-bolero feel at slower tempos. This common misinterpretation has little or no connection with the music of Latin America.

See the subtitled sections "Afro-Cuban Roots" and "Brazilian Roots" for instructions on playing ten popular Latin-American rhythmic patterns.

ORIGINS OF THE LATIN JAZZ FUSION

Many Latin-American countries have contributed to the development of jazz; however, Cuba and Brazil have made the greatest impact. Before the term *Latin jazz* was used to describe this music, it was called *Afro-Cuban Jazz* or, as Dizzy Gillespie and other bebop musicians called it, *CuBop.*

Mario Bauza

One of the first to develop this fused Latin jazz style of music was Cuban trumpeter, composer, and arranger Mario Bauza.

Bauza played with such big bands as those of Chick Webb and Cab Calloway when he first came to the United States from Cuba in the 1930s. During that time, he composed a tune called "Tanga," the first known composition that used a jazz melody and jazz harmonies with a Cuban clave feel and rhythm section.

Later, with his brother-in-law Jose "Machito" Grillo's band, and then with his own band, he continued to compose and record numerous albums of Latin jazz and dance music until his death in 1993.

Dizzy Gillespie

Another important influence a decade later was Dizzy Gillespie and his composition "Manteca," which he composed in collaboration with Chano Pozo, a Cuban percussionist introduced to Dizzy by Mario Bauza. Through his love for Afro-Cuban music and by openly associating himself with it, Dizzy Gillespie attracted many other great bebop players of the era to this exciting music.

Additional Influences

A number of other U.S. and Latin American musicians have been instrumental in the blending of jazz with Latin-American music. In addition to Mario Bauza, Machito, and Dizzy Gillespie, the list includes Tito Puente, Mongo Santamaria, Stan Kenton, Cal Tjader, Horace Silver, Claire Fischer, Chick Corea, Paquito D'Rivera, Dave Valentine, Sergio Mendes, Antonio Carlos Jobim, Toninho Horta, and many, many more. Afro-Cuban jazz/CuBop caught on quickly, and its evolution continues today.

AFRO-CUBAN ROOTS

Afro-Cuban music was developed when African slaves brought their drums, rhythmic patterns, and chants (call-and-response) to Cuba. These African musical elements combined with the mixture of Spanish harmony, melody, song, and dance forms and evolved into Afro-Cuban music.

Afro-Cuban music is rich in variety, substance, and spiritual significance. Authentic forms include danzon, guaguanco, rumba (not what North Americans call rumba, which is actually closer to a bolero), son (also referred to as salsa), son montuno, cha-cha-cha, mambo, and one of the most recent forms to evolve, songo, a blend of son montuno and American funk.

Understanding Clave

The single most important aspect of traditional Afro-Cuban music is its strict adherence to the rhythmic pattern known as **clave.** In order to understand Afro-Cuban rhythms, we need to establish a clear concept of clave (which literally means "key").

Two Major Clave Styles

There are two major clave styles in Afro-Cuban music: the *son clave* and the *rumba clave*. Both the *son clave* and the *rumba clave* are two-bar (eight-beat) rhythmic patterns that occur in two forms: (1) the 3-2 forward clave and (2) the 2-3 reverse clave.

The 2-3 *son clave* is the most widely used clave style in salsa music. In the *rumba clave* the note played on beat 4 is delayed a half beat and played on the "and" of the fourth beat.

Every component of Afro-Cuban drum patterns, piano montuno, bass lines, melodic phrasing, and horn lines has to be in sync with clave.

Examples of the Various Forms of Clave

In 3-2 son clave, the accents fall on the first beat, the "and" of the second beat, the fourth beat of the first bar, and the second and third beats of the second measure.

3-2 *son clave* (forward)

3-2 *rumba clave* (forward)

In 2-3, or reverse clave.

2-3 *son clave* (reverse)

In 2-3, or reverse son clave.

2-3 *rumba clave* (reverse)

Clave in Latin Jazz

It is worth reiterating that in traditional Afro-Cuban music the clave is the sacred foundation to the style. As you read this chapter, keep in mind we are discussing Latin jazz, as opposed to either traditional Latin music or traditional jazz. When merging these two kinds of music, some of the basic elements of each genre are retained and some are omitted.

For example, in Latin jazz the clave is not always the sacred element that it is in traditional Latin music. Composers such as Bob Mintzer have written Latin-flavored compositions while using jazz conventions, and some of these works make use of odd meters, which negate the flow of the clave. While this kind of odd-meter rhythm forces a traditional Latin song off clave, it is acceptable in Latin jazz.

Cuban Rhythm Instruments

The following is a list of typical Cuban rhythm instruments:
- Bongos
- Claves
- Cowbell
- Congas (tumba, conga, quinto)
- Guiro
- Maracas
- Timbales
- Vibra-slap

Afro-Cuban Musical Styles

Let's look at the basic rhythmic notation for these Afro-Cuban musical styles. Remember, all Cuban styles are danceable and are used by dance orchestras.

- Mambo
- Cha-cha-cha
- Son montuno
- Bolero
- Rumba
- Afro-Cuban

Mambo

Mambo is an up-tempo dance rhythm derived from the mambo section of the danzon. *Mambo* is a term used to describe three musical settings, the vamp section of the danzon, an instrumental interlude in the montuno section of a salsa tune, and arrangements featuring a call-and-response dialog with the horn section and complex jazz harmonies. The essential instruments for this style are congas, cowbell, and timbales.

Example 1

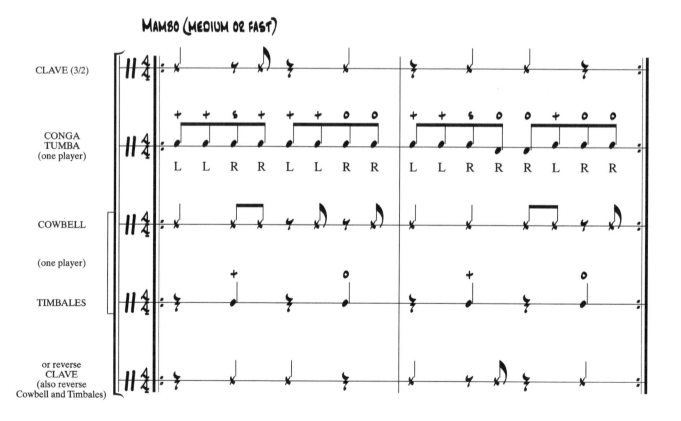

Cha-Cha-Cha

Cha-cha-cha is perhaps the most simple of the Cuban rhythms. This rhythmic style, written in 4/4 time, has its origins in the second section (nuevo ritmo, later called mambo) of the Cuban danzon. Cha-cha-cha is played at a medium tempo. The essential instruments are congas, guiro, and timbales. The cha-cha-cha was made popular by the charanga orchestras, which also used flutes and violins. The group Santana is well known for combining cha-cha-cha with rock rhythms.

Example 2

𝄖 - slap
+ - muted
o - open
L - left hand
R - right hand

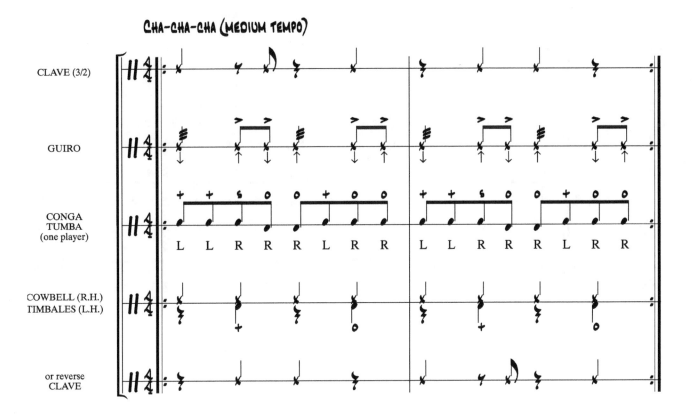

Son Montuno

The **son** rhythmic style is the most popular and the oldest Cuban music and dance genre of the twentieth century. The son does not have a single-meter rhythmic pattern or instrumental set-up that characterizes the genre. The heart of the performance style is the bass rhythm pulse that precedes the expected downbeat. Son rhythms can be played with either a two feel or with a 4/4 feel. The tempo is medium to medium fast. The essential instruments for this style are bongos, maracas, conga, and cowbell.

Example 3

SON MONTUNO (MEDIUM TO MED. FAST)

A - stroke on rim
B - stroke near close end

Bolero

Bolero is a ballad-like, danceable song style originating in Cuba in the early 1900s. In a bolero the typical bass line rhythmic pattern is a half note followed by two quarter notes. The essential instruments for this style are bongos, congas, maracas, and/or timbales.

Example 4

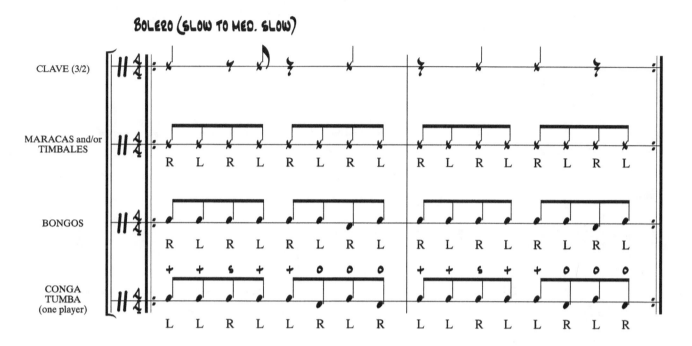

Rumba

Rumba was played originally on boxes instead of drums. It is one of the oldest of the Cuban rhythms. This Cuban folkloric secular form consists of drumming, dancing, and call-and-response singing. There are three forms of rumba: columbia (fast tempo), yambu (slow tempo), and guaguanco (medium to fast tempo). Of these three forms, the guaguanco is the most commonly used. The essential instruments for this style are clave, congas, bongos, and timbales.

Example 5

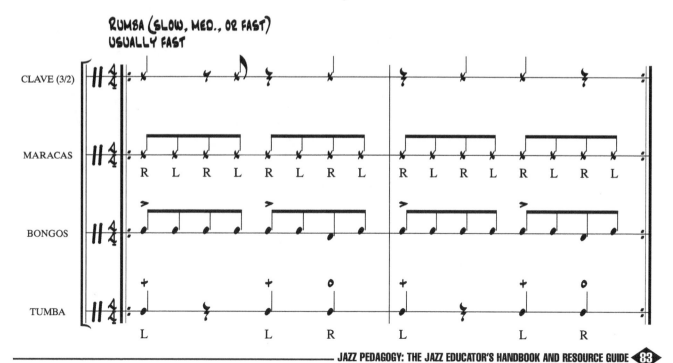

Afro-Cuban

Afro-Cuban $\frac{6}{8}$ uses the rhythms that come from the musical rituals that include drumming, dancing, and singing. It is played in a two-bar form (in the same way the previous $\frac{4}{4}$ rhythms were). The essential instruments for this style are claves, congas, and cowbell.

Example 6

The authors recommend these highly regarded Afro-Cuban jazz recordings:

Mario Bauza - *Tanga* - Messidor 15819
Cachao - *Master Sessions,* Volume 1 - Crescent Moon/Epic 64320
Caribbean Jazz Project - *The Caribbean Jazz Project* - Heads Up 3033
Cubanismo - *Jesus Alemany's Cubanismo* - Hannibal 1390
Paquito D'Rivera - *Reunion* - Messidor 15805
40 Years of Cuban Jam Sessions - Messidor 15826
Dizzy Gillespie - *The Complete RCA Victor Recordings* - Bluebird 66528
Ruben Gonzalez - *Introducing...Ruben Gonzalez* - World Circuit/Nonesuch 79477
Giovanni Hidalgo - *Worldwide* - RMM/Tropijazz 81585
Irakere - *The Best of Irakere* - Columbia/Legacy 57719
Machito - *Mucho Macho* - Pablo 2625-712
Kenya - Roulette 22668
Chico O'Farrill - *Cuban Blues* - Verve 314533256
Chano Pozo - *Legendary Sessions* - Tumbao 017
Tito Puente - *El Rey* - Concord Picante 4250
Salsa Meets Jazz - Concord Picante 4354
Gonzalo Rubalcaba - *The Blessing* - Blue Note 97197
Poncho Sanchez - *Para Todos* - Concord Picante 4600
Arturo Sandoval - *The Latin Train* - GRP 9818
Mongo Santamaria - *Watermelon Man* - Milestone 47075
Cal Tjader - *Monterey Concerts* - Prestige 24026
Chucho Valdes - *Briyumba Palo Congo* - Blue Note 98917

BRAZILIAN ROOTS

Brazilian music is a beautiful blending of musical styles and influences from outside Brazil and within. African slaves and Portuguese and Brazilian Indians contributed instruments and musical forms to Brazil's culture. In Brazilian music there are many forms that are typically linked with certain instrumentations, occasions, song forms, and even chord progressions. Each of these forms has its place in the evolution of Afro-Brazilian music. Some emanate from particular regions of Brazil, such as the states of the northeast, Bahia, Minas Gerais, and Rio. These forms include xaxado, frevo, baião, choro, batuque, samba, and bossa nova, to name a few. Since it is virtually impossible to distinguish between folk music and popular music, both forms are called Música Popular Brasileira.

Brazilian music, with its rich harmonies and infectious rhythms, is a natural fit for jazz. It is also important to note the tremendous importance and value placed on music by the people of Brazil. This is so much so that the airport in Rio de Janeiro is named after its famous composer, Antonio Carlos Jobim. He is affectionately called Tom Jobim, and his legacy and importance lives in almost every corner of this great city.

Brazilian Instrumentation

The combination of instruments in the Brazilian orchestras and groups are more varied than those of Cuba. The guitar is the most popular instrument and is often accompanied by vocalists and/or rhythm instruments. Small groups often use an accordion. Flutes are often used and are a very popular part of the samba and bossa nova orchestras. Marching bands have been a part of the culture from the early days and have made popular the trumpet, saxophone, and other marching instruments. The samba groups and orchestras all use percussion as the dominating element. Since the rhythm instruments are so important, a list follows with a loose description of each where needed.

Brazilian Rhythm Instruments

- Surdo - (SOOR-doh) the bass drum (floor tom can be used as a substitute)
- Chocalho/Ganza - (sho-CAHL-yoh/GHAN-sah) a Brazilian shaker
- Reco-reco - (reh-koh-REH-koh) a Brazilian guiro
- Pandeiro - (PON-DAEE-roh) a Brazilian tambourine, one-sided
- Tamborim - (tam-boh-RIM) a small hand-held Brazilian drum with a single head
- Ago-go - (ah-goh-GOH) the go-go bells
- Cuica - (koo-EE-kah) a Brazilian drum played with a damp cloth; produces a sound that resembles a barking dog
- Cabasa - (kah-BAH-sah)
- Triangle
- Caixa - (GUY-shah) a Brazilian snare or marching drum
- Caixeta - (guy-SHEH-tah) wood block
- Apito - (ah-PEE-toh) whistle
- Atabaque - (ah-tah-BAH-kee) a Brazilian conga drum
- Bongos - only used for samba

Basic Pulse

Brazilian music is built on a *basic pulse* provided by many instruments but does not have a clave rhythm like that found in Cuban rhythms. A list of musical styles with rhythmic notation for each of the Brazilian instruments follows. Each is the most basic of forms found. Many variations of each rhythm are used.

Brazilian Musical Styles

Here are the basic rhythms for the following popular Brazilian styles:
- Samba (samba batucada)
- Samba moderno
- Bossa nova
- Baion

Samba

Samba is the most well-known and most popular rhythm of Brazil. The various samba groups use a variety of instruments, but all use percussion as the dominant element. Although there are many different types of samba, they all have the same basic pulse. Typical percussion instruments in the **samba batucada** are surdo, chocalho, reco-reco, tamborim, and ago-go.

Samba Batucada

Example 7

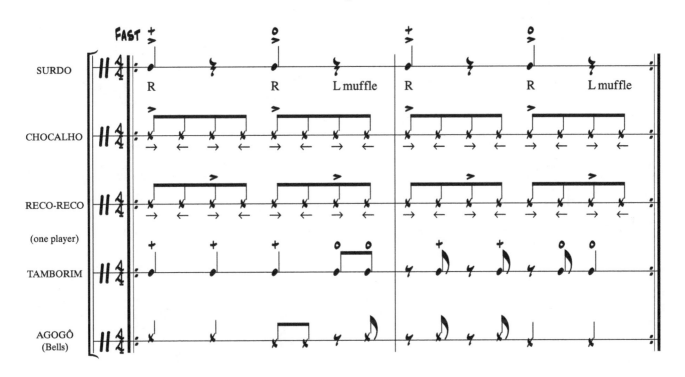

Samba Moderno

Samba moderno has become a part of the modern samba. The Cuban bongos and the cowbell are added to the Brazilian congas (atabaques).

Example 8

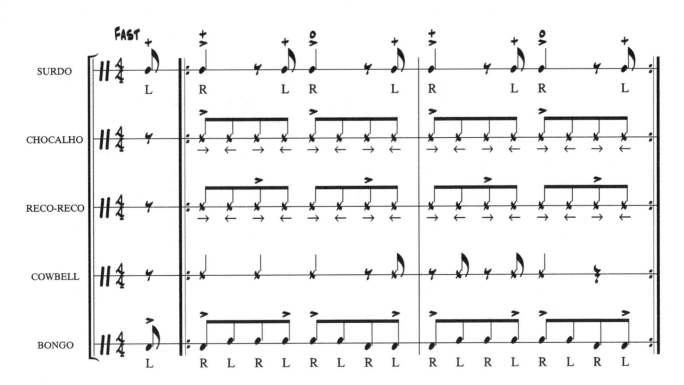

Bossa Nova

Bossa nova was made popular by Antonio Carlos Jobim and João Gilberto. It was a mixture of musical cultures, and it created a change in the structure of the samba groups: guitar, bass, drum set, and piano. The example below shows the drum set, because it has become an important part of the bossa nova instrumentation. The percussion instruments used include cabasa, triangle, and maracas.

Example 9a – Bossa nova for drum set

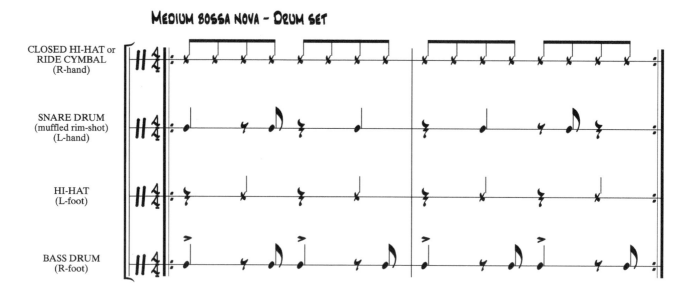

Example 9b – Bossa nova for percussion

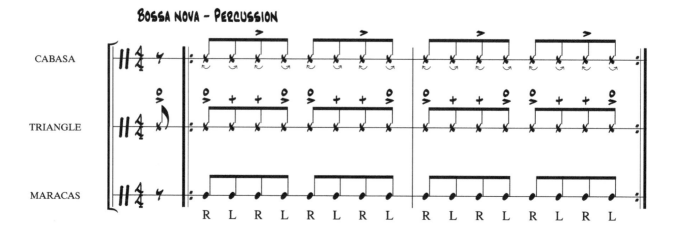

Baion

Baion became popular in the folk music from the northeastern part of the country. Baion is played by all types of orchestras. The essential instruments for baion are surdo and triangle. The surdo is replaced by the bass drum of the drum set in modern groups.

Example 10

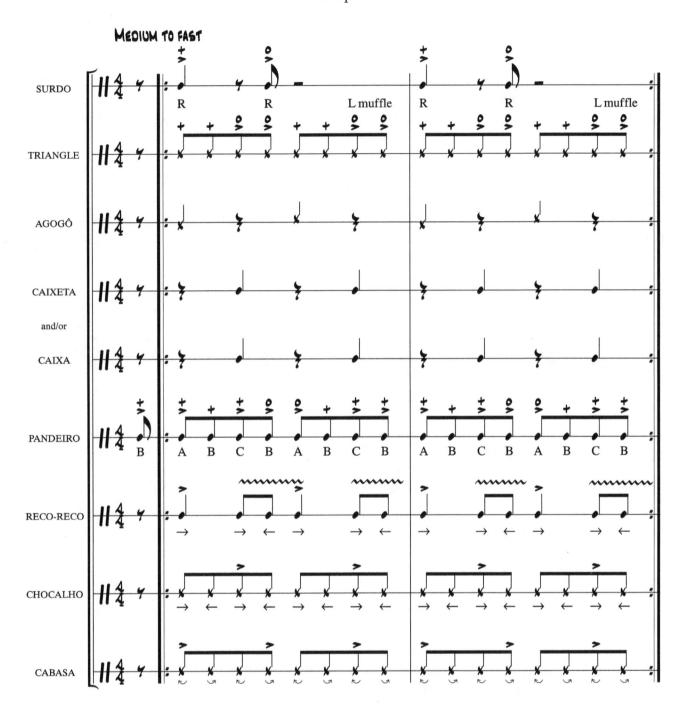

The authors recommend these highly regarded Brazilian recordings:

Antonio Carlos Jobim - all of his recordings
Dorival Caymmi - *Serie Coletanea*, Vol. 6 - EMI/SC 10093
João Gilberto - *Brazil* - Warner Bros. BSK 3513
Luiz Gonzaga - *Asa Branca* - RCA 1070216
Airto Moreira - *Identity* - Arista AL 4068
Gilberto Gil - *Realce* - Elektra BR 32038
Milton Nascimento - *Milton* - A&M SP 4611
Edu Lobo and Tom Jobim - *Edu & Tom* - Philips 6328478
Flora Purim - *500 Miles High: Live at Montreux* - Milestone M 9070

INTRODUCING LATIN JAZZ TO YOUR JAZZ ENSEMBLE

Incorporating Latin jazz into the jazz ensemble begins with understanding how to use the various instruments in the rhythm section. It will help to add Latin percussion instruments, as the prior information in this chapter indicates.

In addition, we must know what each of the other instruments in the rhythm section must do. Here are some tips on how to best accomplish this.

The Role of the Drum Set

The drummer has the responsibility of translating the rhythmic figures originally played on various rhythm section instruments (timbales, congas, and bass) onto the drum set. The instrumentation of the rhythm section determines the approach used by the drummer. In the absence of a conga player, the drummer must replace that part with the tom-toms; if there are no timbales, the drummer should play the timbale part (cascara) on the shell of the floor tom, cymbals, or cowbell. Typically, the bass drum is used to reinforce the tumbao played on the bass.

Example 11 shows a basic cha-cha-cha pattern on the drum set.

The cascara pattern played on the timbales (or the drum set; see illustration in Example 11) varies depending on which clave is being played.

Recommended Video Resources

Video resources for drums that will greatly assist the director and all rhythm section students are:
- Berroa, Ignacio - *Mastering the Art of Afro-Cuban Drumming*-VH0215 (Instruction on important Afro-Cuban rhythms, traditional Latin instruments, and drum set), Warner Bros. Publications
- Hernandez, Horacio "El Negro" - *Festival: Horacio "El Negro" Hernandez* - VH0357 (Performance and insights into playing drum set in this style), Warner Bros. Publications

The Role of the Bass

In Latin jazz the bass player does not "walk" (the traditional jazz four-quarter-note-per-measure rhythm) but makes use of lines found in the more traditional types of Latin music. Here are examples of basic bass patterns for the Afro-Cuban styles, son, and cha-cha-cha:

Example 12 shows a basic son bass pattern:

Example 13 shows a basic cha-cha-cha bass pattern:

Although the root and fifth are the predominant chord tones played by the bass regardless of the style, this doesn't mean that other chord tones are not employed. In these examples we are simply pointing out the common usages.

Communication Between Bass and Drums

As with most styles of jazz, there should be cohesiveness among the members of the band, especially between bass and drums. The bassist's main concern is to follow the drummer's bass drum pattern because it is the rhythm that anchors the groove. Once this foundation is established, it is possible for the bassist to embellish the pattern based on some of the rhythms being played on the other components of the drum set.

Be aware that embellishing does not mean overplaying, which is a major problem with most young players who want to show off their new-found chops. Other members of the band will not appreciate this practice. Remind your bassist and drummer that their playing should *complement* the music; it must not *get in the way of* the music. This is certainly true of all members of the rhythm section no matter what style they are playing.

Refer to Example 14 to see how the bass and drum patterns fit together. This cooperative effort creates a strong foundation upon which the harmonies, the percussion, and the solo instruments can build. For in-depth discussions and examples of these concepts, check out the resources listed below.

Recommended Book Resources for Bass Players

- Goines, Lincoln and Robby Ameen, *Funkifying the Clave,* Manhattan Music Publishers.
- Mauleon, Rebeca, *Salsa Guidebook,* Sher Music.

The Role of the Piano

In traditional Afro-Cuban music, the pianist is responsible for establishing and maintaining the rhythmic pulse. One of the basic elements of this music is the montuno, which is a repeated, syncopated phrase, usually of two bars, although it can be extended to four or eight bars depending on the harmonic rhythm. While contributing to the harmony in Latin music, the montuno is also a very important part of the rhythmic element because it (along with the bass, drums, and percussion) is part of a larger rhythmic scheme, much like a single piece of a puzzle: it has its own design yet fits into and contributes to the overall picture.

Example 14 shows the basic montuno rhythm found in the son, mambo, and various other styles. This two-bar montuno consists of a combination of downbeats and upbeats that, when combined with the bass and drums, help to establish the pulse.

Example 14

BASIC MONTUNO PATTERN

In Latin jazz, the two basic elements, montuno and comping, are integrated by most pianists to create a less rigid base from which to work. Comping must be flexible because it is a process requiring the pianist to respond to a given melody or solo.

There are many ways pianists alter the basic montuno pattern in order to personalize it. Example 15 shows one variation.

Example 15

The Role of the Horn Players

When playing Latin jazz, the horn player is not as obliged to the traditional Latin elements and proceeds more according to common jazz practice, particularly regarding harmonic and melodic matters and the extent to which these components are developed through improvisation. However, the underlying Latin rhythms can significantly influence the melodic line.

Characteristic Melodic Lines

Let's compare characteristic melodic lines in the jazz idiom and then in the Latin jazz idiom.

Jazz Melodic Lines

Melodic lines in standard jazz songs are often swing eighth-note based. As discussed in Chapter 7, the typical jazz swing feel is characterized by the walking bass line and the drummer's ride cymbal/hi-hat pattern, creating a strong $\frac{4}{4}$ groove with secondary emphasis on beats 2 and 4. See Example 16.

Example 16

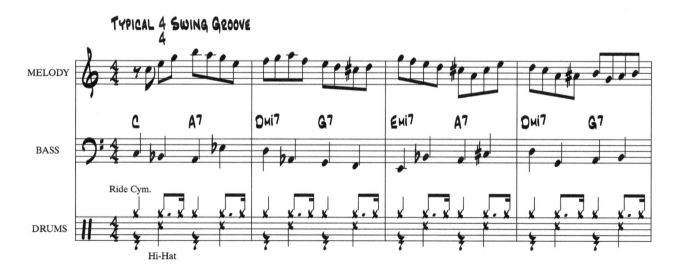

Latin Jazz Melodic Lines

In contrast, Afro-Cuban and Brazilian grooves are more often felt and written in $\frac{2}{4}$ or cut-time meter. For instance, over the samba pattern you commonly find a melody constructed of consecutive upbeats, and it has a nice, light lift. However, if this same melody were placed over a walking $\frac{4}{4}$ jazz groove, it would soon become heavy due to the constant conflict between the downbeats of the rhythm section and the upbeats of the melody. (See Examples 17 and 18.)

Example 17

Example 18

Eighth-note lines also work well over the samba and other Latin grooves; however, they are usually played as straight eighths, as opposed to the swing eighths typical in American jazz. (See Examples 19 and 20.)

Example 19

The concept of swing eighths is very personal to every jazz artist and we refer to it here in a strictly generic sense in order to make a point.

Example 20

Because straight eighth notes do not emphasize upbeats, as do swing eighths, in many cases they are more effective over Latin grooves.

Stylistically, we hear a contrast in the way conventional Afro-Cuban, Brazilian, and American jazz melodies are sung or played. This is not only a result of the different rhythmic activity but also a direct reflection of the language in which each music style has traditionally been sung. For example, compare the singing styles of Celia Cruz, Elis Regina, and Ella Fitzgerald. Horn players should listen to such singers to gain some insight into where these styles are coming from and then apply the concepts when playing the various Latin grooves.

Style Markings on Jazz Ensemble Charts

When charts are marked with specific style indications, Latin jazz music is much easier for your jazz ensemble to perform. Jazz publishers are responding to this need, and as a result, we are seeing less music simply marked "Latin."

Summary

In summary, the style called Latin jazz started as bebop played over a Latin groove such as mambo. Mario Bauza, Dizzy Gillespie, Chano Pozo, Machito, and others introduced this style in the 1930s and 1940s. Since then it has evolved, with the elements becoming more integrated, especially through the work of Weather Report, Chick Corea, Clair Fischer, and others who began in the early 1970s. Today this course continues to intensify, probing deeper into the wealth of Latin forms such as those described in this section of the book. As always, with any style, the bottom line is listen, study, and have fun!

Putting everything together with the jazz ensemble requires models just as in swing style. The various recommended recordings help define the proper Latin styles. All of the following audio recordings are on the included online media.

Mambo example - *Mambo Hot* and *King of Timbales*

Salsa example - *Mondongo*

Merengue example - *Mr. Papi*

Samba example - *Gentle Rain*

Afro-Cuban example - *Miami Spice*

JAZZ IMPROVISATION

AN INTRODUCTION

by Dr. Willie L. Hill, Jr.

Let's discuss the essence of jazz: improvisation. I believe that the jazz educator understands the need for improvisation skills but questions, "How do I teach it?" First, let's put things in perspective. Does the jazz musician know more about music than an opera singer? More than a classically trained saxophone player? More than a conductor of an orchestra? Of course, the answer is no. Jazz players use the same 12 notes as everyone else. The difference is the jazz vocabulary. To begin to learn how to improvise and/or to teach jazz improvisation, you and your students must study jazz vocabulary and language. By developing acute jazz aural skills, students will be able to internalize the jazz language.

JAZZ IMPROVISATION = JAZZ VOCABULARY AND AURAL SKILLS

The ultimate goal for a jazz improviser is to play effortlessly what is heard in the mind. Obviously, this skill cannot result from an overnight process, and having one lesson or using one jazz method or book is not going to make a great jazz player. The finest, most successful and well-established jazz players not only continue to practice their instruments to maintain technical facility but also are constantly seeking to improve jazz vocabulary. Typically, they are not satisfied with a jazz solo and are always striving to play it better. So, consider the process of learning jazz improvisation a cumulative one, taking each opportunity to increase jazz vocabulary. Remember that an accomplished jazz improviser did not just pick up his or her instrument to find, miraculously, that jazz came forth!

STEPS ALONG THE PATH TO JAZZ VOCABULARY AND AURAL SKILLS

- Listening
- Practicing
- Playing
- Transcribing
- Copying
- Analyzing

Listening

The language and vocabulary of jazz are most easily grasped through the process of listening, which has been proven throughout 100 years of jazz history. You and your students can begin by listening to a jazz tune or artist you like or find interesting, as discussed and amplified in Chapter 3. The goal: to develop aural skills and jazz vocabulary.

Practicing

Technical skills are necessary for improvisation. Should improvisers play jazz exercises? Sure, it will help the concept. But more important, a wide variety of all types of exercises should be practiced to gain technique. The goal: to improve technique.

Playing

Aspiring improvisers can play along with jazz recordings, starting simply with just the melody. Have your students sing the tune before playing it. Don't select something so complex as to discourage the students, but rather something accessible, realistic, and attainable. Encourage each student to put on a set of headphones and pop in a CD or try playing along with the radio. This will get the player accustomed to finding the notes on his or her instrument without written music. The goal: aural skills and jazz vocabulary.

Transcribing

You and your class can examine a jazz phrase (or simple solo) and start to discover the process of hearing a note or rhythm pattern (for the drummer). Play the excerpt over and over until it can be written down. Even finding one note is a great start. This exercise will associate hearing the note, finding the note on the instrument, and notating it. I recommend that all players, including rhythm instrument players, participate in this process. The goal: to develop aural skills and learn jazz vocabulary. This can be as simple as a one- or two-note phrase, as in Example 1.

Example 1

Copying

The process of playing along with, or mimicking, someone's playing is essential to internalizing the nuances of jazz language. Of course, the critical point here is to select a good model to copy and to find a simple and accessible tune. An example of a simple tune is shown in Example 5. Mimicking can be done with jazz duet or etude books that include play-along CDs. Another idea concerns simply playing along with a jazz head (melody) from a CD. The melody does not have to be fast, complex, or overly challenging. In fact, the simpler the better, so the student can learn to play it correctly. The goal: to develop aural skills and jazz vocabulary.

As an example, *15 Easy Jazz, Blues and Funk Etudes* by Bob Mintzer includes a great play-along CD to develop the skills discussed thus far. The CD includes a demo version of Bob Mintzer playing each tune (copying) and then a play-along version (playing). Refer to the Resource Guide for additional examples.

Analyzing

Intertwined with all of the above is studying solos in transcription books, which is a great way for students to see how great jazz players play certain notes over chord progressions. Students can trade their transcriptions with each other for further study. Your class should take transcribed solos a step further by figuring out why the notes are selected to be played. Have them search for patterns, sequences, scales, and the outlining of chords. The goal: to develop jazz vocabulary and aural skills.

DEVELOPING JAZZ VOCABULARY AND AURAL SKILLS

Improvising should be a pleasurable experience, and expert players relish each solo opportunity. Yet often, even with the melody, scales and chords provided, an inexperienced improviser will not know what to play or how to play it and generally lacks confidence in attempting to improvise. This trepidation demonstrates a limited jazz vocabulary.

Why do directors who have significant jazz experience (with jazz as their main focus and performance area) instinctively know how to explain and demonstrate the jazz feel, articulation, and improvisation? Because they have jazz vocabulary "under their belt." It's important to know that music educators with limited jazz experience can easily grasp these concepts. Remember, the two critical steps are developing aural skills and building jazz vocabulary.

Example 1 demonstrates a melody using eighth notes and how the concept can differ between the classical style and the jazz style. In the classical style, the figure would be played evenly, such as: tah-tah, tah-tah, tah-tah. In the jazz style, the notes would be played in a swing style, such as doo-dit, doo-dit, doo-dit. The jazz style or concept consists of two elements:

1. The rhythmic approach, i.e., playing the two eighth notes with a swing feel.
2. The articulation.

Examine this example and sing it/play it both ways—classical and jazz style. Vocal syllables are included for jazz style.

Example 2

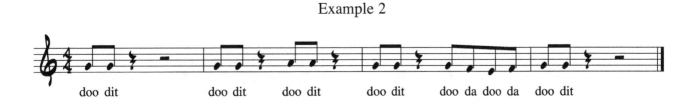

doo dit   doo dit   doo dit   doo dit   doo da doo da   doo dit

Assignment for the teacher/student: Find other examples to demonstrate this concept of playing a melody in a classical and jazz style. Consider reviewing Chapter 7: How to Teach Swing.

What Is Jazz Vocabulary?

Jazz vocabulary is scales, chords, patterns, modes, sequences, riffs, quotes, snippets, melodies, harmonic chord progressions, and so on. Example 3 shows examples of these terms:

Example 3

SCALES AND CHORDS

PATTERNS AND SEQUENCES

RIFF

QUOTE

I GOT RHYTHM
MELODIC AND HARMONIC CHORD PROGRESSION

Music and Lyrics By
George Gershwin
and Ira Gershwin

Just as the impromptu public speaker mentally organizes and draws from internalized information (knowledge and experience), the jazz player can draw from musical information that has been stored and digested and use it while adapting this jazz vocabulary into a musical setting, tempo, key, style, tune, and chord progression.

What Are Aural Skills?

These skills pertain to learning to listen productively—to absorb and learn. Goals for your students should include learning to hear and identify a note, riff, pattern, or musical ideas, and then work on learning to transfer these musical devices to their own instruments. Students then practice, digest, and use these ideas for soloing, which becomes jazz vocabulary. Improvisers generally play without written music, and as I said, the ultimate goal is to play what they hear. Example 4 is a sample of a catchy riff to demonstrate something a listener could identify and then use in a solo.

Example 4

CATCHY RIFF

Listening to an accomplished jazz player improvise using only scale and chord patterns can be impressive from a technical viewpoint. However, this approach can become boring quickly. Why? Because as a listener, it is easy to lose your place in the tune when it all sounds like scale-based exercises, absent of melodic content. Scales and arpeggios are learning tools, not playing tools. An important aspect of creating an interesting improvised solo is creating melodic ideas. Are the scales and arpeggios of the chord progression used? Absolutely, but they are not the only source of melodic content. The improviser's palette consists of development, repetition, harmonic/melodic interest, tension/release, and rhythmic interest/syncopation, all of which can be internalized from aural study.

Example 5 shows a simple melody and sample improvised solo.

Example 5
(Melody)

ON THE TRAIL

Example 5
(Improvised Solo)

C INSTRUMENTS

BY WILLIE THOMAS

The preceding example shows typical ingredients of an improvised solo, which are likely to be present in the original melody as well. Just as most people strive to expand their vocabulary and general knowledge through reading, writing, conversing, and listening, the jazz player does the same with jazz vocabulary—by collecting information both consciously and unconsciously.

Written Solos?

Typically, jazz educators write out solos and musical ideas (licks and tricks) to give their inexperienced improvisers a head start. This is an excellent technique for helping students to begin improvising. As you develop your jazz vocabulary, you will be able to compose written solos for your students. Written-out solos should be a starting point for an inexperienced soloist. However, you should always encourage the student, at least, to embellish what is written and ultimately to create his or her own improvised solo.

Summary

The more exposure your students have to jazz music through listening, practicing, playing, transcribing, copying, studying, and analyzing, the larger their vocabularies will be. When listening to an accomplished jazz soloist improvise chorus after chorus over a standard tune, even a simple blues progression, you may wonder how he or she knows what to play and how he or she thinks of all of those musical ideas. The answer is jazz vocabulary.

DIRECTOR'S CHECKLIST
JAZZ IMPROVISATION: AN INTRODUCTION

- The jazz vocabulary is the ticket to improvisation.

- Know the steps on the path to jazz improvisation: listening, practicing, playing, transcribing, copying, studying, and analyzing.

- Two critical areas to focus on:
  - Developing aural skills—listening productively.
  - Building jazz vocabulary—scales, chords, patterns, modes, sequences, riffs, quotes, snippets, melodies, and so on.

- Chapter 10 offers three lessons to teach jazz improvisation.

Please refer to the Resource Guide Index for improvisation, ear-training, and play-along materials and transcribing aids.

JAZZ IMPROVISATION

SAMPLE LESSONS

by Dr. Willie L. Hill, Jr., and Pete BarenBregge

Many outstanding jazz improvisation books and materials are available; please bear in mind that this chapter offers merely one approach. The art of jazz improvisation is a cumulative process; therefore, each and every opportunity to build jazz vocabulary and aural skills will contribute greatly to the total jazz improvisation experience. In this chapter you will find three outlines to teach jazz improvisation, beginning with the basic improvisation lesson designed to open the doors to the concepts of jazz improvisation.

EASY (BASIC LEVEL) JAZZ IMPROVISATION LESSON

Let's use a simple 12-bar tune as in Example 1. This is a blues in F. The basic blues is a chord progression, usually 12 bars in length and built on three chords. The three chords are the tonic, subdominant, and dominant chords: I-IV-V chords. In this example, however, **all three** of the chords use the lowered 7th and therefore function as dominant sounding chords, i.e., I7-IV7-V7. This lesson is designed for a typical jazz combo that includes piano, bass, drums and a few melodic instruments; however, the director can adapt this lesson to teach various settings and needs. For the first part of this lesson, have the drummer use a piano or mallet instrument to assist with the melodic concept. All musical examples provided in this chapter are in concert key.

1. Using Example 1, start by having all students **play** the melody, or head as it is often called, in unison. This blues should have a swing eighth-note feel. If you are unfamiliar with the swing concept, refer to Chapter 7. After the students become comfortable and secure playing the melody, ask the students to identify rhythmic patterns in this melody.

Example 1

2. In tempo, have the students **clap** the rhythm of the tune (the rhythm pattern repeats every two bars in this blues tune).

3. Ask the students to **clap** a simple variation to the rhythm in this basic blues. Use Example 2 or create your own.

Example 2

4. Have the students **play** the same melody once again, only this time change the rhythm pattern using Example 2 or your own rhythmic variation. This activity will begin to build jazz vocabulary, requiring the students to play rhythms they can easily clap and also melodic ideas they hear in their minds but are not necessarily written down. Ask the students to play this melody from memory.
5. Develop further rhythmic variations. Have the students **clap** and **then play**.
6. Next, using the simple rhythms and melodic notes, teach a call-and-response exercise (another good example of this call-and-response concept is in Shelly Berg's *Chop Monster* improvisation method). To demonstrate, the director can either sing or play an instrument using intervals and rhythms taken from the blues melody. Keep it simple. The purpose here is to have students play without the music and use their ears. Challenge the students by permitting them to offer the call. Example 3 shows a sample two-measure call-and-response exercise.

Example 3

7. Example 4 shows the notes in the scales of each of the three chords in this blues. Ask the students to identify the roots, 3rds, 5ths, and lowered 7th notes of the chords.

Example 4

SCALES AND CHORDS

8. Have the students **play** through the scales and become familiar with the notes in the scales and chords. The students should now be able to identify the roots, 3rds, 5ths, and lowered 7ths of the I7-IV7-V7 chords and the notes in the scales. Have the students identify differences and similarities in each scale and chord. Have the students play the scales without the music.

9. The director should now demonstrate **singing** the root tones of each chord, followed by having the students sing the root tones of the chords. This can be demonstrated with a simple quarter-note rhythm as shown in Example 5. Try expanding this exercise to include the 3rd and 5th, and so on. This exercise builds jazz vocabulary and aural skills.

Example 5

10. Now, it's time to add the rhythm section instruments. Example 6 provides the piano, bass, and drum parts. Have the piano play the chords in a dotted quarter-/eighth-note pattern that is a traditional comping pattern better known as the Charleston rhythm, and have the bass player walk the chords using quarter notes. The bass line can be as simple as the basic chord roots in quarter notes or outline the chord tones. Going a step further, have the bassist add some scale notes that lead smoothly into the next chord. The drummer should play a basic time pattern with quarter notes on the ride cymbal, hi-hat on beats 2 and 4, and, if possible, a cross-stick snare on beat 4. Going a step further, add the bass drum softly on either beats 1 and 3 or all four beats. Example 6a shows a sample piano rhythm/voicing, 6b shows a sample bass line, and 6c shows a sample drum part. For additional information regarding piano voicings, see Chapter 16: Piano. The other students can listen and observe how the rhythm section builds the foundation and chord progression accompaniment to this tune.

Example 6a: Piano

Example 6b: Bass

Example 6c: Drums

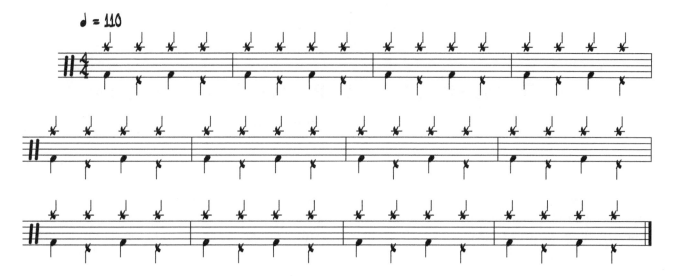

11. Let's put it all together. Using the jazz vocabulary learned so far, the students can now begin to **create** their own improvisation. With the rhythm section and the melodic instruments together, play the original blues melody in Example 1. State the melody two times, and then the rhythm section should continue to repeat the form as needed for the various improvised solos. Students should take turns improvising on the 12-bar form. As the students gain confidence, ask the students to alternate, trading four-bar and then two-bar phrases; this will encourage students to listen to each other and to follow the chord progression closely.
   - For melodic notes, the students can use the written scale/chord notes from Example 4.
   - Students can play (and sing) any note from the appropriate scale.
   - For rhythmic ideas, the students can use either the original rhythm pattern of the blues or the variations in Example 2, or they can create their own.
   - Any written scale note is correct, but as the director and the students will hear, the most desirable notes in each scale are the chord tones root, 3rd, 5th, and lowered 7th.
   - Challenge the students to create a variety of rhythms to include syncopation and sustained notes as well.
   - The only caution here is that beginning improvisers tend to linger on the fourth of the major scale, which can cause dissonance because it creates a minor second interval with the third of the chord. One solution to this is to ask the student to raise the fourth scale degree by one half step as a passing tone.

As for solos in the rhythm section, the piano can play the chord voicings with the left hand and improvise with the right hand. The bass can add variations to the bass line or create a melodic solo. The drummer can embellish the drum pattern while keeping the hi-hat as the constant timekeeper.

By now the students will have achieved the following:
   a. Learned a simple blues melody.
   b. Learned to vary the rhythms and rhythm patterns.
   c. Learned to hear and sing the blues chord progression.
   d. Learned the 12-bar blues form.
   e. Learned the scales and (dominant) chords to the blues chord progression.
   f. Learned to embellish the melody and rhythm.
   g. Played without the music, using their jazz vocabulary and aural skills.
   h. Played as a group.
   i. Begun to improvise—to create new melodic ideas over a chord progression.

Next, try this entire process in a different key! Have the students transpose the blues chord progression into other keys. Playing this exercise in a different key will bring all of the above concepts into clearer focus. For additional practice, the director and/or the students can compose a new melody using the same basic blues chord progression.

INTERMEDIATE JAZZ IMPROVISATION LESSON

This intermediate-level lesson will use the jazz standard "Cantaloupe Island" by Herbie Hancock. The form consists of a 16-bar structure and has a modal sound using minor, minor 7th, and dominant 7th chords. This composition is ideal for the intermediate-level player because the melody is easy to learn and there are only three chords. The basic feel or groove of "Cantaloupe Island" is a straight eighth-note feel, not swing eighth notes. This lesson is designed for a typical jazz combo consisting of piano, bass, drums, and a few melodic instruments. The director can adapt the lesson for various settings and needs. All musical examples are in concert key. The music for this lesson is taken from the *Approaching the Standards Jazz Improvisation Series,* Volume 1, by Dr. Willie L. Hill, Jr. (Warner Bros. Publications). All *Approaching the Standards* books include an accompanying CD with demonstration and play-along tracks.

Steps:
1. Observe "Cantaloupe Island" on the video section titled "Teaching Jazz Improvisation." If possible, further prepare yourself by listening to the original recording of "Cantaloupe Island" by Herbie Hancock.
2. Have the students **listen** and **observe** the demonstration of the melody or head of "Cantaloupe Island" on the video, as provided in Example 7. Students will hear jazz phrasing and articulation.

Example 7

CANTALOUPE ISLAND

MEDIUM ROCK

BY HERBIE HANCOCK

3. Have students **sing** the melody along with the video (rhythm section sings also). Use simple scat syllables like *doo, da, dit, dot,* and so on.

4. Without the video, have all students **play** the head to "Cantaloupe Island," including the drummer playing on a mallet instrument or piano. If needed, review and copy jazz phrasing and articulation as demonstrated on the video.

5. Add the rhythm section. Ask the piano, bass, and drums to play individually and then together as a rhythm section. If needed, have the rhythm section copy jazz phrasing and articulation as demonstrated on the video. The other students can observe as the rhythm section builds the harmonic and rhythmic foundation.

6. Have the full ensemble **sing and then play** the head. After the ensemble begins to feel comfortable playing the head, have them play "Cantaloupe Island" without the music.
7. Have the students play the written example improvisation as provided in Example 8. The purpose here is to develop jazz vocabulary. Melodic instruments can play the example solo as the rhythm section plays their parts. Listen to the video for ideas for jazz phrasing and articulation. This can be an etude assignment.

Example 8

8. Ask students to transcribe jazz solos. Transcription is critical to developing the aural skill of hearing and recognizing notes on each individual instrument. Transcription tasks can be simple or complex, depending on the student ability level. It is suggested that the director write out and play simple intervals and rhythms for the students to transcribe—this is time well spent! Additional opportunities for transcribing demonstration solos are provided in the *Approaching the Standards* books.

9. Familiarize your students with licks and tricks, as shown in Example 9. Brief musical ideas in jazz are often referred to as licks. Three examples are provided in the music for "Cantaloupe Island." *Licks and tricks* are simple and brief musical ideas that can be incorporated into improvised solos. Have students play through these licks and tricks to become familiar with the musical ideas. More experienced students can play these ideas as the rhythm section plays the form of the tune.

Example 9

LICKS AND TRICKS

C INSTRUMENTS

Lick #1 is a two-bar phrase written as it fits in each of the three chords in this tune. Lick #2 is based on a blues scale written here for each of the three chords Lick #3 is an eighth-note line outlining the three chords using the ninth.

10. Practice call-and-response exercises. These should be **sung first and then played.** They consist of simple melodic and rhythmic riffs (call) with easy intervals for the instrumentalist to play (response) without music—use the ears! Create these call-and-response exercises by using snippets from the head, using the licks and tricks, or using snippets from the example improvisation. More advanced groups can then add call-and-response exercises as the rhythm section plays the form of the tune. Challenge the students to provide the call to each other.

11. Examine the scales and chords for "Cantaloupe Island," as shown in Example 10. All students should **play** through the scales and identify similarities and differences and the overall sound of each scale. Try playing the scales in tempo with the rhythm section playing the form of the tune. The chords in this tune consist of minor 7th (Dorian) and dominant 7th (Mixolydian). All scale notes can be used in a jazz solo; however, remember to avoid lingering on the fourth of a dominant scale. In a minor scale, using the fourth is fine.

Example 10

SCALES AND CHORDS

12. **Identify** the root notes of the chord progression and recognize the 16-bar form of this composition. Have the students **sing and then play** root tones of chord progression.

13. Have students identify notes 1, 3, and 5 of each chord and then the 7ths. Students should demonstrate recognition of these intervals by **singing and then playing** them individually and collectively. This step is known as outlining the chords.

14. At this point, students have learned the head, established some phrasing/articulation concepts, and recognized the form and the chord progression.

15. Now the students are ready to play the head and begin to improvise.
    • Play "Cantaloupe Island" from the top with the repeat.
    • The rhythm section should continue to repeat the form for solos.
    • Solos should be played over the entire 16-bar form.
    • Students will have accumulated melodic, rhythmic, and harmonic vocabulary, which they can use to begin to create their own ideas.
    • The improvisation can be as simple as playing and/or embellishing the melody, using the licks-and-tricks ideas, and playing snippets from the example improvisation.
    • Don't forget to include the rhythm section as soloists! Try having the rhythm section alternate or trade solos every four bars.

16. Have the students transpose this composition into another key, and repeat the process. This exercise will be a tremendous help in furthering their understanding of chord progressions and form.

Some students will easily grasp these ideas and begin to use them creatively, whereas other students will have difficulty improvising. If students need additional help and/or challenges, here are a few suggested supplemental improvisation teaching techniques:
    • Have students review and outline the basic chord notes, and then expand to other scale notes.
    • Focus on only the simple licks-and-tricks ideas.

- Discuss and compare other song forms, such as AABA and other 32-bar song forms. Additional examples of various song form types are presented in the tunes of the *Approaching the Standards* books.
- Suggested recordings of "Cantaloupe Island" by jazz masters are:
  - Herbie Hancock – *Cantaloupe Island* – Blue Note 29331.
  - Herbie Hancock – *Best of Herbie Hancock (The Blue Note Years)* – Blue Note 91143.
- There are many other excellent books and materials that teach jazz improvisation listed in the Resource Guide Index.

Although it is unlikely that any student will sound like Charlie Parker, Miles Davis, Herbie Hancock, or Duke Ellington at this point, the process of building jazz vocabulary has begun. Everything and anything students hear is vocabulary!

INTERMEDIATE–ADVANCED JAZZ IMPROVISATION LESSON

This lesson uses "Billie's Bounce" by Charlie Parker and is based on the video chapter "Teaching Jazz Improvisation." It is recommended that you observe the video prior to teaching this lesson. This lesson, along with the musical examples, is based on the *Approaching the Standards Jazz Improvisation Series,* Volume 1, by Dr. Willie L. Hill, Jr. (Warner Bros. Publications). There are many other outstanding books and materials concerning jazz improvisation. Please keep in mind that the ideas discussed here offer only one approach. Directors are encouraged to use this basic lesson format and tailor it to specific settings and needs. All musical examples for "Billie's Bounce" are in concert key and located at the end of this chapter.

Note: The lesson described here is a step-by-step outline of the video session "Teaching Jazz Improvisation"

1. Observe "Billie's Bounce" on the video section titled "Teaching Jazz Improvisation." If possible, further prepare yourself by listening to the original recording of "Billie's Bounce" by Charlie Parker.
2. Listening is critical to learning jazz vocabulary—the melody, rhythm, and harmony. Students should listen to the jazz masters on all the instruments.
3. Students play the head to "Billie's Bounce" without the rhythm section. See **Example 11.**
4. Students sing the melody (rhythm section sings also), using simple scat syllables like *doo, da, dit, dot,* and so on.
5. Students can play again after singing, now hearing the melody in the mind's ear.
6. Discuss the form, recognizing the 12-bar blues.
7. Add the piano, bass, and drums individually and then as a rhythm section.
8. The full ensemble sings and then plays the head. Play "Billie's Bounce" without the music!
9. Outline the chords, with students identifying the root notes of the chord progression. See **Example 12.**
10. Students should sing and then play root tones of the chord progression.
11. Students identify notes 1, 3, and 5 of chords and then add flat 7th. Students should demonstrate recognition of these intervals by singing them individually and collectively.
12. Key elements learned at this point: melody, form, and chord progression.
13. Students should play the chord notes.
14. Discuss solo approaches. Have a starting note in your mind.
15. Listening helps develop the creative process.

16. Listen to the demonstration of example improvisation. See **Example 13.**
17. Discuss transcribing jazz solos. Transcription is critical to developing aural skills and hearing/recognizing notes on each individual instrument. Transcription tasks can be simple or complex, depending on student ability level. Consider writing out and playing simple exercises for the students to transcribe.
18. Create call-and-response exercises. They should be sung first and then played. They consist of simple rhythmic riffs (call) with easy intervals for the instrumentalist to play (response) without music—use the ears!
19. Play the jazz ideas known as licks and tricks. These are brief ideas, or jazz vocabulary, to incorporate into improvised solos.
20. Examine the scales. Students will play through all scales and identify similarities and differences and the overall sound. Notice that all chords in this blues have a lowered 7th. A major chord with a lowered 7th functions as a dominant chord. The scales in this tune are dominant scales (Mixolydian) or minor 7th scales (Dorian). See **Example 12.**
21. Students play the head and begin to improvise. Solos can be the entire 12-bar form or shorter sections. Students will have accumulated melodic, rhythmic, and harmonic vocabulary, which they can use to begin to create their own ideas. This can be as simple as playing and/or embellishing the melody, using the licks-and-tricks ideas, or using the snippets/ideas from the example improvisation.
22. Review.
23. Learn other tunes in a similar fashion by following steps 1 through 22.

As with the other sample lessons, some students will easily grasp these ideas and begin to use them creatively, whereas other students will have difficulty improvising. Here are a few suggested improvisation teaching techniques to assist and/or challenge students:

- Have students review outlining the chord notes, focusing on the 3rd and 7th and then expanding to other scale notes.
- Focus on only the simple licks-and-tricks ideas.
- Discuss/compare other song forms such as AABA and other 32-bar song forms. Additional examples of various song form types are presented in the tunes in the *Approaching the Standard*s books.
- Suggested recordings of "Billie's Bounce" by jazz masters are:
  ○ Charlie Parker – *The Charlie Parker Story* – Columbia 65141.
  ○ John Coltrane – *Blue Trane: John Coltrane Plays the Blues* – Prestige 11005.
  ○ Red Garland/John Coltrane – *Dig It* – OJC 392.
- There are many other excellent books and materials that teach jazz improvisation, which are listed in the Resources section at the end of this chapter.
- All scale notes can be used; however, avoid lingering on the fourth note of the dominant scale. In a minor scale, using the fourth is fine.
- Have the students transpose the blues into various keys. This will help further their understanding of chord progressions and form.
- Have students compose a blues head.
- Don't forget to include the rhythm section for the solos!

This lesson can be expanded and modified in many ways and is provided to offer a step-by-step method for building jazz vocabulary and aural skills. Directors are encouraged to follow this format and apply it to learning other tunes.

Approaching the Standards for jazz vocalists is also available and is correlated to the instrumental books.

Additional Information

The jazz educator can easily transfer this lesson format to learn other jazz tunes. Typical sources are from fake books, recordings, or other jazz educational sources, methods, or books. While engaged in the process of building jazz vocabulary, the director and the students must remember to be consistent. Establishing a solid daily practice routine will help develop positive habits that should ensure faster progress toward the students' goals. This routine should include listening, practicing, playing, transcribing, copying, analyzing, and learning/memorizing tunes. Apply each of these steps to a particular tune that: 1) you are working on in class, 2) your students are playing with a band outside of school, or 3) a student is interested in learning simply because he or she likes the tune. Sometimes it speeds up the process to learn tunes with a purpose in mind (a concert that's coming up soon, a gig, and so on). The song should really move your spirit or excite your inner soul.

To bring the creative process of learning to improvise to fruition, design a practice schedule that the student of jazz will adhere to each day. Here is an example of a practice routine:

1. Practice long tones (or the equivalent rhythmic exercise) every day to get your body physically ready for the task (build those chops).
2. Play overtones (or the equivalent rhythmic exercise).
3. Memorize major and minor scales in F, B♭, C, and G, adding others as you feel comfortable (work toward covering all keys).
4. Memorize licks and tricks (build your jazz vocabulary).
5. Work on a variety of jazz phrasings and articulations as they apply to a particular tune or to build vocabulary.
6. Practice patterns and commit them to memory.
7. Transcribe solos, at least one to two choruses of your favorite artists (a chorus is one time through the progression). Start this process slowly, one note at a time. Hear the note, identify it, find it on your instrument (or the piano), and then write it down.
8. Try applying work done so far to other keys: transpose it.
9. For the more advanced, try practicing the cycle of 4ths, 5ths, chromatics, or whole tones with bebop and blues scales, and so on.

In order for a jazz artist to become a successful player in the world of jazz, the musician has to be technically proficient on the instrument. Whatever is heard in the individual's mind's ear, he or she is executing that idea on the instrument or with the voice. When you hear master musicians like Joe Henderson, Louis Armstrong, Oscar Peterson, Art Tatum, Dizzy Gillespie, Stan Getz, Lester Young, John Coltrane, Dave Brubeck, Ella Fitzgerald, Sarah Vaughan, or Billie Holiday, you hear consummate musicality. In addition to great technical prowess, you also hear beautiful tone quality from the instrument. A musical voice, or the characteristic sound of the instrument, that is generated is just as important as good technique. Encourage your students to work to develop a beautiful tone or sound.

DIRECTOR'S CHECKLIST FOR JAZZ IMPROVISATION LESSONS

• Can the student demonstrate jazz phrasing and articulation?

• Can the student sing the head?

• Can the student identify and play the scales notes?

• Can the student respond to call-and-response exercises? Can he or she create his or her own call-and-response pattern?

• Can the student identify and play the chord notes? How about the dominant and minor scales?

• Can the student improvise simple embellishments of the melodic, harmonic, and rhythmic aspects of the head?

• Can the student compose a simple blues head?

RESOURCES

Currently, these are the most widely used books on jazz improvisation:

• *Approaching the Standards* by Dr. Willie L. Hill, Jr., Warner Bros. Publications.

• *New Approach to Jazz Improvisation* by Jamey Aebersold, JA Jazz.

• *Chop Monster* by Shelly Berg, J Frazer Collection.

For additional resources, refer to the Resource Guide Index.

Example 11

BILLIE'S BOUNCE

C INSTRUMENTS
HEAD

Medium blues

By Charlie Parker

Example 12

SCALES AND CHORDS

Example 13

EXAMPLE IMPROVISATION

C INSTRUMENTS

BY JAVON JACKSON

THE JAZZ COMBO

OBJECTIVES AND BENEFITS

by Arthur Dawkins

Throughout the more than one hundred-year history of jazz, small group combos have provided a setting for crystallizing the art of improvising, arranging, and composing. Consequently, the role of combos cannot be overemphasized. Combos represent a core foundation around which almost everything in jazz music revolves.

WHAT, WHY, WHEN

The jazz combo is a small musical ensemble typically comprised of five to eight performers. Stellar small groups have been a mainstay of jazz since its beginnings.

- Early instrumental music labeled "jazz" was essentially played by combos, and some of the most influential recordings in those early years featured small groups such as Louis Armstrong's Hot Five.
- Jazz scholars often cite combo performance as a core formation around which essential elements of jazz music revolves.
- While large jazz groups usually require notated arrangements and often restrict opportunities for improvisation, combos more effectively encourage individual musical freedom and individual expression.

Jazz Ensemble vs. Jazz Combo

If you have time for only one jazz group, should it be the jazz ensemble or the jazz combo? There is no clear answer to this question. You will have to weigh all of the factors listed here and plan accordingly.

In a typical school setting, philosophy, experience, tradition, and personnel are often factors in determining the need and desire to organize a jazz combo. Does your schedule permit rehearsal time for the combo? Are you comfortable with combo instrumentation? Are the expectations of the administration, community, and instrumental students that you will have only a traditional full-size 18-piece jazz ensemble? Are there enough students in the program to form a traditional jazz ensemble? Are there too many students interested in the jazz ensemble but not enough for a second full band?

If there is a functioning and successful jazz ensemble in the school, often the addition of a combo to the schedule is a challenge to both the director and the students. Here are a few thoughts (and perhaps incentives) to consider:

- Small groups are logistically less complicated with regard to organizing and maintaining stable personnel.
- There is less dependence on music notation for maintaining cohesion of musical statements, allowing more individual expression.
- Fewer performers imply a more open "sonic canvas" upon which the musicians can express themselves.
- Organization of music materials (i.e., musical arrangements) is generally less complex with fewer instrumentalists.
- Within a small group context there is greater potential for improvisational experience for each participant.

- Combo experiences often encourage students to work independently of a teacher. This tradition is usually found in productive jazz programs and can serve as an effective motivational tool.
- Combos become a viable alternative when the instrumental program lacks sufficient instrumentation for a big band.
- Combos provide opportunities for participation when there is a wide range of ability levels.
- Combos provide additional opportunities when there is a need to challenge students beyond the typical jazz ensemble.
- Combos focus on individual expression (improvisation, style, etc.), group interaction, and relatively abstract musical concepts—such as less reliance on music notation.
- Combos require less physical space for rehearsals and performances.
- Combos require less complicated logistics regarding transportation and performances.

Objectives

Goals are essential! Here are a few ideas to consider for a jazz combo. These objectives could be posted on the rehearsal room walls, used for administrative purposes, shared with a student director, or for your own personal use.
- Combos should provide opportunities for a small group of musicians to interact as soloists, accompanists, and ensemble participants.
- Combos should strive for a high level of musicianship—good tone quality and intonation, rhythmic precision, technique, and understanding musical context.
- Combos should provide opportunities for improvised solo development.
- Combos should focus on individual expression as well as group cohesiveness.
- Combos should be presented in public performances as often as possible.
- Combos should ideally be self-directed (they should not depend on a conductor).

INSTRUMENTATION

The number of performers in a jazz combo typically ranges from five to eight; however, duos, trios, and others are common as well. Some historians cite ten as a maximum number of performers for a combo. Since solo opportunities are expected from each member, the maximum group number should be a major consideration. Using six to eight performers offers the possibility of three-part harmony, which has the potential for a big sound. In the body of important modern jazz recordings, the typical instrumentation is saxophone, trumpet, piano, bass, and drums. Often a third melodic voice (i.e., trombone) is added to the ensemble for more flexibility. Variations of this instrumentation include combinations of two, three, or four melodic instruments and rhythm section.

Rhythm Section

The rhythm section may include any or all of the following: piano/keyboard, bass, drum set, percussion instruments, and guitar. Although these are typical instruments, they are by no means required.
- Piano: acoustic or electronic keyboard with amplifier (discussed further in Chapter 16A: Piano)
- Drum set (discussed further in Chapter 16C: Drums)
- Bass: acoustic or electric, with amplifier (discussed further in Chapter 16B: Bass)
- Guitar: electric and acoustic (discussed further in Chapter 16D: Guitar)
- Latin percussion

Creatively gifted artists produce outstanding jazz without standard rhythm sections. A good example is the Dirty Dozen Brass Band's CD, *This Is Jazz No. 30*, Sony/Columbia (this group does not use a drum set, string bass, or piano).

Traditional Horns

The traditional wind instruments in a combo are:
• Tenor saxophone or alto saxophone or baritone saxophone: discussed in Chapter 17A: Saxophone
• Trumpet: discussed in Chapter 17B: Trumpet
• Trombone: discussed in Chapter 17C: Trombone

Others Welcome

Understand that the combo does not have a fixed instrumentation like the jazz ensemble. You can use virtually any combination of melodic instruments desired. Considering individual expression as an overall objective, any combination of instruments is acceptable. Therefore, instruments not commonly associated with jazz (strings, double reeds, various percussion instruments) can and should be used in combos. This is especially effective in training situations such as classroom activities and non-performance circumstances. If you have talented and motivated players interested in being in a jazz combo who play violin or French horn or whatever, go for it! You or your students may have to transpose or adapt parts for these non-traditional instruments, but it can be well worth the effort.

Don't forget the vocalists that have some understanding of instrumental jazz. They should be encouraged to participate in combos as well.

COMBO LAYOUT

The combo typically sets up in two tiers or rows. The melodic wind instruments or horns are in the front tier, usually in a semicircle depending on the number of players. The rhythm section is in the second tier or row.

Horn Section

The horn section stands in front of the rhythm section. Both aural and visual communication is critical between the rhythm section and the front line horn section. Example 1 is a typical rhythm section set-up. During rehearsals, consider having the horn section face the rhythm section to lock in aural and visual communication.

Example 1 (Rhythm section set-up diagram)

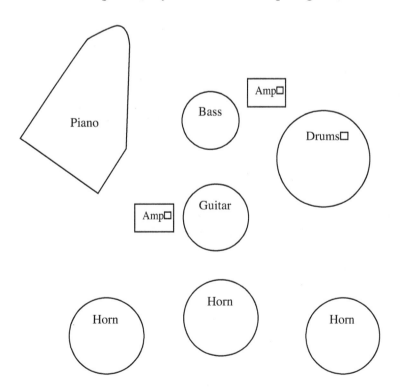

Rhythm Section

The rhythm section is divided into two segments. The bass and drums are the primary timekeepers. The piano and guitar are the harmonic voices responsible for comping—accompanying soloists with chord progressions as required by the composition. The piano and guitar have a critical role as timekeepers too. The rhythm section set-up should reflect these roles. Visual and aural site lines are extremely important. The functions of instruments in the rhythm section dictate their placement.

Piano and Guitar

The pianist and guitarist provide the harmonic structure and need to be close enough to clearly hear as well as see each other. As shown in the seating chart, the guitarist is seated just off the right side or the upper register of the keyboard. This encourages working together and allows for good communication to determine alternating comping responsibilities.

Bass and Drums

The same is true for the bass and drums. Depending on the preference of the director and the needs of the band, the bass can be on either side of the drummer. The drummer is generally placed between the piano and bass or between the bass and the winds. The latter is the preferred set-up because it separates the drums from the piano and prevents possible bleed-through when the piano is miked. Even with an inexperienced drummer, this set-up is still the best because it forms the most cohesive setting for the rhythm section. Another option, although less desired, is placing the bass on the other side of the drummer. Either way, the bass player must be able to see and hear clearly the drummer's ride cymbal to help lock in the time. It is also important that the drummer is able to see the bass player's right hand for the same reason.

All rhythm section instruments should be close to one another so they can function as a compact section. Notice the placement of amps in the set-up diagram because their placement is important so that all players can hear and maintain the balance of sound. It is through these lines of communication (aurally and visually) that individual rhythm section players become a unified and cohesive rhythm section.

LISTENING

Music is one of two major methods of communication used by all human societies. Another method of human communication is spoken language. Consequently, music and language systems are learned first through hearing it and then by practicing and perfecting skills needed to speak properly within the cultural context for which it was designed. This concept is especially appropriate when examining jazz education.

Critical listening is an all-important first step in acquiring aurally discriminatory skills in making culturally rooted musical choices. Listening to quality jazz—music that has stood the test of time—is an important way to develop "an ear." This is particularly relevant as one acquires an affinity for a given style or artist.

Getting Started

Some fundamental considerations for optimizing music listening are as follows:
- As often as possible, listen to live musical performances. It is sometimes difficult to perceive dynamics of great jazz artists listening to recordings. Live performances provide overall reception that is auditory as well as visual; this adds considerably to listening experiences.
- Early listening techniques may include identifying the melody. Attempt to sing along. If melodies are too complicated, as many are on an initial hearing, try to identify with anther aspect (i.e., rhythm, dynamics) that may be of interest or appreciated.
- Seek recommendations for listening to live or recorded music from respected, mature musicians.
- Listen with a goal of being able to identify some musical aspect.

Goals

Long-term and short-term goals of listening should include developing an ability to transcribe and imitate solo and ensemble elements. Specifically, an integral part of combo training should be the development of students' skills in transcribing melodies of standard jazz compositions, particularly material not available in fake books. Transcribing jazz solos is an extremely important skill for developing jazz musicians.

IMPROVISATION

The beauty of a combo lies in its players' ability to work independently as well as together to create jazz in an organized ensemble. Improvisation is probably the most challenging aspect of the combo experience; therefore, while big bands most often feature a small number of soloists, combos require much more improvisation from all members, including rhythm section players. Each member of a combo should expect greater opportunity to experiment and improvise without the restricted structure of the typical big band arrangement.

For further discussion of the art of improvisation, please refer to Chapters 9 and 10.

SELECTING PERSONNEL

Selecting personnel is especially critical in a combo. Although the audition process is discussed in Chapter 12, the director should add one additional criterion to the combo audition process: *desire*. The combo may occasionally rehearse/perform without the director, so the members of the group should be self-motivated to rehearse on their own and ultimately to create music beyond the written note.

Creativity, self-expression, and intimacy within the ensemble are other abstract elements of the combo that also should be considered.

Selection of players for the combo is not as dependent on sight-reading skills as the jazz ensemble. Although sight-reading is important, it is sometimes not as critical because of the focus on improvisation. The overall structure of the combo is not as confining as the larger ensemble.

In conclusion, the members selected for a combo should be creative and motivated to make music. Student performers interested in writing are ideal for a combo because this is the ideal opportunity to create, write, and experiment with blend, color, and texture.

SCHEDULING

Except in extraordinary situations, combo rehearsals will be scheduled outside the regular school day. Combos usually meet before school, after school, during periods in the regular school day when musicians can meet, or on weekends. Once students become aware of what is expected, many combos rehearse without the director.

Duos

There are numerous recorded examples featuring duets or duos. Three outstanding examples of duos are the following:

- Clark Terry, *One-on-One*, Chesky Jazz

- Kenny Barron/Regina Carter, *Duet Project*, Verve

- Ellis Marsalis/Branford Marsalis, *Loved Ones*, Sony/Columbia

Duos require more advanced and creative players. Most duos consist of a chordal instrument (piano, keyboard, guitar, etc.) and a non-chordal instrument (brasswind, woodwind, etc.).

DIRECTOR'S CHECKLIST JAZZ COMBO

- Ensemble size: Five to eight usually works best, but creative options abound.

- Improvisation: The combo can be the ideal musical palette for the essence of jazz. Always be thinking about jazz vocabulary and aural skills.

- Using talented and mature student directors can often solve scheduling challenges. The right student leader can make the combo happen!

- Jazz ensemble vs. jazz combo: Weigh the factors such as program size, student leadership, philosophy of the administration, community, scheduling, and the expectations of the students.

- Set goals and share them with students. Post them and update regularly.

- Instrumentation/equipment. Don't automatically limit to standard instrumentation.

- Layout: Use the standard diagram or design creative alternatives. Aural and visual communication is essential.

- Listening must be a priority. Learn style, phrasing, concept, and melody (sing along) and train your ear. Challenge yourself and the students daily.

- Personnel consideration for a combo offers unlimited potential. Interested, talented, and motivated performers on any instrument should be considered. Think outside the box.

- Fake books are perfect tools for the jazz combo. Learn melodies/rhythms/harmonies, create arrangements, and expand jazz vocabulary and aural skills.

- Embrace the technology.

COMBO RESOURCES
See the Resource Guide Index

Play-along books
Music publishers
Fake books
Technology-related resources

More About Fake Books

A fake book is an essential resource for the combo. The term *fake book* is a hold-over expression from the not-so-distant past when a collection of standards and other songs would be sold under the counter because the publishing copyrights were not listed, recorded, or documented. These books were unauthorized and therefore illegal. Not listing and crediting copyright-holders cheats the composers of compensation for their creative work. Most professionally published fake books are legal with documentation, credits, and compensation tracked for the copyright owners. The following fake books, or real books as they are often called, are enormous resources of outstanding titles with standard chord changes and often with suggested alternate and more harmonically interesting chord changes. The use of these books is highly recommended to learn, study, analyze, and provide an instant arrangement of thousands of titles. However, you should be aware of the standard publisher's statement that any duplication, adaptation, or arrangement of the compositions in these collections requires the written consent of the publisher.

FAKE BOOKS

101 Montunos, Sher Music.

50 Essential Bebop Heads, Hal Leonard Publications.

African Percussion, Sher Music.

Best Fake Book Ever, 2nd Edition, Hal Leonard Publications.

Best of the Brecker Brothers, Hal Leonard Publications.

Bill Evans Fake Book, Hal Leonard Publications.

Billie Holiday Anthology, Music Sales Corporation.

Blues Fake Book, Hal Leonard Publications.

Brazilian Guitar, Sher Music.

Chicago Fakebook, Hal Leonard Publications.

Choice Jazz Standards, Hal Leonard Publications.

Concepts for Bass Soloing, Sher Music.

Definitive Jazz Collection, Hal Leonard Publications.

Disney Fake Book, Hal Leonard Publications.

Esterowitz, Michael, *How to Play From a Fake Book*, Warner Bros. Publications.

Great Jazz Classics, Hal Leonard Publications.

Greatest Legal Fake Book of All Time, Warner Bros. Publications.

Hyman, Dick, *All the Right Changes*, Ekay Music.

Hyman, Dick, *Professional Chord Changes and Substitutions for 100 Tunes*, Ekay Music.

Jazz Bible Series, Hal Leonard Publications.

Jazz Etudes to Rhythm Changes, JA Jazz.

Jazz of the '50s, Hal Leonard Publications.

Jewish Fake Book, Hal Leonard Publications.

Just Blues Real Book, Warner Bros. Publications.

Just Jazz Real Book, Warner Bros. Publications.

Just Standards Real Book, Warner Bros. Publications.

Latin Bass Book, Sher Music.

Latin Fakebook, Sher Music.

Latin Real Book, Sher Music.

Levine, Mark, *Jazz Piano Book*, Sher Music.

Mantooth, Frank, *Best Known Chord Changes*, Hal Leonard Publications.

Mantooth, Frank, *The Best Chord Changes for the Most Requested Standards*, Hal Leonard Publications.

Mantooth, Frank, *The Best Chord Changes for the World's Greatest Standards*, Hal Leonard Publications.

Muy Caliente! Sher Music.

Neely, Blake, *How to Play From a Fake Book*, Hal Leonard Publications.

New Real Book, Vol. 1, Sher Music.

New Real Book, Vol. 2, Sher Music.

New Real Book, Vol. 3, Sher Music.

Pat Metheny Songbook, Hal Leonard Publications.

Pocket Changes, Jeffersonville, IN.

Professional Pianist Fake Book, Hal Leonard Publications.

Professional Singer Pop/Rock Fake Book, Hal Leonard Publications.

R&B Fake Book, Hal Leonard Publications.

Ragtime & Early Jazz 1900–1935, Hal Leonard Publications.

Real Jazz Book, Hal Leonard Publications.

Real Jazz Standards Fake Book, Hal Leonard Publications.

Real Little Ultimate Fake Book, Hal Leonard Publications.

Salsa Guide Book, Sher Music.

Standards Real Book, Sher Music.

Straight Ahead Jazz Fakebook, Music Sales Corporation.

Swing Era 1936–1947, Hal Leonard Publications.

The Antonio Carlos Jobim Anthology, Hal Leonard Publications.

TV Fake Book, Hal Leonard Publications.

Ultimate Fake Book, 3rd Edition, Hal Leonard Publications.

Various Styles Fake Book, Country, Rock, Pop, R&B, etc., Hal Leonard Publications.

World's Greatest Fake Book, Jazz/Fusion, Sher Music.

World's Greatest Fake Book, Sher Music.

World's Greatest Fake Book, Warner Bros. Publications.

Yellowjackets Song Book, Sher Music.

SUGGESTED RECORDINGS OF SMALL GROUPS

Twenty Influential Small Group Jazz Recordings

Adderley, Julian "Cannonball," *Cannonball: Somethin' Else,* Blue Note, 95392-2, Recorded 3/1958.

Armstrong, Louis, *Hot Fives,* Vol. 1, Columbia, 44049, Recorded 11/12/1925–6/23/1926.

Blakey, Art, *A Night at Birdland,* Vols. 1 and 3, Blue Note, 46519-2; 46520-2, Recorded 2/21/1954.

Brecker Brothers, *The Brecker Brothers Collection,* Vol. 1, RCA-ND, 90442, Recorded 1975/1981.

Coltrane, John, *My Favorite Things,* Atlantic, 812275350-2, Recorded 10/1960.

Crusaders, *Live at the Lighthouse '66,* Pacific Jazz, 37988, Recorded 1/1966.

Davis, Miles, *Kind of Blue,* Columbia, CK 64935, Recorded 3–4/1959.

D'Rivera, Paquito, *Tico! Tico!* Chesky, 034, Recorded 7–8/1989.

Gillespie, Dizzy, *Bird and Diz,* Verve, 521436-2, Recorded 6/1950.

Hargrove, Roy, *Parker's Mood,* Verve, 527907, Recorded 4/1995.

Henderson, Joe, *Page One,* Blue Note, 98795, Recorded 6/1963.

Lewis, Ramsey, *In Person,* Chess, 0518142 2CD, Recorded 1960–1967.

Marsalis, Wynton, *J Mood,* Columbia, 468712, Recorded 12/1985.

Metheny, Pat, *Road to You: Live in Europe,* Geffen, GED, 24601, Recorded 1992–1993.

Parker, Charlie, *The Charlie Parker Story,* Savoy, SV-0105, Recorded 11/1945.

Peterson, Oscar, *Night Train,* Vol. 1, Verve, 521440-2, Recorded 12/16/1962.

Redman, Joshua, *Joshua Redman,* Warner Bros., 945242-2, Recorded 5–9/1992.

Return to Forever, *Light as a Feather,* Verve, 557115-2, Recorded 10/1972.

Silver, Horace, *Song for My Father,* Blue Note, 99002-2, Recorded 10/1964.

Weather Report, *Live in Tokyo,* Columbia, 489208, 2-CD, Recorded 1/1972.

SIGNIFICANT COMBO PLAYERS AND GROUPS

Small Groups of the 1930s and Before:

New Orleans-Style Early Jazz

Louis Armstrong's Hot Five

King Oliver

McKinney's Cotton Pickers

Washboard Rhythm Kings (Alabama Washboard Stompers)

The Buddy Bolden Quartet

Preservation Hall Jazz Band

Rebirth Jazz Band

Small Groups of the 1940s, 1950s, and 1960s:

Bop
Charlie Parker/Dizzy Gillespie Quintet
Thelonious Monk
Bud Powell

New Thing - Free Jazz
Ornette Coleman Quartet
Art Ensemble of Chicago
Eric Dolphy

Hard Bop
Max Roach/Clifford Brown Quintet
The Jazz Messengers (Art Blakey)
Horace Silver Quintet
Cannonball Adderley Quintet
Jazztet (Benny Golson, Art Farmer)
Freddie Hubbard Quintet
Wes Montgomery (Groups)

Piano Trios
Oscar Peterson Trio
Ramsey Lewis Trio
Nat Cole Trio
Ahmad Jamal Trio
Bill Evans
Brad Mehldau
Joanne Brackeen

Chamber Jazz

Modern Jazz Quartet

Les Jazz Modes

Progressive Jazz

John Coltrane Quartet

Miles Davis Quintet (Early/Middle/Kind of Blue)

Small Groups of the 1970s, 1980s, and 1990s:

Fusion

Weather Report

Prime Time

Herbie Hancock (Groups)

Return to Forever

Miles Davis (1960s–1990s)

Funk/Pop

Stanley Turrentine (Groups)

Fourplay

Crusaders

Family-Based

Heath Brothers

Ethnic Heritage Ensemble

Black/Note

Stan Getz Quartet

B Sharp Quartet

Joe Lovano (Groups)

Roy Hargrove Quintet

Branford Marsalis (Groups)

Wynton Marsalis (Groups)

Harper Brothers

Clayton Brothers

Brecker Brothers

General

World Saxophone Quartet

M'Boom

New York Jazz Quartet

Circle

Giants of Jazz

Sphere

Dameronia

Mingus Dynasty

Paquito D'Rivera (Groups)

Joshua Redman (Groups)

Dave Brubeck Quartet

Joe Henderson (Groups)

Tito Puente (Groups)

David Murray (Groups)

Dave Holland Quintet

Pat Metheny (Groups)

THE JAZZ ENSEMBLE
ORGANIZATION AND AUDITION BASICS

by J. Richard Dunscomb

Chapter 12

Have you ever had the experience of hearing a really good big band live? It's thrilling! Whatever catches the fancy of the listener—the rhythm, the many colors, the various textures, the simplicity or complexity, the finesse, the hot improvisation, or just the pure energy and power of the ensemble—it is a unique experience. Let's explore how to pass those sensations on to our schools' most valuable assets, our students.

Most educational institutions have at least one jazz ensemble, whether at a middle school, junior high school, secondary school, prep school, community college, or university. The jazz ensemble has great tradition, popularity, and wide acceptance. As a result, it has excellent visibility in the community and, in turn, has the responsibility to represent the entire music program positively.

> *A jazz ensemble is also called a big band or jazz band. The terms "stage band" and "dance band" are rarely used today.*

PREPARE FOR SUCCESS

It was through the persistence and hard work of early jazz educators that big bands were included in educational music programs. These trailblazers were successful because they kept the lines of information and communication open with their fellow educators and administrators.

One of the most realistic points of view we can maintain is that the jazz ensemble is part of a well-rounded music program. If we present our jazz teaching in this manner, and adhere to it, we will be on the road to success. The popularity of the jazz program, as well as the positive visibility that a jazz ensemble imparts, can be an important feather in the cap of the informed music department. Working with your colleagues to let them know that you are a part of the team continues to be very important not only to the success of your jazz program but also to the overall success of jazz education.

INSTRUMENTATION

The instrumentation makeup of the big band contributes to its appealing sound and emotional impact. The instrumentation of the standard jazz ensemble is: five saxophones, four trombones, four trumpets, piano, guitar (optional), bass, drums, and auxiliary percussion (optional). The instrumentation may be expanded to five trombones, five trumpets, vibes, and any other instrument specified on a musical composition or arrangement.

One-on-a-Part

The manageable size of a 17- to 20-piece jazz ensemble provides students with a challenging one-on-a-part experience. It stimulates them to know that if they don't play their part, it affects the entire ensemble's success. They develop a keen sense of confidence and teamwork. As a result, they grow musically and socially and become better all-around players. They also progress in the areas of creativity, individuality, and responsibility. The jazz ensemble will reward your more advanced players and provide an incentive for them to stay involved in the entire music program.

Performance Set-Up

The performance set-up is also vital to the sound and success of your jazz ensemble. Example 1 shows the jazz ensemble performance set-up that has evolved over the years. It is accepted universally as the standard one. Experiments with other set-ups have been tried and discarded. This includes simple variations of the traditional set-up and extreme variations like the Kenton "Flying V." Only in rare situations are variations used today.

Positioning the trombone and trumpet sections on tiered risers behind the saxophones will significantly improve the sound quality at concerts. If risers are not available, have your trombone players sit on stools rather than chairs and ask your trumpet players to stand.

Example 1: Standard Jazz Ensemble Performance Set-Up Chart

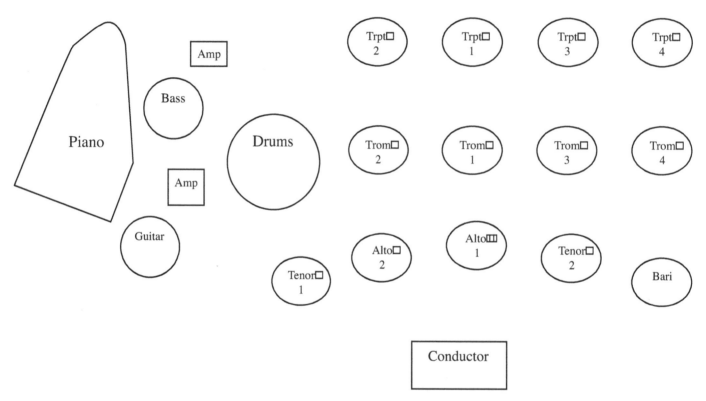

Rehearsal Set-Up

A rehearsal set-up that is gaining much favor is the box set-up shown in Example 2. This set-up is often used in recording sessions. The advantage is that the players can all hear and see each other. It also places the director in the middle of everyone. It's a great way to rehearse, but caution yourself to move from this set-up several rehearsals before a performance so that you and your musicians can adjust to hearing and seeing the ensemble in a performance set-up.

Example 2: Box Set-Up for Rehearsal

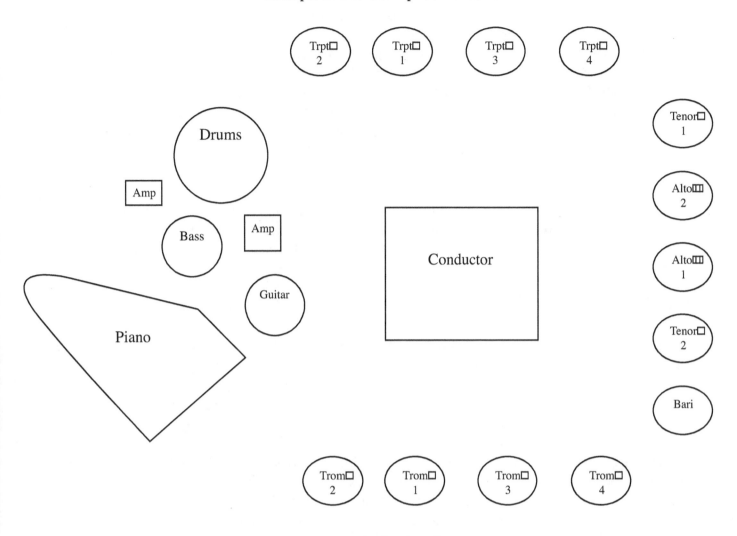

AUDITIONS

Auditions provide a forum to evaluate your students' musical progress. Auditions are also the best way to evaluate potential talent for your jazz ensemble. Well-organized and fair auditions are critical to the success and growth of the ensemble. Most successful jazz programs hold auditions every semester or twice a year.

Announcing Auditions

The process begins with getting the word out. Flyers or posters announcing auditions for your group need to be posted throughout areas where students congregate on a daily basis. This certainly includes the band room/music areas. Flyers should also be posted in other areas as well since it is sometimes necessary to attract the piano, bass, guitar, or drum participants from outside the current music program. This process can also help create a high profile for the jazz band.

What, Where, When, and Why

One of the most important aspects of your announcement is to make it very clear to the students, in advance, what to expect during the audition.

Posted flyers need to contain helpful information about what, where, when, and why the auditions are being held. The flyers present a great opportunity to share information about the prestige of the band, the one-on-a-part playing, the day and time the band will rehearse, upcoming performance dates, and a listing of the audition requirements. It is a good idea to indicate how many of each instrument will be selected so that students have an idea of the size and instrumentation makeup of the ensemble.

When clear and concise information is imparted through this first step, more interest will be generated and students will be more prepared on audition day.

Prepared Selection Portion

Jazz auditions need to include a prepared selection. Create a list of several pieces that would be acceptable to play for the prepared selection. See the additional information in "The Music" section of this book, Chapter 15, for ideas in the appropriate category and grade level. Certainly a selection of jazz standard heads for each of the wind instruments will put them on the right track from the beginning. Have recordings available of each tune so students have a model from which to work.

The prepared selection gives students the opportunity to perform at the highest level possible and begin the learning process even before the first rehearsal. The procedure will identify each student's level of desire, which can be an important indicator of his or her potential impact on the group.

Sight-Reading Portion

Each audition also needs to include sight-reading. Prepared materials that progress from easy to more difficult are required. Many materials are available that will fill this need, such as Lou Fischer's book *Stylistic Etudes in the Jazz Idiom* (Hal Leonard Publications). This book contains several selections for each instrument in swing style, several in ballad style, and several in Latin/rock style. While you want the audition sight-reading materials to reflect the level you expect students to be able to perform, you also need some simpler music for the less advanced players and more challenging music for the more advanced players.

Improvisation Section

The decision to audition improvisation skills must be made according to the level of the students in your program. It can be a vital element for more advanced and well-prepared students. On the other hand, it can intimidate. You may decide that only the more advanced players are required to improvise and it is an option for younger, less experienced players. Once again, providing complete information in advance to students is essential if you intend to audition improvisation skills.

At the college level, this should be a required part of all auditions. Please refer to the information on *Approaching the Standards* or similar improvisation books for samples of improvised solos. Remember, copying someone else's playing style is okay in jazz. This used to be the only way jazz players learned to improvise. As we say in jazz, if you copy, copy from the best! Additional information about improvisation is available in Chapters 9 and 10.

Rhythm Section

Rhythm section auditions for piano, bass, drums, and guitar may be programmed in a similar fashion as described above. Avoid putting rhythm section students in a confrontational situation where they are asked only to sight read, because some may have little or no experience or training in this area. Some of the finest jazz musicians have absorbed their musicality by listening and, therefore, do not have strong reading skills. Allowing these students to play music with which they are familiar will certainly show you their talent level. Perhaps playing along with a recording would suffice. Through the years this is the way many of the great jazz masters learned to play. It is best to have the drummers play time in various styles to show their time and feel abilities.

Ultimately, auditioning rhythm section players together as a rhythm section will often show the best combination of students.

Audition Forms

Audition forms are a vital link to help students understand the audition requirements. The audition form should be simple and well articulated in describing the various areas being evaluated. These forms should be posted prior to the auditions so students can see the musical aspects on which they will be judged.

Retain all of the audition forms after the audition. Hold a private meeting with each student to discuss positively his or her audition. This feedback will provide them with an accurate evaluation of their musicianship as well as encourage their continued progress.

A sample audition form is shown below. Feel free to use it, or better yet, tailor it to meet your specific needs. Using such a form will ensure a smooth audition process for you and your students.

AUDITION EVALUATION FORM

Name_____ Date_____Grade_____

Instrument_____ Phone_____

Address_____

_____

5 = Excellent, 4 = Good, 3 = Average, 2 = Below Average, 1 = Not Ready

Skill	5	4	3	2	1
Prepared music					
Jazz time, feel, and style					
Rhythmic accuracy					
Tone					
Intonation					
Dynamics					
Articulation					
Intonation					
Sight-reading					
Improvisation					
Other					

Total points _____

Comments_____

_____

Selecting the Players

Selecting the players for the parts becomes the next job. It is vital to match up players to their roles in each section. In addition to the level of musicianship, take into consideration each student's sound, personality, leadership qualities, and so on. Successful matching of players and parts can greatly strengthen the ensemble. There are some great suggestions on how to assign parts in the individual instrument chapters. Each player also needs to have a commitment to listening to jazz.

Key Player Characteristics

Here are some characteristics to look for when selecting key players:
- 1st Alto – consistent, responsible, strong reader, leadership skills, strong sound and pitch, conceptual skills.
- 1st Tenor – strongest soloist, ability to blend, team player.
- Bari Sax – strong sound, ability to blend, good intonation.
- 1st Trumpet – consistent, responsible, strong reader, leadership skills, strong sound and pitch, good upper range, conceptual skills.
- 2nd Trumpet – probably strongest soloist, strong sound and pitch, team player, able to match phrasing and articulation, ability to play 1st on some tunes.
- 1st Trombone – consistent, responsible, strong reader, leadership skills, strong sound and pitch, good upper range, conceptual skills.
- Bass Trombone – consistent, responsible, good reader, strong sound and pitch, good lower range.
- Drummer – great time, good ears, consistent, responsible, team player, makes a commitment to listening to jazz.
- Bass – good ears, great time, consistent, responsible, team player.
- Guitar – team player willing to learn the guitar playing style needed for the jazz ensemble style. This consists of often playing in the background much of the time yet being an exciting soloist when called upon to do so.
- Piano – team player willing to learn the piano playing style needed for the jazz ensemble style. This consists of often playing in the background much of the time yet being an exciting soloist when called upon to do so.

Avoid Doubling Parts

Assigning more than one player to a part becomes a problem for the jazz ensemble. Any doubling of parts is detrimental to the characteristic jazz ensemble sound. Although it may be a difficult decision to make, you must make it nevertheless. Avoid being one of the groups that arrives at festivals with an overbalanced instrumentation (i.e., eight saxophones, more brass than needed, multiple rhythm section players). Here are alternative ways to handle additional players if necessary for your situation:
- Rotate players in rehearsal and concert: Results are the best musically since it allows only one player on a part at all times.
- Have everyone play in rehearsal but rotate players in concert: Results are positive and students all have a chance to play.
- Form a second band: Results are positive if enough players are available.

Post Audition Results Quickly

It is best to post the jazz ensemble personnel as quickly as possible. Remember to schedule private meetings with all students to review the audition forms.

SECTIONAL REHEARSALS

Sectional rehearsals are valuable to the jazz ensemble. Many programs do not have ample time/resources to schedule section rehearsals for each section of the jazz ensemble. It would be ideal for each sectional to be run by the director, but the reality of most situations finds either student section leaders in charge (a good idea) or outside musicians, graduates, or area musicians (another good idea) running the sectionals.

In this setting the sections are able to pinpoint problem areas and resolve them in a short period of time. While the director may not have time to actually be in each sectional, he or she can prepare a list of items to work on. Such a checklist gives direction to the leader of the sectional in terms of what to deal with and at the same time allows him or her the ability to develop independence in coming up with solutions. See Chapter 14 for rehearsal tips.

DIRECTOR'S CHECKLIST FOR JAZZ ENSEMBLE

- Use the performance seating chart and the rehearsal seating chart; hear the difference.

- At all rehearsals, check the set-up of your jazz ensemble for consistency.

- Establish a fair audition process.

- Provide students with complete information about the content of the auditions.

- Post an audition form (and explain what it means) prior to the auditions.

- Always attempt to place students in the most suitable position based on the demands of the part, personality, and personnel.

- One player per part is a key to the jazz ensemble sounding accurate.

- Explore scheduling (student-led) sectional rehearsals for the jazz ensemble.

- Know the historical progression of jazz ensembles.

Please refer to the Resource Guide Index.

Chapter 13

BIG BAND HISTORY

AN OVERVIEW

by J. Richard Dunscomb

Place yourself in New York City almost any weekend evening in the latter half of the 1930s. You could have gone to hear the big bands of Benny Goodman, Jimmy Dorsey, Artie Shaw, Les Brown, Woody Herman, Duke Ellington, Glenn Miller, or Jimmy Lunceford. Big band jazz was king! There were swing bands, sweet bands, and almost any other kind you could imagine. The *Metronome* poll, in which readers voted for their favorite big band, listed almost 300 entries in each of three categories for four years from 1937 through 1940.

People throughout the United States were filling ballrooms to dance to the music of the big bands. Bands were on the road constantly and developed a following much like movie stars or sports stars. The great popularity was a result of the communication between the big bands and their fans. Tommy Dorsey once compared his band to a football team. He put his soloists in the backfield, and on the line he put his lead men, first trumpet, first sax, and first trombone, along with the four men in his rhythm section — piano, guitar, bass, and drums.

HISTORICAL CHRONOLOGY

It is important to trace the development of the big band through the years. Organized chronologically, the chart starting on page 138 provides an historical overview. The first column shows the bandleader's name and the years as a big band leader. The second column shows the instruments and roles the leader played in his big band. The third column shows some of the sidemen in those particular bands. The fourth column adds general dates of interest and important dates in the evolution of that band, its director, and/or band members.

Origins

The earliest big bands developed in New York City in the mid-1920s. While many orchestras and larger ensembles had been experimenting by incorporating jazz into their repertoire, none had been successful until Fletcher Henderson. (It is important to note that for the purposes of this book, dance bands preceded big bands, so some dance bands are included in the following chronology.)

Leaders and Arrangers

The two people directly responsible for the style of a band were the leader and its arranger. I trace this evolution of leaders and arrangers through the big bands. I also follow the migration of the multitude of jazz musicians, or side men.

The development of the big band created an influential role for musical arrangers. Don Redman filled that role for the Fletcher Henderson Orchestra. Redman is credited with being the first important arranger for big band and for establishing the standard instrumentation of the jazz band. It is interesting to follow the individual progression of arrangers in the chronology as they move from one group to another and eventually into leadership roles of their own.

It is also fascinating to trace individual musicians as they move from being a sideman in one group to eventually leading their own group. For example, Don Redman's charts for the Fletcher Henderson Orchestra led to his becoming leader of McKinney's Cotton Pickers, one of the most successful big bands of the late twenties. Redman then formed his own successful group. Fletcher Henderson began writing his own charts after Redman left and then became the staff arranger for Benny Goodman, whose radio shows introduced Fletcher Henderson's arrangements to the nation.

Although the chart beginning on page 138 is not meant to be a complete history, it will give you a good understanding of the overall development of the big band.

A HISTORY OF BIG BANDS

by Marcia F. Dunscomb

LEADER YEAR BORN & DIED BIG BAND YEARS	INSTRUMENT	NOTABLE SIDEMEN	COMMENTS
Paul Whiteman b. 1890 Denver, CO d. 1967 Doylestown, PA 1918–1930	Violin Leader	Red Nichols, Tommy Dorsey, Bix Beiderbecke, Frankie Trumbauer, Bing Crosby, Eddie Lang, Bunny Berigan, Jack Teagarden, Charlie Teagarden	World War I: Led a large Navy band. 1918: Organized his first dance band in San Francisco. 1924: Introduced "Rhapsody in Blue" with George Gershwin on piano in Aeolian Hall in New York City. 1920s: Press agents dubbed him the "King of Jazz." Whiteman's bands were always dance bands and never played jazz.
Fletcher Henderson b. 1897 Cuthbert, GA d. 1952 New York, NY 1921–1935 1936–1939	Piano Composer Arranger Leader	Louis Armstrong, Joe Smith, Tommy Ladnier, Rex Stewart, Cootie Williams, Red Allen, Roy Eldridge, J. C. Higginbottham, Dickie Wells, Buster Bailey, Coleman Hawkins, Ben Webster, Lester Young, Chu Berry, Benny Carter, Russell Procope, Sid Catlett, Fats Waller. Arrangers: Don Redman, Benny Carter, Fletcher Henderson, Horace Henderson	Leader of the first great jazz big band. Henderson's orchestra had no close competitors artistically until the rise of Duke Ellington in 1927. Henderson's all-star outfit was recorded relatively little during its peak (1927–1930). Don Redman wrote the bulk of the arrangements until he left in 1927. Henderson then developed as arranger and composer in the 1930s. 1934: Henderson began contributing his better arrangements to Benny Goodman's orchestra. 1936: Henderson put together a new orchestra, which recorded "Christopher Columbus," which would go on to became a big hit. "Christopher Columbus" would be part of the Goodman hit "Sing, Sing, Sing." 1939: Henderson broke up his band and became staff arranger for Benny Goodman.
Don Redman b. 1900 Piedmont, WV d. 1964 New York, NY 1922–1946	Clarinet Alto Sax Voice Composer Arranger Leader	Joe Smith, Coleman Hawkins, Benny Carter Arranger: Don Redman	First great arranger in jazz history. Redman's arrangements established the size and relationship of the brass, reed, and rhythm sections. Redman's innovations as a writer essentially invented the jazz-oriented big band with arrangements that left room for solo improvisations. 1922: Joined Fletcher Henderson's orchestra as arranger. 1924: Armstrong joined Henderson's orchestra. Redman's arrangements began to swing more. 1924: Recorded the first ever scat vocal on "My Papa Doesn't Two Time." 1927: Left Henderson to become musical director of McKinney's Cotton Pickers. 1931–1941: Led his own group. 1946: Led an all-star orchestra that became the first band to visit postwar Europe. 1950s: Pearl Bailey's musical director. First black band to play a sponsored radio series
Walter Page b. 1900 Gallatin, MS d. 1957 New York, NY 1925–1931	Bass Leader		1925–1921: Led the Blue Devils, Bennie Moten's main competition. Most of the Blue Devils were eventually hired by Moten. After Moten's death, Count Basie took over as leader. Page became a member of Basie's All American Rhythm Section.

Ben Pollack b. 1903 Chicago, IL d. 1971 Palm Springs, CA 1926–1934 1942–1949	Drums Leader	Glenn Miller, Benny Goodman, Jimmy McPartland, Harry James, Mugsy Spanier, Jack Teagarden, Frank Teschemacher, Bud Freeman, Mel Torme	Pollack's band played primarily in the New Orleans style. 1934: When Pollack's band broke up, many members became the core of the Bob Crosby band, which continued to play New Orleans-style jazz. Played himself in the movie *The Benny Goodman Story*. 1942: Pollack organized a big band for Chico Marx to front.
William McKinney McKinney's Cotton Pickers 1926–1934		Fats Waller, Don Redman, Coleman Hawkins, Benny Carter, Doc Cheaham, Rex Stewart Arranger: Don Redman	1923: Drummer, William McKinney formed his first big band. 1926: McKinney's band became known as McKinney's Cotton Pickers. 1927: McKinney hired Don Redman away from Fletcher Henderson. This band competed successfully with the bands of Henderson and Ellington and made several important recordings, including "Four or Five Times" and "Gee Baby Ain't I Good to You." 1928–1931: One of the best big bands. 1931: Redman left to form his own band. Benny Carter took over as musical director.
Bennie Moten b. 1894 Kansas City, MO d. 1935 Kansas City, MO 1926–1935	Piano Leader	Count Basie, Walter Page, Ben Webster, Eddie Durham, Jimmy Rushing, Hot Lips Page	1934: The band broke up. Set the standard for Kansas City jazz. 1929: Count Basie joined Moten's band. The Moten Band played mostly head arrangements.
Duke Ellington b. 1899 Washington, D.C. d. 1974 New York, NY Real name: Edward Kennedy Ellington 1926–1974	Piano Composer Arranger Leader	Sidney Bechet, Bubber Miley, Tricky Sam Nanton, Harry Carney, Barney Bigard, Johnny Hodges, Cootie Williams, Rex Stewart, Ivie Anderson, Ben Webster, Jimmy Blanton, Ray Nance, Shorty Baker, Cat Anderson, Oscar Pettiford, Sonny Greer, Louie Bellson, Willie Smith, Juan Tizol, Paul Gonsalves, Clark Terry, Russell Procope Arrangers: Ellington and Billy Strayhorn	Ellington considered his orchestra to be his main instrument. He wrote for his very individual players rather than for an anonymous horn section. Ellington's first group was called The Washingtonians. 1926: Ellington's 11-piece orchestra was formed. 1927–1931: Ellington's orchestra had a permanent gig at the Cotton Club. 1943–1950: Ellington's orchestra presented annual concerts at Carnegie Hall.
Jimmie Lunceford b. 1902 Fulton, MS d. 1947 Seaside, OR 1927–1947 (band until 1949)	Alto Sax Leader	Sy Oliver, Trummy Young, Willie Smith, Joe Thomas, Gerald Wilson, Snooky Young, Tommy Stevenson (screech trumpet) Arranger: Sy Oliver	1927: Lunceford's band originated as a high school band in Memphis. 1930s: Lunceford's band was considered an equal to Ellington's and Basie's orchestras. 1934: Played at the Cotton Club. 1934: Lunceford's was the first orchestra to feature high-note trumpeters. This was to have a strong influence on the early Stan Kenton Orchestra. 1939: Sy Oliver left to join Tommy Dorsey. 1939–1949: Orchestra was not as strong after Oliver left. 1949: Band broke up.

Benny Carter b. 1907 New York, NY 1928–1944	Alto Sax Trumpet Composer Arranger Leader	J. J. Johnson, Miles Davis, Max Roach	Contributed arrangements to Fletcher Henderson and Duke Ellington. 1931: Musical director of McKinney's Cotton Pickers. 1932–1934: Led his own big band again. 1935: Staff arranger for the BBC dance orchestra until 1938. 1943 Returned to Los Angeles where he again led a big band.
Luis Russell b. 1902 Careening Clay, Panama d. 1963 New York, NY 1929–1934 1943–1948	Piano Arranger Leader	Henry "Red" Allen, J. C. Higginbottham	1920: Moved to New Orleans from Panama after winning $3,000 in the lottery. 1925: Moved to Chicago and played in King Oliver's band. 1929: Russell's band backed Louis Armstrong on a few of his early recordings with big band. 1935: Armstrong took over this band as his own. 1943–1948: Russell led a new band that played at the Savoy.
Louis Armstrong b. 1901 New Orleans, LA d. 1971 New York, NY 1929–1947	Cornet Trumpet Voice Leader	Earl Hines, J. C. Higginbottham, Lionel Hampton (on drums)	1924: Left Chicago to join Fletcher Henderson's big band in New York. 1925: Moved back to Chicago. 1927: Switched from cornet to trumpet. He was featured nightly in Chicago with big bands led by Erskine Tate and Carrol Dickerson. 1929: Began leading his own big band. 1947: Broke up the big band and formed the All-Stars.
Cab Calloway b. 1907 Rochester, NY d. 1994 DE Real Name: Cabell Calloway	Drums Voice Tap Dancer Leader	Doc Cheatham, Cozy Cole, Danny Barker, Milt Hinton, Mario Bauza, Chu Berry, Dizzy Gillespie, Johan Jones, Tyree Glenn	1931: Calloway's orchestra began playing at the Cotton Club. In *Porgy and Bess* George Gershwin modeled the character Sportin' Life on Cab Calloway. 1950: Played Sportin' Life in *Porgy and Bess*.
1929–1948 Chick Webb b. 1909 Baltimore, MD d. 1939 Baltimore, MD Real Name: William Henry Webb 1931–1939 (band until 1942)	Drums Leader	Ella Fitzgerald	1935: Hired Ella Fitzgerald after she won the talent contest at the Apollo theater. 1942: After Webb's death, Ella led the band until it broke up later that year.
Gil Evans b. 1912 Toronto, Ontario, Canada d. 1988 Cuernavaca, Mexico Real name: Ian Ernest Gilmore Green	Piano Composer Arranger Leader	Jimmy Cleveland, Lee Konitz, Paul Chambers, Curtis Fuller, Howard Johnson, Billy Harper Arranger: Gil Evans	One of the most significant arrangers in jazz history. 1933–1938: Led his own big band in California. 1941–1942: Gained recognition for his futuristic charts for Claude Thornhill's Orchestra. 1946: Met Miles Davis. Contributed arrangements to Davis's *Birth of the Cool* on the Nonet label. 1957–1987: Led his own band. Also wrote arrangements for Kenny Burrell and Astrud Gilberto. 1970s: One of the first to use electronics. 1980s: Led his jazz orchestra in New York City at various jazz clubs.

Jimmy Dorsey b. 1904 Shenandoah, PA d. 1957 New York, NY 1934–1935 1953–1957	Clarinet Alto Sax Trumpet Leader	Bob Eberle, Helen O'Connell, Maynard Ferguson	1920s: Played with Red Nichols' Five Pennies, Frankie Trumbauer, and Paul Whiteman. 1928: Co-led with brother Tommy a studio group known as the Dorsey Brothers Orchestra. 1934: Dorsey brothers formed full-time big band. 1935: Argument between the Dorsey brothers led to Tommy's leaving. Jimmy took over as leader of this band. 1940s: Band became very successful. 1953: Broke up this band to join Tommy in a new Dorsey Brothers Orchestra that played sophisticated dance music. 1957: Tommy died and Jimmy continued to lead this band.
Tommy Dorsey b. 1905 Shenandoah, PA d. 1956 Greenwich, CT 1934–1956	Trombone Leader	Frank Sinatra, Jo Stafford, Bunny Berrigan, Bud Freeman, Sy Oliver, Buddy Rich, Charlie Shavers	The Dorsey bands played primarily dance music. 1934: Co-leader with brother Jimmy of the Dorsey Brothers Orchestra. 1935: Left Dorsey Brothers band and formed his own orchestra from what had been the Joe Hames orchestra. 1937: Had major hits "Marie" and "Song of India." 1940s: Hired Sy Oliver as chief arranger as well as Buddy Rich and Jo Stafford. 1953: Renamed the band the Dorsey Brothers Orchestra when Jimmy joined this group. This group played dance music.
Bob Crosby b. 1913 Spokane, WA d. 1993 La Jolla, CA 1934–1942	Vocalist Leader	Jess Stacy, Billy Butterfield, Joe Sullivan, Muggsy Spanier, Bob Haggart	Crosby led a big band playing New Orleans-style jazz. The orchestra also featured the Bobcats, a Dixieland group within the Crosby Orchestra.
Benny Goodman b. 1909 Chicago, IL d. 1986 New York, NY 1935–1946 1949–1962	Clarinet Leader	Teddy Wilson, Lionel Hampton, Gene Krupa, Harry James, Artie Shaw, Glenn Miller, Charlie Christian, Jess Stacy, Cootie Williams, Georgie Auld, Mel Powell, Red Norvo, Stan Getz, Wardell Gray, Helen Forrest, Peggy Lee. 1950s: Terry Gibbs, Buck Clayton, Roland Hanna, Jack Sheldon, Flip Phillips, Andre Previn, Herbie Hancock, George Benson	1933–1934: Played in Ben Pollack's orchestra. 1935: Goodman's success in 1935 launched the swing era. Goodman became known as "The King of Swing." 1935–1938: Goodman's orchestra was the most popular band in the world. 1938: Carnegie Hall concert. 1940: Goodman commissioned Béla Bartók to write "Contrasts" and Aaron Copland and Paul Hindemith to write clarinet concertos. 1962: The Goodman orchestra performed in Russia (the first U.S. group to be invited by the Russians).

Count Basie b. 1904 Red Bank, NY d. 1984 Hollywood, FL Real Name: William Basie 1935–1949 1952–present (the band)	Piano Leader	Walter Page, Freddie Green, Joe Jones, Harry "Sweets" Edison, Dicky Wells, Jimmy Rushing, Billie Holiday, Lester Young, Don Byas, Illinois Jacquet, Lucky Thompson, Paul Gonsalves, Wardell Gray, Buddy DeFranco, Joe Williams, Joe Newman, Thad Jones, Frank Wess, Frank Foster, Al Grey <u>Arrangers:</u> Neal Hefti, Ernie Wilkins, Frank Wess, Frank Foster, Thad Jones, Sammy Nestico	1927: Started in Walter Page's Blue Devils and then moved to Bennie Moten's Kansas City Orchestra. 1935: Formed his own nine-piece group known as the Barons of Rhythm, which had a regular radio program. 1936: John Hammond heard the band on his car radio. He went to Kansas City to sign the Basie band to Columbia Records and bring them to New York City. When Basie began to play nightly radio shows from the Grand Terrace in Chicago, he had practically no book. The band had been playing mostly head arrangements. Since this was not allowed at the Terrace, Fletcher Henderson graciously loaned Basie a good portion of his library. 1984: After Basie's death, the Count Basie Orchestra continued to perform all over the world.
Woody Herman b. 1913 Milwaukee, WI d. 1987 Los Angeles, CA 1936–1946 1947–1949 (Four Brothers Band) 1950–1956 1959–1986	Clarinet Soprano Sax Alto Sax Voice Leader	Pete Candoli, Bill Harris, Flip Phillips, Chubby Jackson, Conte Candoli, Stan Getz, Zoot Sims, Herbie Steward, Al Cohn, Serge Chaloff, Shorty Rogers, Jimmy Giuffre, Gene Ammons, Lou Levy, Oscar Pettiford, Terry Gibbs, Shelly Manne, Dave McKenna, Carl Fontana, Phil Wilson, Nat Pierce, Sal Nistico <u>Arrangers:</u> Ralph Burns, Neal Hefti	1934: Played in the Ishal Jones Orchestra. 1936: Formed his own orchestra. 1939: First hit: "At the Woodchoppers Ball." 1943: Herman's band began to show the influence of the Ellington Orchestra. 1970s: Herman's band was one of only four surviving jazz-oriented bands from the swing era that was still touring the world with a big band. 1976: Carnegie Hall concert.
Glenn Miller b. 1904 Clarinda, IA d. 1944 English Channel 1937–1942 1942–1944	Trombone Arranger Leader	Bobby Hackett, Tex Beneke	1926–1928 Miller joined Ben Pollack's band. 1928: Freelance arranger in New York. 1935: Helped organize Ray Noble's American Orchestra. 1937: First time as leader. 1938: Developed his trademark sound: having a clarinet double the melody of the saxophones an octave higher. 1939: Began a regular radio broadcast, which led to the band's popularity nationwide. 1939–1942: Miller's band was the most popular in the world. 1942: Organized the first military jazz band playing in Europe.
Earl Hines b. 1903 Duquesne, PA d. 1983 Oakland, CA 1938–1948	Piano Composer Leader	Ray Nance, Trummy Young, Budd Johnson, Omer Simeon, Billy Eckstine, Charlie Parker, Dizzy Gillespie, Sarah Vaughan, Wardell Gray	Worked briefly in Louis Armstrong's big band and in Jimmy Noone's Apex Club Orchestra. 1928: Debuted with his big band at Chicago's Grand Terrace.

Artie Shaw b. 1910 New York, NY Real Name: Arthur Jacob Arshawsky 1938–1941 1944–1946 1949–1955	Clarinet Leader	Roy Eldridge, Billie Holiday, Zoot Sims, Al Cohn, Hank Jones, Hot Lips Page, Georgie Auld, Helen Forrest, Billie Holiday, Buddy Rich	Primarily a dance band. Shaw was a pioneer in leading integrated bands.
Gene Krupa b. 1909 Chicago, IL d. 1973 Yonkers, NY 1938–1943 1944–1951	Drums Leader	Anita O'Day, Roy Eldridge *2nd band:* Red Rodney, Roy Eldridge Arranger: Gerry Mulligan	First drummer to be a superstar. Prior to Krupa, drum solos were a rarity, and the drums were thought of as a supportive instrument. 1927: First drummer to use a full drum set on records. 1934: Joined Benny Goodman's orchestra. 1937: Historic lengthy drum solo on "Sing, Sing, Sing." 1943: Re-joined Goodman band. 1944: Worked with Tommy Dorsey for a while and then put together another big band. Welcomed the bebop influence into arrangements for this band.
Charlie Barnet b. 1913 New York, NY d. 1991 San Diego, CA 1939–1946	Tenor Sax Soprano Sax Alto Sax Leader	Lena Horne, Kay Starr, Buddy DeFranco, Barney Kessel, Roy Eldridge, Maynard Ferguson, Clark Terry, Doc Severinsen	One of the few jazzmen to be born a millionaire. One of the few white big band leaders of the swing era to openly embrace the music of Duke Ellington and Count Basie. 1935: Barnet was a pioneer in leading integrated bands
Harry James b. 1916 Albany, NY d. 1983 Las Vegas, NV 1939–1950s	Trumpet Leader	Buddy Rich, Louie Bellson Arranger: Ernie Wilkins	1942–1946: Harry James was the most famous trumpeter of the swing era, and his band was the most popular in the world. James was not as much a jazz player as an entertaining showman.
Claude Thornhill b. 1909 Terre Haute, IN d. 1967 New York, NY 1940–1950	Arranger Leader	Lee Konitz, Red Rodney Arrangers: Gil Evans, Gerry Mulligan	Claude Thornhill's main contribution to jazz was the influence of his arrangements. Also important was the influence his orchestra's sound had on the cool jazz of the late '40s. 1934: Sideman in Paul Whiteman and Benny Goodman Orchestras. 1937: Recorded as a leader. 1940–1942: Put together his own orchestra. Instrumentation featured two French horns, one tuba, and six reeds playing in unison. 1945: Organized a band with Gil Evans as one of the arrangers. Many of Miles Davis's *Birth of the Cool* nonet arrangements were based on the cool-toned principles of the Thornhill big band.

Stan Kenton b. 1911 Wichita, KS d. 1979 Los Angeles, CA 1941–1949 1950–1979	Piano Composer Arranger Leader	Art Pepper, Stan Getz, Anita O'Day, June Christy, Kai Winding, Buddy Childers, Bud Shank, Shelly Manne, Lee Konitz, Conte Candoli, Frank Rosolino, Zoot Sims, Bill Perkins, Mel Lewis, Pete Candoli, Maynard Ferguson, Carl Fontana, Pepper Adams, Jack Sheldon, Peter Erskine <u>Arrangers:</u> Pete Rugolo, Maynard Ferguson, Shorty Rogers, Gerry Mulligan, Lennie Niehaus, Johnny Richards, Bill Holman, Hank Levy, and Bill Russo	1930s: Kenton played in the dance bands of Vido Musso and Gus Arnheim. 1941: Kenton formed his first band—influenced by Jimmie Lunceford who, like Kenton, enjoyed high-note trumpeters and thick-toned tenors. Calling his music "progressive jazz," Kenton sought to lead a concert orchestra as opposed to a dance band at a time when most big bands were starting to break up. 1950: Kenton led the 39-piece Innovations in Modern Music orchestra that included 16 strings, a woodwind section, and two French horns. 1951: Reverted to a 19-piece lineup and began a "swing period." 1960–1963. Kenton led the Mellophonium Band with five mellophoniums. 1964: Kenton turned his attention to jazz education, conducting a countless number of clinics.
Billy Eckstine b. 1914 Pittsburgh, PA d. 1993 Pittsburgh, PA 1943–1947	Voice Trumpet Valve Trombone Guitar Leader	Dizzy Gillespie, Charlie Parker, Sarah Vaughan, Wardell Gray, Dexter Gordon, Miles Davis, Kenny Dorham, Fats Navarro, Art Blakey <u>Arrangers:</u> Tadd Dameron, Gil Fuller	1939: Sang in Earl Hines' Grand Terrace Orchestra. The first black singer to sing romantic ballads (previous black bands were forced to stick to novelty or blues vocal numbers). The first big band to play bebop.
Gerald Wilson b. 1918 Shelby, MS 1944–present	Trumpet Arranger Leader	Melba Liston, Snooky Young, Bud Shank, Jack Wilson, Joe Pass, Harold Land	1939–1942: Played in Jimmie Lunceford's band. Replaced Sy Oliver as arranger, conductor, and trumpet soloist. Later played in the bands of Les Hite, Bennie Carter, and Willie Smith. 1944: Organized his first big band. 1947–1948: Played for Count Basie and Dizzy Gillespie. 1960: Formed a very successful new jazz orchestra. 1980s: Led the orchestra on Redd Foxx's NBC show.
Buddy Rich b. 1917 New York, NY d. 1987 Los Angeles, CA Real Name: Bernard Rich 1945–1947 1966–1987	Drums Leader	Harry "Sweets" Edison, Ernie Watts, Bobby Shew <u>Arrangers:</u> Bill Holman, Phil Wilson, Oliver Nelson, Shorty Rogers, Bob Florence	1919: Buddy Rich started playing drums in vaudeville as "Traps, the Drum Wonder" when he was 18 months old. 1938: Rich was playing in Bunny Berigan's Orchestra. 1939–1945: Played with Artie Shaw and Tommy Dorsey. 1945–1947: Led a bop-influenced band that did not catch on. 1953–1966: Played as a sideman in bands of Harry James, Tommy Dorsey, Les Brown, Charlie Ventura, and others. 1966: Organized a highly successful big band that toured until his death.

Dizzy Gillespie b. 1917 Cheraw, SC d. 1993 Englewood, NJ Real Name: John Birks Gillespie 1946–1950 1956–1958 1990–1992	Trumpet Voice Trombone Piano Leader	1946 band: Chano Pozo, Milt Jackson, John Lewis, Ray Brown, Kenny Clarke, James Moody, J. J. Johnson, Yusef Lateef, John Coltrane 1956 band: Lee Morgan, Joe Gordon, Melba Liston, Al Grey, Billy Mitchell, Benny Golson, Ernie Henry, Wynton Kelly <u>Arrangers:</u> Quincy Jones, Melba Liston, Benny Golson 1990 band: Paquito D'Rivera, Arturo Sandoval, Jon Faddis	Gillespie was an enthusiastic teacher who was eager to explain his musical innovations to the next generation. He was one of the key founders of bebop and Afro-Cuban jazz. 1937: Played in Frankie Fairfax's band and then in Teddy Hill's Orchestra (replacing Roy Eldridge). 1939: Joined Cab Calloway's Orchestra. 1940s: Dizzy was harmonically ahead of everyone. 1941–1943: Played in bands led by Ella Fitzgerald, Coleman Hawkins, Benny Carter, Charlie Barnet, Fess Williams, Les Hite, Claude Hopkins, Lucky Millinder, and Duke Ellington. Contributed arrangements to Benny Carter, Jimmy Dorsey, and Woody Herman. 1942: Joined Earl Hines' big band, which included Charlie Parker and Sarah Vaughan. 1945: Led an unsuccessful big band. 1946: Assembled his first successful big band that played in the bop style. 1956: Gillespie was authorized to form a big band and play a tour overseas sponsored by the U.S. State Department. 1990: Led the United Nations Orchestra.
Ray Charles b. 1930 Albany, GA 1956–present	Piano Voice Arranger Leader	David "Fathead" Newman, Joseph Bridgewater, Marcus Belgrave, Hank Crawford, Lee Harper, Edgar Willis, Richie Goldberg	1936: Blinded by glaucoma. 1951: First R&B Top Ten Hit, "Baby, Let Me Hold Your Hand." Charles records and performs in many genres, including jazz, rock, and popular music.
Maynard Ferguson b. 1928 Verdun, Quebec, Canada 1957–1965	Trumpet Leader	Slide Hampton, Don Ellis, Don Sebesky, Willie Maiden, Joe Zawinul, Joe Farrell, Jaki Byard, Lanny Morgan, Rufus Jones, Billy Berry, Don Menza	1949: Came to the U.S. and played in the bands of Jimmy Dorsey and Charlie Barnet. 1950: Joined Kenton's Innovations Orchestra, playing higher than any other trumpeter in jazz history. 1953: Ferguson left Kenton to work in the studios of Los Angeles. 1957: Ferguson put together a big band that lasted until 1965. 1987–1988: Led a pop band called High Voltage. 1989: Returned to jazz with Big Bop Noveau Band, a medium-sized group that still tours the world.
Bob Florence b. 1932 Los Angeles, CA 1958–present	Piano Arranger Composer Leader	Bud Shank, Bill Perkins, Buddy Childers, Bill Holman, Lanny Morgan, Kim Richmond, Rob McConnell, Don Shelton	1959–1964: Pianist and arranger in Si Zentner's band. Musical director for Julie Andrews.
Quincy Jones b. 1933 Chicago, IL 1959–1969	Trumpet Arranger Composer Leader	Zoot Sims, Harry Sweets Edison, Sam "The Man" Taylor, Phil Woods, Clark Terry, Art Farmer, Lee Morgan, Freddie Hubbard, Curtis Fuller	1951–1953: Played trumpet and arranged for Lionel Hampton's Orchestra. 1956: Toured with Dizzy Gillespie's big band. 1959–1960: Toured Europe with his all-star big band.
Gerry Mulligan b. 1927 New York, NY d. 1996 Darien, CT 1960–1996	Baritone Sax Piano Composer Arranger Leader	Bob Brookmeyer, Zoot Sims, Clark Terry, Mel Lewis	1944: Wrote for Johnny Warrington's radio band. 1946: Staff arranger for Gene Krupa. 1948: Staff arranger for Claude Thornhill. 1948–1950: Performed in Miles Davis's "Birth of the Cool" nonet. For this group he wrote the arrangements for "Godchild" and "Darn That Dream." He also composed "Jeru," "Rocker," and "Venus de Milo." 1952: Formed piano-less quartet with Chet Baker. 1960–1964: Led his Concert Jazz Band.

Doc Severinsen b. 1927 Arlington, OR Tonight Show Orchestra 1962–1992	Trumpet Leader Arranger	Snooky Young, Conte Candoli, Clark Terry, Tommy Newsom, Pete Christlieb, Ernie Watts, Ross Tompkins	Late 1940s: Soloist in Tommy Dorsey's band. Brief stints with Charlie Barnet and Benny Goodman. 1949: Joined NBC Jazz Orchestra, which became the Tonight Show Band. 1962: Named assistant leader of the NBC Orchestra (Skitch Henderson was leader). 1967: Became leader when Henderson left. 1992: Jay Leno brought in a new band for "The Tonight Show."
Sammy Nestico b. 1924 Pittsburgh, PA 1963–present	Composer Arranger Trombone Leader		1950s: Staff arranger for the U.S. Air Force Band. 1963: Worked with the U.S. Marine Band and led the orchestra that performed for functions at the White House. 1968: Retired from the military and moved to Los Angeles. 1967: Began contributing arrangements to Count Basie's orchestra. 1970s–present: Achieved great success as an arranger in the recording studios and as a jazz educator.
Don Ellis b. 1934 Los Angeles, CA d. 1978 Hollywood, CA 1965–1978	Trumpet Leader	Tom Scott, John Klemmer, Sam Falzone, Frank Strozier, Dave MacKay, Micho Leviev Arrangers: Don Ellis, Hank Levy	Performed in the big bands of Maynard Ferguson, Ray McKinley, and Charlie Barnet. 1965: Organized his first orchestra. Ellis's big bands were distinguished by their unusual instrumentation, which sometimes used three bassists and three drummers. Ellis was interested in unusual meters (7/8, 9/8, 15/16) and electronic devices. Ellis invented a four-valve trumpet. 1971: His orchestra consisted of an eight-piece brass section that included a French horn and tuba, a four-piece woodwind section, a string quartet, and a two-drum rhythm section.
Thad Jones (with Mel Lewis) b. 1923 Pontiac, MI d. 1986 Copenhagen, Denmark 1965–1978 1984–1985	Trumpet Flugelhorn, Cornet Composer Arranger Leader	Bill Berry, Danny Stiles, Richard Williams, Marvin Stamm, Snooky Young, Jon Faddis, Bob Brookmeyer, Eddie Daniels, Joe Farrell, Pepper Adams, Hank Jones, Roland Hanna,	Brother of Hank Jones and Elvin Jones. 1954–1963: Played with Count Basie. 1965: Formed Thad Jones/Mel Lewis orchestra with Mel Lewis. 1978: Jones moved to Denmark where he wrote for a radio orchestra. 1984–1985: Jones led the Count Basie Orchestra for one year.
Mel Lewis (with Thad Jones) b. 1929 Buffalo, NY d. 1990 New York, NY Real Name: Melvin Sokoloff 1965–1978	Drums Leader	George Mraz Bill Berry, Danny Stiles, Richard Williams, Marvin Stamm, Snooky Young, Jon Faddis, Bob Brookmeyer, Eddie Daniels, Joe Farrell, Pepper Adams, Hank Jones, Roland Hanna, George Mraz	1948: Performed with Boyd Raeburn, Alvin Rey, Ray Anthony, and Tex Beneke. 1954–57: Performed with Stan Kenton. 1957: Performed with Terry Gibbs, Gerald Wilson, and Gerry Mulligan. 1961: Toured Europe with Dizzy Gillespie. 1962: Toured Russia with Benny Goodman. 1965: Formed Thad Jones/Mel Lewis Orchestra with Thad Jones. 1979: Continued to lead the above orchestra after Jones left for Denmark.
Rob McConnell b. 1935 London, Ontario, Canada 1968–1990s	Valve Trombone Slide Trombone Arranger Leader	Guido Basso, Ian McDougall, San Noto, Moe Koffman	1965–69: Performed in Phil Nimmons' big band. 1968: Formed the Boss Brass. The original group was comprised entirely of brass instruments plus rhythm section and played pop music. 1971: Saxophone section added to Boss Brass. Group began to play McConnell's swinging charts. Late 1980s: Group broke up. 1991: Boss Brass reorganized.

Patrick Williams b. 1939 1970s–present	Trumpet Composer Arranger Leader	Eddie Daniels, Bill Watrous, Peter Erskine, Michael Forman, Warren Luening, Hubert Laws, David Sanborn, Tom Scott, Phil Woods	1961–1967: Active in the studios in New York City. 1968: Moved to Los Angeles and began career as composer/arranger, writing scores of more than 60 films and countless television shows. 1970s–present: Occasionally leads a big band made up of LA's best studio musicians to record his charts.
Toshiko Akiyoshi b. 1929 Darien, China Toshiko Akiyoshi/ Lew Tabackin Big Band 1972–present	Piano Arranger Leader	Bobby Shew, Gary Foster, Lew Tabackin	1946: Moved to Japan. 1956–1959: Studied at Berklee after being noticed and encouraged by Oscar Peterson. 1962: Worked with Charles Mingus. 1965: Performed on a radio series in New York. 1970: Formed a quartet with her husband, Lew Tabackin. 1972: Established a big band
Bill Watrous b. 1939 Middletown, CT 1973–present	Trombone Leader		1962–1967: Made his debut in Billy Butterfield's orchestra. 1960s: Played in big bands of Quincy Jones, Maynard Ferguson, Johnny Richards, and Woody Herman. 1965–1968: Played in Merv Griffin's television show band. 1973–1977: Formed and led big band called the Manhattan Wildlife Refuge.
Jon Faddis b. 1953 Oakland, CA Carnegie Hall Jazz Orchestra 1992–present	Trumpet	Lou Soloff, Byron Stripling, Ryan Kisor, Slide Hampton, Dick Oatts, Gary Smulyan	1970s: Performed with Charles Mingus and Lionel Hampton. 1980s: First trumpet in the Thad Jones/Mel Lewis Orchestra. 1988: Became the musical director of the Carnegie Hall Jazz Orchestra.
Wynton Marsalis b. 1961 New Orleans, LA 1988–present Lincoln Center Jazz Orchestra	Trumpet Leader Composer Arranger	Seneca Black, Ryan Kisor, Marcus Printup, Vincent Chandler, Andre Hayward, Ron Westray, Wess "Warmdaddy" Anderson, Walter Blanding Jr., Victor Goines, Ted Nash, Joe Temperley, Farid Barron, Rodney Whitaker, Herlin Riley, Marcus Roberts, Branford Marsalis, Delfayo Marsalis, Kenny Kirland, Eric Reed	1967: Received his first trumpet from Al Hirt. 1979: Entered Juilliard. 1980: Made his first recordings with the Art Blakey Big Band and joined the Jazz Messengers. 1988–present: Musical director of the Lincoln Center Jazz Orchestra and very active in jazz education.

Contemporary Big Bands

Bob Brookmeyer

Matt Catingub

Clayton-Hamilton Jazz Orchestra

John Fedchock

Gordon Goodwin's Big Phat Band

Bill Holman

Tom Kubis

Frank Mantooth

Jim McNeely

Bob Mintzer

Roger Neumann

Rob Parton

Kim Richmond Concert Jazz Orchestra

Maria Schneider

Bill Warfield Big Band

UMO Jazz Orchestra (Finland)

WDR Big Band (Cologne)

NDR (Hamburg)

BBC Big Band (UK)

U.S. Air Force Airmen of Note

U.S. Army Blues

U.S. Army Jazz Ambassadors

U.S. Navy Commodores

MILITARY SERVICE BANDS

by Pete BarenBregge

Military service bands provide a valuable service to music education. The basic organizational structure consists of the premier bands stationed in the Washington, D.C. area and regional bands stationed at various bases throughout the United States and the world. Musicians in service bands are all full-time active-duty military.

The United States Air Force, United States Army, United States Navy, United States Marines, and United States Coast Guard have music programs. In addition to their military protocol duties, these bands typically provide public community relations concerts along with recruiting performances. Some units provide outreach music clinics to schools.

Premier Bands

Located in the Washington, D.C. area, the premier bands have full-time jazz ensembles with outstanding musicians: the Airmen of Note from the U.S. Air Force, the Army Blues and the Army Field Band Jazz Ambassadors, and the Navy Commodores from the U.S. Navy. The Marine Band (Washington, D.C.) and the Coast Guard Band (Groton, Connecticut) currently do not have full-time jazz units.

Becoming a member of the premier bands requires a rigorous audition process. Winning an audition and accepting the position requires enlistment in that branch of the service. Enlistment requires all of the standard testing and basic training.

Regional Bands

The regional bands have superb jazz groups of various sizes that are extracted from larger ensembles, but they usually do not have full-time dedicated jazz ensembles. Members of the regional bands are provided with musical training at all levels. The Army, Navy, and Marine band programs have an outstanding music school. Located at the Naval Amphibious Base in Norfolk, Virginia, the Armed Forces School of Music provides specialized training for selected personnel of the Army, Navy, and Marine Corps and is the first stop after basic training for instrumentalists and vocalists seeking to join the ranks of America's military bands.

This unique facility, the largest of its kind in the world, provides basic to advanced levels of instruction geared toward preparing soldiers, sailors, and marines for the challenges of performance within a wide variety of military ensembles. Graduates of the Armed Forces School of Music go on to become musical ambassadors throughout the United States and abroad as members of U.S. Army, Navy, and Marine Corps Bands.

Vocalists

Opportunities for vocalists in jazz, pop, and classical styles is another consideration. Vocalists in the regional bands are typically required to perform in a variety of vocal styles, while the premier jazz groups usually have featured jazz vocalists. Like the instrumentalists, vocalists are full-time active-duty members of the military.

Jazz Outreach Programs and Community Performances

Currently, the Airmen of Note and the Jazz Ambassadors have jazz outreach programs that provide concerts, clinics, and jazz education materials/recordings to schools.

Performances are usually free to the public and sometimes at no cost to the sponsor; however, the sponsor should expect to provide the venue, promotions, advertisement, programs, and so on. The bands rotate geographic tour areas throughout the U.S., and careful planning by a jazz educator may provide the opportunity for a school or an organization to host or at least hear one of these outstanding jazz groups.

Recordings

These bands produce superb recordings, and although these recordings are not available for sale to the general public, the bands often provide recordings for recruitment, educational purposes, public libraries, and promoting public performances. Contact the band public affairs office for further information. The authors strongly recommend your seeking the world-class recordings from the premier band jazz ensembles.

Employment Opportunities

Employment opportunities (must enlist prior to the age of 35) for instrumentalists, vocalists, technical personnel, support staff, and conductors abound at all levels. Further information is available directly from the bands or the local recruiter.

Resources

Links:
U.S. Air Force Bands: www.af.mil/band/home.shtml
U.S. Army Bands: www.bands.army.mil
U.S. Navy Bands: www.bupers.navy.mil/navymusic
U.S. Marine Band: www.marineband.usmc.mil
U.S. Coast Guard Band: www.cga.edu/band/default.html
Armed Forces School of Music: www.cnet.navy.mil/som

JAZZ REHEARSAL TECHNIQUES
THE KEY TO A SUCCESSFUL REHEARSAL

by J. Richard Dunscomb

Duke Ellington had it, Count Basie had it, Stan Kenton had it, Bob Mintzer has it, and so do many others. What is it? It is the pride and thrill of standing in front of a jazz ensemble and being able to shape and mold the musicians into a great-sounding collective. You can have it too! Let's identify keys to successful rehearsals and performances.

THE KEEPERS OF THE FLAME

The shift in location of the jazz classroom from the jazz clubs to the schools has put a huge responsibility on jazz educators to keep the music alive and moving forward. Remember that most jazz greats learned their craft by hearing the music over and over again in clubs or on recordings and then working at home to transcribe and internalize it. With jazz groups in nearly every public and private school and the proliferation of jazz studies programs at the university level, jazz educators are charged with upholding this great legacy. The current generation of great jazz performers has come mostly from the school jazz setting. This is not to say that all jazz is or will be learned in schools, but jazz educators will certainly be at the forefront of providing information. To put it another way, the next Charlie Parker, Dizzy Gillespie, Michael Brecker, Ella Fitzgerald, Dave Brubeck, or Wynton Marsalis could come from your classroom!

Your Role in the Classroom

Good performances come from good rehearsals; therefore, the better the rehearsal, the better the performance. Also, weak performances are typically traced to rehearsal problems. Rehearsing and performing jazz music should be fun for the students and the directors. Jazz is a valid, vital, and valuable component in music education, and each jazz experience should be rewarding musically. Based on growing sales figures from various music publishers, we know that students are enjoying the art form and are participating in increasing numbers. Your responsibility is to ensure that they are given the best possible instruction.

Your teaching can impart love for, respect for, and a good understanding of jazz music. If you have enthusiasm for jazz, it is contagious and can create a vibrant center for learning. Next, it is essential that you not only study the musical score of each selection to be rehearsed but also listen repeatedly and critically to a recording of the specific arrangement (or at least music in the style of the chart performed). The more prepared you are, the more rewarding, educational, and fun it can be for everyone. When you do your job successfully in rehearsals, the band will be (almost) able to perform the concert without you. Of course, we won't necessarily tell the students that!

How often in a jazz rehearsal do we realize that things are not going right and find the only solution is to offer generalizations such as "make it swing," "listen more to each other," "make it precise," or "rhythm section, play together"? Check out Chapter 7, How to Teach Swing, for additional information on this topic. We must discover the precise reasons for the problems and solve them with specific suggestions, which is how great musical conductors have operated throughout the years. In other words: hear the problem, identify the problem, and solve the problem. It sounds simple, and it really can be once you are prepared. Every jazz rehearsal should be a worthwhile musical experience for the students; they shouldn't have to wait until the concert to enjoy the rewards of a great performance. Even in a rehearsal, the playing of music should communicate some emotional experiences to the students: exhilaration, excitement, energy, and joy. If you are relaxed and patient, stay involved, and have consistently high expectations, the students will respond in a similar manner. Always, the end goal should be a professional level of performance, no matter the age of the participants.

Three Ps of Rehearsing: Planning, Planning, Planning

Setting goals before your rehearsal is very important. Approach each rehearsal with a positive attitude, and be sure it carries through to the end. You must know what is to be rehearsed, and determine whether to read the entire piece or spot-rehearse the troublesome places. Be certain that you understand and can teach the characteristic interpretations of what the ensemble is going to play, which should include specific ideas and routines for problem-solving. Having a written plan for action is the best way to proceed because planning the rehearsal in advance encourages a more productive and fun session for you and the students. A suggested form is included below that serves as a template for each rehearsal. Here are some tips to get you started:

- Date and save the rehearsal form. There are several reasons for this, such as notating the ensemble's progress while learning the music and also having a file for your lesson plans (as required in some schools).
- Be sure to place the order of selections to be rehearsed on the chalkboard before class begins because this demonstrates an organized and well-planned rehearsal.
- The first item of the rehearsal schedule is not the announcements, but *tuning*. This signals that at the beginning of the session your students are required to listen, whether to a single tuning pitch or through playing warm-up exercises and then tuning.
- Make sure the tuning is done without any talking by the students because it sets the stage for a serious musical rehearsal.

Rehearsals Must Be Flexible and Spontaneous

Although planning is a must, don't be afraid to change rehearsal plans if doing so will provide a better jazz education experience. You can experiment, or improvise, when necessary. For instance, you may find that the overall caliber of the performance is not up to your expectations on a given day. In that case, it is better to have a few measures sound professional so the students know they are capable of it than to rehearse a large amount of music with mediocre results. Once the students hear how great they can sound, they will always be motivated to strive for the professional sound.

Rehearsals Must Be Paced, Varied, Balanced, and Fun

If you approach the rehearsal as an informal concert, you would program the rehearsal so that there is a variety of styles and tempos. Strive for balance: alternate the new additions to the folder with the pieces almost ready for performance; the music that emphasizes open solo sections with the more intricately arranged; the driving, loud, and furious with the subtle, delicate, and lightly swinging compositions. It is always a good idea to begin and end the rehearsal with music that the group plays well. A simple outline for a rehearsal could include the following:

- A chart the band is familiar with and plays well.
- Sight-reading a new chart.
- A moderately difficult chart that will require some time to rehearse.
- A chart that is difficult and will require more time to rehearse.
- A chart they know and play well.

By the way: a *chart* is jazz jargon for a composition or arrangement.

JAZZ REHEARSAL PLAN

Date:_____

Tuning:_____

Announcements:_____

_____

_____

_____

Selections to rehearse:

1. _____ Measures _____ Time allowed ____ CD or video example ____

2. _____ Measures _____ Time allowed ____ CD or video example ____

3. _____ Measures _____ Time allowed ____ CD or video example ____

4. _____ Measures _____ Time allowed ____ CD or video example ____

5. _____ Measures _____ Time allowed ____ CD or video example ____

6. _____ Measures _____ Time allowed ____ CD or video example ____

Comments on above for next rehearsal:

_____

_____

_____

_____

_____

_____

Note that beginning and ending with charts that sound good creates a feeling of self-confidence that will carry through the rehearsal and into the performance.

Student musicians expect the director to be critical in a rehearsal, but the trick is to do it in a positive, nonthreatening manner. Convey to them that you and they are all in it together and are striving for the best possible results. There is really nothing to win or lose in music, except the joy of playing the best we can. This can be achieved by working fruitfully toward common goals. The form on the preceding page is a suggested rehearsal plan. Try creating your own customized rehearsal plan.

THE JAZZ ENSEMBLE SOUND

Identify the jazz sound for each instrument and for the overall sound of the jazz ensemble. What makes up the overall jazz sound of a jazz group? If you heard a single chord played by an orchestra, wind ensemble, or jazz ensemble, would you know the difference? Of course you would. Here are a few obvious and distinctive characteristics of a jazz ensemble, as compared to an orchestra or wind ensemble:

- The jazz ensemble has only one player to a part, which produces a more transparent sound.
- The standard instrumentation is five saxes, eight brass, and four rhythm.
- The five saxophones give a powerful and centered core sound.
- The size, 17 or 18 players, gives a unique character to the ensemble sound.
- Each jazz wind player typically has a bigger and rounder sound.
- The drum set is sized and tuned for a more compact jazz sound, as compared to the drums in a rock band.
- The cymbals are selected for a variety of sounds, all to cut through the ensemble.
- The bass and guitar have amplified equipment designed to cut through, but not overpower, the ensemble.
- The saxophones (with equipment designed for jazz) produce a much larger and brighter sound with more overtones often played with a looser embouchure.
- The brass (with equipment designed for jazz) have a focused, brighter, louder, more brassy sound with more overtones.
- The traditional set-up has all the wind players facing forward, directly toward the audience, delivering a focused wall of sound.
- The jazz harmonies produced have more clarity because of the traditional jazz voicings and the one-to-a-part sound.

ARE YOU LISTENING?

Listening to jazz ensemble recordings is essential. In fact, there really is no hope for having a great jazz ensemble without listening. You can start by having recorded music playing as the students enter the room each day. The recording should be music that is a model for them to aspire to and could include professional renditions of music and/or styles on which they are working. Listening is the biggest key to successful jazz teaching and can unlock the door to comprehending (and loving) the world of jazz. Intuitively, the time spent listening will further the understanding of jazz and will ultimately save redundant explanations in rehearsals. Listening also makes your explanations more meaningful since you can reference comments back to the professional examples.

Demo Recordings

It is most effective and productive to use the recorded examples of the charts you are working on, which most jazz publishers now provide on high-quality demo CDs. If one of the pieces you are rehearsing is a jazz standard, you can also find it recorded by one of the top jazz artists. By all means, use that recording as well. Remember, aural skills are essential to inspired and characteristic performance! Only through listening will your students learn what they are supposed to sound like.

Directed Listening

In addition to the casual listening described above, plan to spend class time on focused listening. It is critical for you to point out what to listen for, which will make a huge difference for your young and inexperienced students. Direct them to listen to the overall sound of the ensemble, the sound of the individual sections and instruments, the articulations, the phrasing and style, the balance, the impact, and so forth. Listening to professional playing will help your students lock into a mental concept of sound and to ultimately imitate that sound.

Below is a list of some professional jazz ensemble recordings that can provide proper examples for your ensemble. This short list is not meant to be all-inclusive but rather a starting point. You will notice that these are contemporary big bands and that the recordings are primarily of straight-ahead (swing feel) jazz in a modern style. Any recordings by the great Count Basie Orchestra could accomplish optimum results.

Basie & Beyond – Quincy Jones–Sammy Nestico Orchestra

Homage to Count Basie – Bob Mintzer's Big Band

Sinatraland – Patrick Williams Big Band

Swingin' for the Fences – Gordon Goodwin Big Phat Band

A Time for Love – Bill Watrous Big Band

A View From the Side – Bill Holman Band

With All the Bells and Whistles – Bob Florence Limited Edition

Check out Chapter 13, Big Band History: An Overview, and the list of professional players in Appendix A.

It is astounding to realize how little listening occurs in most programs. Listening helps you inject some idea of history into the music. By increasing and influencing the listening, the jazz IQ of students goes up in rapid proportions. While listening, your students can grasp the concept of what they hear much easier than just through hearing you speak of something that sounds like another language. You must keep working on the listening aspect every day!

DOES THE BAND LOOK RIGHT?

How's Your Set-Up?

Here are things to remember and check at each rehearsal:
- The rhythm section should be right next to the horns and on the left side as you face them, with the bass player next to the drummer's ride cymbal. The guitarist and pianist should be next to each other, and amps are placed behind the players at least three feet and positioned so the entire band can hear them.
- Saxes are set in a semicircle.
- Bass trombone and bari sax should be on the right side of the band as you face the group.
- Lead players should be in the middle of their sections and seated in a line down the middle of the ensemble.
- Brass players: bells up!
- If possible, have the brass section standing, with trumpets on a riser.
- Okay, let's go!

YOUR REHEARSAL

Transfer of Knowledge

The rehearsal needs to impart the transfer of stylistic concepts from one situation to another. For your students, learning to apply knowledge to various situations is a must if you are to make progress away from rote teaching. Be sure that the introduction of each new pattern or phrase has lasting value. Like any music, jazz is repetitive, and you will see the same rhythmic figures many, many times. Students are quick to pick up on this transfer of knowledge, so after you have taught the interpretation of some rhythm or device, quiz the students about it the next time it occurs. Make *them* tell you how it is supposed to be played. This exercise helps them categorize mentally the various styles and the rules of performing in each jazz idiom.

Rehearse Easy and Challenging Music

Know how to rehearse both the easy and the more challenging music in your folder. Most of the easier charts in your book will play themselves and only require some general comments at the end. These pieces provide a good way to get the students accustomed to the flow of a complete selection. As more difficult charts are encountered, the rehearsing of smaller segments is necessary. This repertoire requires a very efficient technique. For instance, when problems are within the horn section, have them play without the rhythm section. In doing so, you and the students will hear each instrument more distinctly. This practice will also ensure that wind players use their internal time instead of relying on the rhythm section. While doing this, have the drum tap the rhythmic pulse until the students become secure without it. Be sure to review the entire piece after rehearsing the segments so the students have the flow and feel of the entire chart.

Sing It, Baby!

Vocal examples can be the keys to the kingdom of articulation and phrasing. Sing often and have the students sing with you. Singing is a superb way to learn jazz styles and interpretations. Singing imitates the sound on the recordings you've heard, which is a quick and creative way to get the class to understand the proper conceptual approach of style, articulation, feel, and jazz nuance. Insist that the band sing with you, and neither you nor they should be bashful. Insist that they learn to standardize patterns as they sing, since jazz figures will recur in many other charts. The proper singing of phrases, articulations, and so on, will immediately transfer to their playing. Although you may not be confident at first using jazz syllables when singing jazz examples to the group, by practicing at home you will become more comfortable and ultimately will succeed. Articulation and inflection are the most important elements to impart to the band. A good voice is not necessary, but your vocal examples *are*. Getting the students singing, and comfortable with the articulations and phrasing, will greatly add to their confidence level. Check out the rehearsal techniques video for examples. There is also a more complete discussion on how to put these techniques into action in Chapter 7, How to Teach Swing, and Chapter 18, How to Sing It.

Marking the Parts

Marking the parts is essential to your ensemble's performance. Students should have, and use, pencils to mark the music. A good rule to follow is to have students mark in their music anything that they misplay more than twice in rehearsal. Teach the students a consistent marking method and be firm that they all use it. Examining the techniques from professional jazz ensembles, we can learn how they mark music. Here are a few examples:

- A drawing of eyeglasses at any point means "watch out" and can draw the player's attention to some rhythm, dynamic, or note he or she might otherwise miss.
- A minus sign followed by a number indicates a release on that beat; thus, "–4" means off on beat 4.
- A circle (or parentheses) around a note (or a series of notes) means do not play (or tacit).

- "3X" would simply indicate to play that section three times.
- Count-off numbers written before the first measure can remind the students of any unusual pick-ups.
- Students should write in reminders for mute changes, switching to woodwind doubles, and so forth.
- Circling or using a highlighting pen to indicate key and meter changes is also a good idea.

The results of music marking will be a more polished and professional-sounding ensemble.

Record Your Rehearsals

Recording rehearsals can be eye-opening. In addition to the value of teaching the students to hear themselves, recording your rehearsal can also bring back to earth the students who think they have it all under control. It is also very beneficial to record the rhythm section and background parts for each soloist to work with at home. Technology has made it much easier to get a representative recording during rehearsal, and this is time well spent.

CONDUCTING THE ENSEMBLE

Conducting the jazz band is a visual reflection of the band's sound. Traditional conducting techniques are used sparingly in a jazz ensemble; however, there are specific jazz techniques that can help the performers. For instance, jazz conductors use a count-off for most selections, and here are some tips for counting off a tune:
- Start the band with confidence and a reflected sense of the groove. This is critical in jazz because it has to feel good in order for the band to swing.
- Use the count-off to dictate style, tempo, dynamic levels, and starting point.
- It is essential to get the tempo set in your head before beginning the count-off. To get this right, think about passages in the music that exemplify the tempo in your mind.
- You can use a metronome to set the correct tempo, which will create a consistent time pulse for each performance of a piece.
- The inflections you impart need to imply the type of chart you are performing. An up-tempo burner should be counted off with enthusiasm and strong voice inflection. On the other hand, a ballad would be much more quiet and reflective.

Conducting Patterns

Conducting a piece requires a different approach in jazz ensembles than in band, wind ensemble, and orchestra. Do not conduct the jazz band using the continuous patterns you would for a concert band or orchestra. In jazz ensembles, the conductor is needed for tempo setting, cues, dynamics, balance, attacks, phrasing, musical interpretation, cut-offs, and much more, but *not* continuous meter patterns. You should conduct in a traditional manner when there are ritardandos, rubatos, or meter changes and for cueing entrances. But even in these situations, you should conduct the beats only as long as needed. You will find that all of these gestures are needed more in rehearsal than in concert. There is a noticeable degree of confidence displayed by students playing well without a conductor beating time in front of them.

Hand Signals

Proficient jazz directors cue the end of an open section (such as repeated solo choruses) by hand signals. The last time through an open section is cued with a closed fist. This can be further clarified, if necessary, with hand signals showing a reverse countdown of measures—4, 3, 2, 1—until the ensemble comes back in to start the next section.

Stage Presence

When not conducting, concentrate on developing a relaxed but appropriate position. Snapping on 2 and 4 can help convey energy throughout the piece. However, avoid the overkill of clapping loudly on 2 and 4 while the band is playing because anything that diverts attention from the musicians to the conductor is inappropriate. Although many jazz ensemble conductors appear glued to a spot in front of the lead alto, it is far better for you to move around. For example, stand in front of the rhythm section when you want to step aside to feature a soloist. Do not be timid about moving to other places on stage as you feel the necessity. Avoid watching your music throughout so that you will be free to do the more appropriate jazz ensemble director tasks.

The Art of Public Speaking

Your spoken introductions to the music during a concert should provide a learning experience for everyone, including the listeners as well as the students playing the music. Each introduction should have information about the music, its composer, its style, and so on. To be a good master of ceremonies at all performances, you should have a general knowledge of public speaking techniques. Speak clearly and with good articulation. Work for a balance between saying too little or too much. Announcing a tune should not overshadow the music but rather enhance it. Be relaxed and speak with self-assurance regarding the music. Take time to research what you will say and be sure it makes sense. There is another compelling reason for well-timed introductions: a talk at the right place in the concert can rest your ensemble and revitalize the brass chops!

It is just as important to give meaningful information in a rehearsal because it will enrich the understanding of the music. Many jazz publishers are making an effort to include this kind of annotation in the score. Publishers also provide conductor's notes that give information about rehearsing the chart. By slightly revising the wording and adding the names of soloists, these notes could become your announcement at a performance. Another concept is not making an announcement before every selection but rather "back announcing" after a few selections, which will give some variety to the announcing pace. Below is a sample taken from a publisher's program notes and modified for use as an introduction during a concert:

> "Grace" is from the Quincy Jones–Sammy Nestico CD titled *Basie & Beyond*. Composed by the Grammy-winning composer/producer Quincy Jones, this is an emotional ballad for tenor saxophone that will touch your hearts. Lush chords and a tender piano introduction set the mood for this superb chart arranged for the 1984 Summer Olympics. Tonight we feature _____ on the tenor saxophone.

SOUND REINFORCEMENT

Microphones

The miking of your ensemble can make or break the performance. If microphones are used, be sure they are used properly and that they are properly situated for consistent sound reinforcement. The sound engineer should be aware of the director's requirements, tastes, and expectations. It is imperative that the sound engineer know the function of sound reinforcement and not only sound amplification. Have your audio engineer listen to big band recordings, preferably ones that represent the sound you would like for your ensemble. For instance, you can use any of the big band recordings listed earlier in this chapter. Here are some ideas to keep in mind for sound reinforcement:

- Less is better; the band must sound acoustic, not electronic.
- The unique sound of a big band, with only one to a part, means that miking each instrument can throw off the balance. Often, area mikes are more effective in capturing the blend of your ensemble.

- Consider several levels of blend: the overall ensemble blend, the blend of each section, and blend within sections.
- Strive for a balanced sound image, with the presence of the lead trumpet and bari sax prominent in the overall ensemble sound.
- The rhythm section should not overpower the ensemble.
- Soloists need to be heard from the first note to the last.
- Refer to Chapter 3, The Importance of Listening.

Perceptions of Dynamics

Another issue is reality versus the audience's perception that the band is too loud. Is the band too loud on stage? Is the band too loud for the room? Is the audio engineer amplifying the band too much? Sometimes the presence of a lot of audio equipment on stage will cause the audience to perceive excessive amplification/volume even if the mikes are off. This perception of volume by the audience can mar an otherwise outstanding performance and leave a bad experience of the jazz program in the minds of the community. However, it is possible for the music actually to be too loud, and this can lead to permanent hearing damage for you and your students.

ENLISTING JAZZ TUTORS AND GUEST LECTURERS

All of the really great teachers find resources that can assist their teaching. After all, nobody knows it all. Local professional players, good college players, touring military jazz groups, and other teachers in the area are all assets to incorporate into your program. Any professional assistance, when structured properly, can inspire your students. The authors have found that many jazz musicians enjoy helping students and are willing to do so if asked. It is wise to inform the guests of the concepts you are working on so they can reinforce those areas. Trade off with individuals in your area who you can help, and they will help you in return. The students will benefit greatly.

SELF-EVALUATION

In a recent article in *The LeBlanc Bell* (autumn 2000) by Donald DeRoche, the eminent director of bands at DePaul University in Chicago, Illinois, the author points out that *good teachers learn to evaluate themselves as well as their students*. His logical approach states that teaching involves:

1. *Having a philosophy for teaching, or "What and why am I teaching?"* The music you choose to work with, the emphasis you put on various kinds of performances, the standards you demand, and the way you interact with students should all flow from your philosophical point of view.

2. *Who are these kids?* Understanding your students and the environment they live in will help you make educational and artistic choices when developing your plan and choosing materials.

3. *What is my plan for teaching?* Knowing what you want to teach the students by the time they graduate should help you develop your one-year plan and your daily rehearsal schedules.

4. *What materials can I use?* Do the materials you choose for performance reflect your musical goals as stated in your plan?

5. *How do I teach?* Walk into class knowing what music you will work on, what measures you will work on, and what you want to accomplish in that music. Start on time, work hard, and stop on time.

6. *How good was my teaching?* Did your students learn what you had hoped? Was your plan a good one? Did you find the right materials to execute the plan? Did you get the highest level of skill development possible? Did you provide the best music possible?

DIRECTOR'S CHECKLIST
OF REHEARSAL AND PERFORMANCE TECHNIQUES

• Have a rehearsal plan for each rehearsal. Schedule charts in an order that will be most effective. Start and end with charts that sound good.

• Don't waste time in rehearsal. Pinpoint problems and solve them. If it's important to you, it will be to the students.

• Be sure you can identify the jazz sound, both that of individual instruments and the entire ensemble.

• Program with variety in mind—ballad, rock/fusion, swing, shuffle, Latin, and so on. Have emotional peaks in the concert and try to leave the audience wanting more. Use as many soloists as possible.

• Listen to select professional big band CDs as a point of reference for the proper sound of a big band.

• Understand proper set-up for the band. See the set-up charts in Chapter 12, The Jazz Ensemble.

• Encourage your lead trumpet, lead trombone, and lead alto to establish a constant line of communication with each other concerning articulation and phrasing. Establish musical rules and abide by them.

• Work on releases as well as attacks.

• Dynamics can make or break an arrangement. A ff is effective only if contrasted with softer dynamics. Don't let the electronic instruments overpower the band. Constantly strive for dynamic contrast.

• Keep the bells out of the stands.

• Have all lower parts blow up to the lead players (but not overpower), with good air support.

• Rehearse without the rhythm section at times so the horn players develop time by themselves.

• Sing it, baby! Understand jazz articulation and phrasing. Learn how to interpret jazz figures; sing them to the band. Teach the band to sing the figures, too, with appropriate jazz syllables.

• Mark the music. Kick off a tune the right way. Use different emotional devices in your count-off that correspond with the type of chart being played. For example, a count-off for an up-tempo barnburner would be not only fast but also aggressive in volume. On the other hand, a ballad would be less emotional and softer in the count-off.

• Avoid conducting a time pattern during the chart, unless the music will be enhanced by it. The jazz band conductor's main responsibility lies in rehearsing the music; don't get in the way or distract during the performance.

• Be a good master of ceremonies at all performances. General knowledge of public speaking techniques work well for the conductor. Speak clearly with good articulation. Don't say too little or too much. The idea of announcing a tune should not overshadow the music but rather enhance it. Be relaxed and speak with self-assurance regarding the music. Take time to research what you will say and be sure it makes sense. Know how to pace the brass. A well-placed talk at the right place in the concert can revitalize the brass chops.

• Encourage students to study privately, listen to recordings, and attend clinics and workshops. Do this by sharing information you receive in the mail with all of your students.

Chapter 15

THE MUSIC
HOW TO EVALUATE AND SELECT
MUSIC THAT FITS YOUR ENSEMBLE

by J. Richard Dunscomb

How many times have you heard another jazz ensemble play a chart and wish you had picked it? Or wish you directed that band? Well, it happens to all of us. Although the selection of music that fits your group is no mystery, there is a process that is both logical and practical, and it's easy to do. Here are some suggestions for selecting the right music.

WHERE TO BEGIN

One of the most important aspects of our jobs as jazz ensemble directors (and the most difficult at the same time) is the selection of music. When done properly, this process makes a significant impact on the success of the ensemble.

Build Morale

We have all heard bands that attempt to play music that's too difficult. These charts can harm the students' morale as well as their chops. If a group spends all of its rehearsal time on just learning the notes, it is impossible to get a good, solid musical performance.

Choose Quality

We are fortunate in jazz education to have many outstanding professional writers involved in providing jazz music for our educational programs. We applaud this healthy situation and encourage continuing cooperation among composers/arrangers, publishers, and educators to maintain the momentum.

Still, there is a concern with how both publishers and jazz directors view the jazz ensemble's function in the school. A large number of charts are published each year that have very little educational value; most of these fall into a category of pop music or "why do we need an arrangement of this?" We have to assume that publishers are printing large quantities of this kind of music because directors are buying it.

Although we understand the need to purchase a nominal amount of pop music, using a steady diet of such material is simply an unacceptable educational practice—especially in these times of economic accountability in our schools. We must not lose sight of the goal of the jazz program: to have our group play jazz—America's classical music. Each school needs a solid philosophy of jazz education that will ensure a well-balanced diet of good music for the students. (See Chapter 4, Goals and Success Stories, for a sample jazz program mission statement and philosophy.)

The Classic Jazz Standards

Although jazz is only about one hundred years old, we are fortunate to have accumulated an enormous body of standards or classic jazz compositions and arrangements. In this way, jazz parallels the orchestral field where the richness of the proven "classic" literature contrasts with the more recent compositions. While the classic literature has proven the test of time, many of the more recent compositions will soon become classics as well.

Taking advantage of this same approach in selecting jazz music for performances will not only enrich the art form of jazz but will also expand the horizons of all of our students as well as listeners. This is another way to keep jazz history alive, and it is equally important as an effective teaching tool for jazz educators.

For example, there is certainly much to be learned from the way the Count Basie Orchestra interpreted "Basie Straight Ahead." The original arrangement is available for advanced students; however, younger students playing a simplified arrangement of the same tune will gain much as well.

It is difficult to imagine a jazz library without music by great jazz arrangers such as Sammy Nestico, Quincy Jones, Bill Holman, Bob Mintzer, Dominic Spera, Gordon Goodwin, Mark Taylor, Claire Fischer, Dave Wolpe, Lenny Niehaus, Dean Sorensen, Maria Schneider, Jim McNeeley, Doug Beach, Mike Tomaro, Mike Sweeney, Peter Blair, Victor Lopez, and Mike Story, to name but a few.

The classic jazz standards should be present in all jazz band libraries. We encourage you to purchase them for yours.

Your Jazz Music Library

If you are just starting a jazz library or adding to your current library, the charts you select need to be based on the educational and performance needs of your program as you perceive them. Certainly one of your most important tasks as jazz director is selecting music that fits your group. This requires a complete knowledge of the strengths and weaknesses of your group.

Evaluating Your Group's Level

Here is a suggested list of information that can help you determine the ability level of your group so you will be ready to select appropriate music. If your group does not have standard instrumentation, look for charts that are playable with reduced instrumentation.

- Know the practical range of each player in your group, particularly the lead trumpet, lead bone, first alto, and bass bone.
- Who are the weak players and/or sections?
- Who are the strong players and/or sections?
- Can your saxes double on other instruments (flute and clarinet)?
- What is the endurance of the wind players?
- Do the rhythm section players need written-out parts? If so, who?
- Who are the soloists, how advanced are they in their knowledge, and what do they need in the music — changes, suggested solos, scales, and so on?
- What are the limitations of the group in terms of playing in different musical styles?
- Match the music to your performance needs (concerts, festivals, dances, etc.).
- Do you need to include non-traditional instruments such as flute, clarinet, horn in F, baritone horn, tuba, and so on?

Published Charts

Since there are so many charts available today, the selection process might at first seem overwhelming. The publishers of jazz ensemble music have made this job easier thanks to their commitment to publishing quality charts at all levels. A listing of recommended charts grouped by level follows at the end of this chapter.

Publisher Demo Recordings

Publishers also provide another helpful tool — professionally recorded demo recordings of their new charts. These are not only a great aid in selecting music, but also they can and should be used to teach style, concepts, and performance standards to the students.

Professional Recordings and Videos

Encourage your students to start their own jazz libraries of CDs and videos. This suggestion will be met with much enthusiasm and will indicate your students' seriousness toward preparing their music.

A jazz library will also set the tone that there is only one standard to aim for: a professional-level performance of the music. If you aim for being only the best middle school/high school/university jazz band in the area, so will the students. Having a professional sample of the music they are playing will allow them to hear the professional standard.

The jazz library will also put the students on the right track toward developing their aural skills. The process of learning through listening is the way it has been done throughout the history of jazz and something we need to continue to underscore with our students.

Music Reviews

In addition to the information on charts provided by publishers, music reviews provide information on selecting jazz charts. Check out the new music reviews in the following magazines: *Jazz Educators Journal, Instrumentalist,* and *School Band & Orchestra,* as well as some state music journals.

Reading Sessions

New jazz music reading sessions are presented annually at music conferences. Several universities are also beginning to host new music reading sessions on their campuses, and some state music conventions are also having reading sessions. A number of key music dealers also sponsor jazz music reading sessions. At a reading session, a "reading band" comprised of directors and other professionals sight-read through new charts. It is a great way to get a first-hand look at the parts and scores and plan your purchases.

Another good idea is to keep an ongoing list of your favorite charts that you hear played by other groups.

Conferences

The Midwest International Band and Orchestra Clinic

The Midwest International Band and Orchestra Clinic is held in Chicago, Illinois (the third Tuesday through Saturday of every December). This is the largest instrumental music convention in the United States. There are concerts and clinics on all aspects of the band and orchestra field, including jazz. It now offers college credit and has an annual New Jazz Music Reading Session with performances of new jazz charts by one of the outstanding Washington, D.C. service jazz bands. This is a clinic that serves the band directors who have to do everything in their programs: concert, jazz, marching, and so on. Attendance at the clinic is strongly recommended. Further information can be gained by contacting the Midwest Clinic at 828 Davis Street, Suite 101, Evanston, IL 60201-4423, or by email: info@midwestclinic.org.

International Association for Jazz Education

The International Association for Jazz Education (IAJE) hosts an annual in-service conference (the second weekend of every January). It deals strictly with jazz. The conference is held in a different city each year. This way, all parts of the country are served on a regular basis.

Two valuable reading sessions to read new jazz music are slated at the IAJE conference every year. This conference is highly recommended for all and is a must for directors who focus on jazz in their schools.

The IAJE also presents annual Teacher Training Institutes in three or four locations throughout the United States. Each of the three-day TTI sessions is a great training ground for teachers who are new to jazz as well as for teachers who have skills they want to upgrade. Further information on activities of the IAJE can be obtained by contacting them at P.O. Box 724, Manhattan, KS 66505, or by email: info@iaje.org.

Commissioned Works

Many directors are commissioning works for their bands. This is a clear and significant way to set your band apart from the others. In addition to featuring your outstanding players, commissioning a work also allows you to downplay the weaker spots in your band. Be sure that a dedication to your group and you is included in the title.

Commissioning a work allows for great creativity in the same manner Duke Ellington did with his band. He wrote to showcase the individual talents of his players, even to the point of writing their names on the parts instead of the part they played. Although you can't have Duke write for your group, many qualified composers are eager to do this type of work.

The range of cost will vary with the composer, but expect to pay a minimum of $250 for a short piece, with fees increasing rapidly. Be sure to get a clear understanding if copying the parts is included in the fee.

Your contacts will come in handy in this area. Introduce yourself to all of the composers/arrangers you admire at the next IAJE convention.

PUBLISHED MUSIC

Level Rankings

Publishers rank music in various levels of difficulty. Rankings vary from publisher to publisher; the table below describes the grading process used by most. Selecting a balance of musical styles is recommended at each grade level.

Grade 1 or Very Easy	For beginning players
Grade 2 or Medium	Easy primarily for first- and second-year players
Grade 3 or Medium	Advanced middle school, junior high, and/or easy high school
Grade 4 or Medium-Advanced	Advanced high school with good ranges
Grade 5 or Advanced	Very advanced high school, university
Grade 6 or Difficult	Advanced university, professional

Published Charts

Selecting charts for Grade 1, 2, and 3 jazz ensembles is much easier if you use music from established publishers. Key elements that should be present in these grade levels are:
- Full score
- Full recording of chart
- Notes to the conductor, with rehearsal suggestions
- Clear information on the style of the chart
- Written-out rhythm section parts
- Reasonable ranges for all players
- Reasonable and repeated jazz figures for the ensemble
- Complete dynamic and jazz articulation markings throughout
- Solo sections with simple chord changes that can be opened up for more instruments
- Suggested solos or chord changes
- Consistent notation of chord symbols

Repertoire Suggestions

Following are suggested repertoire lists for each grade level with the name of the arranger and the publishing company. Various jazz publishing companies were contacted and asked to submit charts in each style and grade level. Final decisions on including the listed charts were made by the authors. All of the music listed was available for purchase at the time of this book's writing. However, publishers sometimes take music out of print based on sales.

Style Categories

We've sorted charts into four basic categories within each grade level:

1. Swing/shuffle
2. Ballad
3. Latin/rock
4. Special

The first three categories are self-explanatory. The Special category covers anything from an educational aid (such as a warm-up chart) to an unusual chart that will serve as an encore or add spice to a program. A brief description is included for these charts.

Further Designations

In addition to being sorted by musical style and level of difficulty, listings are also designated as Jazz Ensemble Classics and Other Suggested Arrangements.

Jazz Ensemble Classics are arrangements of recognized jazz standards or arrangements of outstanding original compositions for big band that have proven to be timeless. Other Suggested Arrangements are not necessarily jazz standards, but they will make outstanding additions to any program.

SELECTING MUSIC FOR GRADES 1 AND 2

Grade 1 or Very Easy	For beginning players
Grade 2 or Medium	Easy primarily for first- and second-year players

Selecting music for Grades 1 and 2 should emphasize "educational" material—both in theory and practice. Therefore, selections in this category should lean heavily on the basic "swing-teaching" tunes. Use the Latin-rock-pop tunes to take the students' current level of musical interest and use them as a bridge to swing-style jazz. Of course, it is important that the mainly "educational" tunes stand on the musicality of the chart and are appropriate for concert and festival programs. It is also important at this level to have and to use warm-up exercises or selections at the start of every rehearsal.

Categories

Publisher Legend	Style Categories
• WB – Warner Bros. Publications	Charts are sorted into four basic categories within each grade level:
• HL – Hal Leonard Music	1) Swing/shuffle
• HJW – HJW Music	2) Ballad
• Kjos – Kjos Music	3) Latin/rock
• Kendor – Kendor Music	4) Special
• UNC – University of Northern Colorado Press	They are designated as:
• Sierra – Sierra Music	*Jazz Ensemble Classics:* These are arrangements of recognized jazz standards or arrangements of outstanding original compositions for big band that have proven to be timeless.
• Barnhouse – Barnhouse Music	*Other Suggested Arrangements:* These are not necessarily jazz standards, but they will make outstanding additions to any program.
• Queenwood – Queenwood Publications	
• Beach – Doug Beach Music	

GRADES 1 AND 2

Swing/Shuffle
Jazz Ensemble Classics

Ain't Misbehavin' - Ralph Ford - WB
All of Me - Jeff Holmes - HL
All the Things You Are - Mike Sweeney - HL
April in Paris - Bob Lowden - WB
April in Paris - Mike Sweeney - HL
Blue Monk - Mike Sweeney - HL
Bye Bye Blackbird - Kris Berg - WB
C Jam Blues - Paul Cook - WB
C Jam Blues - David Pugh - WB
Cute - Mike Story - WB
Don't Get Around Much Anymore - Paul Cook - WB
Don't Get Around Much Anymore - Ralph Ford - WB
Fly Me to the Moon - Jerry Nowak - HL
I Got Plenty o' Nuttin' - Joe Jackson - WB
I Got Rhythm - Ralph Ford - WB
In a Mellow Tone - Paul Cook - WB
In a Sentimental Mood - Paul Cook - WB
It Don't Mean a Thing - Paul Cook - WB
It Don't Mean a Thing - Mike Sweeney - HL
In the Pocket - Robert Woods - HJW
Jada - Oliver Nelson - Sierra
Jumpin' at the Woodside - Paul Cook - WB
Leap Frog - Paul Cook - WB
Mercy, Mercy, Mercy - John Edmondson - HL
Moten Swing - Mike Sweeney - HL
Night and Day - David Pugh - WB

On Green Dolphin Street - Victor Lopez - WB
One O'Clock Jump - Paul Cook - WB
Opus One - Paul Cook - WB
Opus One - Jerry Nowak - HL
Perdido - Mike Lewis - WB
The Preacher - Carl Strommen - WB
Satin Doll - John Edmondson - HL
Sing, Sing, Sing - Paul Cook - WB
Smack Dab in the Middle - Sammy Nestico - Kendor
Splanky - Mike Sweeney - WB
Stella by Starlight - Peter Blair - HL
Stolen Moments - Peter Blair - HL
Summertime - Calvin Custer - WB
Sweet Georgia Brown - Chuck Sayre - WB
Swingin' Shepherd Blues - Roy Phillippe - WB
Take Five - Mike Lewis - WB
Take the "A" Train - Bob Lowden - HL
Woodchoppers Ball - Mike Lewis - WB
Woodchoppers Ball - Peter Blair - WB

GRADES 1 AND 2 (continued)

Swing/Shuffle
Other Suggested Arrangements

Blue Dinosaurs - Dean Sorenson - Kjos
Blue Note Special - Mike Tomaro - Beach
Blufoladas - Mark Taylor - UNC
Comfort Zone - Lenny Niehaus - Kendor
Do It Right - Rich Matteson - UNC
Doctor Cool - Peter Blair - HJW
Easy Street - Carl Strommen - WB
Front Burner - Sammy Nestico - Kendor
Just You, Just Me - George Stone - UNC
Leap Frog - Paul Cook - WB
Lines for Lyons - Bob Curnow – Sierra
Miles Mood - Shelly Berg - Kendor
Minor Mystery - Ellen Rowe - Sierra
Singing in the Rain - John Denton - WB
Something Like That - Peter Blair - HJW
Steppin' Up to the Blues - Fred Sturm - HJW
Take Me Out to the Ballgame - Mike Story - WB
Vamoose Your Caboose - Bob Washut - Barnhouse
Walrus Walk - Dean Sorenson - Kjos
Won't You Come Home, Bill Basie - John Edmondson - Queenwood
Yes, No or Maybe? - Ken Harris - Barnhouse

Ballads
Jazz Ensemble Classicss

A Child Is Born - Thad Jones - Kendor
Embraceable You - Roy Phillippe - WB
Georgia on My Mind - Mike Sweeney - HL
God Bless the Child - John Berry - HL
Here's That Rainy Day - Bob Curnow - Sierra
Here's That Rainy Day - John Edmondson - HL
Killer Joe - Mike Sweeney - HL
Li'l Darlin - Neil Hefti - WB
Li'l Darlin - Roy Phillippe - WB
Misty - Mike Lewis - WB
Mood Indigo - Paul Cook - WB
My Funny Valentine - Steve Tyler - UNC
A Nightingale Sang in Berkeley Square - Jeff Holmes - HL
Over the Rainbow - Paul Cook - WB
'Round Midnight - Bob Washut - UNC
The Shadow of Your Smile - Roy Phillippe - WB
When Sunny Gets Blue - Jeff Holmes - HL

Ballads
Other Suggested Arrangements

At First Light - Ellen Rowe - Sierra
Beyond the Shadows - Russ Michaels - HJW
Carli - John Edmondson - Queenwood
Dreamsville - Mike Lewis - WB
For My Dad - Greg Yasinitsky - Kendor
If You Never Look My Way - Les Alrich - Barnhouse
If I Could - Bob Curnow - Sierra
Little Ol' Softly - Rich Matteston - UNC
Natalie's Song - Mike Tomaro - Kendor

Samantha - Sammy Nestico - Kendor
Soft 'n' Gentle - Dean Sorenson - Kjos
Traces - Sammy Nestico - HL

Latin/Rock
Jazz Ensemble Classics

Caravan - Roy Phillippe - WB
Chilli Pepper – Doug Beach and George Shutack - Beach
Corcovado (Quiet Nights) - Ralph Ford - WB
The Girl From Ipanema - Victor Lopez - WB
A Night in Tunisia - Ralph Ford - WB
A Night in Tunisia - Mike Sweeney - WB
Oye Como Va - Victor Lopez - WB

Latin/Rock
Other Suggested Arrangements

Chad Happens - Victor Lopez - WB
Down Roberto's Way - Les Sabina - Kendor
El Rey del Sol - Greg Yasinitsky - Kendor
Finger Lakes - Doug Beach - Kendor
Gospel John - Bob Lowden - Barnhouse
Iroquois Dance - Fred Sturm - HJW
James Bond Theme - Mike Story - WB
Latin Lesson - Mike Carubia - WB
Linus and Lucy - Tom Davis - WB
Lovely Lady - Mark Taylor - UNC
Peter Gunn - Mike Lewis - WB
Rock This Town - Mike Story - WB
Rush Hour - Bruce Pearson - Kjos
Sierra Sunset - David Caffey - UNC
Softness - Les Hooper - Sierra
Soul Bossa Nova - Mike Lewis - WB
Theme From the Pink Panther - Mike Lewis - WB
Wild Oats - Mark Taylor - UNC
When I Fall in Love - Mike Carubia - WB
Zach Attack! - Fred Sturm - HJW

Special

Christmas: The Joy and Spirit - Sammy Nestico - Kendor (seasonal)
Daily Warm-Up Exercises for Jazz Ensemble - Mike Lewis and Jack Bullock - WB (warm-up)
Five Minutes a Day Jazz Warm-Ups - Andy Clark - Barnhouse (warm-up)
Instant Warm-Ups - Mike Sweeney - HL (warm-up)
Ivory Moon - Larry Neeck - Barnhouse (piano solo feature)
Just a Closer Walk With Thee - Dean Sorenson - Kjos (Dixieland funeral and celebration)
Red Baron - Tom Davis - WB (Charlie Brown and Peanuts gang favorite)
Stick Shift - Andy Clark - Barnhouse (drum solo)
Take Five - Mike Lewis - WB (simplified jazz standard in 5/4)
This Little Light of Mine - Andy Clark - Barnhouse (trombone section feature)

SELECTING MUSIC FOR GRADE 3

Grade 3 or Medium	Advanced middle school, junior high, and/or easy high school

Grade 3 is a great level to encourage and emphasize "swing and shuffle" styles. This is a very special level because it's where most directors at the high school level begin to have a chance to share the joy of jazz music with their students. With younger high school and middle school students we can certainly use music they know as a starter to get them comfortable and then introduce them to the jazz concepts. Music used for that purpose should include shuffle, an excellent bridge, since students at this age hear it often on TV and radio. Obviously funk, rock, and Latin can fill a similar bill in bringing the student into jazz. This is also a great time to use ballads, particularly ones for which you have the words. The students are ready to understand how they can convert the phrasing of lyrics into instrumental phrasing.

Categories

Publisher Legend

- WB – Warner Bros. Publications
- HL – Hal Leonard Music
- HJW – HJW Music
- Kjos – Kjos Music
- Kendor – Kendor Music
- UNC – University of Northern Colorado Press
- Sierra – Sierra Music
- Barnhouse – Barnhouse Music
- Queenwood – Queenwood Publications
- Beach – Doug Beach Music

Style Categories

Charts are sorted into four basic categories within each grade level:
1) Swing/shuffle
2) Ballad
3) Latin/rock
4) Special

They are designated as:

Jazz Ensemble Classics:
These are arrangements of recognized jazz standards or arrangements of outstanding original compositions for big band that have proven to be timeless.

Other Suggested Arrangements:
These are not necessarily jazz standards, but they will make outstanding additions to any program.

GRADE 3

Swing/Shuffle
Jazz Ensemble Classics

Alexander's Ragtime Band - Dave Wolpe - WB
April in Paris - Dave Barduhn - HL
Autumn Leaves - Peter Blair - HL
Basie Straight Ahead - Sammy Nestico - Kendor
Birth of the Blues - Sammy Nestico - WB
Blue Rondo à la Turk - Calvin Custer - WB
Blues in Hoss's Flat - Mark Taylor - WB
C Jam Blues - Dave Wolpe - WB
Cute - Calvin Custer - WB
Days of Wine and Roses - Mike Lewis - WB
Do Nothin' 'til You Hear From Me - Joe Jackson - WB
Fly Me to the Moon - Mark Taylor - HL
Four - Mark Taylor - HL
Four Brothers - Peter Blair - HL
Georgia - John Clayton - UNC
Groovin' High - Mark Taylor - WB
Groovin' High - Greg Yasinitsky - WB
I Got Rhythm - Mike Lewis - WB
I'm Beginning to See the Light - Mark Taylor - HL
It Don't Mean a Thing - Mark Taylor - HL
It Had to Be You - Tom Davis - WB
Ja-Da - Sammy Nestico - HL
Jumpin' at the Woodside - Mike Lewis - WB
Just Friends - Joe Jackson - WB
Killer Joe - John Higgins - HL
Leap Frog - John Berry - WB
Lester Leaps In - Mark Taylor - HL
Lullaby of Birdland - John Denton - WB
Mack the Knife - Sammy Nestico - WB
Mack the Knife - Dave Wolpe - WB
Moanin' - Mark Taylor - HL
Moonlight in Vermont - Dave Wolpe - WB
Moten Swing - Sammy Nestico - HL
Moten Swing - Ernie Wilkins - Sierra
My Funny Valentine - Dave Wolpe - WB
Night and Day - Dave Wolpe - WB
St. Louis Blues - Tom Davis - HJW
St. Thomas - Mike Lewis - WB
Satin Doll - Frank Comstock - WB
Satin Doll - Mark Taylor - HL
Sing, Sing, Sing - Roy Phillippe - WB
Splanky - Calvin Custer - WB
Splanky - Sammy Nestico - WB
Stolen Moments - Mark Taylor - HL
Stompin' at the Savoy - Roy Phillippe - WB
Straight No Chaser - Mark Taylor - HL
Strike Up the Band - Ralph Ford - WB
Summertime - Frank Mantooth - WB
Sweet Georgia Brown - Mike Sweeney - WB
Take Five - Dave Wolpe - WB
Take the "A" Train - Dave Barduhn - HL
Tenderly - Mark Taylor - HL

Swing/Shuffle
Other Suggested Arrangements

Anything Goes - Frank Mantooth - WB
Blue Note Special - Mike Tomaro - Kendor
Bluebari - Kevin McElrath - Kjos
Blues for Kapp - Marty Paich - Sierra
The Heat's On - Sammy Nestico - WB
Hot House - Jack Cooper - WB
Hog-Squeelin', Rip-Snortin', Belly-Achin' Blues -
    Mike Sweeney - HL
Hot Dog - Greg Yasinistsky - Kendor
Low Down, Nitty Gritty - Mike Tetlebaum - HJW
The Messenger - Paul McKee - UNC
No Scuffle Shuffle - Dominic Spera - Barnhouse
Orange Sherbert - Sammy Nestico - HL
Slam Dunk - John Edmondson - Queenwood
Tweak It - John Edmondson - Queenwood
We're Off to See the Wizard - Jack Cooper - WB
Work Song - Geoff Keezer - Sierra

Ballads
Jazz Ensemble Classics

A Child Is Born - Thad Jones - Kendor
Embraceable You - Roy Phillippe - WB
Here's That Rainy Day - Dave Barduhn - HL
I Remember Clifford - Mike Vax - HL
I'm Getting Sentimental Over You - Dave Wolpe - WB
It Ain't Necessarily So - Victor Lopez - WB
Lil' Darlin' - Neil Hefti - WB
My Funny Valentine - Dave Wolpe - WB
My Funny Valentine - Sammy Nestico - HL
My Romance - Mark Taylor - HL
Naima - Manny Mendelson - Kendor
Quiet Nights of Quiet Stars (Corcovado) - Mark Taylor - WB
'Round Midnight - Dave Barduhn - WB
'Round Midnight - Victor Lopez - WB
Spring Can Really Hang You Up the Most - Frank Mantooth -
    Kendor
Stardust - Dave Wolpe - WB
When Sonny Gets Blue - Dave Barduhn - HL

Ballads
Other Suggested Arrangements

Cerulean Blue - Greg Yasinitsky - Kendor
Closin' Time - Howard Rowe - Barnhouse
Emily - Bob Washut - UNC (jazz waltz, trombone solo)
Firstborn - Dean Sorenson - Kjos
It Had to Be You - Tom Davis - WB
Kelly's Theme - Bob Curnow - Sierra
Only Forever - David Caffey - UNC
A Penthouse Dawn - Oliver Nelson - Sierra
Send in the Clowns - Dave Wolpe - WB
That Warm Feeling - Sammy Nestico - Kendor

GRADE 3 (continued)

Latin/Rock
Jazz Ensemble Classics

Mercy, Mercy, Mercy - Paul Jennings - HL
A Night in Tunisia - Roger Holmes - WB
One Note Samba - Frank Mantooth - WB
One Note Samba - Jerry Nowak - WB
Quiet Nights of Quiet Stars (Corcovado) - Mark Taylor - WB
St. Thomas - Mike Lewis - WB

Latin/Rock
Other Suggested Arrangements

A Night in Havana - Victor Lopez - WB
The Chicken - Kris Berg - WB
Children of the Sun - Bob Curnow - Sierra
Children of Sanchez - Dave Wolpe - WB
Cross Currents - Ellen Rowe - Sierra
El Taco Loco - George Shutack - Kendor
Engine #9 - Les Hooper - Barnhouse
Everytime It Happens - Dave Eshelman - Kjos
Horsepower - Fred Sturm - HJW
Mambo Hot - Victor Lopez - WB
Mr. Papi - Victor Lopez - WB
MWA (Musicians With Attitude) - David Benoit - WB
Night of the Living Chili Pepper - George Shutack - Kendor
Night in Havana - Victor Lopez - WB
Reunion in Rio - Peter Blair - HJW
Santo Sencillo - Bob Washut - UNC
Skydance - Dan Gailey - UNC
Smooth - Mike Lewis - WB

Special

Blue Bones - Dominic Spera (trombone section feature)
Bones Tones - Dean Sorenson - Kjos (trombone section feature)
Christmas Classics, Vol. 1 - Peter Blair - HJW (seasonal)
Emily - Bob Washut - UNC (jazz waltz, trombone solo)
I'll Be Home for Christmas - Greg Yasinitsky - WB
I Only Have Eyes for You - Frank Mantooth - UNC (fusion)
Salsa Caban - Neil Finn - UNC (contemporary)
St. James Infirmary - Tom Davis - WB (traditional jazz)
Tunes From 'Toons - Roy Phillippe - WB (cartoon favorites)
When the Saints Go Marchin' In - Dean Sorenson - Kjos (traditional)

SELECTING MUSIC FOR GRADE 4

Grade 4 or Medium-Advanced	Advanced high school with good ranges

Selecting charts for Grade 4 (and up) creates more room for flexibility. We should now begin to see a more balanced diet of styles. These charts should include some of the items listed for the earlier grades. It will not be necessary to have completely written-out rhythm section parts or suggested solos.

Grade 4 charts may include:
- Full score
- Full recording of chart if possible
- Notes to conductor
- Clear information on the style of the chart
- Complete dynamic and jazz articulation markings throughout

Grade 4 and 5 charts will most likely include some or all of the following:
- Expanded ranges (know your players' limitations)
- More complex figures
- Occasional doubling of woodwind parts
- More complex chord changes and longer solos

The Jazz Classics

Grade 4 provides music for more mature musical students who are generally ready for charts related to the jazz classics. Students are ready, both mentally and musically, to appreciate the importance of this step. In addition to demo recordings by publishers, whenever possible it is important to use recordings by the jazz masters of the selected music. Solid musical publications are available for bands such as Duke Ellington, Count Basie, Woody Herman, Buddy Rich, Stan Kenton, Maynard Ferguson, Thad Jones/Mel Lewis, Rob McConnell, Bob Mintzer, John Fedchock, Maria Schneider, Gordon Goodwin, and Jim McNeely.

Categories

Publisher Legend

- WB – Warner Bros. Publications
- HL – Hal Leonard Music
- HJW – HJW Music
- Kjos – Kjos Music
- Kendor – Kendor Music
- UNC – University of Northern Colorado Press
- Sierra – Sierra Music
- Barnhouse – Barnhouse Music
- Queenwood – Queenwood Publications
- Beach – Doug Beach Music

Style Categories

Charts are sorted into four basic categories within each grade level:
1) Swing/shuffle
2) Ballad
3) Latin/rock
4) Special

They are designated as:

Jazz Ensemble Classics:
These are arrangements of recognized jazz standards or arrangements of outstanding original compositions for big band that have proven to be timeless.

Other Suggested Arrangements:
These are not necessarily jazz standards, but they will make outstanding additions to any program.

GRADE 4

Swing/Shuffle
Jazz Ensemble Classics

All the Things You Are - Stan Kenton - Sierra
All the Things You Are - Mike Tomaro - HL
April in Paris - Jeff Hest - WB
Avalon - Dave Wolpe - WB
Basie-Straight Ahead - Sammy Nestico - Kendor
Cherokee - Dave Wolpe - WB
Cottontail - Dave Wolpe - WB
Cute - Bob Mintzer - WB
Don't Get Around Much Anymore - Dave Wolpe - WB
Don't Get Around Much Anymore - Sammy Nestico - HL
Fly Me to the Moon - Sammy Nestico - HL
A Foggy Day - Lennie Niehaus - Sierra
Harlem Nocturne - Earl Hagen - HL (original edition)
I Got Plenty o' Nuttin' - Mike Lewis - WB
I'm Beginning to See the Light - Gordon Goodwin - HL
I'm Beginning to See the Light - Sammy Nestico - HL
In a Mellow Tone - Roy Phillippe - WB
It Don't Mean a Thing - John Fedchock - WB
Jada - Oliver Nelson - Sierra
Kids Are Pretty People - Thad Jones - Kendor
Killer Joe - Les Hooper - HL
Ladybird - Maria Schneider - Kendor
Lullaby of Birdland - Lennie Niehaus - Sierra
Lullaby of Broadway - Lennie Niehaus - Sierra
Mean to Me - Frank Mantooth - Kendor
Moten Swing - Ernie Wilkins - Sierra
Ol' Man River - Dave Wolpe - WB
One O'Clock Jump - Bob Mintzer - WB
Opus One - John Fedchock - Kendor
Opus One - Sammy Nestico - HL
Perdido - Dave Wolpe - WB
Perdido - Ray Wright - Kendor
Seven Steps to Heaven - Manny Mendelson - Kendor
Sing, Sing, Sing - Mike Lewis - WB
Sophisticated Lady - Dave Wolpe - WB
Speak Low - George Stone - HL
Stella by Starlight - Bill Holman - Sierra
Stolen Moments - Paul Jennings - HL
Straight No Chaser - John LaBarbera - HL
Struttin' With Some Barbeque - Alan Baylock - WB
Take the "A" Train - David Berger - HL
Take the "A" Train - Sammy Nestico - HL
Things Ain't What They Used to Be - David Berger - HL
Things Ain't What They Used to Be - Mark Taylor - HL
Until I Met You (Corner Pocket) - Dave Wolpe - WB
Woodchoppers Ball - Mike Carubia - WB
You Go to My Head - Bill Holman - Sierra

Swing/Shuffle
Other Sugggested Arrangements

Big Al Meets the Barnyard Gals - Dan Gailey - UNC
Duke It Out - Dominic Spera - Barnhouse
Hay Burner - Sammy Nestico - Kendor
Miss Fine - Oliver Nelson - Sierra
The Queen Bee - Sammy Nestico - Kendor
Rhythm of the Masses - Frank Mantooth - HJW
Sonny's Place - Carl Strommen - WB
Stumblin' and Shufflin' - Neal Finn - UNC
Whisper Not - Mike Abene - Sierra
Wind Machine - Sammy Nestico - HL

Ballads
Jazz Ensemble Classics

Angel Eyes - John Fedchock - Kendor
Body and Soul - George Stone - HL
Chelsea Bridge - Phil Wilson - Kendor
Come Rain or Come Shine - George Stone - HL
Darn That Dream - Frank Mantooth - Kendor
Georgia on My Mind - Dave Barduhn - HL
God Bless the Child - Sammy Nestico - HL
I Loves You Porgy - Lisa DeSpain - WB
In a Sentimental Mood - Mike Tomaro - HL
I Remember Clifford - Sammy Nestico - HL
I've Never Been in Love Before - Lennie Niehaus - Sierra
Lush Life - Phil Wilson - Kendor
My Funny Valentine - Willie Maiden - Sierra
My One and Only Love - Lennie Niehaus - Sierra
My Romance - Mark Taylor - HL
'Round Midnight - Dave Wolpe - WB
Sophisticated Lady - Bob Mintzer - Kendor
Stella by Starlight - Bill Holman - Sierra
Willow Weep for Me - Bob Brookmeyer - Kendor

Ballads
Other Suggested Arrangements

All the Way - Mike Lewis - WB
Cerulean Sky - Fred Sturm - HJW
From the Eyes of a Child - Andy Classen - Barnhouse
Hey There - George Stone - UNC
If I Could - Bob Curnow - Sierra
Midnight in Manhattan - Jeff Jarvis - Kendor
Rachael - Sammy Nestico - Kendor
Slowly and Quietly Please - Don Sebesky - Barnhouse
Strayhorn - Dave Eshelman - Kjos
What's New? - Eric Richards - UNC
Whispered Elegy - Frank Mantooth - HJW

GRADE 4 (continued)

Latin/Rock
Jazz Ensemble Classics

Begin the Beguine - Jeff Hest - WB
Blue Bossa - Johnson - Kendor
Caravan - Mike Tomaro - HL
Caravan - John Wasson - WB
Manteca - Mike Tomaro - HL
A Night in Tunisia - Sammy Nestico - HL
One Note Samba - Mike Tomaro - WB
St. Thomas - Bill Holman - Sierra

Latin/Rock
Other Suggested Arrangements

Black Orpheus - Eric Richards - UNC
Brass Machine - Mark Taylor - HL
Chick on the Grill - Victor Lopez - WB
Dewey - Vince Mendoza - UNC
Dominga - Jeff Jarvis - Kendor
High Impact - Robert Woods - HJW
Minuano - Bob Curnow - Sierra
Puffy Taco - Victor Lopez - WB
Rain Codes - Vince Mendoza - UNC
Saturday Night Blues - Les Hooper - Barnhouse
Tijuca - Mike Crotty - WB

Special

Alternate Route - Dominic Spera - Barnhouse (trumpet section feature)
Basie Straight Ahead - Sammy Nestico (simplified edition)
Channel One Suite - Tom Davis - WB (from the Buddy Rich suite)
Harlem Nocturne - Earl Hagen - HL (original edition)
Jefferson Blues - Doug Beach - Kendor
Lassus Trombone - Dave Wolpe - WB (trombone section feature)
Off the Cuff - Jim McNeely - UNC (contemporary)
Second Thought - Steve Weist - UNC (street band style)
Struttin' With Some Barbeque - Alan Baylock - WB (traditional)
Trombone Boogie - Andy Clark - Barnhouse (trombone section feature)

SELECTING MUSIC FOR GRADE 5

Grade 5 or Advanced	Very advanced high school, university

Grade 5 contains many of the same comments as the previous level. Let's also assume that these students are eager for a good look at some of the more contemporary styles in the Latin and rock area. At the same time, it is important to keep a balance of charts in the swing-shuffle category. It's also time for some experimentation in the contemporary writing of the current hot big bands and their composers.

Categories

Publisher Legend

- WB – Warner Bros. Publications
- HL – Hal Leonard Music
- HJW – HJW Music
- Kjos – Kjos Music
- Kendor – Kendor Music
- UNC – University of Northern Colorado Press
- Sierra – Sierra Music
- Barnhouse – Barnhouse Music
- Queenwood – Queenwood Publications
- Beach – Doug Beach Music

Style Categories

Charts are sorted into four basic categories within each grade level:
1) Swing/shuffle
2) Ballad
3) Latin/rock
4) Special

They are designated as:

Jazz Ensemble Classics:
These are arrangements of recognized jazz standards or arrangements of outstanding original compositions for big band that have proven to be timeless.

Other Suggested Arrangements:
These are not necessarily jazz standards, but they will make outstanding additions to any program.

GRADE 5

Swing/Shuffle
Jazz Ensemble Classics

After You've Gone - Michael Abene - Sierra
All of Me - Billy Byers - HL
All of Me - Lenny Niehaus - Kendor
All the Things You Are - Don Sebesky - Sierra
All the Things You Are - Mark Taylor - HL
Basie Straight Ahead - Sammy Nestico - Kendor
Blues and the Abstract Truth - Oliver Nelson - Sierra
Cherokee - Mark Taylor - HL
Donna Lee - Rick Lawn - Kendor
Don't Get Around Much Anymore - Sammy Nestico - HL
Four - Willie Maiden - Sierra
Four Brothers - Jimmy Giuffre - HL
Goodbye Pork Pie Hat - Sy Johnson - HL
Just Friends - Bill Holman - Sierra
Limehouse Blues - Tom Davis - WB
Love Walked In - Lennie Niehaus - Sierra
Love Walked In - Kim Richmond - Sierra
Moanin' - Sy Johnson - HL
On Green Dolphin Street - Michael Abene - Sierra
Over the Rainbow - William Russo - Sierra
Satin Doll - Sammy Nestico - HL
Speak Low - Johnny Richards - Sierra
Stolen Moments - Oliver Nelson - Sierra
Stompin' at the Savoy - Matt Catingub - UNC
Stompin' at the Savoy - Bill Holman - Sierra
Take the "A" Train - Don Sebesky - Kendor
Take the "A" Train - Frank Foster - WB
Tenderly - Mark Taylor - HL
Things Ain't What They Used to Be - Dave Lalama - HL

Swing/Shuffle
Other Suggested Arrangements

Belly Roll - Quincy Jones - WB
Delta City Blues - Dave Eshelman - Kjos
Got Rhythm? - Doug Beach - Kendor
Hard Sock Dance - Quincy Jones - WB
How Sweet It Is - Sammy Nestico - WB
I-80 Shuffle - Andy Classen - Barnhouse
The Joy of Cookin' - Sammy Nestico - WB
No Time Like the Present - Sammy Nestico - WB
Speed Trap - Dominic Spera - Barnhouse
Step It Up Blues - Dave Eshelman - Kjos
Swingin' on the Orient Express - Sammy Nestico - WB
Witching Hour - Quincy Jones - WB

Ballads
Jazz Ensemble Classics

A Nightingale Sang in Berkeley Square - Frank Mantooth - HL
Angel Eyes - Frank Foster - WB
Angel Eyes - John Fedchock - Kendor
Georgia on My Mind - Sammy Nestico - HL
Here's That Rainy Day - Dee Barton - Sierra
What's New - Bill Holman - Sierra

When Sunny Gets Blue - Frank Mantooth - HL
Yesterdays - Bill Holman - Sierra

Ballads
Other Suggested Arrangements

Ballad for P.J. - Dominic Spera - Barnhouse
Central Park West - John Fedchock - Kendor
Decision - Jim McNeely - UNC
First Child - Bob Curnow - Sierra
For Lena and Lenny - Quincy Jones - WB
Grace - Quincy Jones - WB
In Your Tender Care - Steve Owen - UNC
It's a Raggy Waltz - Dave Wolpe - WB
Lisette - Sammy Nestico - WB
A Long Time Ago - Bob Mintzer - Barnhouse
Quintessence - Quincy Jones - WB
Samantha - Sammy Nestico - HL
To You - Thad Jones - Kendor

Latin/Rock
Jazz Ensemble Classics

Brazil - Chip McNeil - WB
Caravan - Michael Abene - HL
It Don't Mean a Thing - Matt Harris - Kendor
Mercy, Mercy, Mercy - Phil Wilson - Kendor
St. Thomas - Bill Holman - Sierra
Tanga - Mark Taylor - HL
The Peanut Vendor - Stan Kenton and Pete Rugolo - Sierra

Latin/Rock
Other Suggested Arrangements

Big Al's Boogie - Dominic Spera - Barnhouse
Coconut Champagne - Denis DiBlasio - HL
Granada Smoothie - Mark Taylor - HL
It's the Gospel Truth - Denis DiBlasio - WB
Los Gatos - Jeff Jarvis - Kendor
Miami Spice - Victor Lopez - WB
Samba Mozart - Dave Eshelman - Kjos
The Sleaze Factor - Mike Crotty - WB
Some Skunk Funk - Mark Taylor - HL

Special

Big Dipper - Thad Jones - Kendor (from the Thad Jones/ Mel Lewis book)
Cajun Cookin' - Denis DiBlasio - WB (New Orleans flavor)
Computer - Bob Mintzer - Kendor (simulates computer sounds)
New Rochelle - Bob Mintzer - Kendor
Pullin' Punches - Les Hooper - Barnhouse

SELECTING MUSIC FOR GRADE 6

Grade 6 or Difficult	Advanced university, professional

Grade 6 charts are written for professional bands and have no limitations. Many will be manuscript writing and many do not have full scores. In Grade 6, although the scope of the charts is limitless, you will find even in this most advanced category that a balanced representation of styles will be present.

Categories

Publisher Legend
- WB – Warner Bros. Publications
- HL – Hal Leonard Music
- HJW – HJW Music
- Kjos – Kjos Music
- Kendor – Kendor Music
- UNC – University of Northern Colorado Press
- Sierra – Sierra Music
- Barnhouse – Barnhouse Music
- Queenwood – Queenwood Publications
- Beach – Doug Beach Music

Style Categories
Charts are sorted into four basic categories within each grade level:
1) Swing/shuffle
2) Ballad
3) Latin/rock
4) Special

They are designated as:

Jazz Ensemble Classics:
These are arrangements of recognized jazz standards or arrangements of outstanding original compositions for big band that have proven to be timeless.

Other Suggested Arrangements:
These are not necessarily jazz standards, but they will make outstanding additions to any program.

GRADE 6

Swing/Shuffle

On Green Dolphin Street - Michael Abene - Sierra
Pete's Feet - Jim McNeely - UNC
Second Cousins - Neal Finn - UNC
Soupbone - John Clayton - UNC
Ya Gotta Try Harder - Sammy Nestico - WB

Latin/Rock

Entropical Paradise - Eric Richards - UNC
Guarabe - Claire Fischer - UNC
Malaguena - Bill Holman - Sierra
A View From the Edge - Eric Richards - UNC

Special

Empty House - Jim McNeely - UNC (contemporary)
The First Circle - Bob Curnow - Sierra (contemporary, includes challenging hand clapping)
Night Visitors - Steve Wiest - UNC (contemporary)
Orange Guitars - Vince Mendoza - UNC (fusion)

ESSENTIAL JAZZ EDITIONS

A unique and special group of charts has come out recently from the Jazz at Lincoln Center program. *Essential Jazz Editions* is a comprehensive series of arrangements that was conceived by Jazz at Lincoln Center, the Smithsonian Institution's National Museum of American History, and the Music Division of the Library of Congress and is published by Warner Bros. Publications. Five scores are produced annually, beginning with the masterworks of early jazz and continuing to the present. Transcribed from classic recordings, the goal of *Essential Jazz Editions* is to document America's music and make the scores available for performance and in-depth study by musicians and scholars. The end result will be a comprehensive library of some of the greatest jazz compositions and arrangements ever recorded. The following editions are currently available:

All of these *Essential Jazz Editions* arrangements are Grade 4.

Set #1: New Orleans Jazz, 1918–1927
Black Bottom Stomp - as recorded by Jelly Roll Morton's Red Hot Peppers, 1926
The Chant - as recorded by Jelly Roll Morton's Red Hot Peppers, 1926
Grandpa's Spells - as recorded by Jelly Roll Morton's Red Hot Peppers, 1926
Potato Head Blues - as recorded by Louis Armstrong and His Hot Seven, 1927
Tiger Rag - as recorded by the Original Dixieland Jazz Band, 1918

Set #2: Louis Armstrong, 1926–1929
Cornet Chop Suey - as recorded by Louis Armstrong and His Hot Five, 1926
Hotter Than That - as recorded by Louis Armstrong and His Hot Five, 1927
West End Blues - as recorded by Louis Armstrong and His Hot Five, 1928
Tight Like This - as recorded by Louis Armstrong and His Savoy Ballroom Five, 1928
Mahogany Hall Stomp - as recorded by Louis Armstrong and His Savoy Ballroom Five, 1929

Set #3: Music of the 1930s
From A-flat to C - as recorded by the John Kirby Sextet, 1938
For Dancers Only - as recorded by Jimmie Lunceford & His Orchestra, 1937
Big Jim Blues - as recorded by Andy Kirk & His Twelve Clouds of Joy, 1939
Lonesome Road - as recorded by Tommy Dorsey & His Orchestra, 1939
Symphony in Riffs - as recorded by Benny Carter & His Orchestra, 1933

JAZZ AT LINCOLN CENTER LIBRARY

Another group of special charts is from the Jazz at Lincoln Center Library. These arrangements are transcribed for the Jazz at Lincoln Center Essentially Ellington High School Jazz Band Competition and Festival. To date, 48 arrangements have been published by Warner Bros. Publications and are available for purchase. All of the charts listed below are exact transcriptions of recordings by Duke Ellington and His Orchestra prepared specifically for high school bands. The transcriptions are all medium to medium-advanced in difficulty. All of the J@LC charts are transcribed by David Berger. Each score includes performance notes on how to play Ellington's music as well as specific notes on each piece by Wynton Marsalis and transcriber David Berger.

All of these J@LC arrangements should be identified as Grade 4; the stylistic considerations are often the key here more than technical challenges. The following are currently available:

Across the Track Blues - Duke Ellington
All Heart - Duke Ellington/Billy Strayhorn
Almost Cried - Duke Ellington/Billy Strayhorn
Anitra's Dance - Edvard Grieg/Duke Ellington/Billy Strayhorn
Black and Tan Fantasy - Duke Ellington/Bubber Miley
Blue Cellophane - Duke Ellington
Blue Feeling - Duke Ellington
Boy Meets Horn - Duke Ellington/Rex Stewart
C-Jam Blues - Duke Ellington
Caravan - Duke Ellington/Juan Tizol
Concerto for Cootie - Duke Ellington
Cottontail - Duke Ellington
The Eighth Veil - Duke Ellington/Billy Strayhorn
Half the Fun - Billy Strayhorn/Duke Ellington
Harlem Airshaft - Duke Ellington
I Got It Bad (And That Ain't Good) - Duke Ellington
I Let a Song Go Out of My Heart - Duke Ellington/Henry Nemo/John Redmond
In a Mellow Tone - Duke Ellington
It Don't Mean a Thing (If It Ain't Got That Swing) - Duke Ellington
I've Just Seen Her - Charles Strouse/Billy Strayhorn
Jump for Joy - Duke Ellington
Kinda Dukish/Rockin' in Rhythm - Harry Carney/Duke Ellington
Ko-Ko - Duke Ellington
Launching Pad - Clark Terry/Duke Ellington
Main Stem - Duke Ellington
The Mooche - Duke Ellington/Irving Mills
Mood Indigo - Duke Ellington/Billy Strayhorn
Never No Lament (Don't Get Around Much Anymore) - Duke Ellington
Oclupaca - Duke Ellington
Old King Dooji - Duke Ellington
The Peanut Vendor - Moises Simons/Dick Vance
Perdido - Juan Tizol/Duke Ellington
Portrait of Louis Armstrong - Duke Ellington
Prelude to a Kiss - Duke Ellington
Pyramid - Duke Ellington/Juan Tizol
Raincheck - Billy Strayhorn
Rockabye River - Duke Ellington
Rocks in My Bed - Duke Ellington/Billy Strayhorn
Rumpus in Richmond - Duke Ellington
The Shepherd (Who Looks Over the Night Flock) - Duke Ellington
Solitude - Duke Ellington
Sophisticated Lady - Duke Ellington
The Star-Crossed Lovers - Duke Ellington/Billy Strayhorn
Such Sweet Thunder - Duke Ellington/Billy Strayhorn
Sultry Sunset - Duke Ellington
Things Ain't What They Used to Be - Mercer Ellington/Duke Ellington
Tutti for Cootie - Duke Ellington/Jimmy Hamilton
Zweet Zurzday - Duke Ellington

JAZZ ENSEMBLE WITH VOCAL SOLO

The following are vocal solos with big band accompaniment. All of these charts have a moderate vocal range and most have an optional tenor sax part as a substitute for the vocal solo.

These arrangements are Grades 3–4 and are all published by Warner Bros. Publications. The following are currently available:

Vocal With Big Band

All the Way - Dave Wolpe (Vocal range: F below staff to 3rd line Bb, treble clef)
Almost Like Being in Love - Dave Wolpe (Vocal range: Bb below staff to 3rd space C, treble clef)
And the Angels Sing - Dave Wolpe (Vocal range: A below staff to 3rd line Bb, treble clef)
Do Nothin' 'til You Hear From Me - Dave Wolpe (Vocal range: F below staff to 3rd line Bb, treble clef)
Don't Get Around Much Anymore - Dave Wolpe (Vocal range: F below staff to 3rd space C, treble clef)
Have Yourself a Merry Little Christmas - Dave Wolpe (Vocal range: G below staff to 3rd space C, treble clef)
The Lady Is a Tramp - Dave Wolpe (Vocal range in two keys: Female key [low] - G below middle C to 3rd line B; Male key [high] - Bb below middle C to 4th line D)
Makin' Whoopee! - Dave Wolpe (Vocal range: G below staff to 3rd line Bb, treble clef)
The Man I Love - Dave Wolpe (Vocal range: Ab below middle C to 2nd space Ab)
Moonglow - Dave Wolpe (Vocal range: G below staff to 3rd line Bb, treble clef)
Nice Work if You Can Get It - Dave Wolpe (Vocal range in two keys: Female key [low] - E below middle C to 2nd line G; Male key [high] - A below middle C to 3rd space C)
Over the Rainbow - Dave Wolpe (Vocal range: G below staff to 3rd space C, treble clef)
'S Wonderful - Dave Wolpe (Vocal range: Ab below staff to 3rd line Bb, treble clef)
Someone to Watch Over Me - Dave Wolpe (Vocal range: G below staff to 2nd space A, treble clef)
Summertime - Dave Wolpe (Vocal range: G below staff to 3rd space C, treble clef)

These arrangements are all Grades 3–4 and are all published by Kendor Music, Inc. The letter at the end of each line indicates the key of the chart. The following are currently available:

Vocal With Big Band

Ain't Misbehavin' - Jeff Jarvis - C
All of Me - Lennie Niehaus - F
Almost Like Being in Love - Lennie Niehaus - Ab
Angel Eyes - Matt Harris - C minor
Darn That Dream - Matt Harris - F
Fly Me to the Moon - John La Barbera - Ab
For Once in My Life - Lennie Niehaus - Ab
Here's That Rainy Day - Jeff Jarvis - F
Imagination - Bob Lowden - Bb
It Don't Mean a Thing - Matt Harris - Bb
Like Someone in Love - Hanson - Bb
Mean to Me - Manny Mendelson - Eb
Moonlight in Vermont - Frank Mantooth - Eb
Opus One - Lennie Niehaus - Eb
Polka Dots and Moonbeams - Bob Lowder - C, Db
Sophisticated Lady - Bob Mintzer - Eb
Three Little Words - Frank Mantooth - Db
Tuxedo Junction - David Caffey - Bb, F
What Kind of Fool Am I? - Scott Strommen - C
When the Saints Go Marching In - Dick Lieb - Bb, F, C, Db
Who Can I Turn To? - Matt Harris - C
Willow Weep for Me - Matt Harris - F
Yesterday, When I Was Young - Dick Lieb - A minor

These arrangements are all **Grades 3–4** and are all published by Hal Leonard Music. The letter at the end of each line indicates the key of the chart. The following are currently available:

Vocal With Big Band

All by Myself - Mark Taylor - A♭, C
All the Things You Are - Jeff Holmes - A♭
Alright, Okay, You Win - Sammy Nestico - C, D♭
Beauty and the Beast - Mark Taylor - E♭, F, A♭
Beyond the Sea - Jerry Nowak - E♭
Birdland - Jeff Holmes - F
Blue Skies - Jeff Holmes - C minor
Call Me Irresponsible - Jerry Nowak - F
Can't Help Lovin' Dat Man - Jeff Holmes - C, D♭
Come in From the Rain - Jerry Nowak - F
Don't Get Around Much Anymore - Mark Taylor - A♭
Endless Love - Jerry Nowak - A♭
Every Day I Have the Blues - Jeff Holmes - F
Fever - Jeff Holmes - B♭ minor
Fly Me to the Moon - Sammy Nestico - A♭
Georgia on My Mind - Dave Barduhn - C, D♭
The Girl From Ipanema - Jeff Holmes - F
God Bless the Child - Jerry Nowak - C
How High the Moon - Jerry Nowak - F
How Sweet It Is - Mark Taylor - C
I'm Beginning to See the Light - Mark Taylor - C, E♭
In a Sentimental Mood - Jerry Nowak - C
It Don't Mean a Thing - Jerry Nowak - C minor
It's Only a Paper Moon - Jerry Nowak - B♭
I've Got You Under My Skin - Mark Taylor - C
Misty - Jerry Nowak - C
My Funny Valentine - Jerry Nowak - B♭ minor
A Nightingale Sang in Berkeley Square - Mike Tomaro - E♭
Send in the Clowns - Jerry Nowak - E♭
Skylark - Jerry Nowak - B♭
Smoke Gets in Your Eyes - Jeff Holmes - C
Stella by Starlight - Jerry Nowak - A♭
Tuxedo Junction - Jerry Nowak - C, D♭
The Way You Look Tonight - Jeff Holmes - C
What a Wonderful World - Jerry Nowak - E♭
When I Fall in Love - Jerry Nowak - C
When Sunny Gets Blue - Jerry Nowak - C
Yesterday - Jerry Nowak - B♭
You're Nobody 'til Somebody Loves You - Jerry Nowak - E♭

These vocal quartets with big band accompaniment are arranged for SATB, SSAA, and vocal solo. **All of these are Grades 3–4** and published by Warner Bros. Publications.

Jazz Ensemble With Jazz Vocal Quartet

As Time Goes By - Mike Carubia (Vocal solo range: C below staff to 4th line D, treble clef)
Chattanooga Choo Choo - Mike Carubia (Vocal solo range: B♭ below staff to 3rd space C, treble clef)
Don't Get Around Much Anymore - Mike Carubia (Vocal solo range: F below staff to 3rd line B♭, treble clef)
I've Got a Gal in Kalamazoo - Mike Carubia (Vocal solo range: C below staff to 3rd space C, treble clef)
It Don't Mean a Thing (If It Ain't Got That Swing) - Mike Carubia (Vocal solo range: C below staff to 4th line D, treble clef)
Just Friends - Mike Carubia (Vocal solo range: B below staff to 4th line D, treble clef)
Moonlight Serenade - Mike Carubia (Vocal solo range: F below staff to 3rd line B♭, treble clef)
Satin Doll - Mike Carubia (Vocal solo range: 1st line E♭ to 3rd line B♭, treble clef)
Stompin' at the Savoy - Mike Carubia (Vocal solo range: F below staff to 3rd line B♭, treble clef)

DIRECTOR'S CHECKLIST
FOR SELECTING CHARTS FOR YOUR ENSEMBLE

• Make an accurate assessment of the performance range of the brass section. Check for doubles in the woodwinds.

• Determine where the solo strengths are in your band.

• Can the rhythm section players comp or do they need written-out parts?

• Is your instrumentation complete or should the material be able to work with fewer parts than called for in the score? Much material of this nature is now available.

• What is the overall technical skill level of the winds and rhythm section?

• Do the solos have written-out suggested lines that the players can use as a guide if necessary?

• Does the music being considered have interesting musical qualities or is it just technically easy?

• Is a recorded example available?

• Does the music fit into your balanced, varied program?

Summary

Although the information in this chapter will help you determine the level of your group and appropriate charts at that level, you must decide upon a balance of easier charts and more difficult charts to fill out your book. A jazz ensemble needs some easy charts that they can have success with immediately. These easy charts are great for their confidence and also can make great warm-up selections for rehearsals. The band could become bored, complacent, and frustrated without challenging music that makes them stretch beyond their current ability level.

Following is a comprehensive list of jazz publishers that provide music for educational jazz groups. Most of these publishers' music can be found at your local music retailers. Order directly from those publishers with an asterisk (*) after their name.

Alfred Publishing
16380 Roscoe Blvd.
P.O. Box 10003
Van Nuys, CA 91406
www.alfredpub.com

Caris Music Services*
2206 Brislin Rd.
Stroudsburg, PA 18360

C.L. Barnhouse
P.O. Box 680
Oskaloosa, IA 52577
www.barnhouse.com

Educational Programs Publications
1784 W Schuykill Rd.
Douglassville, PA 19518

J. Fraser Collection
P.O. Box 705
Verdugo City, CA 91046-0705
www.jfraser.com

Kendor Music, Inc.
P.O. Box 278
Delavan, NY 14042
www.kendormusic.com

Hal Leonard Publishing Corporation
7777 W Bluemound Rd
PO Box13819
Milwaukee, WI 53213
www.halleonard.com

Jazz at Lincoln Center
33 W 60th St
New York, NY 10023-7999
www.jazzatlincolncenter.org

Kjos Music Publishers
4382 Jutland Dr.
San Diego, CA 92117
www.kjos.com

Otter Music Distributors
P.O. Box 1910
Pismo Beach, CA 93448-19109
www.ottermusicsales.com

Second Floor Music
(available through Hal Leonard)
130 W 28th St., 2nd Floor
New York, NY 10001-6108
www.secondfloormusic.com

Sierra Music Publications*
P.O. Box 928
Port Townsend, WA 98368
www.sierramusic.com

UNC Jazz Press*
School of Music
University of Northern Colorado
Greeley, CO 80639
www.arts.unco.edu/UNCJazz

Walrus Music (see Otter Music Distributors)

Warner Bros. Publications
15800 NW 48th Ave
Miami, FL 33014
www.warnerbrospublications.com

Please refer to the Resource Guide Index.

Chapter 16

THE RHYTHM SECTION

PREFACE

by J. Richard Dunscomb

As with most recipes, sometimes the ingredients a cook adds that are not in the printed recipe are what make it taste exceptional. Read on for those rhythm section ingredients.

Recipe for a Great Rhythm Section

• Mix equal parts: 1 drummer, 1 bassist, 1 pianist, 1 guitarist.
• Sprinkle on the various jazz styles.
• Blend together for as long as possible.
• Let cook on low, medium, and high until ready.
• Voila! The foundation for your jazz ensemble!
• Serve with equal parts of saxophones, trumpets, and trombones.

Many jazz educators say that the rhythm section is the most important section in a jazz band. For sure, it is the least understood by many directors. Therefore, this chapter is quite detailed and full of useful reference materials. Fortunately, many good books and videos are now available for every instrument in the rhythm section, and you can refer to the Resource Guide for additional information. It is imperative that the director get to know the rhythm section as a whole as well as each instrument in the section intimately. Piano, bass, drum set, and guitar players often have little structured ensemble experience, so they may need extra guidance. Always keep in mind that every player in a jazz ensemble benefits from a listening program that identifies musical role models. Listening to recorded examples by professional rhythm section players is particularly important for those students. Although each instrument will be discussed in more detail later, this preface will get you hipper than most of the students.

Metronome Basics

Keeping a steady beat is such an important element of jazz music that I recommend that all players own and practice with a metronome. *This is essential for the rhythm section members*. Using a metronome is absolutely essential for all young jazz players, but rest assured that many if not all professional jazz players still use metronomes as well.

Regarding rhythm, using the metronome allows the student to practice with confidence and purpose. The ultimate goal is for every player to develop a sense of internal time that will allow the individual to play without the assistance of the metronome. The more advanced nuances of jazz that involve playing slightly on top, in the middle, or on the back side of the beat can never be accomplished without a steady internal beat.

A simple battery-powered metronome will do fine; however, there are a variety of other rhythmically advanced metronomes available today. Whatever the choice of device, using it on a regular basis will help the student realize the essence of steady beat.

Big Band and Small Group Functions

The rhythm section has two functions in every jazz chart. First, they must think of themselves as part of a big band ensemble when they are playing together with the winds. Second, they must think of themselves as a combo when soloists perform with only them. This requires additional knowledge and logically expands the listening program for the rhythm section to big bands and combos.

Clarity of Sound

One of the most immediate goals is to achieve clarity of sound in the rhythm section. This can be accomplished efficiently if everyone knows their roles, as well as each other's roles, in the rhythm section.

The word *comping* will come up many times and is simply short for accompanying, or being complementary to all that's going on. This can apply to a variety of settings, such as playing chord changes behind a soloist or supporting a vocalist to help him or her sound good. The number one priority for a good rhythm section always is to complement.

We have all heard young rhythm sections that are not cohesive, where everyone is doing his or her own thing. This creates confusion and can lead to further chaos when the winds are added to the mix.

Make the first rehearsal of the beginning rhythm section as simple as possible. Involve many repeated patterns and repeated chord changes. Concentrate on clarity of sound, balance, and their roles during the performance.

Timekeepers and Harmonic Voices

As described in Chapter 11: The Jazz Combo, the rhythm section is divided into two segments. The bass and drums are the primary timekeepers; the piano and guitar are the harmonic voices responsible for comping. The piano and guitar have a critical role as timekeepers too. The rhythm section set-up should reflect these roles. Proper placement of instruments in the jazz band is extremely important and none is more important than those in the rhythm section. Visual and aural sight lines are extremely important. The functions of instruments in the rhythm section dictate their placement.

JAZZ ENSEMBLE SET-UP

<u>PERFORMANCE</u>

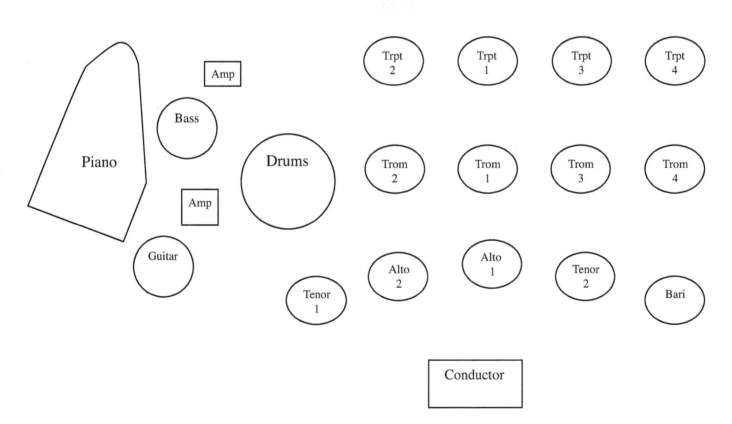

Piano and Guitar

The pianist and guitarist provide the harmonic structure and need to be close enough to hear as well as see each other clearly. As shown in the seating chart, the guitarist is seated just off the right side or the upper register of the keyboard. This placement encourages working together and allows for good communication to determine alternating comping responsibilities.

Bass and Drums

The same is true for the bass and drums. Depending on the preference of the director and the needs of the band, the bass can be on either side of the drummer. The drummer is generally placed between the piano and bass or between the bass and the winds. The latter is the preferred set-up because it separates the drums from the piano and prevents possible bleed-through when the piano is miked. Even with an inexperienced drummer, this set-up is still the best because it forms the most cohesive setting for the rhythm section.

Another option, although less desirable, is placing the bass on the other side of the drummer. Either way, the bass player must be able to see and hear the drummer's ride cymbal clearly to help lock in the time. It is also important that the drummer is able to see the bass player's right hand for the same reason.

Keep Them All Together

All rhythm section instruments should be positioned close to one another so they can function as a compact section. Notice the placement of amps in the set-up diagram. This is important so all players can hear and maintain the balance of sound. It is through these aural and visual lines of communication that a rhythm section of individuals will become a unified and cohesive rhythm section.

In addition, there should not be a large space between the rhythm section and the wind section. Such a gap will lead to a lack of tightness of the whole ensemble.

Dynamics

It is imperative that you insist your rhythm section play with dynamics—the same as you expect from the winds. Actually, the rhythm section is quite capable of playing much louder than the winds. As we know, the winds can only play so loud and then they lose their tone quality and focus. Therefore, it is important that the rhythm section is aware that their dynamics play a very important role in the overall balance of the band.

There are typically two places in every chart where the rhythm section should automatically get softer: (1) on the head or melody, immediately following the introduction, and (2) in the solo section. In both instances, the volume and activity will naturally increase along with the activity of the melody and the soloist. This musical conversation with the soloists and rhythm section is part of the spontaneous musical dialogue of jazz.

Troubleshooting

Each instrument will be discussed individually in the following section of the book, but for now, here are some troubleshooting suggestions that will get your rhythm section students off to a good start in jazz ensemble playing. Although some of the comments here apply to both swing/shuffle and rock/Latin styles, they are primarily aimed at the swing/shuffle style of playing.

Bass

If your bassist plays an electric bass, the bass sound needs to simulate the sound of an acoustic instrument as closely as possible. You can come close to approximating the acoustic sound by working with volume, tone, and reverb controls on the electric bass and the amp. We will discuss amps in detail later, but the following comments will get the electric player off to a good start.

- Set the tone as flat or in the middle of the range (about 5 on a scale of 10).
- Do the same with the treble and bass settings.
- If there is reverb, turn it off.

- To get a cleaner sound, adjustments can be made from that point.
- If the sound is still not satisfactory, turn the bass control down a bit more and the treble control up, which should get rid of the boomy sustained sound of the typical electric bass.
- Do not overcompensate; otherwise, the sound with become twangy.
- It is generally helpful to set the volume below the desired level and have the bass player dig in to create a more articulate sound.
- The player should get started as soon as possible playing an acoustic bass.

The bass is the heartbeat of the band, and it is important that all players, especially the rhythm section, clearly and cleanly hear its pulse. When the bass player is playing a walking bass line, the notes should not be too short. The aim is to create a smooth feel and to lock in with the ride cymbal. Lining up notes and overall time between the drummer and bass player is an ongoing job that will create a solid foundation for the rhythm section. Most published charts have fairly accurate written bass parts; however, jazz bassists will eventually want to learn how to create their own bass lines. See Chapter 16: Bass.

Drums

The drummer often has drum set experience, although it may be in rock, funk, or Latin styles. With or without experience, the drummer will need a lot of help making the transition to jazz playing. Nothing is more detrimental to the overall effect of a jazz band than hearing a drummer play an incorrect style, for instance, a rock beat on a swing chart.

Most drums in a jazz band are smaller that those found in a rock/funk band. The pitch of the drums should gradually ascend from bass drum to large tom-tom to small tom-tom to snare. The snare should have the good, crisp sound that comes from having a snare head that is tighter than the batter head.

The basic cymbals are hi-hat (pair), ride, and crash; others can be added for special effects. An in-depth discussion of drums and cymbals can be found later in this chapter. When purchasing a drum set, test the sound of the drums and cymbals in the music store. If the drum set is not your area of expertise, take along a local pro for advice.

The first order of business will be to have your drummer work on playing the hi-hat and ride cymbal together at various tempi. Although this may seem very elementary, the idea of creating a smooth, flowing sound with just these two instruments is essential. It will add to the foundation that you are trying to create when you combine the drums and the bass.

Once your drummer is comfortable with playing the cymbals correctly, he or she may add the bass drum to mark the phrases. This will give the right overall effect, especially for a young drummer. In this way, you eliminate his or her inclination to use the bass drum as a four-on-the-floor approach, or the typical rock-style pattern. It is essential to encourage your drummer to play along with recordings of good jazz drummers. See Chapter 16C: Drums.

Guitar

The instrument most often used by incoming guitar players in school bands is unfortunately not a hollow-body jazz guitar, so again you are challenged to create a sound that fits the idiom. The proper jazz guitar sound is warm, fat, mellow, and full-bodied with very little treble. Start the same way you did with the bass guitar and its amp. Also be sure the student is using the upper pickup switch on the instrument.

When comping, guitarists should play only the upper four strings, which creates a clean, uncluttered sound and frees up the lower octave range for the bass. Encourage your guitarist to try the Freddie Green style of playing: downstrokes on each of the four beats in a swing chart. It is imperative that he or she achieve an acoustic guitar sound while doing this. In this style, the guitar becomes primarily a rhythmic cog while still maintaining a chordal function. A complete description of how to achieve this technically is included in the guitar segment of this book.

Some jazz arrangements are beginning to include a chord-voicing chart, which is extremely useful. By all means, get your guitarist started on one of the outstanding methods listed in the reference section.

These books provide information on guitar comping and proper jazz voicings.

When comping for solos, the guitarist should keep the volume at a level complementary to the piano, and keep in mind that it is generally preferable for the guitar and piano not to comp behind solos at the same time. Creating an awareness of blend and balance with others in the rhythm section is very important for younger guitarists to understand from the start. See Chapter 16D: Guitar.

Piano

The sound of an *acoustic* piano should serve as the basis for setting the volume level of the entire rhythm section; the other rhythm section members should not overbalance the piano.

Most of the easy to medium-level difficulty charts have piano parts that are written out but are usually somewhat generic. Listen to the demo recording to find out what that piano player did or did not use from the written part. The best parts have comping on chords built from the 3rd or 7th, with no note lower than C below middle C. Generally avoid doubling the bass in the left hand, even though the piano part is often written that way. Also, if you have a chart showing only chord changes, remember that four slashes per bar does not mean you must play a quarter note on each beat.

An inexperienced pianist tends to play way too much in a big band. Everyone wants to be heard, but one of the challenges and rewards of a big band rhythm section is being part of the big musical picture. Many times while the full ensemble is playing, the piano should not play at all. Also, the pianist should not use the sustain pedal unless the music specifically calls for that sound.

Eventually, your pianist will want to learn to comp on his or her own, using good jazz voicings. See Chapter 16A: Piano.

DIRECTOR'S CHECKLIST FOR THE RHYTHM SECTION

- Have all players purchase and use a metronome.

- The bass is the heartbeat of the jazz band.

- The bass and drums are the timekeepers of the jazz band.

- The guitar and piano should take turns comping behind solos.

- The guitar and piano have both harmonic and rhythmic functions in the jazz band.

- Every player in the rhythm section is a timekeeper.

- The players should be able to play as a combo or a big band.

- The acoustic piano volume sets the overall rhythm section volume.

- Dynamics are a must.

- Players should listen to professional recordings of top players on their respective instruments.

- Use a proper rhythm section set-up.

- Get the right equipment (specific details in the piano, bass, drums, and guitar sections of this chapter).

Please refer to the Resource Guide Index.

THE PIANO
ITS ROLE IN THE JAZZ RHYTHM SECTION

by Jerry Tolson and Mike Orta

The primary role of the pianist in a jazz rhythm section is to work with the entire rhythm section to establish a solid time feel and rhythmic groove. Additionally, his or her role is to provide color and depth to the harmonic texture as well as rhythmic punctuation to complement whatever else is going on. This is where we get the word *comp,* which is what the piano player does to accompany and complement the rest of the ensemble. Much of the time, the pianist in your jazz ensemble will play chords in three- to six-part textures. In some cases, however, it may be appropriate for your pianist not to play at all. Alternatively, it may be effective to encourage your pianist to play simple one-line fills or play melodic lines along with another section of the ensemble. Unraveling the mystery of what and when your jazz pianist should play is the goal of this chapter.

Style and Nomenclature

In order to play well within a jazz rhythm section, pianists, guitarists, and bassists must develop an understanding of the jazz language. They must become familiar with the system of chord symbols that jazz composers use. They must then interpret what those symbols mean and create appropriate sounds and rhythms. Pianists must learn to creatively voice lead the notated chords and develop note arrangements, called voicings. Different styles of jazz require different approaches to both chord voicing and comping rhythms. A good jazz pianist must be able to play a variety of styles authentically. Those styles include swing, bebop, fusion, funk, and Latin, which includes Afro-Cuban, samba, salsa, bossa nova, mambo, and others.

Getting Started

The Resource Guide lists a number of excellent books and videos that will help aspiring jazz pianists develop their understanding of jazz nomenclature, patterns, and techniques for playing the jazz styles listed above. Among those resources are *The Jazz Piano Book* by Mark Levine, *The Contemporary Jazz Pianist* by Bill Dobbins, and *101 Montunos* by Rebecca Mauleon-Santana. Mauleon-Santana's book is especially helpful for understanding Afro-Cuban styles.

Listening to Recordings

The most effective way to learn the nuances of playing piano in all jazz styles is by listening to recordings of the great jazz masters and emulating their playing.

For solo piano, the *Smithsonian Collection of Jazz Piano* is an excellent reference that is particularly helpful for understanding the historical development of solo piano styles from ragtime and stride to contemporary jazz. To study small group playing, a recommended starting point is the *Smithsonian Collection of Classic Jazz,* which provides a historical perspective as well as excellent examples to emulate. To hear and understand the swing concept and the pianist's role in big band settings, listen to swing bands such as the Count Basie Orchestra, the Duke Ellington Orchestra, and the Thad Jones/Mel Lewis Orchestra. Good examples of more contemporary stylings are the Stan Kenton Band, the Maynard Ferguson Band, the Woody Herman Orchestra, and the Bob Mintzer Big Band. Finally, for a quick introduction to authentic Latin style, begin by listening to Tito Puente, Pancho Sanchez, Bob Mintzer, and Stan Kenton. The personnel in all of these bands provide excellent examples for students to follow.

Listening is not only the key to understanding style, but it is also the key to a better functioning rhythm section. Concepts of interaction with the other rhythm section members, time feels, and establishing grooves are best learned via aural example. That means listening to each other and listening to professional rhythm sections as models. Each member of the rhythm section should understand and know the roles of each other member of the section so that the section does not sound cluttered and no one is overstepping his or her role within the section.

INTERPRETING WRITTEN PIANO PARTS

Many directors and aspiring players find it daunting to interpret the written piano parts typically published with jazz ensemble charts. One must begin with the understanding that rhythm parts are seldom complete as written. The written parts are merely a guide from which rhythm section players create their parts. Whereas written parts for the horn sections provide specific notes, rhythms, and articulations to play, rhythm parts only occasionally provide that same information. There is no simple way for a composer to notate accurately everything that the rhythm section is expected to provide, particularly for the pianist. On occasions where composers have attempted to provide that information, it is generally not conducive to the creation of a good-sounding part anyway.

Troubleshooting

What a jazz pianist plays beyond the written notes defines a successful player. Here are several typical challenges that may arise when your pianist tries to interpret the written part and how to address them:
1. **Root-position chords** in closed voicings.
2. **Chord symbols** include wrong notes due to unfamiliarity with structure or nomenclature.
3. **Chord voicings** played in an unsuitable register of the piano.
4. **Chord progression** is hampered by awkward movement from chord to chord.
5. **Comping patterns** are not stylistically appropriate.
6. **Cluttered comping patterns** detract from, rather than add to, the texture.

Root-Position Chords

Playing the piano part in a jazz arrangement requires the player to determine what notes to play based on the given symbols. He or she must also decide how to voice these notes for the most appropriate sound in the given context. Root-position chords in closed voicings (within one octave) are generally not suitable for jazz ensemble charts, even if written out that way. As a first step, encourage your pianist to play spread, or open, voicings (greater than an octave), which are much more effective.

Chord Symbols

A written jazz piano part provides information about basic chord information via chord symbols. A combination of letters and numbers identifies the root of the chord and the quality of the sonority (major, minor, and so on). In essence, chord symbols are a shorthand system for chords.

A written jazz piano part also indicates the duration for each chord via chord slashes. The slashes on a piano chart do not indicate specific rhythms but merely the duration that each chord lasts:

Example 1A

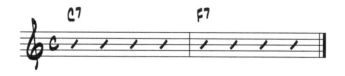

A possible interpretation of the chord slashes on the same chart is indicated below:

Example 1B

When specific rhythms are desired, the well-written chart will indicate the composer's intention:

Example 2

Likewise, when a specific voicing or specific notes are desired, the well-written chart will have them written on the staff:

Example 3

Chord Structure

Most piano players already have the knowledge necessary to develop an understanding of jazz chords. If your pianist understands the notes in the major scale, you can help him or her develop competent jazz piano voicing skills. Jazz chords are based on the foundation of notes 1-3-5-7 of the major scale, and they occur in four categories, Major, Minor, Dominant, and Diminished.

Example 4

The chord symbol consists of a capital letter and signs indicating one of the four basic chord categories. Because of how they usually function, half diminished chords (1-♭3-♭5-♭7) fall under the Minor category while augmented chords (1-3-♯5-♭7) fall into the Dominant category.

Example 5

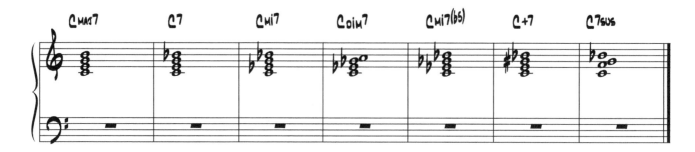

Chord Spellings

Quality	Symbols used	Scale degrees (from the Major scale)
Major	C Maj 7, C MA, CΔ	1, 3, 5, 7
Major	C6	1, 3, 5, 6
Dominant	C7	1, 3, 5, ♭7
Dominant	C7+5, Caug7	1, 3, ♭5, ♭7
Dominant	C7sus	1, 4, 5, ♭7

Note: Dominant chords are frequently notated with upper extensions such as 9, 11 and 13. In a dominant chord the upper extensions can also be raised or lowered. Beginning pianists can ignore the upper extensions at first. These scale degrees can easily be found by realizing that 9 = 2, 11 = 4 and 13 = 6. Therefore C7 ♭9 would contain the notes C, E, G, B♭ and D♭. See "Chord Extensions" below

Minor	Cm7, C-7	1, ♭3, 5, ♭7
Minor	Cm7♭5, Cm7-5	1, ♭3, ♭5, ♭7 (half-diminished chord)
Diminished	Cdim7, C°	1, ♭3, ♭5, ♭♭7

Essential Chord 3rds and 7ths

Notes 3 and 7 of each chord are most crucial for the pianist to play because they outline the harmonic function of the sound. These notes should almost always be included in the voicing. All other notes of the scale are available for color.

The chord root and the 5th add the least amount of color. Therefore, the pianist may omit them from the chord. This is particularly true when a bass player is present because the bass is generally already playing the root and the 5th. The exception is that when 5 is altered, it should be present in the chord sound.

Suspended Chords and Polychords

A sus chord is a dominant chord with note 4 suspended or substituted for 3 and not resolved (Csus, C7sus4, or C11). Polychords, which call for the combination of two different chord sonorities, are indicated with one chord above the other separated by a horizontal line: D7.

                       C

Different Bass Note

Chords to be played over a different bass note from the root are indicated with a slash, i.e., C/D, which implies a C triad over a D in the bass. *If there is a bass player, the piano player need not play the bass note.*

Chord Extensions

Many jazz chord symbols also include numbers such as 6, 7, 9, 11, or 13. *A chord symbol that has only a capital letter and a number 7, 9, or 13 is a dominant-quality chord with a ♭7. Note that the major-quality category is the only one that uses a natural (major) 7.*

When scale notes such as the 2nd, 4th, and 6th are used above the foundation notes, they are called extensions and are respectively referred to as the 9th, 11th, and 13th.

Extensions enhance the color of the chord and may be altered for additional color and tension. These alterations are indicated with ♭ or ♯ signs in parentheses next to the rest of the chord symbol [C7(♯9)]. Note that when the 5th is lowered or raised, there is an indication in the chord symbol in parentheses as well. [Cm7(♭5)]. The 11th, if added to major or dominant chords, is always raised [CΔ7(♯11) or C7(♯11)] to avoid an augmented octave between the 3rd and the 11th. However, adding the 11th to minor or diminished chords provides a nice colorful addition without causing any undesirable dissonances.

Chord Voicing

There are many ways to voice chords, and a number of books are published that deal with chord voicing techniques (see Resource Guide). Ultimately, the style and rhythmic groove of a piece should determine how chords are voiced. Different pieces and different sections of a particular arrangement may require different voicing textures ranging from three to six or more notes. One basic technique is discussed below and on the next page, which establishes either the 3rd or the 7th as the lowest sounding note. By alternating voicings with the third of the chord as the lowest note (shown as Voicing A below and on the next page) with voicings that use the 7th (Voicing B), the voice leading is smooth and continuous. Voicings can be adjusted according to the ability of the individual student. For novices, a three-note voicing is sufficient. The three-note voicing may also be used in the left hand when a solo or melodic line is necessary in the right hand. As described below, this voicing technique is flexible enough to be used in a variety of settings, and will, with a player with basic scale knowledge, allow you to create a functional pianist for your jazz ensemble.

Recommended Voicing Range

The range of chord voicings should generally fall between C below middle C to the second C above middle C. Lower than that, the sound is too muddy. Higher than that, the sound is too thin.

Suggested Three-Note Voicings

C7 (dominant chord) is used as the example for the voicings.

Three-note voicings: [A] 3-7-9   [B] 7-3-5 (6)

Example 6

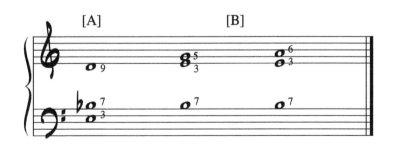

Note that the 9th is used in voicing A instead of the root. Likewise, in voicing B you may substitute 6 for 5. Both of these substitutions provide more color to enhance the sound. Since the root and 5th are not essential notes for the quality identity and as long as there is a bass player, the use of other notes by the piano player is preferred to give the sound a fuller texture. Extensive doubling of notes such as the root and the 5th should be avoided.

Suggested Four-Note Voicings

Four-note voicings: [A] LH 3-7 RH 9-5 [B] LH 7-3RH (5) 6-9

Example 7

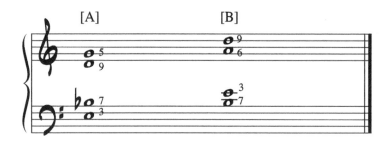

Suggested Five-Note Voicings

Five-note voicings: [A] LH 3-7 (6) RH 9-5-1   [B] LH 7-3 RH 6-9-5

Example 8

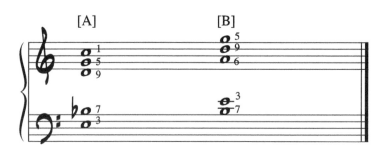

With major chords, substitute 9 for 1 or 6 for 7 (Voicing A) to avoid an augmented octave between the major 7th and the root.

With minor chords, you may substitute 5-9-4 RH (Voicing B) for additional color.

Suggested Six-Note Voicings

Six-note voicings: [A] LH 3-7-9 RH 6-1-5   [B] LH 7-3-6 RH 9-5-1
Note that in Voicing A, 6 replaces 5 at the bottom of the RH to avoid doubling notes.

Example 9

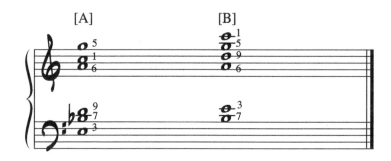

Voicing in 4ths

Another effective chord voicing technique is comprised of 4ths and works for several chord symbols. This voicing technique is often heard in fusion and more contemporary style arrangements.

Example 10

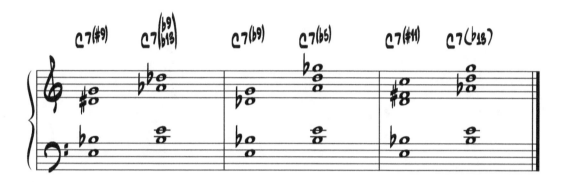

Alterations

Alterations (♭5, ♯5, ♯11, ♭9, ♯9, ♭13) provide increased tension and harmonic interest and are easily inserted into voicings:

Example 11

Substitute Chords

This paragraph applies to a more advanced player. Another way to increase harmonic interest and create tension is to use substitute chords. One of the most common substitutions is the tritone substitution, which allows you to interchange chords with the same 3rd and 7th (i.e., C7 and G♭7). Chords with significant common tones can also be substituted for each other. An example of this type of substitution would be to use an Em7 in place of a CΔ9. The use of passing chords, which involves inserting diatonic or chromatic chords when moving from one chord to another, is another way to increase harmonic interest and create variety. This technique is called chord interpolation.

Example 12

Chord Progressions

In general, chord progressions move in one of three ways according to the relationship of the roots of each chord. When moving from chord to chord, smooth voice leading is important to remember. Root movement occurs either by major or minor 2nd, major or minor 3rd, or perfect or augmented 4th. By maintaining either the A voicing or the B voicing or alternating from one to the other, smooth voice leading can be achieved with a minimum effort. The application of three rules of thumb will help in the selection of the chord voicing to use.

1. When the chord root moves by a 4th or 5th, switch to the other voicing.

Example 13

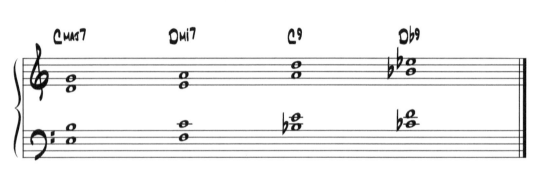

2. When the chord root moves a 2nd (minor or major), maintain the same voicing.

Example 14

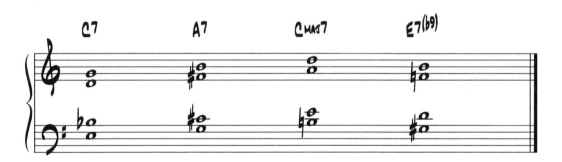

3. When the chord root moves by a 3rd, choose the voicing that involves the smoothest movement and leads best to the next chord.

Example 15

When applying these rules of thumb, it is important to keep the voicing range in mind. Register changes, when they are necessary to avoid going beyond the recommended voicing range, are best executed on chords that last for a measure or more. Shifting the register or changing the voicing on a given chord can also provide a needed color or texture change.

Routine practicing of drills will help your pianist become proficient at playing open-voice, rootless chords. A very successful practice drills is to alternate Voicings A and B while playing chords of one quality around the circle of 5ths. While Example 16 shows minor 7th chords, the same should be done with dominant and major quality chords.

Example 16

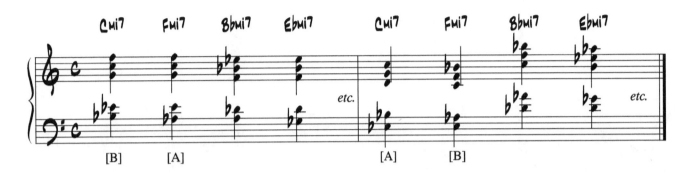

Example 17 demonstrates chromatic movement with major 7th chords. Practice this drill with the other quality chords as well.

Example 17

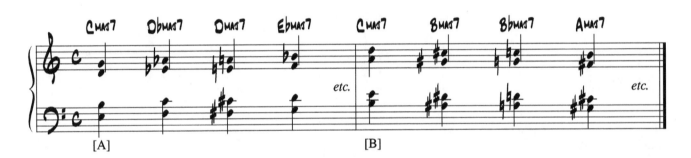

Practicing voicing drills in chord patterns as they normally resolve in compositions is extremely helpful. Example 18 demonstrates dominant-major resolution, while Example 19 demonstrates minor-dominant.

Example 18

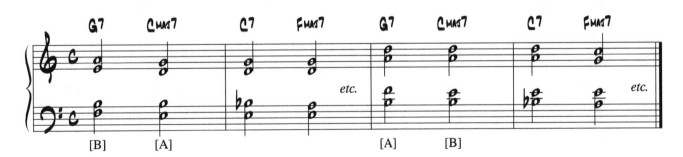

Example 19

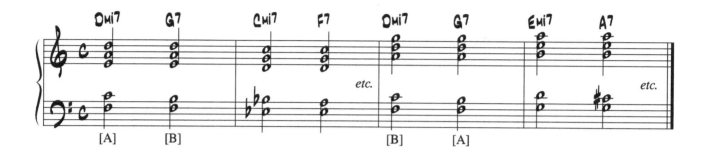

Example 20 is for practice of ii-V-I chord progressions.

Example 20

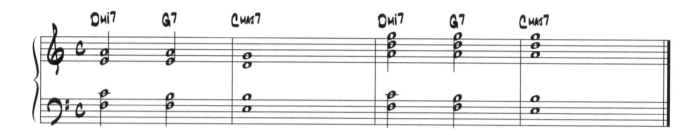

Example 21 demonstrates the I-vi-ii-V chord progressions used so often in popular music.

Example 21

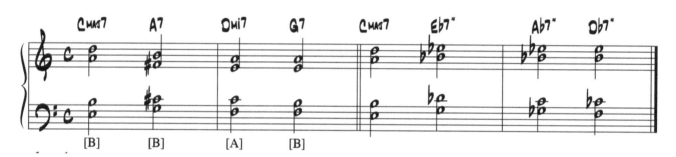

Practice of all the previous drills as well as other typical chord progressions such as blues changes and "Rhythm changes" will ensure that your pianist develops excellent technique. In the real world, however, your pianist will probably practice only the chords found in the charts the jazz ensemble is currently playing. He or she should be encouraged to create a practice routine for those chords.

Comping Textures

The above examples are shown in whole notes; however, the pianist should develop a vocabulary of comping rhythms to be used with these voicings. One of the most difficult tasks of a developing jazz pianist is knowing what to play and when to play. When comping for a soloist, whether in a combo or big band setting, he or she must listen to the soloist and adjust the rhythm patterns, register, style, dynamics, and melodic fills to the melody being played by the soloist. The pianist's role here is to make the soloist sound good, and great care should be taken not to play too much or get in the way. The pianist will have plenty of opportunities as soloist to display all of his or her virtuosity.

Incorporate Rhythmic Patterns

It is also important to incorporate rhythmic patterns that are appropriate to the style of the music. That means if the selection has a swing feel, the piano comping rhythms should swing as well. It is easy to derive such comping rhythms from rhythms heard in the horn section. Rhythms should be repetitive but not too busy, especially if the full band is playing. Often a two- or four-measure repeated rhythmic pattern is effective.

Leave Breathing Room

When the full ensemble is playing, it is not necessary for the piano player to play all of the time. This applies even if the written part does not indicate rests. The decision of when and how much to play should be made by your pianist as he or she listens to what is going on in the remainder of the ensemble.

Comping does not mean that your pianist should play on all beats for the duration that the chord lasts, or that a chord must sound on the downbeat of each chord change. Leaving space is important to allow the sound texture to breathe.

Avoid the Damper Pedal

Use of the damper pedal (sustain pedal) on an acoustic piano allows all the piano strings to vibrate sympathetically with everything being played by all the horns as well as the drum set. The result is a very muddy sound for your ensemble. Most pianists have played only in solo situations prior to joining the jazz ensemble and are accustomed to using the damper pedal generously. They will not be aware of the problems this creates for the overall sound and will have difficulty breaking the damper pedal habit and learning to play with finger legato. Some directors have found it helpful to place a book under the pedal to disable it during rehearsals.

Swing Comping

Example 22 shows sample swing comping rhythms.

Example 22

Blues Comping

Example 23 shows sample comping for a 12-bar blues.

Example 23

Block Chord Comping

In swing styles, the block chord approach is often used. Listen for holes in the texture where chords can be inserted. Occasionally anticipating the chord change by playing on the "and" of beat 4 of the previous measure can help propel the rhythmic feel. Changing the comping pattern every eight measures or for different sections of the form of the tune prevents monotony in the rhythm section sound.

Tension and Release

Moving the entire voicing up or down a half step, whole step, or minor 3rd and then returning to the original sound is an effective way to achieve harmonic and rhythmic variety. This technique of introducing and resolving tension is called planing (Example 24). This technique is very effective when the chord progression is relatively static. Many fusion and rock-oriented tunes have such chord progressions.

Example 24

Latin Styles

For Afro-Cuban and other Latin styles, the montuno, a repetitive linear pattern, is commonly used. A montuno is usually two, four, or eight measures long. Although it is less dense harmonically, the montuno provides basic harmonic information and establishes a definitive rhythmic foundation.

Example 25

Often, tunes in Afro-Cuban style have simple harmonic structures with a limited number of chords. Therefore, the establishment of a solid rhythmic groove becomes more important in the style. The upbeat is significantly emphasized in a montuno, which corresponds with the rhythmic emphasis on upbeats in the entire rhythm section. Refer to the chapter on Latin jazz for a more complete discussion of the various styles and how to interpret them. Mark Levine's *The Jazz Piano Book* and Rebecca Mauleon's *The Salsa Guidebook* and *101 Montunos* as well as the other books listed at the end of chapter are suggested references for understanding Latin jazz piano style. Important professional models of Afro-Cuban and Latin styles of playing include Bebo Valdes, Chucho Valdes, Emiliano Salvador, Gonzalo Rubalcaba, Eddie Palmieri, and Danilo Perez.

Comping Greats

The best sources for rhythmic comping ideas are recordings of jazz greats. The comping of pianists Wynton Kelly and Bill Evans on Miles Davis's "Kind of Blue" is an excellent small group example to follow. Another example of small group comping can be found on Horace Silver's "Song for My Father." Likewise, the uncomplicated work of Count Basie with his orchestra demonstrates the effective use of space and simplicity. Another example of big band piano comping is the work of Alan Broadbent, Harold Danko, and Andy Laverne with the Woody Herman Orchestra on recordings in the 1960s and 1970s. Transcriptions of the comping found on the *Jamey Aebersold Play-a-long* series of recordings are a very effective source for studying voicings and the concept of planing.

Remove the Clutter

If both piano and guitar are present, as a general rule, they should not both comp at the same time. Since the concept of comping implies the freedom to respond to the sounds of the moment, it is disastrous to have both guitar and piano comping at the same time. To avoid cluttered comping, one player should provide a consistent or sustained rhythm (called a pad) while the other player comps. Another solution is to have one player rest while the other player comps.

IMPROVISATION

Improvisation is one of the most important elements in jazz. The ability to create melodies extemporaneously over a given harmonic progression is a desirable skill for not only pianists but also for all jazz players. When soloing, the jazz pianist primarily uses the right hand for the solo line while the left hand provides the harmonic foundation. As noted in the voicing section above, the use of three-note comping voicings in the left hand is sufficient for accompanying the right-hand solo line. Developing solo technique involves learning scales, modes, arpeggios, and jazz licks that are part of the jazz vocabulary. Imitating the masters, assimilating the information garnered from imitation, and then applying that information in creative ways to the given harmonic situation is the best way to learn soloing.

ELECTRONICS

There are often situations where an electronic keyboard is necessary or preferred. Out-of-tune acoustic pianos can compromise the best of performances. Likewise, for some performance venues, an acoustic piano may not be available. In this case, one should consider an electronic keyboard. While budget is always a consideration, directors should invest in the best equipment possible. With proper care, the investment will pay long-term benefits and savings.

It is preferable that an instrument with weighted keys be selected to give the player a touch and feel that is as close to an acoustic piano as possible. Companies such as Roland, Korg, Kurzweil, and Yamaha offer many good choices. They offer a variety of sound options including an acoustic piano sound that approximates well the authentic acoustic sound. It is also important to purchase a good solid keyboard stand and a good keyboard amplifier. Roland and Yamaha offer good amplifier choices. The amplifier should have multiple tone controls to achieve the optimum sound from the keyboard. Special effects such as reverb and delay are desirable but not necessary for fusion or contemporary pieces. It is best to test the keyboard and amplifier together in the showroom and also in your performance venue. Prices for the better keyboards range from $1,000 and up. The range for a quality amplifier is from $300 and up. If used properly, the electronic keyboard is a good alternative.

Summary

By combining knowledge of jazz vocabulary, listening, and practice, the road to a successful jazz ensemble pianist is readily traveled. Keep in mind the following tips to help your pianist achieve success:

DIRECTOR'S CHECKLIST FOR PIANO

• The pianist's role as an accompanist is to provide harmony, color, rhythmic interest, and fills.

• Comping should fit with the style, dynamics, register, and rhythm patterns created by the soloist.

• The appropriate range for comping is from the C below middle C to the second C above middle C.

- The damper pedal should not be used in jazz ensembles in 99.9% of performance situations. Learn finger legato.

- Open-voiced, rootless chords should be used for comping.

- The 3rd and 7th of each chord are essential for defining the chord quality and should be present in each voicing.

- 13ths (6ths) and 9ths (2nds) can be added for color and tension.

- Roots and 5ths are least important and may be omitted unless the 5th has been altered.

- Move from chord to chord as efficiently as possible. Go to the nearest inversion of the next chord with the smallest amount of intervallic movement.

- When chords last for four beats or more, harmonic interest can be added by change of register, change of voicing, and/or planing.

- Playing too little is preferable to playing too much.

- Study with a professional jazz piano teacher.

Suggested Recordings

COLLECTIONS FEATURING PIANISTS

The Instrumental History of Jazz; N2KE-10004

Smithsonian Collection of Classic Jazz; RD033 A519477

Jazz Piano: A Smithsonian Collection; RD039 A421010

SMALL GROUPS FEATURING PIANISTS

Adderley, Cannonball; *The Cannonball Adderley Quintet in San Francisco;*
    Bobby Timmons, piano; Riverside 1157.

Brown, Clifford; *Compact Jazz;* Richie Powell, piano; EmArcy 842933-2.

Brown, Ray; *Some of My Best Friends Are Singers;* Geoff Keezer, piano; Telarc 83441.

Corea, Chick; *Light as a Feather;* ASIN 0000046YK.

Davis, Miles; *Kind of Blue;* Wynton Kelly and Bill Evans, piano; Columbia CK 40579.

Evans, Bill; *The Village Vanguard Sessions;* Milestones 47002; and *Waltz for Debby;* Riverside 9399.

Garland, "Red"; *A Garland of Red;* Prestige 7064; and *Groovy;* Prestige 7148.

Hancock, Herbie; *Maiden Voyage;* Blue Note CDP 546339; and *Speak Like a Child;*
    Blue Note 84279.

Kelly, Wynton and Wes Montgomery; *Smokin' at the Half Note;* Verve 829578.

Palmieri, Eddie; *Azucar Pa' Ti;* Tico 1122.

Rubalcaba, Gonzalo; *Live in Havana;* Messidor 15960.

Shew, Bobby; *Salsa Caliente;* Mark Levine, piano; MAMA Records MMF 1023.

Silver, Horace; *Song for My Father;* Blue Note CDP 584185.

Valdes, Bebo; *Sabor de Cuba;* Palladium PLP-123.

Valdes, Chucho and Arturo Sandoval; *Straight Ahead;* Jazz House JHR 007.

Walton, Cedar with Art Blakey; *Mosaic;* Blue Note 46523.

BIG BAND FEATURING PIANISTS

Count Basie Orchestra; *Basie Straight Ahead; Essential Basie,* 3 Vols., Columbia.

Dizzy Gillespie United Nations Band; *Manteca;* Quintessence GJ-25211.

Duke Ellington Orchestra; *Ellington at Newport;* Columbia CK 40587.

Maynard Ferguson Band; *MF Horn 4 & 5, Live at Jimmy's;* Pete Jackson, piano; Columbia PG 32732.

Bob Mintzer; *Latin From Manhattan;* DMP 523.

Tito Puente; *El Rey;* Concord Picante 0118.

Stan Kenton Orchestra; *Kenton '76;* Creative World Records; ST 1076; and *Cuban Fire;* Capital CDP 96260 2.

Thad Jones/Mel Lewis Orchestra, *New Life;* Roland Hanna, piano; A&M Records; SP 707.

Woody Herman Orchestra; *The Raven Speaks;* Harold Danko, piano; Fantasy 9416.

PIANO SOLOISTS

Barron, Kenny; *Autumn in New York;* Uptown 2726.

Ellington, Duke; *Duke Ellington and John Coltrane;* MCA Impulse 39103.

Flanagan, Tommy; *...Plays the Music of Harold Arlen;* Inner City 1071.

Garner, Erroll; *Concert by the Sea;* Columbia CK 40589.

Green, Benny; *Prelude;* Criss Cross 1036.

Harris, Barry; *Bulls-Eye;* Prestige 7600.

Hines, Earl "Fatha"; *Harlem Lament;* Portrait Masters RK 44119.

Jamal, Ahmad; *Ahmad's Blues;* Chess GRD 803.

Jarrett, Keith; *Standards,* Vol. 1; ECM 811966.

Monk, Thelonious; *Monk's Dream;* Columbia CK 40786.

Miller, Mulgrew; *Wingspan;* Landmark 1515.

Powell, Bud; *Jazz Giant;* Verve P229937; and *The Amazing Bud Powell;* Blue Note 81503/81504.

Peterson, Oscar; *Night Train;* Verve 68538.

Tatum, Art; *Piano Starts Here, 1933 and 1949;* Columbia CS 9655.

Tyner, McCoy; *Time for Tyner;* Blue Note 84307.

Please refer to the Resource Guide Index.

THE BASS
ITS ROLE IN THE JAZZ RHYTHM SECTION

by Nicky Orta

The jazz rhythm section's responsibility is to establish a solid time feel and rhythmic groove for the entire jazz ensemble. Naturally the bassist must have good technique. Let's explore exactly what that means in the context of a big band or jazz combo. To start with, the bassist's sense of time must be very accurate yet flexible. He or she must have the ability to read some basic rhythms and lines and have a good ear to grasp quickly the parts that he or she cannot read at sight. The bassist should be able to construct a decent walking bass line. Finally, the bassist must listen to other members of the band and have an understanding of the styles they are going to be playing. Here's how to get your bass player heading down the right path in these areas.

STYLE AND NOMENCLATURE

The only way your bassist can become truly adept at playing jazz is by *listening* to the artists that are representative of the various jazz styles. Jazz is one of the most inclusive music forms ever. It incorporates traditional straight-ahead jazz, rock/funk influences, a vast array of Latin styles, classical music, and so on. The same applies to the more current types of charts. For instance, great contemporary composers/arrangers like Maria Schneider and Bob Mintzer run the gamut of styles in their compositions. This means that your bassist has to be able to play convincing grooves in many different styles. Similarly, if you're going to play a Duke Ellington chart, your bassist needs to listen to the Ellington band to be able to emulate the sound of the bass and the kinds of bass lines that are going to fit that particular style.

Getting Started

The Resource Guide lists books and videos that will help aspiring jazz bassists develop their understanding of jazz style, nomenclature, chord structure, constructing walking bass lines, and so on. See also the section entitled "Interpreting the Written Bass Part" later in this chapter for a basic overview of part reading.

The serious bassist should consider studying with a private teacher. Learning on one's own or playing by ear can take one only so far. A good teacher can help a student develop good technique; time feel; sight-reading abilities; ear-training; knowledge of theory, harmony, and rhythm; understanding of various styles; and other important musical concepts. The less practice the bassist has with these concepts, the more difficult and time-consuming it's going to be for you to convey these ideas during your rehearsals.

INTERPRETING WRITTEN BASS PARTS

Learning the jazz idiom involves the issue of *nomenclature*. There are specific chord names, scale names, and chord symbols, as well as concepts, like playing "in 2," or various groove indications with which the bassist needs to become familiar.

Troubleshooting

The written bass parts published with jazz ensemble charts are generally intended as a guide to help the bass player create his or her own part. Following are several typical areas that need attention by less experienced players.

- Chord symbols
- Playing "in 2"
- Time feel
- Walking bass lines
- Memorization
- Hand technique
- How to practice

Chord Symbols

There are various ways to notate the same chord. For example, here are several different ways you might see a D minor 7 chord written on a chart:

D-7

Dmi7

Dmin7

Dm7

All of those different notations mean the same thing. Also, the bassist needs to know that when he or she sees that chord, he or she will probably be using a *Dorian* scale to play over that particular chord. This kind of information is part of what one will learn in jazz theory and is essential to creating effective bass lines, particularly walking bass lines.

Playing "in 2"

At some point when conducting swing tunes, you will come across the direction to the bassist to play "in 2." This means that instead of playing four quarter notes to the measure, the bassist should play two half notes to the measure. Playing roots and 5ths of the chords is both acceptable and effective in these sections. The more experienced player may choose other notes, of course.

Time Feel

Time feel is undoubtedly the most important element for a bassist since, along with the drums, the bass is the foundation upon which the groove is laid. There are two essential components of developing good time: pulse and feel.

Pulse

One component is having a good pulse—that is, laying down the quarter-note pulse in a precise way. Practicing technical studies and grooves using a metronome will allow the bassist to gauge how well or poorly he or she follows the basic pulse.

Another option is using a drum machine as a practice tool. This has its advantages since one can play bass to a set groove programmed on the machine. (Much studio work involves playing to a prerecorded drum track, so this kind of training is both beneficial and practical.)

When playing along with a metronome or drum machine, one should use a wide range of dynamics. Bass players commonly speed up when playing louder and slow down when playing softer. Practicing dynamics with the metronome can help prevent this problem.

Feel

The other component is the time feel. When playing swing, it can be helpful to set the metronome at half the speed of the actual pulse and think of the clicks as beats 2 and 4, which is often what the drummer will play on the hi-hat when playing jazz.

Note length is an important factor in swing feel as well as other styles. Patterns where one note is played legato and the following note is staccato may sound a great deal different and can create very disparate results.

Straight vs. Swing Eighth Notes

The inexperienced big band bassist needs to learn the difference between straight eighths and swing eighths. The best way to describe swing eighths is to take an eighth-note triplet figure and tie the first two partials of the triplet together.

Example 1

Try playing straight eighths and then playing swing eighths to feel the difference. It is a good idea for the bassist to practice all scales, arpeggios, and other technical studies both with straight feel and swing feel. Keep in mind that the slower the tempo is, the more pronounced the swing eighths are; the faster the tempo, the less pronounced they are.

Interaction With the Drummer

Finally, bass players should analyze drummers as well as bassists when learning the jazz idiom. In the rhythm section, the drummer and the bassist together form the foundation of the groove. Note how they interact. When the drummer is playing busy patterns, does the bassist tend to anchor the groove more? Are there times when the drummer may be the one anchoring the groove, thus allowing the bassist to play more freely? What you want to help your bassist avoid is overplaying and getting in the way of the other musicians. Remember: the function of the bass is to *support* the music.

Walking Bass Lines

Since the big band bassist will frequently be dealing with walking bass lines, let's examine some of the elements in their construction:
- Scales and arpeggios
- Chromatics, non-chord tones, inversions
- Note length

Scales and Arpeggios

Scales and arpeggios form the essential basis of the waking bass line. However, using only one of these tools is insufficient. Quite often, an inexperienced bassist will play something like Example 2 on a blues progression. This bass line is laden with arpeggios, which makes it sound predictable, forced, and generally uninteresting.

Example 2 shows excessive use of arpeggios.

Example 2

Now, let's look at the same progression in Example 3, but this time we'll add the scalar element to the bass line. You can see that by using both scales and arpeggios, we already improve the overall sound and flow of the line.

Example 3 shows scales and arpeggios combined.

Example 3

Chromatics, Non-Chord Tones, and Chord Inversions

To make the lines more smooth and interesting, we should add chromatic lines, non-chord tones, and chord inversions as shown in Example 4. Notice in measures 8 and 12 how we approach the roots of each chord by a half step, from either above or below the roots. These different approaches allow us to create long, flowing lines that are musically interesting and keep the momentum of the line going. Try looking at simple tunes from a fakebook and experiment with creating your own bass lines using the examples as guides.

Example 4

Note Length

An important factor regarding walking bass lines is note length. In general, you want the notes to be played long (legato). You don't want to hear space between the notes because this creates a very thumping, disjointed sound.

An exception to this would be when trying to emulate the sound of the upright bass in very early big-band styles. The best way to get the kind of control that allows a bassist to be in command of note length is to practice doing it with all scales, arpeggios, and technical studies. For example, if you are playing a C-major scale, play the first note C, making sure you keep that note pressed until your next finger plays the D. *Do not remove your finger* from the C until you play the D. If you do this from note to note, you will be playing legato. You should be able to do this at all tempos.

Walking Bass Lines Summary

As a general rule for the young bassist learning to play walking bass lines, he or she should play consonant scale and chord tones and lay down the root on the downbeat of each new chord. With practice, analysis, and experience, more chromatic tones and other embellishments may be added to his or her bass lines.

Memorization

A very helpful element in chart reading is memorization. Too often the young bassist buries his or her head in the chart and is so concerned with the paper that he or she cannot listen to the other musicians who are part of the music-making process. Furthermore, the bassist needs to make frequent eye contact with you as conductor, since you will be giving cues throughout the chart. The less your bassist needs to rely on the chart, the more relaxed he or she will be to give attention to other important areas. The chart should ultimately be used as a guide to the music. If you see familiar patterns or things that repeat quite often like open solo sections, encourage your bassist to memorize the rhythms and the progression.

Hand Technique

Lack of good hand technique is going to be the first obstacle for the inexperienced bassist. A lot of the jazz repertoire includes quick tempos for which the bassist is going to have to be able to create a bass line for a sustained period of time. If his or her technique is poor, he or she will not be able to keep up. The time will drag and the groove will come to a halt. If the bassist is playing a ballad and hasn't used the metronome creatively as part of his or her studies, he or she is going to have a difficult time dealing with the slower tempos as well. So it is imperative that the bassist have a good teacher or at the very least a good method book.

How to Practice

The best way to develop a good technique is to practice correctly. The esteemed guitar and bass instructor Vince Bredice often told his students, "Practice doesn't make perfect. *Perfect* practice makes perfect." Here's how you might help your bassist focus his or her practice sessions.

Slow and Accurate

You can practice all day long, but if you're not practicing correctly, you're basically wasting a lot of valuable time. The golden rule is to do everything slowly and accurately. When you first come across a new scale or arpeggio, analyze it, sing it, learn good fingerings for them, and set the metronome to the slowest tempo at which you can play them accurately. Through constant repetition, you will eventually commit these scales, arpeggios, and concepts to memory. Once memorized, you can increase the tempo on the metronome slightly each day. You'll notice your technique improving if you follow these basic rules.

Environment and Practice Tools

Other important factors that will help you get the most out of your practice sessions are environment, practice tools, planning, and mental preparation. Your environment should be conducive to focused practice. A quiet place free from distractions like the TV, noise, and concurrent activities is essential. A practice room is ideal—a place where you go specifically to practice. Everything you're going to need for your practice sessions should be there and ready to go: stool, music stand with light, amplifier, tuner, metronome, study books, manuscript paper, a sound system, and a keyboard. If all of these things are in place, then you only have to deal with having a focused practice plan.

Set Specific Goals

Having specific, realistic practice goals is important. You don't want to have an all-encompassing goal like "I want to learn jazz" when you step into the practice room. Instead, you need to focus on maybe two or three specific things that you want to work on that week, say several scales and arpeggios, or a bass soli in a big band chart. By narrowing down your goal, you can realistically achieve what you set out to do. Also, don't waste time by working on things that you can already do. Focus on those things that give you trouble, and plan your lesson for the week to target those problem areas.

Encouragement

Finally, once you begin practicing, make that your sole priority for the two hours or so that you devote to it each day. It is only through immersion, concentration, and diligent practice that you will learn music.

Remember that everything you learn in music is a process of accumulation. Be patient. Don't expect to digest everything immediately. Even though we live in a culture that thrives on fast and instant everything, some things cannot be rushed. If you take your time, listen, study, and diligently get involved with the music, you'll surely achieve your goals. Now, get to it and enjoy the excitement, beauty, and interaction of making music!

EQUIPMENT

Electric Bass

The young bassist playing in a big band for the first time will probably own an electric bass. There are many great sounding basses available in all price ranges: Carvin, Peavey, Fender, Yamaha, Warwick, Pedulla, Alembic, Sadowsky, and Fodera. The bassist needs to shop around for the bass that accommodates his or her aesthetic sense as well as financial situation. Some things to consider are available tone controls on the bass (many of the better basses have controls for bass, treble, bass boost/cut, and treble boost/cut), weight of the bass, scale length, and type of bass, for instance, fretted, fretless, four-string, five-string, six-string. Your bassist's ears and hands should be the ultimate guide in what he or she decides to buy.

Authentic Sounds

How do you produce an authentic sounding Basie or Ellington groove with an electric bass? Clearly the electric bass sounds different from the acoustic bass, but through sufficient experimentation with the tone controls on the bass as well as with the available EQ options on a decent amplifier, you can approximate the sound of an acoustic bass. This can be achieved, for example, by cutting some treble on both the bass and the amp to about the midway setting, adding bass boost, and placing the striking hand closer to the end of the fingerboard where the sound is fatter than when you are playing closer to the bridge. On the amplifier, I'll usually set the output level to the midway point (or a little past the midway point) and work with the volume control to get a clean sound. I make sure the volume setting on the amp is high enough to give me room to adjust the volume on my bass. This way I don't have to go to the amp during a performance to make adjustments. The bassist will probably find himself or herself working out several EQs for different stylistic situations (slap/funk sound, Jaco Pastorius type of sound, upright sound, and so on). This is largely an area of experimentation. Explore your bass and gear to work out the sounds you're aiming for.

Acoustic Bass

The bassist should also pursue acoustic bass studies. Many universities and high schools have practice basses, but the student would have to invest some money to purchase an upright bass for home study. There are vast differences in electric and upright technique, so the student who is going from one to the other should be prepared for changes in fingerings, hand positions, body position, special techniques such as bowing, and amount of physical effort required. It is definitely an asset to be able to double on electric and acoustic. For one thing, there will be more job opportunities if your bassist is adept at both. In terms of big-band playing, being a doubler means he or she will be able to offer a greater amount of authentic sounds.

Amplification

Amplification is the next major consideration. Again, there are many types of amplifiers for all kinds of situations. Combo amps are popular since they combine a good, powerful sound for most situations and are both portable and affordable. Here's a short list of some of the many available combo amps. Most good music stores have them in stock for you to try out.
- Hartke Kickback series
- Hartke 2115
- SWR Workingman's series
- GK 400RB / 112
- GK 400RB / 115
- GK 150S-112 Micro-Bass Combo
- Trace Elliott 712-7 Combo

For more power necessary for gigs in large halls or concert settings, you can purchase separate speaker cabinets, bass heads, and power amps according to necessity. Some popular companies that make both speaker cabinets and bass heads are Hartke, Eden, Trace Elliott, Ampeg, and SWR. A common basic set-up for a larger rig is usually a couple of speakers, say a cabinet with two 10-inch speakers and another cabinet with a 15-inch speaker powered by a bass head. This kind of set-up is usually quite sufficient for most kinds of gigs. You can enhance this basic set-up with various effects like a reverb unit, a compressor, a noise reduction unit, a parametric equalizer, and many other configurations.

As an aside, it should be noted that a good sound begins with the hands. If your bassist has bad technique and lack of control of his or her instrument, good amplification is only going to make those defects more audible.

DIRECTOR'S CHECKLIST FOR BASS

• Listen to jazz bassists in all styles of jazz.

• Work on establishing authentic grooves in each style, including proper sound.

• Purchase and use a metronome in individual practice time.

• Develop a consistent practice setting and routine.

• Work on becoming a good reader of both notes and chord changes.

• Understand how to construct walking bass lines.

• Work on improving your ear; the bass is the foundation of the harmonic structure for the jazz ensemble.

• Learn to play both upright and electric bass.

• Study with a private teacher.

• Use good equipment.

• Enjoy the excitement, beauty, and interaction of making music!

Suggested Listening

Chick Corea, *Friends,* 1978 Polydor (849 071-2).
Miles Davis, *Kind of Blue* (remastered), 1959 Sony Jazz (CK64935).
Miles Davis, *Miles Ahead,* 1957, Columbia (CK 65121).
Bill Evans, *Portrait in Jazz,* 1959, Riverside (OJCCD-088-2).
Herbie Hancock, *Maiden Voyage* (remastered).
Keith Jarrett, *Standards,* Vols. 1, 2, 3.
Bob Mintzer, *Incredible Journey,* 1985, DMP Records.
Charlie Parker, *Confirmation: Best of the Verve Years,* Verve (314 527 815-2).
Weather Report, *Heavy Weather,* 1977, Columbia (CK 34418).

Please refer to the Resource Guide Index.

THE DRUM SET

ITS ROLE IN THE JAZZ RHYTHM SECTION

by Remy Taveris

The drum set is the driving force not only within the rhythm section but also for the entire jazz ensemble. Its primary role is to be a time-keeper and work in tandem with the entire rhythm section to establish a solid time feel and rhythmic groove. Second, the drum set has the critical responsibility of controlling the dynamics and setting the style and mood in the band. Third, the drum set acts as a gel among the different colors of the band with various cymbals that serve as a constant carpet of sound for the band.

Regardless of complexity, the drummer needs to be as clear as possible, both with what is played and how it sounds. When the drummer makes the form of the arrangement clear and effectively sets up and plays certain section and ensemble figures with the band, everybody is confident, and it becomes a living team effort.

A famous drummer giving a clinic to a group of drummers said he believes "if the phone doesn't ring, it's you." His meaning was simple: The drummer's role is to make everyone sound good, and as a result, the drummer's reputation will speak for itself.

Let's explore specific ways to coach your drum set player to become a more solid time-keeper, mood-setter, and team player.

STYLE AND GROOVE

In order to play well within a jazz rhythm section, drummers, pianists, guitarists, and bassists must develop an understanding of the jazz language. A good jazz drummer must be able to create authentic grooves in a variety of jazz styles, such as swing, shuffle, bebop, fusion, funk, and Latin (such as samba, salsa, bossa nova, and mambo) and perform them at a variety of tempos.

Getting Started

The Resource Guide lists a number of excellent books and videos that will help aspiring drum-set players develop their understanding of jazz nomenclature, patterns, and techniques for playing the jazz styles listed above. Among those resources are *The Drummer's Guide to Reading Drum Charts* by Steve Houghton; *Playing, Reading and Soloing With a Band* by Gregg Bissonette; and *Essential Styles for Drummers and Bassists* by Steve Houghton and Tom Warrington.

Listening to Recordings

As mentioned throughout this text, the most effective way to learn the nuances of playing in all jazz styles is by listening to recordings of the great jazz masters and emulating their playing. Check out the drummers on the following recordings.

Classic Jazz Recordings
A good place to start, as recommended by Shelly Berg

• Miles Davis – *Kind of Blue, Seven Steps to Heaven*

• Count Basie – *Basie Straight Ahead, April in Paris*

• Charlie Parker – *Yardbird Suite*

• Chick Corea – *Light as a Feather*

• Dexter Gordon – *Go*

• Wayne Shorter – *Speak No Evil, JuJu*

• Art Blakey – *Art Blakey and the Jazz Messengers*

• Thad Jones – *Solid State*

• Oscar Peterson – *The Trio*

• Weather Report – *Heavy Weather*

• Duke Ellington – *The London Concerts*

• Ella Fitzgerald – anything of hers

• Bill Evans – *Bill Evans and Tony Bennett*

• John Coltrane – *John Coltrane and Johnny Hartman, Giant Steps*

Big Band Recordings
A good place to start, as recommended by J. Richard Dunscomb

• Count Basie – *Basie Straight Ahead, April in Paris*

• Duke Ellington – *The London Concerts*

• Bob Mintzer – *Homage to Count Basie*

• Quincy Jones and Sammy Nestico – *Basie and Beyond*

• Bill Watrous – *A Time for Love*

• Bill Holman – *A View From the Side*

• Bob Florence – *With All the Bells and Whistles*

• Patrick Williams – *Sinatraland*

Time, Feel, and Groove

Concepts for interaction with other rhythm section players and establishing good **time, feel,** and **groove** may also be learned through aural example. Younger rhythm section players should spend a great deal of time listening to professional rhythm sections with the goal of identifying the roles of each member as described in the "Rhythm Section Preface" (Chapter 16) section of this book.

The drummer's duty, along with the rest of the rhythm section, is to be able to provide the correct feel and groove when presented with a new chart. The way your drummer grooves to whatever style your band is playing will set the overall confidence and comfort for the band. For example, while playing a shuffle, it can be very tight, straight-ahead, and in the pocket, or it can be loose, laid-back, and with an open feel. In either case, this interpretation will dictate the way the band interprets the shuffle groove. It is important for your drummer to learn and feel the difference.

Spend time with your drummer to make sure he or she is obtaining good information on different jazz styles and the history of those styles. The Ken Burns *Jazz* video/DVD series is an excellent place to start. If you are new to teaching jazz, refer to Chapter 7: Swing, and Chapter 8: Latin, for information on teaching styles.

Time

Good **time** is crucial for a drummer. Being a good time-keeper requires vigilant practice at internalizing and maintaining a steady beat.

Practicing with a metronome is essential for developing good time. However, some drummers get used to practicing with a metronome to the point where they let the metronome keep time for them, a task that must be done by the drummer, not the metronome. Encourage your drummer (and all instrumentalists in your band for that matter) to think about time even when they are away from the instrument. A good exercise to help internalize the pulse away from the instrument is to take the metronome and walk with the beat of it and then against it.

Another good idea for the drummer is to use a drum machine or some other programmable time reference device for practice sessions. He or she should play along with a style pattern for a number of bars, then continue keeping time alone for another number of bars while the device is silent, and then evaluate when the machine comes back in if he or she has strayed from the original tempo. Exercises like this one help strengthen one's internal clock so that it becomes second nature, making time-keeping in the band not a task but rather something that happens naturally.

Feel

The **feel** of any piece of music is dictated by the style and the tempo. It doesn't require a lot of technical facility. For instance, when playing a jazz chart at $\quarternote = 100$ beats per minute, the drummer has to make the decision between playing an open, triplet-based feel, which would start on the ride cymbal with a relaxed sound, or on the other hand, playing a more tight and bouncy shuffle, with the ride cymbal pattern more based on sixteenth notes. Or he or she might consider breaking up the cymbal pattern to make it sound more open and spacey, creating a floating feel. All of these little nuances will make the rest of the band decide on how to swing their phrases and how the rest of the rhythm section supports the feel being established by the drummer. For this reason, a proven teaching tool is to expose drummers to older recordings and all the musicians on them who have set standards for different feels.

Groove

The **groove** of the entire band starts from the rhythm section. All players must agree on the time and feel; otherwise, the music will not groove. If the drummer is playing the right style pattern and even the right feel but does not agree time-wise with the bass or the piano, then no matter what, it is not going to groove. Conversely, if everybody is playing time in the same manner but the drummer's feel is wrong, it is not going to groove either. The job of the drummer is to lay down the time with the correct feel so that he or she can bond musically with the rhythm section to lay a foundation so all the members of the whole band can find their places in the groove.

SET-UP BASICS

Even though the drum set is a combination of many parts (cymbals, hi-hat, bass drum, snare drum, toms), it is essential to view it as a single unit. The importance of this is conceptual. Most people would not think of the piano as a combination of keys or the guitar as a combination of strings. Yet many beginning drummers, or individuals exposed to classical music more than jazz, tend to think of the drum set as a combination of percussion instruments, and this view takes away from understanding the role of the drum set in the jazz ensemble.

To avoid fatigue, encourage your drummer to set up or adjust the drum set comfortably so he or she is not reaching too far for any individual component. The following diagram shows a basic jazz set-up used by many professionals.

Diagram 1

A BASIC DRUM SET

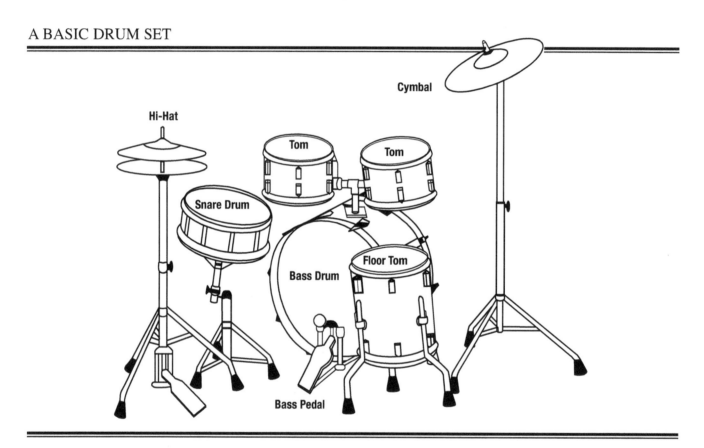

Since jazz drummers primarily drive the band with the cymbals, they should take care to position their cymbals at a height that provides maximum comfort and stick control. It is generally best for jazz ensemble drummers to avoid set-ups that position cymbals very high, despite the flashy stage appearance. Such high cymbals may block the drummer's visual line of communication with the director and the rest of the rhythm section.

In addition, less experienced players may be inclined to position the drum throne too high, resulting in fatigue during extended performance. A good rule of thumb is that a drummer's thighs should be parallel to the floor when seated with his/her feet on the bass drum pedal and the hi-hat pedal.

The following section provides specific information about each drum set component that may be helpful to you while trouble-shooting your drummer's set-up or when selecting new instruments.

Bass Drum

A bass drum with a clear, round tone is optimal for a jazz ensemble, with a clear attack, not a dead sound. A foot pedal with an attached beater is used to produce the sound.

Many young drummers tune the bass drum the way they hear it in pop music recordings. In the jazz setting, there should be a real difference between what sound engineers call a kick drum sound and a bass drum sound. A bass drum sound for a jazz band should have a bit of sustain that will enable it to blend with the acoustic bass sound or even an electric bass. A 20-inch drum is ideal for the jazz ensemble, and an 18-inch is fine for combo use. *Try to avoid the 22-inch bass drum because it is too large and overpowers the set.*

The bass drum beater is important because it has a lot to do with the attack sound. The foot pedal is usually equipped with a felt beater that produces a traditional jazz sound. You may encounter some instances where a drummer has changed the beater to a plastic beater or even a wood beater for a sharper attack.

Snare Drum

A versatile snare drum is one that fits different styles and produces different colors depending on how and where on the drum head it is played. Young drummers tend to emulate contemporary recordings, and the most common mistake is to use a piccolo snare drum sound with a jazz band. Although a high popping snare drum will certainly cut through the band, it serves properly only for backbeats or accents. Ghosted notes will sound a little choked and awkward, and brushes will barely get a sound out of the drum.

A good snare drum size for jazz band is either $5\frac{1}{2}$" x 14" or $6\frac{1}{2}$" x 14". Drums of these sizes will produce a full musical sound and get different tones depending on where you strike the head. It should have a dry, controlled sound if you strike the head dead center, and as you strike closer to the rim, more overtones should be noticeable that will blend very well with the band in different situations for a more wet sound.

Also, rim shots (striking the head and the rim at the same time) result in a distinct sound projection that cuts through the entire band. Rim shots are great for backbeats or very loud brass kicks or accents. Playing the rim with the stick across the head (side stick) is often used to simulate a clave sound, resulting in yet another color from the drum. Either of the recommended drum sizes should have a very nice sweet spot for the side-stick sound.

It is also important to pay attention to the position and condition of the snares themselves, which give the drum the quality of a snare drum. If the snares are too loose, the drum will have little definition. If the snares are too tight, the drum will sound choked and unnatural. Overall, drum head choice and tensioning are two critical areas for drummers.

Toms/Floor Toms

When tuning or selecting toms for the jazz ensemble, aim for a clear tone with sustain. Tune each drum to its characteristic sound. A 10-inch drum should not be so loose that it has wrinkles on the head or so tight that it sounds totally dead, and vice versa with a larger head. Many jazz drummers prefer a legato sound with sustain.

Also, when tuning toms and floor toms for a jazz band, the preferred sound is a bit on the high side so that the toms sing better with the band. Young drummers usually try to tune the toms to match their favorite rock band, and that's characteristically low and deep with very little sustain. The rock kind of tuning doesn't work well with a jazz ensemble because it lacks definition and can create confusion as to where the time is.

Often times, you'll encounter toms that are too big or deep, which makes it difficult to position them above the bass drum. A good tom size is 10" x 8" or 12" x 8". A good floor tom size is 14" x 12" or 14" x 14".

Cymbals/Hi-Hat

Ride Cymbal

The ride cymbal is a big part of the sound of the jazz band. Just as the lead trumpet player's sound is critical to the overall ensemble sound, the tone of the ride cymbal is equally important. The ride cymbal penetrates the ensemble; therefore, the tone of the ride cymbal must be a quality sound with good overtones and wash.

The wash is the lingering sound after the initial strike by the drumstick. Cymbals ring constantly and serve as a sound carpet underneath all of the other instruments in the band. The actual hit of the stick on the cymbal is of utmost importance, because if it is not clear, then the rest of the band tends to get confused as to where the drummer's time is. A very thin cymbal produces too much wash and usually the stick gets lost. Conversely, a very heavy cymbal tends to be too dry and does not fulfill its function of carrying the band. Sometimes rivets (sizzle cymbals) work great to soften the sound of the cymbal and fill up the band with a constant hum. An old trick to achieve the rivet effect is to tape a coin, preferably a dime or a penny, loosely to the cymbal.

The playing area of the cymbal is also an issue, because if struck too close to the edge, it will have crash cymbal qualities, and too close to the bell tends to give a dryer, less resonant sound. In any case, the ear is the best guide to where to play the ride cymbal.

Crash Cymbals

Crash cymbals can be very different from the ride cymbal. Many drummers tend to go for a higher, sharper attack that won't get lost in the sound of the band. Overall, the sound of cymbals is a very personal issue that relates to the drummer's style and musical tastes. However, you the director can and should have some control of the cymbal sound. More cymbals does not always mean better quality. There are many excellent big band drummers who play with only two ride cymbals and make them suit all musical styles.

Hi-Hat

A pair of hi-hat cymbals (controlled by a foot pedal) should have a nice "chick" sound, should blend well with the band, and be very easy to discern at any volume. Fourteen-inch hi-hats work well as all-around cymbals for a variety of jazz styles. You may find that 15-inch hi-hats are a bit too big for inexperienced players and as a result will be too loud. Thirteen-inch hi-hats may be too small and simply not create enough sound for the band to notice while playing. Generally, thinner cymbals are better for recording and medium to thick cymbals are best for live performances.

Music Stand

As your drummer sets up, don't forget to take care of a very basic issue, the position of the music stand. Although reading the chart is important, it is more important to have your drummer's senses paying attention to everything that's happening in the band, both musically and visually. Eye contact is very important while performing, which allows no room for a drummer to have his/her face buried in the music and not paying attention to anything else. For this reason, the music stand should be at a level where the drummer can see and be involved with the band and the conductor for any change or signal that may happen while performing. A logical place to set the music stand is to the left of the hi-hat, since usually no other equipment is there. Also, be careful not to have the stand so high that it covers the drummer's face.

Balance

Now that we've defined the whole drum set, it is important to go back and review the concept that all of these components are part of one single unit. For this reason, the drummer should be aware of dynamic balance in all four limbs while he or she plays the drum set, much like when a quartet plays.

For example, he or she should listen for how loud he or she is playing the snare drum in comparison to the ride cymbal and the hi-hat and how the whole drum set blends together as a single instrument.

To use the same analogy as in the beginning of the chapter, a piano player wouldn't play one hand dramatically louder than the other, or a guitar player wouldn't hit one of the strings harder than the others while playing a chord. Similarly, a drummer shouldn't play one volume on the ride cymbal and then play the snare obnoxiously loud since this would upset the balance of the sound.

Check out the Resource Guide for books and videos with detailed information on drum tuning, cymbals, and balanced playing.

HIRE TEAM PLAYERS

Ideally, your rhythm section will work as a team, and you can encourage it with good coaching. A common mistake by young drummers is to play for themselves and not understand that they are part of a team. Complex rhythmic patterns or fast technique demonstrations do nothing to establish or enhance the groove, which the whole band is counting on for phrasing.

Help your drummer realize that many times he or she is looked upon to take the initiative to start this team effort, setting the time and feel from the moment the music starts. Here are four ways to get him or her started on the right path:

1. Have a union of drums and bass.
2. Place the time in three time zones.
3. Interact with the piano and/or guitar.
4. Support the soloist.

Union of Drums and Bass

One of the most important things in the rhythm section is the union of the drums and the bass. *The union of the drums and bass is critical.*

This combination is certainly the heartbeat of the band. For instance, while the drummer is playing a standard jazz ride cymbal pattern and the bass player walks a bass line, it is of utmost importance to have a symbiosis of the sounds. The drummer and bassist must agree on where the time is in order to set a pulse for both the rhythm section as a unit within the band as well as for the whole band. This is the foundation upon which to build the rest.

Encourage your drummer and bassist to rehearse together to better lock in. Eye contact between the players is essential. The drummer should watch the bass player's hands, and the bass player should watch the drummer's ride cymbal.

Three Time Zones

The concept of "where the time is" can be simplified and explained as the pulse per beat and can usually be described in three distinct zones. Those three zones are (1) on top or slightly ahead of the beat, (2) dead center or in the middle, and (3) on the back or behind the beat. For clarification, playing on top of the beat is to play on the forward side of dead center. Believe it or not, this can be accomplished without rushing the tempo, but usually only if another rhythm section member counters with playing dead center. For example, if the bass player is dead center or slightly on the backside of the beat, the drummer can play on top and it will still swing. Conversely, if the bassist pushes on the topside, the drummer must hold the time back.

Ideally, especially for young jazz ensembles, both the bass and drums should play dead center. As you listen to professional jazz recordings, you will often hear fluctuations in the time, and within reason, this is normal. In a jazz ensemble or in a small group, the rhythm section can be playing together with consistent and comfortable time, and when the brass and saxophones enter, the time may change dramatically. This is not normal and underscores why the sound of cymbals is critical. Each member of the ensemble must hear and know where the time is so he or she can play within that zone. This is the foundation upon which to build everything else.

Interaction With Piano and/or Guitar

The drummer's interaction with the comping instrument, usually piano or guitar and piano, is a third building block for their development as a team player. A drummer is wise to pay attention to the rhythms the comping instrument is playing to better define the style and feel of the music. Sectional rehearsals are a great way to encourage this type of listening.

After the drummer understands the above concepts, the way to achieve a tighter groove in the rhythm section is for the drummer to try to lock in with the bass player subconsciously so that not a lot of conscious attention is employed doing this task.

Supporting a Soloist

Behind a soloist, the drummer should be very aware of the aforementioned concepts but also accept that a new leading voice has entered the music, which takes priority over what is already established. The soloist should be allowed the space to build on his or her improvised solos and then be supported on any direction he or she takes. This is the job of the rhythm section as a team, and the drummer can support or push the soloist with interaction, dynamics, and rhythmic intensity, always making sure that the time and the feel are very comprehensible. This is one of the unique aspects of the jazz art form: the sound, feel, and energy can change instantly with each addition or subtraction of individual players or sections in the ensemble.

INTERPRETING WRITTEN DRUM CHARTS

Playing the music should clearly be a priority over reading the music. The drum chart is just information on how to make this music happen. It is easy to complain that the typical jazz ensemble drum part does not provide much information for the player. In reality, much can be made of a simple chart with proper attention and understanding on the drummer's part. However, it is ultimately the drummer's responsibility to mark any of the following information in the part that may be missing. For the inexperienced drummer, this might require your assistance.

Troubleshooting

Your drummer should not view reading and interpreting a drum chart as a difficult chore. He or she should get used to routinely absorbing certain basic information as soon as the written music is on the music stand.

1. **Style and Tempo:** Determine the style and tempo of the tune, indicated usually at the top left corner of the chart.
2. **Road Map:** Quickly check out the road map: repeats, jumps, signs, the first steps of analyzing the overall form.
3. **Form:** For a drummer, reading a chart is not the same as, say, the piano and bass player reading their charts. The drum chart usually will not indicate the chord changes, so the drummer at this point should figure out the form: intro, head/melody (and how many bars in the head, and different sections of the head), transitions between parts of the arrangement and ending. Recognizing, understanding, and hearing the form are critical for the drummer. As the director, you should draw special attention to the overall form and discuss any unusual variations to the established form, if present, including tags or codas, and so on.
4. **Fills:** To help define the form further, the drummer should outline different sections of a chart with fills at the end of each section, making sure the sections sound different. A logical extension of this concept is that an intro should sound like an intro, and when the melody of the chart comes in, the drums should sound different in order to acknowledge that the main musical idea is being presented.
5. **Dynamics:** The drummer should clearly write in the dynamics on the part that you are conducting so the drum volume is in sync with the rest of the band. The rhythm section traditionally plays softer in two places in every piece: (1) on the head/melody and (2) in the solo sections.

The chart should now sound much better just by the drummer following the above guidelines.

Section and Ensemble Figures

The next part of the drummer's job is to make sense of the figures written on his or her part, and this will challenge his or her creativity. Unfortunately, drum parts are not written or notated in a universal and consistent fashion. A simple rule of thumb is to consider the figures written on the staff to be essential—play them. Figures written above or below the staff are of secondary importance. These figures written above (occasionally below) the staff are usually showing section or melodic accents. Although these section and melodic accents should usually be played, they are not essential. Sometimes these figures are written as smaller cued notes. They can also function as a guide. Another reality to consider is that drum parts are sometimes overwritten and therefore can be confusing to an inexperienced drummer.

Example 1 shows a simple and well-written drum part. This gives the drummer basic information.

Example 1

Example 2 shows a more complex drum part. This specifies what to play throughout the chart. This can be useful to an inexperienced drummer but at the same time confusing because it has so much information.

Example 2

This brings us to realize that there are not many possibilities of rhythmic figure combinations. If it is a dotted quarter with an eighth note after, which is a very common figure, it doesn't mean that the band is going to play the same melodic notes every time, but the drummer will have the same rhythmic figure every time. The band may not play with the same dynamics or with the same combination of instruments every time, but the drummer will have the same figure.

This is when the drummer must use his or her ears to play musically, because if he or she gets locked into playing the same way every time just because it's the same written figure, the music will sound boring and predictable.

So reading drum charts is nothing more than interpreting the rhythmic figures that repeatedly present themselves in different charts and in different styles.

Section Figures

One or more sections of the band, as is quite evident, play section figures. When supporting a section figure, the main concern for the drummer should be to avoid stopping the time flow. The ride cymbal or hi-hat can provide a good continuum so that the section can play along without a break in the music.

A good example of a section figure is to listen to any Frank Sinatra recording with a big band. While he is singing the melody, notice how sections of the band play small riffs supporting his melodic phrases. These are section figures, and the drummer should not make a big deal out of them.

Section figures may be set up with something simple, such as playing a snare or a bass drum hit one beat before the figure, and then playing the section figure with either the snare drum or a combination of snare and bass drum. If the circumstances allow it, maybe use a tom hit, all the time keeping the time flow going just like before the figure started. Not a lot of volume is needed—just enough to give the section figure an added attack.

Another important item to have in mind is that the drummer does not need to play every note in the figure. Often playing the first and last note of the section figure will work better than playing every note as the section is doing. For instance, if faced with a two eighth-note section figure, the drummer could play a snare on the first one, making it sound like a set-up, and a bass drum on the second one, making it sound like an accent. If faced with four eighth notes, the drummer could play a bass drum on the first eighth note and a snare drum, accenting the end of the figure, on the last one. Any number of eighth notes could be played in this same manner, playing only the first one as the beginning of the figure and then accenting the end of the figure with a snare or the like.

Section figures are not supposed to be dramatic and are certainly not solos for a drummer; rather, they are simply cue notes. The key here is to keep the groove going. *To signal that the time flow should not stop, section figures are usually written above the staff.*

Ensemble Figures

Ensemble figures are dramatic and punctuate a rhythmic or melodic figure played by the entire band. *Therefore, ensemble figures are usually written in the staff, signaling the disruption of the time flow.*

For this reason, the drummer must feel comfortable keeping time; otherwise, he or she will either rush or drag when playing an ensemble figure, carried away or dragged down by the weight of the band. The band relies on the drummer during ensemble figures more than ever, so the drummer must be clear and precise in his or her ideas and keep the internal pulse going so the band can feel the time in the fills.

To ensure that the groove still flows throughout, the drummer may choose to play both the set-up of the figure and the figure itself. The set-ups for ensemble figures can be as long and involved as the drummer wants, if played with musicality and clarity.

Drastic ensemble figures (for instance, stopping the time a beat before the figure and after a fill or playing quarter-note triplets before the figure) tend to bring a lot of novelty to the music.

The volume of ensemble figures can range from very soft to very loud. Just because the whole group plays an ensemble figure together does not mean that the drummer needs to play triple forte!

Common Fill Mistakes

One common mistake made by young drummers is to play a fill and then play a cymbal crash incorrectly, for example, in the sixth bar of an eight- or twelve-bar section, which may confuse other band members who may be counting bars to come in at their next entrance. Another mistake by less experienced drummers is to get involved playing complicated patterns or fills, making the time so shaky that the rest of the band can't really understand where the time is, and everything falls apart.

Invest some time helping your drummer interpret the drum parts, especially in analyzing the form and the types of figures, and these errors will diminish dramatically. Listening to the CD recordings included with most published jazz ensemble arrangements will help drummers hear a professional play the arrangement. Listen and learn!

Phrasing and Coloring

The next step is to teach your drummer to pay close attention to how the brass and the reed instruments phrase. When the drummer phrases the same way, the band will sound like a single unit.

Be aware that different sounds from the drum set match nicely in different ways with different colors from the band. Generally speaking, drums have shorter sounds and cymbals have longer sounds.

It is effective to combine different sounds of the drum set with different instruments of the band or different kinds of accents. For example, the trumpets might play a very short, loud note; then a couple of bars later they may play the same voicing, but this time really soft and not as short, making the sound of the trumpets rounder and a bit muffled. A good idea for the drummer would be to hit a rim shot with the trumpets on the first short, loud note (maybe even add a bass drum along to give it the bottom end and make it sound bigger). Then, for the second attack, hit the floor tom or just the bass drum considerably softer. This will make a real distinction between the first note and the second note, all the while supporting the figure so it sounds like everybody is playing together as a team.

The same process can work with cymbals in different sections or phrases of the arrangement by changing the ride beat from one cymbal to another, or crashing different cymbals depending on what instruments are playing at that moment—saxes, trombones, or trumpets.

Dynamics

Dynamically, it is essential for the drummer to control his or her own volume. If a drummer starts out a typical arrangement playing constantly loud, there will be no room to increase the volume at the shout chorus.

Also, it doesn't help the tuning of the band if the brass and reeds have to play loud to be heard over the drums.

It's a good idea for the drummer to ask to himself or herself if he or she can hear everything else happening in the band over the drums. If he or she cannot, then probably the drums are too loud.

DRUM SET SOLOING

A drummer, like the rest of the soloists in the band, should work on improvisation and be aware of different soloing styles in different eras and styles of music. For example, if playing the swing chart "In the Mood," it would be inappropriate to play jazz-rock fusion ideas during a drum solo, which would be out of character in a swing chart. This is another reason why it is very important for a drummer to research the musical language associated with different styles.

A good way to help your drummer learn the jazz language is on a chart-by-chart basis. Your drummer could find out where a particular style came from and emulate what the drummers who defined the style played. This way, he or she will get enough language in that style and perhaps even use the fills he or she admires from contemporary recordings and adapt them to the style at hand.

Drum set soloing needs to be studied from the best historical drum set soloists, as does piano, saxophone, trumpet, or trombone improvisers. There is a tradition that has evolved, and the best way to learn it is through listening. Many excellent videos on this subject are referenced in the Resource Guide.

SUMMARY

Many drummers love the quote by one of the truly admired professional drummers of our time, Adam Nussbaum: "So many drummers I've heard are just drumming away, working on licks, not on playing musically." **Music** is a language. We must remember that we are obliged to serve it, protect it, and honor it. Why do we get the gig? Because we make the other musicians in the group sound good and feel good. If we take a moment to think about it, most of the drummers we admire do that first. When the band sounds good, you sound good. The music is our main priority, our foremost responsibility.

DIRECTOR'S CHECKLIST FOR DRUMS

- The drummer must understand the style and groove of each piece of music.

- The drummer should make listening a priority.

- The drum set player should be a good time-keeper, which requires vigilant practice at internalizing and maintaining a steady beat.

- The feel is dictated by the style and tempo.

- All rhythm section players must agree on the time and feel; otherwise, the music will not groove.

- Have the player adjust the drum set for optimum playing comfort.

- A 20-inch bass drum is ideal for a jazz ensemble.

- A good snare drum size is 5½" or 6½" x 14".

- A good tom size is 10" or 12" x 8".

- A good floor tom size is 14" x 12" or 14" x 14".

- Many drummers choose a ride cymbal that produces a higher, sharper attack.

- Fourteen-inch hi-hat cymbals work well.

- The drummer must place the music stand in a logical place.

- Insist on teamwork.

- Unify the bass and drums, the heartbeat of the band.

- Support the soloist.

- Playing the music should take priority over reading the music.

- The drummer must listen for form and dynamics.

- Help the drummer make sense of ensemble and section figures.

• Share the concepts of color and phrasing with the drummer and the rhythm section.

• Music is the main priority; when the band sounds good, the drummer sounds good.

• Establish and stick to a practice routine that includes working on time, feel, and groove—every day possible.

• Listen to professional jazz drummers in all styles.

• Buy and practice with a metronome.

• Study with a private instructor and/or selected videos.

Recommended Drum Set Videos

(All available from Warner Bros. Publications)

Louie Bellson - *The Musical Drummer* - VH005
Gregg Bissonette - *Playing, Reading and Soloing With a Band* - VH0173
Clayton Cameron - *The Living Art of Brushes* - VH078
Peter Erskine - *Everything Is Timekeeping and Timekeeping 2* - VH0503
Steve Gadd - *Up Close* - VH004
Bob Gatzen - *Drum Tuning* - VH0156
Steve Houghton - *The Drummer's Guide to Reading Drum Charts* - VH0177
Steve Houghton - *The Complete Rhythm Section* - VH0161
Steve Houghton - *Drums in the Rhythm Section* - VH0162
Steve Houghton - *Drum Set Masterclass* - PAS9424
Ed Thigpen - *The Essence of Brushes* - VH0147
Various artists - *Developing a Groove* - VH019

Recommended Drum Set Books and CDs

(All available from Warner Bros. Publications)

Art Blakey by John Ramsay - *Art Blakey's Jazz Messages* - MMBK0059CD
Steve Houghton - *The Drumset Soloist,* Book and CD - EL9602CD
Steve Houghton - *The Drum Set Performer,* Book and CD - PERC9604CD
John Riley - *Beyond Bop Drumming,* Book and CD - MMBK0070CD
John Riley - *The Art of Bop Drumming,* Book and CD - MMBK0056CD

Recommended Rhythm Section Videos, Books, and CDs

(All available from *The Contemporary Rhythm Section Series*
published by Warner Bros. Publications)

Steve Houghton - *Drums in the Rhythm Section* - Video VH0162, Book/CD 0048B
Steve Houghton and others - *The Complete Rhythm Section* - Video VH0161, Book/CD 00478B
Tom Ranier - *Piano in the Rhythm Section* - Video VH0165, Book/CD 0051B
Paul Viapiano - *Guitar in the Rhythm Section* - Video VH0164, Book/CD 0050B
Tom Warrington - *Bass in the Rhythm Section* - Video VH0163, Book/CD 0049B

Please refer to the Resource Guide Index.

THE JAZZ GUITAR
ITS ROLE IN THE JAZZ RHYTHM SECTION

by Lindsey Blair

The guitar has been a part of jazz right from the inception of this style of music. Guitarists like Django Reinhardt, Wes Montgomery, Antonio Carlos Jobim, and John Scofield may seem to have little in common with each other, yet they all fall under the canopy of being called jazz guitarists.

Jazz guitarists tend to favor a specific style of jazz, such as swing, bebop, Latin jazz, fusion, and so on. Regardless of your guitarist's preferred style, he or she should become familiar with the basic elements of different jazz styles in order to participate fully in your ensemble.

This chapter will review the four basic jazz styles that guitarists most often encounter in big band or small group combos and the respective guitar performance practices:
1. Traditional jazz (early jazz through swing)
2. Bebop
3. Fusion
4. Latin jazz

STYLE AND NOMENCLATURE

As mentioned in the piano, bass, and drum chapters, jazz rhythm section players must develop an understanding of the jazz language and become familiar with the system of chord and notation symbols that jazz composers use. Guitarists must learn to interpret what those symbols mean in terms of stylistic sounds and rhythms. Please consult the Rhythm Section Preface (Chapter 16) for an overview of the guitarist's basic role in the jazz ensemble.

Getting Started

The Resource Guide lists excellent books and videos that will help your aspiring jazz guitarists develop their understanding of jazz nomenclature, patterns, and techniques. Highly recommended books from those resources are:
- Deyner, Ralph, *The Guitar Handbook,* Knopf Publishers.
- Galbraith, Barry, *Guitar Comping,* JA Jazz.
- Greene, Ted, *Chord Chemistry,* Warner Bros. Publications.
- Leavitt, William, *Melodic Rhythms for Guitar,* Berklee Press Publishers.
- Montgomery, Wes, *The Early Years,* Mel Bay Publishing.
- Van Eps, George, *Harmonic Mechanisms for Guitar,* Mel Bay Publishing, 3 books.

EQUIPMENT BASICS

Although early jazz guitarists played acoustic guitars, jazz ensembles quickly adopted the electric guitar upon its invention. Guitarists today spend a great deal of time working on their tone for different musical styles. Here are some basic guidelines that you will find appropriate for most jazz situations.

Guitars

The tone a guitarist uses for traditional and bebop jazz styles should be dark and full-bodied with plenty of warmth. To achieve this sound your guitarist will need the proper equipment, ideally a hollow-body archtop electric guitar. The guitar will need to have only one pickup placed at the base of the guitar neck, although most archtops have two pickups.

If the guitarist in your ensemble already owns a solid-body electric such as the popular Fender Stratocaster, they can still roughly emulate a jazz sound by positioning one pickup at the base of the guitar neck and following the amplification suggestions below.

See the Latin jazz section later in this chapter for more tone and guitar specifics related to that style.

Amplifiers

The guitar amp will need to project the warmth of the guitar. *Since most guitar amps are designed to enhance the brighter string attack needed to create a good rock, R&B, or country guitar tone, the jazz guitarist will probably find that he or she needs to turn down the treble on most amps to get a nice tone.* The bright switch on the amp will probably never be needed. There will be no call for any effects or signal processors to get this sound. A little reverb from the amp to add ambiance will be all that is required.

Effects

Guitar effects and processors are used in fusion and contemporary jazz styles. See the Fusion section later in this chapter for a discussion on such effects.

TRADITIONAL JAZZ STYLE

I have loosely grouped the early jazz era and the swing era together here and called it traditional jazz since the guitarist's role in the ensemble was consistent throughout those years. It is not realistic to try to cover all of the fine points, but here are the basics that your guitarist will need to master.

Comping

In traditional jazz, comping is the guitar's primary function. The guitarist plays a quarter-note rhythm that helps define the pulse created by the bass line. This quarter note rhythm is strummed with a pick using voicings from the lower four strings of the guitar (the low E, A, D, and G strings). Voicings usually consist of only the root, 3rd, and 7th of the chord. Guitarists commonly refer to this as the "Freddie Green" style.

Freddie Green Style

Freddie Green was the guitarist with the Count Basie Orchestra. He provided a light, airy quarter-note rhythm that helped propel one of the most swinging rhythm sections ever. The Freddie Green guitar sound is either unamplified or lightly amplified and is just loud enough to add some rhythmic attack and harmonic meat to the bass line. Freddie Green's chord voicings were just three-note voicings, using only root, 3rd, and 7th with no chord extensions. Green's style was often described as being felt more than heard.

All jazz guitarists should learn to play a good Freddie Green-style rhythm guitar part. These voicings will help the guitarist see the basic harmonic elements of the chord changes and serve as a good point of departure for learning more elaborate chord voicings. Let's face it: today's guitarist cannot get by in a big band without knowing this style.

To understand this sound, you must listen to some guitar players play the style. Start by listening to some Count Basie recordings—some of my favorites feature Frank Sinatra. Songs like "The Best Is Yet to Come" and "Fly Me to the Moon" featuring the Basie band playing some great Quincy Jones charts are probably the most familiar examples featuring the Freddie Green style of guitar playing.

Here is an example of how a guitarist might play a 12-bar F blues in the Freddie Green style:

Example 1

Listening Resources

Although Freddie Green is the person most commonly associated with the quarter note rhythm guitar style, he was certainly not the first or the only person to do it. Quarter-note rhythm guitar can be found on some of the earliest jazz recordings like "I Can't Give You Anything but Love" as recorded by Louis Armstrong in 1929 with Lonnie Johnson on guitar.

There were other fantastic guitarists playing during the traditional jazz period. Check out Django Reinhardt with the Quintet of the Hot Club of France, or Lonnie Johnson with Duke Ellington. Eddie Lang made some great recordings with Bix Beiderbecke and Louis Armstrong.

Django Reinhardt, Lonnie Johnson, and Eddie Lang were all great soloists too. They provide an excellent example of how great traditional jazz single-note lines can sound on a guitar.

BEBOP STYLE

When playing the bebop style in the jazz ensemble, a guitarist is expected to play melodies, comp, and play solos, much like in a bebop combo. Although bebop has the same triplet subdivision as swing, it has a much more broken-up rhythmic style and is more unpredictable. Some guitarists that play in the bebop style are Wes Montgomery, Jim Hall, Tal Farlow, Joe Pass, and Jimmy Bruno. The list could go on and on.

COMPING

When playing bebop, the guitar is no longer tied down to the role of the quarter-note rhythm, although it can be used if the guitarist feels the urge to use it. Characteristic bebop comping punctuates rhythmic accents, marks the beginning and ending of phrases, and provides the harmonic structure for the rhythm section in a pianistic punctuation style of comping.

This type of comping is usually played on the upper five strings of the guitar (A, D, G, B, and high E strings). Voicings usually are derived from drop 2 and drop 3 formulas and usually include chord extensions (9th, 11th, or 13th). Example 2 shows an F blues that demonstrates guitar comping in a pianistic punctuation style.

Example 2

When Comping With Piano

In general, it is not a good idea to have the guitar and piano comp at the same time in a big band. With bebop, the function of the guitar is very similar to the role of the piano; therefore, the guitarist and pianist must be careful not to clutter up things. However, when the guitar and piano do decide to comp at the same time, the guitarist should play two- or three-note voicings and make sure to use chord voicings that match or complement what the piano player is doing.

Example 3 shows an F blues using sparser two- and three-note guitar voicings while comping with piano.

Example 3

Listening Resources

Bebop was originally a small-group idiom. Therefore, the best examples of bebop guitar playing are found in small-group recordings. Some post-bebop big bands, such as those led by Woody Herman, Buddy Rich, and Dizzy Gillespie, also featured great bebop guitar playing.

Good examples of pianists and guitarists who work well together in the bebop style are Jim Hall (guitar) and Bill Evans (piano); Wes Montgomery (guitar) and Wynton Kelly (piano); and Joe Pass (guitar) and Oscar Peterson (piano).

Jim Hall and Bill Evans made two duet albums called *Undercurrent* and *Innermodulations*. Jim Hall is a great role model for comping. He uses quarter-note traditional style as well as pianistic punctuation-style comping and single-note countermelody ideas. Hall and Evans seem to have no problem playing together.

Wes Montgomery recorded a few albums using Wynton Kelly on piano. My favorite Wes Montgomery/ Wynton Kelly albums are *Smokin' at the Half Note* and *Full House*. Montgomery's comping consists of block chords and octaves. Wes seems to be the master of the use of riffs. He uses ostinato patterns to create the same effect as a Count Basie horn riff.

Joe Pass and Oscar Peterson recorded many albums together. My favorite of these records are with the Peterson/Pass/Pederson trio made with bassist Niels Pederson.

Although there are only a few good examples of guitar/piano groups from the bebop style, there are many examples of guitar/organ groups. This is a great sound that not many band directors cash in on. Some great guitar/organ combos worth checking out are the Wes Montgomery/Jimmy Smith duo; the George Benson group featuring Dr. Lonnie Smith; and Pat Martino's recordings with Jack McDuff's band.

FUSION STYLE

The idea of jazz fusion is to fuse jazz elements with elements of other genres of music, most commonly R&B or rock. This requires that the players on any instrument understand the nuances of jazz and at least one other style of music in order to incorporate an authentic feel in the music.

Many younger jazz guitarists begin with rock as their first musical inspiration and then progress into the jazz idiom as their thirst for harmonic and rhythmic knowledge leads them into a more fertile environment for growth. Fusion is a natural for this type of player. It often allows the guitarist to expose a more complete picture of his or her musical personality. Since most fusion incorporates elements of R&B or rock (both genres of music that rely heavily on guitar), the guitarist often finds himself or herself being featured as a soloist and/or heavily relied upon for comping during these tunes.

Comping

Fusion really can run quite a large gamut of sounds and styles for the guitar. Players like John Scofield, Pat Metheny, Scott Henderson, Bill Frisell, and Mike Stern have all recorded music that I would place in the category of fusion. Each of these players has a unique and very individualistic sound and style of playing yet still can fit into this category. I would even go so far as to say that an important element of becoming a great fusion guitarist is to find an easily recognizable sound and approach. Though each player will have his or her own version of the fusion sound, here are some elements that I find are common ground for most fusion guitarists.

Choking or muted playing

Picking single strings and at the same time damping the strings with the heel of the right hand will produce a choked or muted sound. This technique is good for adding a rhythmic feel while avoiding or conflicting with the keyboard, which may be providing broader voicings or textures.

Three-note chordal rhythm

Avoid using basic bar chords, which will clutter the texture of the music. Instead, try using the fingers and a pick to produce the three notes at the same time. This technique merely outlines the harmony instead of cluttering the harmonic canvas.

Strumming technique

Rhythmic ideas can be introduced in a fusion or rock setting by strumming. Using a three- or four-note voicing and occasionally damping the chord with your right hand can interject a rhythmic feel similar to the choked technique but with more variety.

Listening Resources

Fusion forged a separate musical identity as a creative jazz style by the early 1970s. Groups like Return to Forever, Weather Report, the Mahavishnu Orchestra, and various bands of Miles Davis were playing first-class fusion that fused the best qualities of both jazz and rock. As time has moved on, fusion gradually has evolved into what is now known as smooth jazz, which can be described as a combination of jazz with easy-listening pop music and lightweight R&B. Here are a few examples of fusion guitar players and significant recordings: John Scofield, *Hand Jive,* 1993; George Benson, *Beyond the Blue Horizon,* 1971; John McLaughlin, *My Goals Beyond,* 1970; Larry Coryell, *Larry Coryell and the 11th House,* 1972; Al DiMeola, *Splendido Hotel,* 1979; Steve Khan, *Evidence,* 1980; and Hiram Bullock, *Give It What You Got,* 1987.

Fusion Equipment

Most fusion guitarists incorporate some type of signal processing to achieve the variety of tones that are required to get the right sound. A typical fusion guitar set-up might include distortion, delay, chorus or flanger, and digital reverb. All of these effects can be achieved several different ways. The effects can be modular little stompboxes that you might find connected on the floor where the guitarist can turn them on and off with his or her feet, or the effects might be rack-mounted or may be incorporated into the design of the amplifier that the guitarist chooses to play through.

As a band director, you are not required to know how these effects are achieved, but you should know a little about what they sound like and what they are good for. The following are brief descriptions of each of these effects:

Distortion

The distortion effect makes a guitar amplifier sound as if it were turned all the way up, except without the bleeding eardrums. Distortion is the guitar tone associated with rock guitar.

Delay

Just as the name implies, delay adds a delayed signal with the original guitar tone. This has an echo type of effect. Delay can add a lot of depth to a guitarist's sound but can cause the sound and rhythm to be less defined if it is mixed in too loud. Most newer delays have a tap tempo feature that allows the guitarist to adjust the tempo of the delayed signal to fit the song tempo.

Chorus/Flanger

The chorus effect creates a second mirror image of the original guitar tone that is repeated just milliseconds after the original signal. This mirror image is then changed slightly in pitch, creating the same effect as a chorus of singers attempting to sing a pitch in unison. Flanging is very similar but creates more of a Doppler effect than chorusing. These effects sound nice for sustained chords or for adding variation to a clean soloing tone.

Reverb

Reverb is one of the oldest effects and has been incorporated in the design of most guitar amps since at least the late 1950s. The classic guitar amp reverb is created by using a spring reverb (literally using springs to make the reverb effect). Reverb can also be created digitally or in several other ways.

Reverb is meant to give the illusion of making a very dry, dead-sounding room sound as if you were in a much larger and more reflective area. Just go to the nearest large tiled room or enclosed stairwell and clap your hands and you will know what natural reverb sounds like.

LATIN JAZZ STYLE

Latin jazz, like fusion, requires the player to incorporate an authentic feel for jazz and another style of music. In this case, jazz is fused with Latin music. However, Latin jazz has been around quite a bit longer than jazz-rock fusion.

There are many different types of Latin jazz, so this is a rather broad term. Applying the term *Latin* to any musical style is about as specific as using the term *American* music. The Latin styles most commonly associated with the guitar are discussed next. See also Chapter 8 for a detailed discussion of Latin jazz concepts.

Brazilian Jazz

The guitar is relied upon heavily for most Brazilian jazz. The bossa nova and samba are two styles that bring to mind the sound of the guitar by the mere mention of their names. These Brazilian jazz styles became popular among American jazz musicians in the early 1960s and have remained popular to this day.

The samba and bossa nova are based on repeated rhythmic patterns or grooves. Once a pattern is established it generally continues throughout the tune with the exception of a few variations that might serve to mark the end of phrases.

Clave Pattern

The clave pattern is a common thread that runs throughout many styles of Latin music and found sometimes in Brazilian jazz guitar patterns. The clave is based on a three-against-two polyrhythm that is two bars long. The polyrhythmic nature causes one of the bars to have three accents and the other bar to have two accents.

- Patterns that have three accents in the first bar are referred to as 3-2 clave patterns (three accents in the first bar and two accents in the second bar).
- Patterns that have two accents in the first bar are called 2-3 clave.
- The clave pattern stands in contrast to the bass line in Brazilian jazz that is generally played on the first and third beat of every bar.

Example 4 shows a 3-2 clave pattern with a bass line.

Example 4

Example 5 shows a 2-3 clave pattern with a bass line.

Example 5

Comping

There are many variations of the clave pattern. However, clave patterns rarely vary once established during a song. The rhythmic pattern, once established, should carry throughout the tune. Although the clave pattern shown above is frequently used, it is not the only type of pattern used in Brazilian jazz. There are hundreds of ways to play sambas and bossas. Newer ways to play these are probably emerging right now.

Listening Resources

The Brazilian jazz style became popular in 1962 with an album featuring guitarist Charlie Byrd and saxophonist Stan Getz, *Jazz Samba*. But the brilliant Antonio Carlos Jobim from Brazil led the way with this Latin style. Jobim was often described as the George Gershwin of Brazil in that he contributed so many brilliant compositions to the jazz repertoire and symbolized Brazilian jazz worldwide. Significant Latin-style jazz guitarists and their most famous recordings include the following: Laurindo Almeida, *Brazilliance,* Vol. 1, 1953; Charlie Byrd, *Latin Byrd,* 1961; Bola Sete, *The Solo Guitar of Bola Sete,* 1966; Antonio Carlos Jobim, *Wave,* 1967.

Latin Jazz Equipment

Most Latin jazz guitar music is played on a nylon-string acoustic guitar. The nylon-string acoustic is also known as the classical guitar or the gut-string guitar. Guitarists who use this instrument still need to amplify the guitar since the natural acoustic sound of the instrument is not loud enough to project in the quietest of jazz ensembles. Fortunately, the acoustic quality of the guitar can be preserved by amplifying the instrument with a piezo pickup.

Classic Recordings

Check out the following CDs for great jazz guitar playing.

- Frank Sinatra/Count Basie, *It Might as Well Be Swing,* Warner Bros. Records.

- Django Reinhardt, *The Classic Early Recordings in Chronological Order* (Box Set), JSP Records

- Wes Montgomery, *Impressions: The Verve Jazz Sides,* Verve.

- Wes Montgomery, *Full House,* Riverside.

- Bill Evans/Jim Hall, *Undercurrent,* Blue Note.

- Bill Evans/Jim Hall, *Intermodulation,* Blue Note.

- Tal Farlow, *Jazz Master 41,* Verve.

- Tribal Tech Scott Henderson/Gary Willis, *Illicit,* Blue Moon.

- John Scofield, *Groove Elation,* Blue Note.

- The Pat Metheny Group, *Still Life Talking,* Geffen.

- Asturd Gilberto, *Asturd Gilberto's Finest Hour,* Verve.

- Toninho Horta, *Moonstone,* Verve Forecast.

DIRECTOR'S CHECKLIST FOR GUITAR

- The guitar player should be familiar with the four basic jazz guitar styles: traditional, bebop, fusion, and Latin.

- Tone, pickups, and hollow body are key elements of the guitar.

- Know what kind of equipment is needed to play in each style.

- Buy the best equipment you can afford.

- Amplifiers and pickups can be adjusted to produce a variety of colors.

- Today's guitarist should learn to read both notes and chord symbols.

- Comping styles vary for jazz styles.

- Voicings vary for jazz styles.

- Students should consider studying with a private jazz guitar teacher.

- Have students establish a practice routine that is consistent and productive.

Please refer to the Resource Guide Index.

THE SAXOPHONE SECTION

by Chris Vadala

The saxophone, a unique and versatile instrument, is a hybrid creation of Belgian inventor Adolphe Sax designed to combine the power of a brass instrument with the flexibility and facility of a woodwind. Its amazing popularity, particularly in jazz and commercial music, has made this instrument a mainstay in the big bands and its literature.

ENSEMBLE BASICS

Since the instrument was built to have a strong musical voice, it is important that each saxophonist in a large ensemble section play with a full, vibrant sound.

Balance

The saxophone section needs to be able to balance with a brass section that is typically twice its size. It addition, it must balance with a rhythm section that often includes electronic instruments. In other words, survival may depend on the strength of all the reed players in the section.

Strive for a Pleasing Sound

Individual and group sound/tone is predicated on an aural concept and an oral concept. Players must strive for a pleasing sound that's in tune and in time with others. It's important to remind your students to *play through,* not just *into* the saxophone. They should play with appropriate air speed and breath/diaphragmatic support. Playing position and posture may have a direct bearing on the final tonal result. It is imperative to achieve a good natural or characteristic sound, with good intonation, in all registers.

Vibrato

That said, vibrato should be an integral part of the saxophonist's tone, not a panacea for a poor tone. There are always exceptions, however. Don't have your saxes tune with vibrato in their sound, and they should generally not use vibrato in unison sections or fast, technical passages. Although there are different procedures for producing vibrato, most saxophonists prefer a jaw or intensity vibrato to throat or diaphragmatic undulations. Speed and usage are also debatable.

For example, the Stan Kenton sax section often used no vibrato (N.V.) or very little vibrato, while the Basie band saxophonists favored a wide, warm vibrato sound employed by all section mates. Ellington saxophonists sometimes had only the lead player use vibrato while others played with a straight sound, or all played with vibrato at varying speeds. Saxists in bands like those of Thad Jones, Buddy Rich, and Maynard Ferguson, among others, used what Louis Armstrong labeled "terminal vibrato," a sustained note with wavering at the end of the note. Whatever the choice, it should be appropriate for the musical setting.

Tone

I recommend a distinct, clear tone with depth or body and a projection that is laser-like, not spreading out or flowering. A typical jazz sound should have a balanced combination of highs (upper partials of sound or edge) and lows (deeper, rounder partials of resonance).

Once again, arguments will arise since certain notable sax sections and players have identifiable tonal signatures. A few classic sound identifications come from the horns of Johnny Hodges, Lester Young, Ben Webster, Charlie Parker, Stan Getz, Phil Woods, Cannonball Adderley, Paul Desmond, John Coltrane, and Sonny Rollins. Many of these soloists were also section players in larger ensembles and had to blend accordingly. These distinct sound personalities are the result of many factors, including equipment preferences (reeds, mouthpieces, ligatures, instrument).

Sectional Synchronicity

Finally, sectional synchronicity in areas of rhythm, intonation, dynamics, balance and blend, phrasing, and the proper use of jazz articulations is important in the success of your woodwind section. See Chapter 14 for specific rehearsal techniques.

STANDARD SEATING PLAN

Depending on the preferred band set-up and instrumentation, the standard seating plan in a traditional format of five saxes is shown below.

JAZZ ENSEMBLE SET-UP

PERFORMANCE

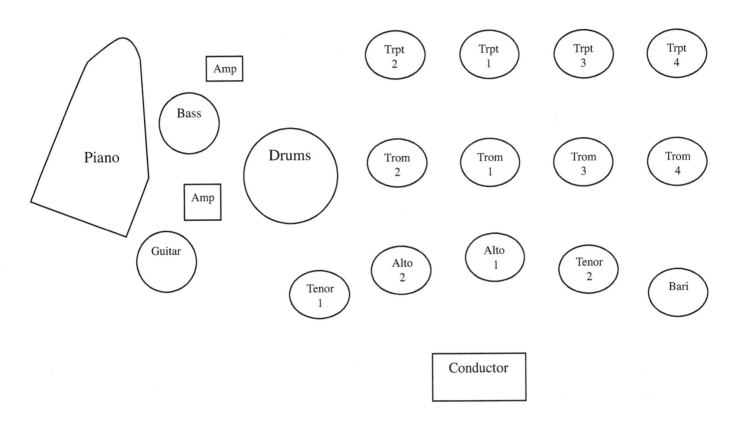

This block set-up helps with balance and blend and aligns the lead players in the horn section in a customary track to the back row. Tuning inward to the lead player enables a better pitch reference (buddy system), and this, in turn, helps the lead player reference the lead trombone and the lead trumpet.

Avoid grouping the tenors because it destroys the balance of the section, especially if the tenors are stronger players than the altos. Since the lead tenor chair is the frequent solo or ride chair, it's preferable to have that player sit on the left side of the section (stage right) near the rhythm section, along with the other usual solo players like trombone 2 and trumpet 2. This, of course, forms a quasi-combo setting, ideal for solo or soli sections.

SPECIFIC ROLES IN THE SAXOPHONE SECTION

Obviously, all saxophonists are integral to the section and yet each has an assortment of roles that are uniquely challenging. However, the main mission in sectional playing is homogeneous sound. Section players must assimilate and match the stylistic concepts, tone (with or without vibrato), attacks and releases, articulations, dynamics, and other elements of musicality set by the lead player. A rule of thumb is to ask the saxophonists to play strong and enthusiastically but not so loud that they can't hear the lead player or the player(s) on the other side. I highly recommend having your students listen to and imitate respected solo and sectional players—it must be part of the practice and learning procedure in this idiom.

Lead Alto

The lead alto player is generally the strongest and most influential player in the section. The mission of this player is to direct the section in stylistic concepts; set the standard for pitch, articulation, and phrasing; and strike a relationship or connection with the brass and rhythm sections. It may be helpful to single out the lead players from each section and rehearse with them and rhythm section personnel to set up a skeleton preview of a chart, clarifying articulations, time placement, tonal concepts, phrasing, and so on.

Second Alto

The second alto supports the lead and sometimes replaces the lead. Being a good listener and an unselfish player are important traits for second alto. Intonation is especially critical with this part, as well the ability to adapt to variations from the lead alto player.

Lead Tenor

The lead tenor is generally the strongest soloist and may get opportunities to lead some soli sections. Blending is obviously vital, as with all chairs, but some lead tenor players have a tendency to be strong and need to adjust accordingly.

Second Tenor

The second tenor (sometimes referred to as tenor 4 or reed 4) is a very demanding and challenging seat. This player helps support the bari on the bottom of the chord structures, sometimes gets solo opportunities, sometimes doubles the lead, and often plays rather disjunct lines (try reading some Thad Jones tenor 2 parts and you'll understand).

Baritone

The baritone sax player is a chameleon: a fifth voice in the reed section playing color tones and roots, doubling the lead, teaming up with the bass trombone or tuba, teaming up with the bass, or playing a solo part. A bari player should be fearless yet flexible.

WOODWIND DOUBLING

Today's market for woodwind playing in the jazz ensemble and studio pit orchestra sections is competitive, and versatility is more of a necessity than an option. The triple-threat instruments (sax, clarinet, flute) are the most common doubles you'll see in jazz ensemble music. However, don't ignore same-family doubling. Some saxophonists sound wonderful on alto or tenor but are very uncomfortable on soprano. Each family member has its own peculiarities and personality, and it's important to sound your best on any choice.

Doubles in the Jazz Ensemble

The woodwind section in the jazz ensemble has often been expanded beyond the usual aggregate of five saxophones, and an increasingly large number of composers and arrangers are requiring woodwind doubling in their compositions.

For example, in the 1920s, the reed section of the Paul Whiteman Orchestra sported an arsenal of woodwinds. Much like today, bands throughout the twentieth century featured an array of talented woodwind doublers, such as the orchestras of Sauter-Finegan, Duke Ellington, Count Basie, Woody Herman, Bob Florence, Maynard Ferguson, and Thad Jones–Mel Lewis.

Writers like Maria Schneider, Vince Mendoza, Manny Album, Fred Sturm, Bob Mintzer, Toshiko Akiyoshi, Mike Crotty, Michael Abene, and a host of others love to explore various combinations of timbres in the front row.

Some reed parts that you are likely to encounter in more advanced charts include:
Alto I (Reed I): soprano sax, flute, piccolo, and clarinet.
Alto II (Reed II): soprano sax, flute, and clarinet.
Tenor I (Reed III): clarinet, flute, alto flute, oboe, and soprano sax.
Tenor II (Reed IV): clarinet, flute, alto flute, and bass clarinet.
Baritone (Reed V): bass clarinet, clarinet, alto flute, bass flute, bassoon.

Getting Started With Doubles

The first step to becoming a doubler is to acquire a broader understanding of your own instrument by studying members of the same family as well as related woodwind families. Closely examine the obvious differences between instruments of the same and different families. It is essential that tone, endurance, and technical facility do not suffer as you or your students proceed in study from one instrument to the next.

Warning: Do not attempt to venture into doubling until you are a strong player on at least a primary instrument. Don't be a dabbler, a jack of all trades, master of none.

Keeping High Standards

Once again, it is important to remember that as you proceed in study from one instrument to the next, you need to approach a new double as seriously, patiently, and as methodically as your primary instrument, always aiming for the highest of standards. In an ideal world, you'd begin doubling on a professional instrument, study with a master, and have ample hours of practice time to excel. Realistically, you should use as fine an instrument as you can afford and take lessons whenever possible to avoid developing any bad habits. Budget practice time accordingly.

EQUIPMENT

For sectional playing, strike a balance by using standardization, not extremism, in equipment and concept. In general, a medium mouthpiece chamber with a medium-hard reed with a medium tip opening is a good place to start. Too soft or too hard a reed choice will adversely affect intonation and may make it difficult for your students to sustain long notes or phrases or even vary dynamics. Some resistance is preferable to attain a full-bodied sound and avoid biting or pinching. Many teachers and performers agree that a medium-hard to hard reed with a fairly close mouthpiece facing may stabilize intonation and tonal quality because there's something to blow against. This helps build stronger chops. As your students mature and become more selective, these general recommendations may change.

Mouthpieces

There is a plethora of mouthpiece, reed, and ligature choices available, and to list them all here is not practical.

Some of the more commonly used jazz alto mouthpieces are Meyer (the cherished New York #5, although the new ones with current serial numbers and the RC models are gaining popularity), Berg Larsen, Brillhart, Beechler, Morgan, Runyon, Hite, Ria, Lakey, and Selmer. Most alto players prefer hard rubber rather than metal, which is more commonly found on the larger saxes.

Tenor saxophonists may favor Otto Link, Berg Larsen, Rovner, Bari, Morgan, and Dukoff mouthpieces, or the designer models by Guardala, Sugal, Barone, and so on, while baritone players may use Berg Larsen, Lawton, Rousseau, and Brillhart, among others.

Advise your students to select a mouthpiece that fits their musical situation; they should not just buy a brand because someone they know or heard has one. *This must be a personal selection process.* They should try to avoid first-impression or impulse buying: encourage them to live with a mouthpiece for a while to attain consistency.

Reeds

There are probably as many reed brands as there are mouthpiece types. Some of the more widely used varieties are Vandoren, Rico (Hemke, Royal), LaVoz, Oliveri, Marca, Alexander Superial, and Glotin. The list goes on and on.

Reeds seem to be a constant source of frustration. It's our Achilles heel. Brands and strengths that work for us today may be problematic next month. There are so many reed players today that some of the precious bamboo cane is harvested before full maturity. Some players have given up and have switched to synthetic (Legere, Fibracell, Fiberreed, Bari, Woodwind) or plasticover options to avoid the search for the perfect Arundo donax.

Ligatures

Ligature manufacturers also present a number of options. Although many players use a variety of Rovner designs, Winslow, Harrison, Oleg, and BG, as well as those made for specific mouthpieces, are popular choices.

Popular Instrument Brands

After you or your students have selected the ideal tone generator, finding the right instrument poses another critical decision. Some current favorites are made by Selmer, including the new Series III, Reference 36 and 54 models, plus Yamaha, Keilwerth, Yanagisawa, and Buffet. Others seek out vintage horns of yesteryear such as the Selmers: Mark VI, Balanced Action, Cigar Cutter, and Radio Improved models, and others such as the King Super 20, Buescher 400, Conn Big Bell, Couf Superba, Martin, and Marigaux.

Instrument Cases

Many varieties of single and double cases, such as the Reunion soprano/alto or tenor/soprano or clarinet soft bag, are available. Some traveling musicians prefer hard cases such as the Walt Johnson, Selmer Flight, SKB, Bam, Pro Tec, or even specially designed Anvil/Calzone road cases. Smaller soft packs are lighter and easier to transport but subject the instrument to damage if dropped or bumped.

Nowadays, any serious woodwind player is looking down the road at hauling around a handful of instrument cases, unless he or she is truly bent on focusing as specialist on one particular instrument. Many of today's recognizable jazz saxophone soloists are proficient doublers, such as Joe Lovano (clarinet, alto clarinet), Michael Brecker (EWI, flute), Phil Woods (clarinet), Bob Mintzer (clarinet, bass clarinet, wind synthesizer), and David Murray (bass clarinet).

Stands, Pegs, and Other Useful Items

Other useful equipment items include gig stands and pegs (Hamilton, Beechler, LA Sax, Konig and Meyer, La Voz, and Oleg). For doubles, make sure you select appropriate stands (don't lay instruments on the floor or a chair). Also useful are reed guards or holders, swabs, a small screwdriver and/or repair kit, reed clippers, and reed adjustment materials (knives, Dutch rush, and sandpaper).

TIPS FOR CONDUCTORS

Many of the finest jazz players and woodwind doublers (in the studios and show bands on cruise ships and in theaters around the world) are too numerous to mention and I would not proclaim to know them all. However, since it is vital for you and your students to listen to significant players and heroes in order to acquaint yourselves with the aspects of the music you're performing, I highly recommend listening to the following jazz artists.

Listen to Jazz Artists

Alto Saxophonists: Johnny Hodges, Benny Carter, Charlie Parker, Sonny Stitt, Julian Cannonball Adderley, Phil Woods, Art Pepper, Lee Konitz, Paul Desmond, Jackie McLean, Ornette Coleman, Kenny Garrett, and Chris Potter.

Tenor Saxophonists: Lester Young, Coleman Hawkins, Ben Webster, Don Byas, Dexter Gordon, John Coltrane, Sonny Rollins, Stan Getz, Al Cohn, Zoot Sims, Sal Nestico, Hank Mobley, Joe Henderson, Johnny Griffin, Stanley Turrentine, Joe Lovano, Bob Mintzer, Joshua Redman, Jerry Bergonzi, Michael Brecker, and Bob Berg.

Baritone Saxophonists: Harry Carney, Serge Chaloff, Gerry Mulligan, Pepper Adams, Nick Brignola, Gary Smulyan, and Ronnie Cuber.

Soprano Saxophonists: Sidney Bechet, Lucky Thompson, Steve Lacy, Jan Garbarek, Wayne Shorter, and Dave Liebman.

Doublers: (not including many above) Eddie Daniels, James Moody, Lawrence Feldman, Eric Dolphy, Anthony Braxton, Lew Tabackin, Joe Farrell, and Ira Sullivan.

This is merely a selected list of inspiring woodwind artists. A more detailed list is available in Appendix A.

Recordings of Charts You Are Conducting

If you're conducting charts from Rob McConnell's *Boss Brass* library, Sammy Nestico and Neal Hefti's famous Basie arrangements, Ellington/Strayhorn's era repertoire, the Buddy Rich band's feature charts, or whatever, access recordings and study the music earnestly. Play the recordings for your students. Listen together to tonal concepts, articulations (ghosting and other inflections), ornaments and embellishments, sectional balance and blend, placement of time (on the beat, ahead or lunging, laid-back feeling), dynamic contrasts, and other aspects in order to be stylistically correct.

For example, David Berger and Wynton Marsalis have helped make many of the Ellington favorites available with precise markings and representative recordings to assist with this process. Take advantage of that! Many publishing companies provide recorded samples of their libraries so you can get specific ideas on performance practices.

There's no saying that certain liberties can't be taken, unless the mission is to capture an exact adaptation. Isn't risk-taking and experimentation essential in jazz playing?

Help Your Students Learn the Jazz Standards

Repertoire is often a matter of personal taste and preference. There are thousands of jazz tunes and standards that your students may select from and learn. Students should acquire music and recordings of established jazz literature.

A good place to start might be a musical setting where a soloist in your ensemble is called upon to be an interpretative player and replicate what someone else has done. Examples are Jimmy Dorsey's "So Rare" alto sax performance, Al Klink's famous tenor solo on "In the Mood," Phil Woods' solo on Quincy

Jones' "Quintessence," or Lester Young's classic big band solo on "Lester Leaps In." Use these recordings to challenge your students to listen with more focus.

Then have your students make a list of tunes that they know well, and note those that they need or want to know. They should learn those songs in the standard key(s) and experiment with transposing to other centers. For starters, they could select:

- Any Ellington/Strayhorn standard.
- Standards by Kern, Porter, Gershwin, Mercer, Van Heusen, V. Duke, Arlen, Rodgers and Hart, plus many, many more depending on their level of experience.
- Charlie Parker heads, especially "Donna Lee," "Confirmation," "Ornithology," and "Anthropology." Some other great standards are: "Body and Soul," "Tune Up," "'Round Midnight," "All the Things You Are," "A Night in Tunisia," "Airegin," "Daahoud," "Joy Spring," "Four," Nica's Dream," "So What" "Impressions," "Mr. P.C.," "Well, You Needn't," "Autumn Leaves," "Skylark," "Just Friends," "Have You Met Miss Jones," "Giant Steps," and "Cherokee."

Improvisation Is the Essence of Jazz

All saxophonists should be encouraged to improvise. See Chapters 9 and 10 for information about teaching improvisation basics. As your students become proficient improvisers, they can expect to see any variety of major or minor key blues changes, various modal progressions, rhythm changes (songs based on the chord changes to "I've Got Rhythm"), and even Coltrane third-relationship compositions. In addition to practicing short harmonic formulas like major and minor turnarounds (ii-V or ii-V-I turnbacks), students should practice improvising to the standards listed above.

FINAL TIPS

1. Don't ignore sight-reading; saxophonists should work on it individually, in sectional rehearsals, as well as in the ensemble setting.
2. Focus and have fun!

Ten Suggested Listening Examples

It would be as presumptuous for me to narrow a list of recommended recordings for saxophonists to just a few. In fact, I suggest that such a list not be limited exclusively to saxophonists since it is important to imitate and learn the jazz language by listening to a variety of instrumentalists and vocalists. Furthermore, my list of ten favorite saxophone recordings is likely to be different from those of other listeners and performers, but these are a select group from my library that have enhanced my appreciation of great saxophone playing:

1. *The Smithsonian Collection of Classic Jazz* (America's Jazz Heritage RJ0010/A519477) includes a host of heroes like Charlie Parker, John Coltrane, Coleman Hawkins ("Body and Soul"), Don Byas ("I Got Rhythm"), Cannonball Adderley, Dexter Gordon, Sonny Rollins, Ornette Coleman, and others. *The Saxophone* (Impulse ASH9253-3) is another wonderful collection of noted jazz saxophonists.
2. Coleman Hawkins and Lester Young, *Classic Tenors* (Doctor Jazz Records FW 38446).
3. Charlie Parker, *Charlie Parker* (Prestige PR24009).
4. John Coltrane, *The Best of John Coltrane* (Atlantic SD 1541).
5. Cannonball Adderley, *Cannonball Takes Charge* (Landmark LP 1306).
6. Phil Woods on *Quintessence* (Quincy Jones, Impulse A-11).
7. Sonny Rollins, *Saxophone Colossus*.
8. Paul Desmond and Gerry Mulligan, *Two of a Mind* (RCA LPM 2624).
9. Michael Brecker, *Two Blocks From the Edge* Impulse IMPD-191).
10. Joe Henderson, *Lush Life* (Verve314-511-779-2).
11. Duke Ellington, *At Newport Diminuendo and Crescendo* (Columbia 934).

DIRECTOR'S CHECKLIST FOR THE SAXOPHONE SECTION

• Use the standard seating plan, preferably in a semicircle.

• Know the specific roles of each member of the saxophone section; this will assist in achieving a homogeneous sound.

• Sound is predicated on both an aural and oral concept.

• Most saxophonists prefer a jaw or intensity vibrato.

• A typical jazz sound should have a balanced combination of highs and lows.

• In general, a medium mouthpiece chamber, reed, and tip opening is a good place to start.

• Mouthpiece selection is a personal choice. Avoid impulse buying.

• Instrument selection is challenging since there are many fine brands of new and vintage brands. Seek assistance from teachers.

• Doubling on other woodwind instruments is necessary at the professional music level. However, students should not venture beyond their primary instrument until proving themselves as strong and consistent players.

• Listening is vital to hearing a model sound. Significant saxophone heroes are plentiful.

• Repertoire is vital to learning style and jazz vocabulary.

• Sight-reading is part of the overall musical package; work on it.

• Study with a private instructor.

Please refer to the Resource Guide Index.

Chapter 17 B

THE TRUMPET SECTION

by Bob Montgomery and Peter Olstad

One of the great musical thrills for trumpet players is the opportunity to perform in a big band where the common goal of the trumpet section is musicality of performance as a *section*. When members of the entire section listen carefully to each other and strive for balance, sound, intonation, time feel, articulation, dynamics, and passion of performance, the resulting music can be absolutely electrifying and can achieve great musical heights.

ENSEMBLE BASICS

Achieving such a heightened level of performance requires a group of musicians whose common goal is to perform as a unified section. A unified section can attain a level of performance far beyond that of an individual performer. When all players bring their own individuality to the music and a high level of musicianship, as well as pay attention to basic ensemble skills, together they become a unified section.

Balance

To play in balance, all players must listen carefully to each other to ensure that all can be heard equally. When one player plays significantly louder or softer than other members of the section, the concept of a trumpet section is lost.

In actual practice, the fourth player in the section will play at the highest dynamic level (since he or she is playing the lower notes), with the third player at a *slightly* lower dynamic level, the second at a slightly lower dynamic level yet, and the lead player at the lowest dynamic level. Because the upper players are playing higher notes in each chord, they will naturally be heard more easily, even if they are *slightly* softer than the players playing lower chord tones.

During a sectional rehearsal, recording the section and listening to the recording as a group can be extremely beneficial.

Help your students identify the components of balance.

- Can they hear all four parts? Does one part stand out from the group, or is there a part that cannot be heard?
- Listen to the recording four times, and each time focus on one specific part.
- What about dynamics? Are all crescendos and decrescendos played together with all members participating in the dynamic change equally? If even one player does not make the dynamic change, the change will be ineffective.
- Next, listen for pitch and quality of sound.
- Listen for accurate articulation. Are the length of notes, attacks, and cut-offs identical within the section? Cutting off notes together is as important as starting notes together.
- Developing this kind of listening within a trumpet sectional will transfer to their listening ability within their section during ensemble rehearsals and performances.

Strive for a Pleasing Sound

Each member of the section must work toward a full, rich, controlled sound, capable of loud, soft, high, low, bright, and dark sounds.

A great way to help students learn to achieve a rich, full sound is by coaching them to play long tones using "warm" air. Have them check to see if they are playing with "warm" or "cold" air by placing a hand in front of their mouth and blowing air against the palm of their hand. Ask, "Is the air warm or cold?" Warm air is achieved, for example, by using the same air that you would use to clean eyeglasses. When you breathe against a glass lens, you use warm, moist air to create a fog on the lens. Teach trumpet players to use that same warm air to produce sound with a trumpet. Another test is to ask them to try playing a long tone on the trumpet using cold air to start and then change the air to warm air. You will hear an immediate change in the quality of the sound to a richer more centered sound.

Next, have each section member take turns playing an identical musical phrase to see if they can achieve a similar sound to each other. This is a first step to producing a pleasing sectional sound.

Remember, always have your trumpet students play with warm air. They will create a fuller, more centered sound, and you will be amazed at the greater projection of their sound. They will also find it much easier to play in tune.

Intonation

Having good intonation means each member of the trumpet section must listen to all other section members to ensure that all are in tune with each other. It also means listening to the bass player to ensure that the trumpet section remains in tune with the band. The bassist is the common denominator for pitch for all of the sections in the big band. This is because the bassist is standing close to the piano and can constantly check the pitch of the bass with the piano (the piano has the only set pitch in the ensemble). The pianist in a big band does not always play during the ensemble sections of a chart (in particular while the horns are performing as sections), which makes the piano a less likely choice for providing a standard of pitch during performance. The bassist is the guide harmonically through the music anyway, so encourage your students to listen to the bassist intently as they perform.

Teach your trumpet players how to tune quickly and accurately

Observe professional performers tune. They play the tuning note for no more than three or four seconds and then will either place the horn on their lap, satisfied that they are in tune, or will adjust the tuning slide of their instrument and then check again with a tone lasting three or four seconds. They will repeat this procedure until they determine that they are in tune.

Observe many young players attempt to tune. They play a long tone while trying to determine whether they are flat, sharp, or in tune. Younger players cannot determine easily whether they are flat or sharp only because they have not trained their ears to identify the difference. They may hear that they are not in tune, but they are not sure whether they are flat or sharp. Here's what to tell them:

- Play the tuning note for three or four seconds.
- Listen to the sound of your instrument compared to the sound of the instrument to which you are tuning. If you feel you might be out of tune, but are not sure whether you are flat or sharp, try the following:
  - Move the tuning slide either in or out and play the tuning note again. You will either sound better or worse.
  - If you sound better, you may continue to move the tuning slide in the same direction until you sound in tune.
  - If you sound worse, you moved the tuning slide in the wrong direction. Move it in the opposite direction and play the tuning note again.
  - Continue this process until you hear your pitch match the instrument to which you are tuning.

By advising them to play short three- or four-second tuning notes and then adjusting the tuning slide out or in, they will gradually train their ears to hear the pitch more accurately. Eventually they will recognize pitches as being in tune or flat or sharp immediately. Playing a long tuning note when their ears are not prepared to determine the difference accurately can be a very frustrating experience. By helping your students train their ears to hear the difference in pitch, they will become very happy trumpet players. Naturally, the ability to hear pitch accurately will be extremely handy for them in other performing situations.

Time Feel

The trumpet section will never swing unless a common time feel is achieved, nor will it swing if everyone just *follows* the strongest player. Each player must internalize his or her own strong sense of time and then listen to the other members of the section to understand their sense of time.

Practicing with a metronome set on 2 and 4 will help achieve this individually and as a section. When you perceive that a metronome is clicking on w and 4, it becomes much like a click track in a recording studio and relates to the sound of the drummer's hi-hat cymbal on beats 2 and 4.

Instruct your students to determine the tempo that they would like to play and set the metronome to half that tempo. The clicks now become 2 and 4 of each measure.

Most professional musicians have practiced in this manner at some point in their careers. Many continue to do so throughout their entire careers, on average 10 to 15 minutes per day. Rufus Reid was once asked why he continued to practice to a metronome set on 2 and 4 after all of his years of success and hundreds of records and CDs. He responded that he contributes his great time feel to practicing daily with a metronome (in his case almost 20 minutes a day). He stated that he plays his music until the metronome begins to swing, or actually begins to feel human; then he knows that he, too, is swinging.

Articulation

Good articulation is an absolute must for any great section. (See Chapter 13 for rehearsal techniques.)

Encourage your trumpet players to listen carefully to each other to ensure that the tongued attack, length of note, and tongued release are identical, as well the identical placement of the attacks and releases within the time feel.

With direction from the conductor, the lead player will determine how each note in a phrase will be played and how the overall phrase will be played, and will ensure that it is always performed the same way. It is up to each section player to listen to the lead player's example and always play in an identical manner. Some school bands fail to rehearse articulation, spending all of their rehearsal time on notes, dynamics, and rhythm. Great bands spend as much time on articulation and accuracy of **placing** notes and rhythms in the time feel as they do on other ingredients of performance. Notice the concept of **placing notes and rhythms within the time feel** rather than just playing rhythms.

Traditionally, we have used the terms *long* and *short* to identify the way we play quarter notes and eighth notes in jazz, and it is important to know what is meant by these terms. *Long* as used in jazz terminology means full value or connected. *Short* means less than full value or separated. When notes are played short in jazz, they are played in a very precise manner and are placed in time accurately. When a quarter note is played with the ∧ accent (daht) in jazz, the sound of the note is begun with a tongued attack and released with a tongued cutoff. The tongue should use the syllable D to begin jazz articulation. If the quarter note is played full *(doo)*, it will be marked with a dash above the note and will be held into the next note. Eighth notes in a group of two or more are played long or connected; however, the last eighth note in a group of eighths is played short *(dit)*. Any note longer than a quarter note is held full value. Example 1 shows some typical jazz articulation and how to approach it on the trumpet.

Example 1

Attention to articulation marks the difference between a good band and a great band. In a professional situation, a musician would never be able to secure a position in a band if he or she did not pay close attention to articulation.

Dynamics

While it is up to the *lead* player to determine how loud any phrase will be played and where crescendos or decrescendos will occur, it is up to the *fourth* player in the section to take charge of these musical events. The fourth player listens to the lead player's direction and then ensures that the appropriate dynamic action occurs. All efforts toward balance and dynamics actually begin with the fourth player and work upward through the section, not the reverse.

The lead player is the leader stylistically, and he or she determines how the music is to be played. The fourth player in the section is the person who ensures that this actually happens and to what degree it will happen. If the lead player wants more or less, he or she will discuss this with the fourth player.

An important consideration when rehearsing crescendos and decrescendos is this: crescendos or decrescendos are rarely performed gradually throughout the length of the note or phrase. They are typically sustained at the original dynamic level for perhaps a third of the duration of the note or phrase, followed by a more marked change for the remaining duration of the note or phrase. This is the most effective method of execution of this musical event and is the most readily observed by the audience.

Passion of Performance

Having a passion for the music is the final ingredient that makes any performance special. I think of passion as being the expression of one's love of the music. It is an excitement that in this sense means playing with exceptional and intense musicianship (and should not be confused with playing louder, faster, and higher). It means playing with fire as well as subtlety.

Believe it or not, a flawless performance without passion can be a rather boring experience. Hearing a musical performance played without passion may be likened to listening to someone read a dictionary as opposed to listening to the reading of a fine novel.

If a love of the music is demonstrated, if the performance contains excitement and musicianship, the resulting performance can be a thrilling, rewarding aural experience, and the performers and the audience may reach a level of ecstasy unobtainable in any other medium.

STANDARD SEATING PLAN

Four-Trumpet Section

In a jazz ensemble with four trumpets, the typical section set-up is shown in Diagram A below. Positioned from left to right (as you are looking at the section) is second, lead, third, and fourth trumpets.

Diagram A

JAZZ ENSEMBLE SET-UP

PERFORMANCE FOUR-TRUMPET SECTION SEATING

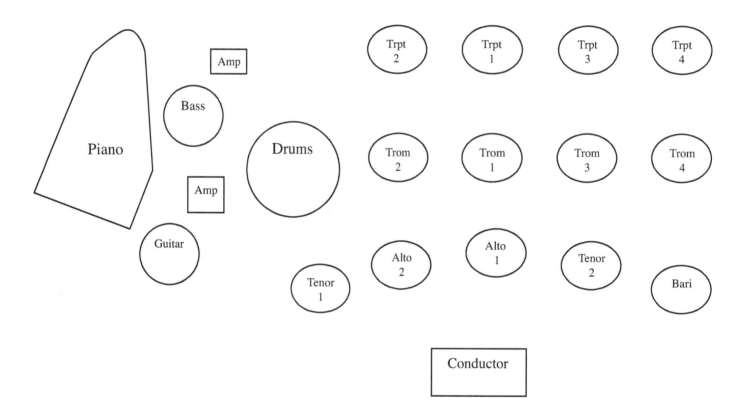

The lead trumpet is always placed as close to the middle as possible in order to line up directly behind the lead trombone and the lead alto so that they can listen carefully to each other to match articulation, phrasing, style, and dynamics.

Depending on the level of difficulty of the music, the second trumpet part often has the improvised solos. Therefore, this section set-up ensures that the second trumpet/jazz soloist is as close to the rhythm section as possible during solos. If a jazz solo is in a different part, that player may want to simply switch positions with the second trumpet so he or she may play at the far-left position, next to the rhythm section.

Five-Trumpet Section

The seating plan for a five-trumpet section is shown below in Diagram B. Usually organized from left to right (as you are looking at the section): fifth, second, lead, third, and fourth trumpets.

Diagram B

JAZZ ENSEMBLE SET-UP

PERFORMANCE FIVE-TRUMPET SECTION SEATING

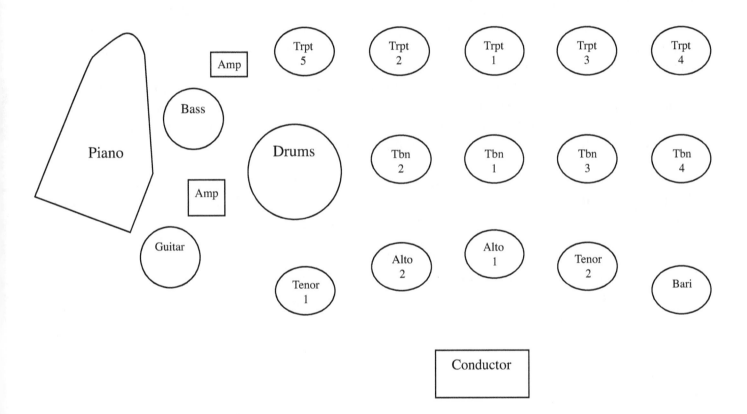

As with the four-trumpet section, the five-trumpet setting may be adjusted depending on which player has jazz solos. However, the lead trumpet should always stay in the center and line up directly behind the lead trombone and lead alto for reasons previously stated.

Once again, the jazz trumpet chair has been placed closest to the rhythm section in each of these examples to accommodate short solos when the soloist does not have time to move to the front of the stage (i.e., solos that are only eight to 16 bars in length, or are just one or two choruses of the blues). When the soloist has a longer solo or a feature, he or she should always come to the front of the stage and stand in front of the rhythm section. This allows the rhythm section to hear and respond to the soloist and, in turn, allows the soloist to hear and respond to the rhythm section.

SPECIFIC ROLES IN THE TRUMPET SECTION

Lead Trumpet

The lead player (also called *1st Trumpet* or *Trumpet 1*) is, as the name implies, the leader of the section. This position carries with it the responsibility of not only musical leadership by example but also leadership applied in a manner that shows respect for each section member, for the section as a whole, and for the section's responsibility within the full ensemble.

The lead player is expected to interpret the music in a manner that enhances the performance of the music. This includes historical and stylistic accuracy, which means a certain amount of preparation is required from the lead player. He or she should listen to many recordings of great bands, attend live performances by great bands, and talk to older, more seasoned lead players about the responsibilities of being a lead player. These are the ingredients of preparing for the job of leading the section.

A great lead player listens to the members of the section during rehearsals and performances and makes suggestions that will improve the section's performance. The lead player works carefully with the lead trombone and lead alto to achieve cohesiveness between the sections and works *closely* with each member of the rhythm section.

The relationship musically between the lead trumpet and the drummer is perhaps the most important relationship in the band. If the lead trumpet and drummer work closely together, an incredible swing can develop for the entire ensemble. When the lead trumpet and drummer are "on," the rest of the ensemble will be pulled into that ring of fire, and the resulting performance can be exceptional.

A note of caution: A great lead trumpet player is not a show-boater who, because of a possible greater command of the upper register, wishes to ensure that the audience knows who is playing lead through such tactics as holding high notes beyond the section cutoff, playing higher unwritten notes to demonstrate his or her great range, or visually scolding or looking askance at section members.

Second Trumpet

The second trumpet (also called *2nd Trumpet* or *Trumpet 2*) is in a close partnership with your lead player. It is the second trumpet's listening and performing skill that allows the lead player to relax and lead the section. He or she walks a fine line between pushing the lead player too much (which makes his or her job much more difficult) and *supporting* the lead player, which is really what the job is all about. Playing in tune with a big well-centered sound and ensuring that phrasing and articulation match the lead player's will allow the lead player's sound to sparkle or sizzle, depending on the musical situation. The second trumpet player often works harder than other members of the section because he or she is playing in the upper register with the lead player; however, the second trumpet does not have as many opportunities to rest and keep his or her chops fresh. The second trumpet is also called upon to play lead on some tunes (usually ballads) to spell the lead player for a tune.

Playing second trumpet is a demanding and often overlooked task, but playing this chair correctly will make your student a better trumpet player and will definitely make the section sound better. It is also great training for becoming a lead player.

Third Trumpet

The third trumpet (*3rd Trumpet* or *Trumpet 3*) has a very important role in the success of the trumpet section yet is perhaps the most difficult position. It requires the ability to judge carefully the balance of the section and play at only slightly a less dynamic level that the fourth player. If the third trumpet plays too softly compared to the fourth player, it will leave the lead and second players with nowhere to go dynamically—they will have to play so softly that they will not be heard. If the third trumpet plays too loudly compared to the fourth player, he or she can single-handedly destroy the balance of the section. This is the chair that actually makes the section balance work. Encourage your third trumpet to listen constantly to his or her dynamic relationship with the fourth player.

Fourth Trumpet

The fourth trumpet (*4th Trumpet* or *Trumpet 4*) in more experienced bands is often thought of as the *strongest* role in the section. The term *role* reflects not necessarily the strongest technical or physical command of the instrument, but the fourth player determines how successful the dynamic variation within the section will be, as well as dynamic level at any point in the chart. The lead player counts on the fourth player to listen carefully to the lead's stylistic and dynamic direction and then take charge of that musical event to ensure that it is played correctly. In younger student bands, however, the fourth trumpeter is usually *not* the most experienced player or the player with the most range or technique; however, the responsibility and demands of this part should not be underestimated. Therefore, the fourth player should not resign himself or herself as the last player in the section but instead strive to develop into a strong, consistent, and confident trumpet player who can deliver the dynamics, intonation, and tone quality needed for this role in the section. Every trumpet section will sound noticeably better with a fourth player who can not only follow the lead player but also play with solid intonation, tone, and dynamics.

Sectional Synchronicity

See Chapter 14 for specific rehearsal techniques. A trumpet section should spend time practicing together outside of regular band rehearsals. Encourage your trumpet players to take turns going to each other's homes once a week to rehearse as a section. They should talk to each other about the music and how they each feel it should be performed. They should listen to recordings together and discuss the musicians and recorded performance, and go to live performances together. Also, record the section during your sectionals and listen together, paying attention to balance, phrasing, dynamics, and articulation.

And trumpet players should practice, practice, practice, and enjoy, enjoy, enjoy!

FLUGELHORN

Music for the flugelhorn is written exactly like music for the trumpet. Although it has a more limited range, its mellow sound is sometimes a welcome contrast to the brightness and edge of the trumpet. The conical construction of the flugelhorn (similar to a bugle) determines its dark and warm sound, especially in the lower register, which makes it ideally suited as a solo instrument. Other useful timbres are in unison with other flugelhorns or as the lead of a brass section passage. Keep in mind that the sound of the flugelhorn is unique; therefore, it should not be used as a substitute for the trumpet.

Flugelhorn Dos and Don'ts

Because the flugelhorn mouthpiece is deeper that that of a trumpet (similar to a French horn), DO try to match rim size to that of the trumpet mouthpiece. This will make the flugelhorn feel more comfortable and compatible and allow the player to maintain a similar embouchure. DON'T use a trumpet or cornet mouthpiece in a flugelhorn. Typically the bore size of a flugelhorn is smaller than that of the trumpet, so the tendency is to overcompensate; DON'T overblow. Simply put, DON'T try to play a flugelhorn loudly. DO be aware that flugelhorns are prone to intonation problems in the extreme low and high registers.

EQUIPMENT

Student Instruments and Mouthpieces

Student musicians should choose a medium-large bore trumpet and a medium to medium-shallow cup mouthpiece. It is not wise for a student musician to play on a large bore or a small-bore trumpet, nor on a very shallow or very deep cup mouthpiece. Middle-of-the-road choices are the most desirable for younger trumpet players.

Any new student-line trumpet built by a reputable trumpet manufacturer will work well for a beginning student. New student line trumpets are typically available through rental or lease programs from your local music stores. By the end of a rental or lease agreement the student will know if he or she desires to continue his or her musical development (this desire will be guaranteed if he or she has studied under an instructor who loves music). At the end of a rental or lease period, most music stores will allow the student to apply the money paid for rental toward the purchase of an instrument.

Stepping Up to Professional Instruments

For students who are continuing their musical studies, most professional trumpet players and educators agree that they will perform and learn more easily on a professional-model trumpet rather than a student model. If a budget will not allow the purchase of a new pro-model horn, it is wiser to purchase a used pro-model horn than to continue with a student-line trumpet.

Trumpets do not wear out quickly, and it is not difficult to tell if a horn has been well cared for. The condition of the lacquer or silver finish on a used trumpet is not necessarily an indication of good or poor care of the instrument. More important is the condition of the valves and slides, along with the presence of bends or dents. The valves and slides should work easily without any sideway play. Look for indications that the horn was kept well oiled on the valves and greased on the slides. Check the compression of the valves by holding down the third valve and then pushing the third valve slide out as far as it will go. Release the third valve and pull the third valve slide in all the way and hold it in. After four or five seconds, push the third valve down, and if the compression is good, you will hear a slight pop. The presence of bends or dents is an indication of poor care; however, slight pings are okay and fairly typical in a used instrument.

Professional Instruments

When choosing a horn and a suitable mouthpiece for a college student or professional musician, there are no set answers. If you look at horns and mouthpieces as tools of the trade, your search for a trumpet will be easier. One would not want to choose the heaviest and darkest horn and the deepest cup mouthpiece to play lead on a four-hour gig. On the other hand, one might not want a smaller, tighter horn and a shallow cup mouthpiece with more sizzle to the sound when playing jazz in a small group.

Choose horns and mouthpieces that work for specific jobs. Some horns are more adept at big band lead and section playing, and others more adept at small group or jazz performance. Also, if you listen to players who you would like to sound like and try to match their sounds, it will help you in choosing the right tools.

If you cannot afford or do not wish to deal with two or more trumpets in your arsenal for the different styles of music you will be performing, you must pick one trumpet that does it all. A trumpet of medium bore and medium weight seems to work in most situations. However, you must experiment with different bore sizes, weights, bell sizes, percentage of copper and zinc in the brass (especially in the bell), taper of the lead pipe, etc. Most important, experiment with how it responds in several different playing situations in order to make the most intelligent choice. It is a good idea to borrow any trumpet that you are interested in purchasing from the music store for a week or more to play in as many musical situations as possible before making your final decision to purchase the instrument. Ask other trumpet players to listen to you play and ask their opinions on the sound, presence, projection, and intonation of the horn.

Professional Mouthpieces

Once you have chosen the right horn, you can achieve the warmth, the sizzle, and the shadings of sound from bright to dark with your choice of mouthpiece or, more typically, mouthpieces.

The depth of the cup and size and the taper of the throat and backbore will determine the suitability of any mouthpiece for your needs. Start with a medium-shallow mouthpiece and, depending on how bright or dark you want to sound, try smaller and larger mouthpieces with different throats and backbores until you find the perfect mouthpiece for you.

Once you have chosen a preferred mouthpiece size, you should play on several mouthpieces of that identical size and choose the mouthpiece that sounds the most clear and has the best ring to the sound. There are differences in the sound of each mouthpiece, even though they might come from the same manufacturer and have identical size markings.

As players progress, they usually feel the need to change equipment as their chops develop and as their ear becomes more aware of subtle differences in their playing.

Mutes

For more than a century, mutes have been an important part of the vocabulary of the jazz artist and subsequently the commercial arranger. In many applications they were often used to imitate the harsh vocal styling of the blues singer. The jazz trumpeter should be familiar with a variety of mutes. There are many available for sale in local music stores and catalogs; however, the average player needs only a few. There are two main types of brass mutes:

1. Mutes that fit into the bell of the instrument include cup, straight, and Harmon. These mutes significantly alter and greatly soften the sound of the instrument.
2. Mutes that fit over or around the bell of the instrument include the plunger, bucket, and felt hat, which touch the instrument, and the loose plunger and metal derby (hat), which are held away from the instrument. The sound is altered much less with the loose plunger, felt hat, and derby. These three mutes serve more to cover the sound.

• Straight: Humes & Berg Stonelined (fibre); match type and brand in the section if possible.

• Cup: Humes & Berg Stonelined. The cup mute is the basic brass mute. There are three variable factors connected with the use of the cup mute: (a) the use of a felt lining on the inside of the cup, (b) the use of rubber edging on the rim of the cup, and (c) the tightness or closeness of fit, which can be increased by shaving down the corks on the side of the mute.

• Plunger: The rubber "plumber's helper" is still the best.

• Bucket: Velvet-Tone by Humes & Berg Stonelined velvet (in 4½" or 5" sizes).

• Practice Mutes: Whispa-Mute; Yamaha Silent Brass. These are great for practicing in hotels, in apartments, and backstage.

Tip: When buying a mute, it is best to try the mute in the bell of your trumpet BEFORE buying the mute. Since there are several different bell diameters and several different mute sizes, it is best to see what works on your particular model.

Mute Tuning Characteristics
• Harmon mute: sharp.
• Cup mute: flat.
• Straight mute: flat but not as extreme as the cup mute.

TIPS FOR CONDUCTORS

It is vital for you and your students to listen to significant players in order to acquaint yourselves with the aspects of the music you're performing. The following recording lists are a place to start but are by no means complete.

Great Lead and Section Trumpet Players

These and many, many others are great trumpet players you will identify as you listen to recordings of the great big bands:

Al Porcino, Bobby Shew, Snooky Young, Jon Faddis, Dave Stahl, Doc Severinson, Bernie Glow, Conrad Gozzo, Johnny Frosk, Lew Soloff, Jimmy Maxwell, Marvin Stamm, Laurie Frink, Peter Olstad, Roger Ingram, Dave Trigg, George Graham, Bill Chase, and Buddy Childers.

Great Big Bands With Great Trumpet Sections

Some of the tightest and cleanest trumpet section playing can be found on the original Benny Goodman Carnegie Hall concert recording, now available on CD. Check out the following additional great bands along with many, many others you will identify as you talk with other musicians:

Jimmie Lunceford, Count Basie, Benny Goodman, Duke Ellington, Woody Herman, Terry Gibbs, Bob Florence, Maria Schneider, and Bob Mintzer.

Improvisation Is the Essence of Jazz

All trumpet players should learn to improvise. See Chapters 9 and 10 for improvisation basics. Usually when soloing with a big band, players are given a set length of time to solo rather than the open space that a soloist in a small group enjoys. A big band soloist will typically have 8, 12, or 16 bars to solo within, or at the most one or two choruses of a tune. The goal of soloing in a big band is to learn to play more concise solos that enhance the style or direction of the arrangement being performed. It is about creativity, yes, but also about creating with a sense of brevity. The ability to express one's individuality within only a few bars of solo space is the goal—much like the *Readers' Digest* version of a creative music solo.

JAZZ TRUMPET DISCOGRAPHY

What follows is a general, but by no means complete, discography of important jazz trumpet players. If I were to narrow this list to ten of the most (in my opinion) important trumpet players in the history of jazz trumpet, they would probably be as follows: Louis Armstrong, Roy Eldridge, Dizzy Gillespie, Fats Navarro, Clifford Brown, Clark Terry, Miles Davis, Lee Morgan, Kenny Dorham, and Freddie Hubbard. I would also include a list of five contemporary players who are important players currently on the jazz scene: Tom Harrell, John McNeil, Terrence Blanchard, Nicholas Payton, and Dave Douglas.

NAT ADDERLEY
Introducing Nat Adderley – Trip; *The Scavenger* – MSP; *Keep It Moving* – Fantasy; *The Cannonball Adderley Quintet in San Francisco* – Riverside; *The Cannonball Adderley Quintet at the Lighthouse* – Riverside.

LOUIS ARMSTRONG
West End Blues (with King Oliver) – CBS; *The Hot Fives & Hot Sevens* (three volumes) – Columbia; *Satch Plays Fats* – Columbia; *Louis Armstrong and His All Stars Play W.C. Handy* – Columbia; *The Louis Armstrong Story* (four volumes) – Columbia; *The Essential Louis Armstrong* (two volumes) – Vanguard; *Ambassador Satch* – Columbia; *What a Wonderful World* – MCA.

CHET BAKER
Mulligan Meets Konitz – World Pacific Jazz; *Carnegie Hall Concert* – CTI; *The Most Important Jazz Album of 1964/65* – Colpix; *Smokin' With the Chet Baker Quintet* – Roulette; *The Touch of Your Lips* – Steeplechase; *I Remember You* – Inja; *Star Eyes* – Marshmallow (Century).

BIX BEIDERBECKE
Bix Beiderbecke – Everest; *At the Jazz Band Ball* – ASV; *Bix Beiderbecke and the Chicago Cornets* – Milestone; *Bix Restored* (three volumes) – Origin Jazz; *The Bix Beiderbecke Collection* – Hallmark; *The Indispensable Bix Beiderbecke* – RCA.

TERRENCE BLANCHARD
Simply Stated – Columbia; *Black Pearl* – Columbia; *Nascence* – Columbia; *V* – Blue Note; *Heart Speaks* – Sony; *Malcolm X Jazz Suite* – Warner Bros.

LESTER BOWIE
Nice Guys – ECM; *Message to Our Folks* – BYG; *The Great Pretender* – ECM; *The Fifth Power* – Black Saint.

RANDY BRECKER
In Pursuit of the 27th Man – Blue Note; *You Gotta Take a Little Love* – Blue Note; *The Guerrila Band* – Mainstream; *Reach Out* – Steeplechase; *In the Idiom* – Passport; *Pendulum* – Artists House; *Into the Sun* – Concord; *Out of the Look* – GRP; *Priceless Jazz* – GRP; *Return of the Brecker Brothers* – GRP; *Randy Brecker Quintet Live at Sweet Basil* – Crescendo.

CLIFFORD BROWN
A Night at Birdland (two volumes) – Blue Note; *Clifford Brown in Paris* – Prestige; *The Best of Max Roach/Clifford Brown in Concert* – GNP; *At Basin Street* – Emarcy; *Brown & Roach, Inc.* – Emarcy; *Clifford Brown Memorial Album* – Blue Note; *Study in Brown* – Emarcy; *More Study in Brown* – Emarcy; *Jordu* – Emarcy; *The Beginning and the End* – KC; *Daahoud* – Mainstream; *Live at the Beehive* – Columbia.

DONALD BYRD
Off to the Races – Blue Note; *The Catwalk* – Blue Note.

DOC CHEATHAM
Good for What Ails Ya' – Classic Jazz; *The Fabulous Doc Cheatham* – Parkwood; *Doc Cheatham & Nicholas Payton* – Verve; *Doc Cheatham & Sammy Price* (two volumes) – Sackville; *At the Bern Jazz Festival* – Sackville; *New Tango '90* – Muze/MTS; *Butch Thompson & Doc Cheatham* – Daring.

DON CHERRY
This Is Our Music – Atlantic; *Ornette* – Atlantic; *Something Else* – Contemporary; *Change of the Century* – Atlantic; *Science Fiction* – Columbia; *Our Man in Jazz* – RCA Victor; *Eternal Rhythm* – MPS; *Symphony for Improvisers* – Blue Note; *Old and New Dreams* – Black Saint.

JOHNNY COLES
Little Johnny C. – Blue Note; *The Prisoner* – Blue Note; *New Morning* – Criss Cross; *The Warm Sound* – Enja.

CONTE CANDOLI
Sweet Simon – Best; *Powerhouse Trumpet* – Avenue Jazz; *Conte-nuity* – Fresh Sound.

MILES DAVIS

Miles Davis (two volumes) – Blue Note; *Workin'* – Prestige; *Cookin'* – Prestige; *Somethin' Else* – Blue Note; *'Round Midnight* – Columbia; *Milestones* – Columbia; *Kind of Blue* – Columbia; *Seven Steps to Heaven* – Columbia; *My Funny Valentine* – Columbia; *E.S.P.* – Columbia; *Cookin' at the Plugged Nickel* – Columbia; *Miles Smiles* – Columbia; *Nefertiti* – Columbia; *Filles de Kilimanjaro* – Columbia; *In a Silent Way* – Columbia; *Bitches Brew* – Columbia; *Live/Evil* – Columbia; *Agharta* – Columbia; *The Man With the Horn* – Columbia; *Star People* – Columbia; *Decoy* – Columbia; *Tutu* – Warner Bros.; *Doo Bop* – Warner Bros.

KENNY DORHAM

The Jazz Messengers at the Cafe Bohemia (two volumes) – Blue Note; *Horace Silver & the Jazz Messengers* – Blue Note; *Coltrane Time* – Solid State; *Una Mas* – Blue Note; *Whistle Stop* – Blue Note; *Trompete Toccata* – Blue Note; *Kenny Dorham 1959* – Prestige; *In 'n' Out* – Blue Note; *Blue Spring* – Fantasy.

DAVE DOUGLAS

Dave Douglas Five – Soul Note; *Parallel Worlds* – Soul Note; *The Tiny Bell Trio* – Songlines; *In Our Lifetime* – New World/Countercurrents; *Convergences* – Soul Note.

ROY ELDRIDGE

Little Jazz – Inner City; *Art Tatum & Roy Eldridge* – Pablo; *After You've Gone* – GRP; *Happy Time* – Original Jazz/Pablo; *Little Jazz & The Jimmy Ryan All-Stars* – Fantasy; *Roy Eldridge & His All Stars* – RCA Victor; *The Nifty Cat* – New World; *The Big Sound of Little Jazz* – Topaz; *Roy Eldridge and His Little Jazz* (three volumes) – BMG.

JON FADDIS

Into the Faddisphere – Epic; *Remembrances* – Chesky Jazz; *Take Double* – Emarcy; *Oscar Peterson & Jon Faddis* – Pablo; *Hornucopia* – Epic; *Legacy* – Concord.

ART FARMER

Modern Art – United Artists; *Homecoming* – Mainstream; *Art* – Argo; *The Summer Knows* – Inner City; *To Duke With Love* – Inner City.

DIZZY GILLESPIE

Bird & Diz – Verve; *Jazz at Massey Hall* – Fantasy; *In the Beginning* – Fantasy; *The Champ* – Savoy; *Concert in Paris* – Roost; *The Greatest of Dizzy Gillespie* – RCA Victor; *Diz and Roy* – Verve; *The Sonny Rollins/Sonny Stitt Sessions* – Verve; *Dizzy on the Riviera* – PHS; *Jambo Caribe* – Verve. (Almost any record or CD with Dizzy's name on it would be good.)

GREG GISBERT

The Court Jester – Criss Cross; *Harcology* – Criss Cross; *Big Lunage* – Criss Cross; *On Second Thought* – Criss Cross.

TIM HAGANS

On the Rise – EMD; *Animation/Imagination* – EMD; *No Words* – Blue Note.

WILBUR HARDEN

Countdown – Savoy.

ROY HARGROVE

Habana – Verve; *With the Tenors of Our Time* – Verve; *Parker's Mood* – Verve; *Approaching Standards* – Novus; *Family* – Verve; *Moment to Moment* – Polygram.

TOM HARRELL

Silver and Brass – Blue Note; *Silver and Voices* – Blue Note; *Silver and Wood* – Blue Note; *Aurora* – Adamo; *Play of Light* – Blackhawk; *Tall Stories* – Contemporary; *Sail Away* – Contemporary; *Moon Alley* – Criss Cross; *The Art of Rhythm* – RCA; *Labrynth* – RCA; *Real Book* – XtraWatt/BMG/ECM; *Playing With Fire* – Mama; *Look to the Sky* – SteepleChase.

EDDIE HENDERSON

Dark of Light – Cobblestone; *Mwandishi* – Warner Bros.; *Sextant* – Columbia; *Realization* – Capitol; *Sunburst* – Blue Note; *Heritage* – Blue Note.

FREDDIE HUBBARD

Free for All – Blue Note; *Ugetsu* – Riverside; *Caravan* – Riverside; *Maiden Voyage* – Blue Note; *Empyrean Isles* – Blue Note; *Speak No Evil* – Blue Note; *The All Seeing Eye* – Blue Note; *Ready for Freddie* – Blue Note; *Open Sesame* – Blue Note; *Black Angel* – Atlantic; *Straight Life* – CTI; *First Light* – CTI; *Super Blue* – Columbia; *Keystone Bop* – Fantasy; *Knucklebean* – Blue Note.

INGRID JENSEN

Here on Earth – Enja; *Vernal Fields* – Enja; *Higher Grounds* – Enja.

THAD JONES

5 by Monk by 5 – Riverside; *The Magnificent Thad Jones* – Blue Note; *Detroit-New York Junction* – Blue Note; *Sonny Rollins and Thad Jones* – Phoenix; *Mean What You Say* – Milestone; *Back Again* – Sonet; *Tangerine* – Prestige.

BOOKER LITTLE

Booker Little 4 + Max Roach – United Artists; *Out Front* – Candid; *Victory and Sorrow* – Bethlehem; *Far Cry* – New Jazz; *Eric Dolphy at the Five Spot* (two volumes) – Prestige; *The Fantastic Frank Strozier* – Vee Jay; *Booker Little* – Time.

BRIAN LYNCH

Back Room Blues – Criss Cross; *In Process* – KEN.

WYNTON MARSALIS

Wynton Marsalis – Columbia; *Think of One* – Columbia; *Black Codes* – Columbia; *Hot House Flowers* – Columbia; *J Mood* – Columbia; *Marsalis Standard Time* – Columbia; *In This House on This Morning* – Columbia; *Citi Movement* – Columbia; *Blue Interlude* – Columbia; *Midnight Blue's Standard* – Columbia; *Blood on the Fields* – Sony.

JOHN McNEIL

Hip Deep – Brownstone; *Fortuity* – SteepleChase; *Brooklyn Ritual* – Synergy; *The Glass Room* – SteepleChase; *Clean Sweep* – SteepleChase; *Embarkation* – SteepleChase; *Faun* – SteepleChase; *Look to the Sky* – SteepleChase; *I've Got the World on a String* – SteepleChase.

BLUE MITCHELL

Silvers Serenade – Blue Note; *Blowin' the Blues Away* – Blue Note; *Horace-Scope* – Blue Note; *Soul Time* – Riverside; *Heads Up* – Blue Note; *Fraffitie Blues* – Mainstream; *Vital Blue* – Mainstream; *Blue Mitchell* – Mainstream; *Boss Horn* – Blue Note; *A Blue Time* – Milestone/Fantasy.

LEE MORGAN

Moanin' – Blue Note; *Meet You at the Jazz Corner of the World* (two volumes) – Blue Note; *Like Someone in Love* – Blue Note; *The Cooker* – Blue Note; *The Sidewinder* – Blue Note; *Search for the New Land* – Blue Note; *Cornbread* – Blue Note; *Lee Morgan* – Blue Note; *Live at the Lighthouse* – Blue Note.

FATS NAVARRO

The Fabulous Fats Navarro (two volumes) – Blue Note; *Good Bait* – Roost; *Boppin' a Riff* – BYG.

NICHOLAS PAYTON

Payton's Place – Verve; *Gumbo Nouveau* – Verve; *From This Moment On* – Verve; *Dear Louis* – Verve; *Gumbo Nouveau* – Verve; *Nick at Night* – Verve.

CLAUDIO RODITI

Milestones – Candid; *Two of Swords* – Candid; *Gemini Man* – Milestone.

RED RODNEY

Live at the Village Vanguard – 32 Records; *Hey, Chood* – 32 Records; *Then and Now* – Chesky; *Fiery* – Savoy.

WALLACE RONEY

Verses – Muse; *Seth Air* – Muse; *Intuition* – Muse; *The Standard Bearer* – Muse; *Evidence* – Landmark; *Village* – Warner Bros.

WOODY SHAW

Cape Verdean Blues – Blue Note; *Unity* – Blue Note; *If You're Not Part of the Solution, You're Part of the Problem* – Milestone; *Love Dance* – Muse; *The Moontrane* – Muse; *Little Red's Fantasy* – Muse; *Rosewood* – Columbia; *The Homecoming* – Columbia.

JACK SHELDON

Smack Up – Contemporary; *The Return of Art Pepper* – Blue Note; *Hollywood Heroes* – Concord; *The Warm World of Jack Sheldon* – Dot.

BOBBY SHEW

Dialogic – Four Leaf Clover; *Telepathy* – Jazz Hounds; *Class Reunion* – Sutra; *Play Song* – Jazz Hounds; *Playing With Fire* – Mama; *Salsa Caliente* – Mama; *Heavyweights* – Mama; *Trumpets No End* – Delos.

MARVIN STAMM

Machinations – Verve; *Bop Boy* – Music Masters.

IRA SULLIVAN

Horizons – Atlantic; *Peace* – Galaxy; *Multimedia* – Galaxy; *Introducing Roland Kirk* – Argo; *J.R. Montrose* – Blue Note.

CLARK TERRY

Swahili – Trip; *Serenade to a Bus Seat* – Riverside; *Oscar Peterson Trio Plus One* – Mercury; *Gingerbread Men* – Mainstream; *Tonight* – Mainstream; *The Happy Horns of Clark Terry* – Impulse; *Out of the Storm* – Verve; *Portraits* – Chesky; *Clark Terry Live at the Village Gate* – Chesky; *Duke With a Difference* – Riverside; *What a Wonderful World* (For Louis & Duke) – Red Baron; *Color Changes* – Candid; *Having Fun* – Delos; *Take Double* – Emarcy; *Ow* (two volumes) – JLR; *Straight No Chaser* – Mainstream; *The Power of Positive Swinging* – Mainstream; *Oscar Peterson & Clark Terry* – Pablo; *A Celebration of Duke* – Pablo; *Summit Meeting* – Vanguard; *Spanish Rice* – Impulse.

DIRECTOR'S CHECKLIST FOR TRUMPET

• Always think as a section.

• Each member should be prepared as an individual to contribute to the ensemble. Practice!

• The balance is dependent on listening.

• Each player should strive for a full, rich, and controlled sound.

• Use "warm air."

• Intonation means listening to the other players and tuning to the bass player.

• Time must be felt together by the entire section; coordinate time within the section.

• Articulation is a must for a great section. A coordinated attack on a note will give life and power to the section and to the band.

• Dynamics are often determined by the fourth trumpet player, not the lead.

• Always play with passion; love the trumpet and love the music!

• The roles of each player have individual challenges.

• Listen to trumpet heroes. Learn from them.

Please refer to the Resource Guide Index.

Chapter 17c

THE TROMBONE SECTION

by Allan R. Kaplan, Ph.D.

Throughout the history of Western music, the trombone has had a long and distinguished reputation as an ensemble instrument. Trombonists worked as members of town bands, as tower musicians, and as members of the opera and symphony orchestras. In the jazz/commercial field, trombones also have a great tradition. In most cases, with a few rare exceptions, the average professional trombonist makes his or her living still as an ensemble player. To develop the skills to become a successful member of a solid trombone section is the focus of this chapter.

ENSEMBLE BASICS

Today, an experienced jazz trombone section may be asked to phrase as the best jazz artists do and to perform authentic versions of many styles within an incredibly broad repertoire ranging from Dixieland to swing to bebop to various Latin jazz styles. Furthermore, today's experienced trombone section is expected to have the serious background of the classical/conservatory–trained player as well as the experience and trained ear of the road band musician.

A few outstanding soloists in the jazz area have made an incredible impact on section players. Because of these great musicians, lead trombonists of today can aspire to play ballads the way Tommy Dorsey, Urbie Green, and Bill Watrous do. The improvising soloists in the section can now expect to keep up with faster tempos, more complex chord changes, and many varied styles due to the virtuosity and flexibility of performers such as Frank Rosolino, Carl Fontana, Bob McChezney, and Conrad Herwig. The newest addition to the section, the bass trombone specialist, can aspire to play notes below the staff that virtuoso Dave Taylor would play.

Although these expectations may be exaggerated with regard to younger trombonists, the question is: How do you help your students prepare for the exciting world of trombone playing? Read on.

Balance

One person per part in the jazz ensemble is best. Performing in a jazz band helps young musicians learn musical independence. Remember that this is not a concert band! If you want to include every trombone in the concert band who wants to participate, then create a second or third jazz ensemble.

Two basic types of balance are helpful for trombone sections in the jazz ensemble: pyramid and column.

Pyramid Balance

To balance most "normal" chords, especially with less experienced trombone sections, it is helpful to encourage them to think of their volume in terms of a *pyramid,* where the lower parts play "louder" than the lead voice. In reality, this way of thinking encourages the lower parts to move more air through their instruments to fully support the lower notes in their naturally softer dynamic range.

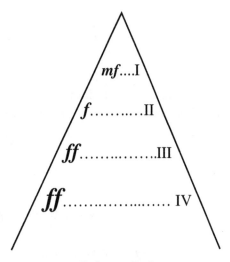

Column Balance

An effective way to balance polychords or very complicated chords is to help your trombone section visualize their parts in a *column,* where they play all parts at the *same* dynamic level for dramatic effect, especially if you do not want the lead part to stand out. This concept is great for complex Kenton-style chords where the roots are "covered."

$$
\begin{array}{cc}
f & \text{I} \\
f & \text{II} \\
f & \text{III} \\
f & \text{IV}
\end{array}
$$

Blend

Combine pyramid balancing and the following tuning method to produce a great sound in your trombone section. It is especially effective for ballads.

Ask your trombone section:

1. What chord note are you playing?
2. Who else is doubling that same note in the band?

Help your trombone section tune chords:

1. To tune major chords, tune the chord root first with an electric tuner and keep in mind that the 5th will be a little sharp and the major 3rd very flat.
2. Tune the root and then 5th for most other types of chords as well. Use a tuner for the root; use your ear for the other notes.

Dynamics

Help your trombone section (and your entire jazz ensemble for that matter) learn to exaggerate dynamics, articulation, and so on. They should strive to send the music "past the footlights." Teach them to play exciting dynamics. If they don't get goose bumps from the music and do not communicate those goose bumps to the audience, then why should the audience get excited by their playing? Before you rehearse a chart, plan the overall dynamics from beginning to end, including the opening and ending, and edit the score when needed.

Dynamics Tips for Trombones

- Begin by finding your best sound/tone quality first and then expand the dynamics from there.
- Practice developing control of tone at the extremes with a tuner: ***ppp*** crescendo to ***fff*** decrescendo to ***ppp***.
- Crescendo means to go from softer to louder. Prepare a crescendo by planning the dynamics ahead.
- Don't play into the stand unless the music says "play into stand."
- Support softer dynamics/phrases. Keep the same energy that you play in loud passages in softer passages.
- Soloists: Do *not* try to out-blow the band. Instead, always keep a centered, good tone and learn to use the microphone. Let the band director balance the band to the solo.

Intonation

Encourage your trombone section to hear the sound they want to produce in their heads *before* they play it. Remind them to let the air do most of the work; they should practice support, using breath attacks in *all* registers and at all dynamics. Trombonists should be encouraged to create a full, rich, beautiful *tone*—and then *tune*.

Great intonation for the trombone section starts with an "oh" breath (a low-sounding, relaxed, yawn-like breath). Good posture will also help your students breathe and prevent injuries to the back, neck, and hands.

Intonation Tips for Trombones

- Practice breathing with an Arnold Jacobs plastic breathing tube. It has a 1"–1½" outer diameter and is 5" long.
- As you practice breathing, "fill up at the gas station" (full, relaxed "oh" breath) and then "waste air" or release some air.
- Do not create forced, uncentered blasts or other ugly sounds.
- Learn and use alternate positions to help with tuning.
- Also, learn to adjust out-of-tune notes in harmonic series. For example: F above middle C is played in flat 1st position.
- Support longer notes—think through long notes.
- Buy an inexpensive tuner such as a Korg CA-20.
- Listen every day to recordings of great wind players—*imitate them!*

Articulation and Phrasing

Good articulation is essential for any great section. See Chapter 14 for rehearsal techniques for the entire ensemble. All trombones need to play with a clean front or attack to the notes (practicing long tones with breath attacks helps this). Low brass can sometimes get in a habit of using lazy air, which may make their attacks sound late. Remind lower parts to play shorter than the lead part.

Make the trombone section sing their parts before you let them play the parts on their instruments. Can everyone sing his or her part correctly? Can the section buzz their parts on their mouthpieces? Also, make sure the section leader has listened to recordings of the charts you are rehearsing, or similar charts by the same composer, and marked his or her part correctly for sectional rehearsals.

STANDARD SEATING PLAN

A common set-up for a jazz band trombone section is based on the traditional three-row stage set-up of saxes in the front row, trombones in the middle row, and trumpets in the back row. The best suggested set-up has the lead trombone in the center, lined up with both the lead alto and lead trumpet. The second trombone is close to the rhythm to hear solo chord changes, and the bass trombone is behind the baritone sax.

JAZZ ENSEMBLE SET-UP

PERFORMANCE FOUR-TROMBONE SECTION

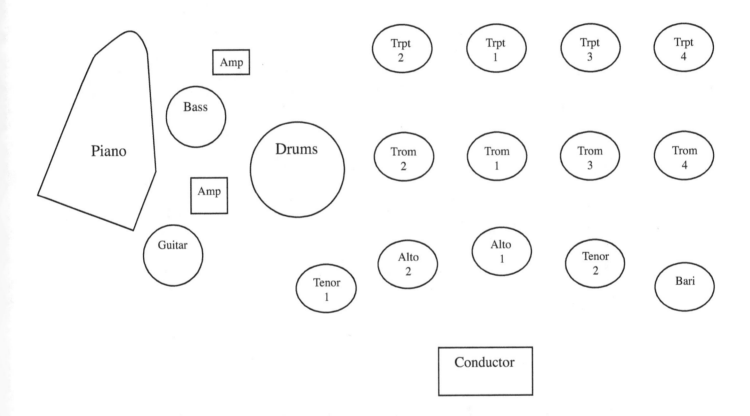

Four-Trombone Section

The diagram above indicates a typical four-trombone section set-up. Positioned from left to right (as you are looking at the section) are second, lead, third, and fourth trombones.

Below is the suggested seating plan for a five-trombone section. Keep the lead trombone aligned in the center of the band with lead trumpet and lead alto sax.

JAZZ ENSEMBLE SET-UP

<u>PERFORMANCE FIVE-TROMBONES SECTION</u>

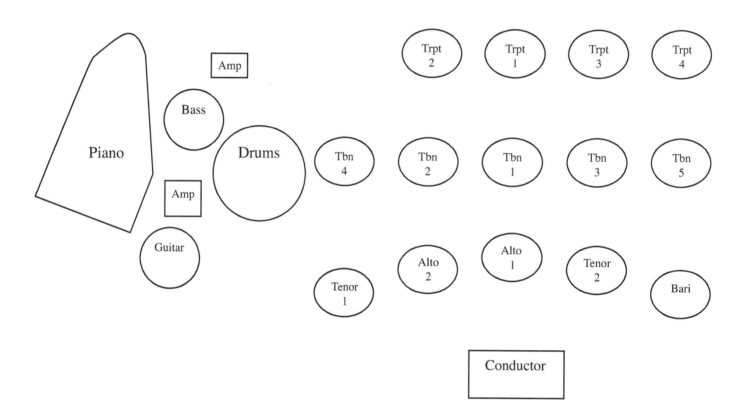

SPECIFIC ROLES IN THE TROMBONE SECTION

Lead Trombone

The lead trombone/section leader (also called *1st Trombone* or *Trombone 1*) is responsible for running the sectional, setting the high standards of performance and professionalism, knowing how each part and style should be performed, and communicating with the director and the other section leaders. Usually this requires strong leadership by example, solid technique, and a very confident upper register. It also helps to be a competent improviser. Usually the pretty ballad solos are written for first trombone. It requires a great deal of additional listening and study to play lead. The lead player is probably the most experienced and sophisticated musician in the section.

Second Trombone

The second trombone (also called *2nd Trombone* or *Trombone 2*) needs to possess the same traits of the lead player in talent, experience, and technique. Like all of the section members, the second trombone must possess the ability to work effectively with other players and to be a good listener. Usually in more advanced-level arrangements, the second trombone requires the most experienced jazz soloist. In many older-style arrangements, the second chair was the solo chair. Both 1st and 2nd Trombone usually require smaller equipment (see the following equipment section) to create a brighter sound in order to blend with the upper voices of the brass.

Third and Fourth Trombones

Trombone 3 and Trombone 4 are the workhorses of the section. In sections consisting of three bones, the third part becomes the bass voice. In a four-bone section, the bass is usually in the fourth part. These are the two chairs where it is permissible to use the larger .547 bore-size horns since they have dual roles.

Fourth (and Fifth) Trombone

Trombone 4 has become the specialized bass trombone chair. In a more advanced ensemble, it is not unusual to have a five-trombone section. Be advised that bass trombones can be quite expensive. Suggested instruments are listed in the equipment section following.

Advice for Bass Trombonists

Aspiring bass trombonists should find a bass specialist/pro to study with as soon as possible. Like lead trumpet-playing a few decades ago, bass trombone-playing has become a specialty with separate method books, sophisticated equipment choices, and superstars. Please refer to the listing of method books in the Resource Guide. Bass trombonists can use the same methods as tenor trombonists, only they also practice down one octave and/or transpose the material in a manner that they get to play even lower than one octave. (For example, play them in tenor clef, down two octaves). Here are some specific texts for bass trombone study: Charles Vernon's *A Singing Approach to the Trombone* will give you some great insights into the Chicago Symphony style of practicing; Paul Faulise's *The F&D Double Valve Bass Trombone* and Aharoni's *Method for Bass Trombone* will give you great workouts with both the valves; any of the major books for tuba published by Robert King, such as the V. Blazevich *70 Studies for Tuba* and the Kopprasch *60 Etudes for Tuba,* are wonderful.

EQUIPMENT

Advise your students to find the best equipment they can afford that suits their individual physical needs as well as their musical needs. It is to be hoped they will not be influenced by the celebrity syndrome. They should not buy a horn or mouthpiece just because they saw it advertised in a magazine or read that their idol uses a certain mouthpiece. All players are different physically and respond to equipment such as mouthpieces on a highly individual level. If your students are interested in a certain product, suggest they try it with you, a trombone teacher, or a respected listener present. Many products may be ordered on a trial basis.

If your students are able to attend major conferences, such as the International Association for Jazz Education (IAJE) conference or the International Trombone Association's Trombone Festival, there are dozens of exhibits that contain instruments, mouthpieces, mutes, and other accessories that they can try out and test. This is a great opportunity to compare makes, sizes, materials, and so on, before making a purchase. There are some suggestions for appropriate equipment listed below. I suggest that students plan their purchases to fit the role (in other words, job description) they plan to play in the section.

Instruments

Suggested lead instrument bores: .508 or .525.

Suggested tenor trombones: King 3B (.508 bore), Bach 16 and 16M (.509 bore), Bach 32 (.530 bore), Edwards T302 (.500 bore), Besson 940 (.500 bore), and 941 (.530 bore). Other excellent brands are Getzen, Yamaha, Benge, Shire, Smelzer, Holton, and Conn.

Note: In many jazz ensemble arrangements, trombones are written as a continuation of the trumpets in the harmony. The top bones form the transition between the higher brass and the lower brass. Many younger players try to play the upper bone parts on so-called baritone trombones (.547 bore horns with F attachments) yet cannot achieve a balance with the trumpets and end up with a rather tubby, unfocused sound. Try to select conservative equipment that will enable your students to achieve a sound that blends easily within the section and band. It is also easier to replace such instruments if damaged or lost. Trombones 3 and 4 are the two chairs where it is permissible to use larger .547 bore-size horns since they have dual roles.

Suggested bass trombones: Holton TR-150 and the Bach 50B, 50B2, and 50B3. The dual bore (.562 - .578) David Taylor Getzen Eterna model is a good choice when the budget prevents purchasing a horn with Thayer valves. The Edwards Bass Trombone also has Thayer valves and an interchangeable leadpipe.

Mouthpieces

Suggested lead trombone mouthpieces: Bach 12C - 6 1/2 AL, Schilke 47 or 49.

Also highly recommended is the new line of mouthpieces by Stork. The Stork tenor trombone mouthpieces, T1 (6.5 AL), T2 (7C), and T3 (12C) are major improvements over the older designs of mouthpieces and will aid in projection, ease in the high register, and flexibility.

For bass trombone, the new #1.5 and the #1 Stork bass trombone mouthpieces were designed with newer bass trombones in mind.

Trombone Stands

Always use a good-quality trombone stand such as Hamilton or UMI.

Mutes

For more than 100 years mutes have been an important part of the vocabulary of the jazz artist and subsequently the commercial arranger. In many applications they were often used to imitate the vocal styling of the blues singer. There are many available for sale in local music stores and catalogs, but not all are needed by the average player. Here is a brief description of the two main types of brass mutes:

1. Mutes that fit into the bell of the instrument include cup, straight, and Harmon. These types of mutes significantly alter and greatly soften the sound of the instrument.
2. Mutes that fit over or around the bell of the instrument include the tight plunger, bucket mute, and felt hat, which touch the instrument, and the loose plunger and metal derby (hat), which are held away from the instrument. The sound is altered much less with the loose plunger, felt hat, and derby. These three mutes serve more to cover the sound.

WHAT TO PURCHASE

The mutes for non-professionals consist of five basic types: straight, cup, plunger, bucket, and practice. Keep in mind that as with most aspects of trombone playing, you need to find recordings that feature jazz artists playing these mutes to begin to get the stylistic sounds in your mind's ear.

1. Straight: Humes & Berg Stonelined, fiber; metal with various bottoms such as copper; Tom Crown; Jo-Ral (J. Alessi); Bach Elite, metal.
2. Cup: Humes & Berg Stonelined; metal such as the Denis Wick.

The cup mute is the basic brass mute. There are three variable factors connected with the use of the cup mute: (1) the use of a felt lining on the inside of the cup, (2) the use of rubber edging on the rim of the cup, and (3) the tightness or closeness of fit, which can be increased by shaving down the corks on the side of the mute.

Note: I do not recommend buying combination mutes that convert from a cup to a straight mute. They never seem to be in the right form at the right time, and usually it is too difficult to change the mute and still make your entrance on time. Buy one good quality mute of each type to be safe. The sound is usually better when the mute designer doesn't try to make a "compromise" mute.

3. Plunger: The rubber "plumber's helper" is still the best.
4. Bucket: Velvet-Tone by Humes & Berg Stonelined (in 7 1/2", 8, and 8 1/2" sizes); Jo-Ral metal Bucket mute (listed as small bore or large bore). These tend to be expensive and are not needed as often as the other mutes.

5. Practice mutes: Denis Wick; Spivak Whispa-Mute; Yamaha Silent Brass. These are great for practicing in hotels, apartments, and backstage. Denis Wick and other great teachers advocate using these mutes to develop a more open sound. His Wick mutes come with a brief music lesson on this subject.

Tip: When buying a mute, it is best to test-drive the mute in the **bell of your trombone** *before* buying the mute. Since there are several different bell diameters and several different mute sizes, it is best to see what works on your particular model. For example, if you purchase a Stonelined straight mute that is the right size for a small-bore jazz tenor trombone, it will probably disappear in the bell of a .547-bore Conn 88-H or similar model. Even though the mute might not fit perfectly, you will be able to find out if it is the right size for your particular model. Keep in mind that for most mutes the corks will have to be adjusted for a better fit by filing them down until the mute fits in the bell exactly as needed.

Bass trombonists note: You may need to find custom-sized mutes that fit the extremely large bells now available. Check your local music stores and those online.

Tuning Tendencies of the Mutes

SHARP: Straight mutes.

FLAT: Cup mute; bucket; metal bucket (in tune).

Adjustments need to be made when playing with mutes. Some people advocate re-tuning when using certain mutes. Unless the problem is extreme, it is possible for a trombonist to adjust the tuning during performance using the slide. Keep in mind that you'll need time to tune back to the standard pitch after using the mute.

TIPS FOR CONDUCTORS

Guiding your trombone section to work independently will make your full jazz ensemble rehearsals more effective. Following are some ways to get your trombone section off to a great start.

Sectional Rehearsals

A good, successful sectional rehearsal is like a good, successful big band rehearsal or a successful personal practice session. Make sure you provide your section leader with the metronome tempo for each piece. Encourage them to select a tempo for each chart that is not too fast so that the section will start out playing everything on the page correctly, accurately, in tune, well phrased, and so on. Then gradually work up to a faster performance tempo. It may take a few sectionals to get there! Remind your students: Do not practice mistakes. If it is too fast, you are only surviving, not learning! Play a recording of the original chart or a similar chart by the same band/arranger/artist. If no recording of the original is available, find a recording of the head (melody) in that style.

Your trombone section should try to include the following in their sectionals:
• Quiet time/meditation (optional).
• Cooperatively set rehearsal goals.
• Warm-ups.
• Using a metronome set on beats 2 and 4 like a hi-hat, if possible.
• Keeping a tuner on at all times and tape recording each sectional and studying the tapes later.
• Marking all parts the same, and in pencil.
• Taking a few moments to evaluate the sectional rehearsal upon completion. Was it a good use of everyone's time? Did you accomplish your goals?

Improvisation Is the Essence of Jazz

All trombone players should learn to improvise. See Chapters 9 and 10 for extensive information about teaching improvisation basics. Encourage your soloists to think vocally (melodically) when they improvise. Do you use Shelly Berg's wonderful text, *Chop-Monster*? It is great for beginners at any age.

Make a rule for soloists: Learn the melody and the chords before you try to improvise! Create a lead sheet for each tune that includes melody and chords transposed as needed.

Beginning Trombone Improvisers

1. Take a melody from a song and make music out of it without adding extra notes or changing anything. Begin learning/memorizing simple solos, and play from memory.
2. Play a melody with passion and expression. Learn the lyrics to songs. Get into the meaning/mood/emotions. (Ballads work well.)
3. Embellish the melody using rhythmic elements: vary the note lengths.
4. Learn the names of the earliest soloists on your instrument and study their style. Who is your favorite soloist? Who were their influences?
5. Create a listening/sharing library. Have the bone section buy five different CDs and share them.

Advancing Trombone Improvisers

1. Transcribe solos. ReedKotler.com has a transcriber program that enables you to slow down the music.
2. Purchase Hal Crook's *Ready, Aim, Improvise* (Advance Music) and Jerry Coker's *Elements of the Jazz Language for the Developing Improviser.*
3. Use Band-in-a-Box and/or Jamey Aebersold's play-alongs to help learn tunes.
4. Attend a summer workshop: Jamey Aebersold's camps are located in various cities. Also of note are the Mile High Jazz Camp (Boulder, Colorado) and Idyllwild Jazz Camp (Idyllwild, California) to name only a few.
5. Band directors: attend the camps along with your students. Many camps have no age limit.

TEN ATTRIBUTES OF SUCCESSFUL TROMBONISTS

1. Become the greatest musician possible.
2. Become the greatest trombonist possible.
3. Become a musical athlete.
4. Strive to develop a background in the jazz language.
5. Study with the four greatest private teachers in the world.
6. Develop the proper attitude toward the music.
7. Study with the masters.
8. Study improvisation.
9. Hear live performances as much as possible.
10. Have a dream.

Become the Greatest Musician Possible

Notice that becoming the best musician possible, not the best trombonist, is the first step. Every day flood your brain with the greatest sounds played by the greatest artists in all styles. Listening to ballads performed by Frank Sinatra, John Coltrane, and Luciano Pavarotti will teach you how to phrase, use the appropriate vibrato/no vibrato, breath control, and so on. Once you have the sound in your head, your job is then to imitate it by trial-and-error until you can play what you hear. Remember: What you want it to sound like is more important than what comes out. Be patient, but strive to play the trombone in your head. Keep an open mind when it comes to listening to music.

Become the Greatest Trombonist Possible

Seek out the best equipment, as discussed earlier in this chapter. Study the trombone with a master teacher who is able to inspire you to put in the enormous amount of time and energy required to become a great trombonist.

Wonderful traditional method books are available that may be used throughout many years of study. Follow the example of such artists as J. J. Johnson, who not only practiced these books, such as the *Melodious Etudes* by Bordogni/Rochut, but who also took lessons from such great symphony brass players as the renowned tubist Arnold Jacobs.

Become a Musical Athlete

It is necessary to be in good health in order to meet the physical demands of the profession and the trombone. Plan organized daily practice sessions that cover all of the basic fundamentals, such as lip slurs, scales, arpeggios, tonguing, and so on, as well as musical challenges, such as etudes, solos, transcribed solos, and jazz studies. Do not neglect the physical aspects of trombone playing. Schedule practice sessions as well as exercise sessions. The physical demands of performing on a professional level or even a college level are enormous.

A smoke-free, drug-free lifestyle that includes a proper diet and regular aerobic exercise is essential. The greatest brass and wind players all over the world use the breathing concepts and exercises explained in *Arnold Jacob's Song and Wind* by Brian Frederiksen. I recommend learning them and/or studying with someone who knows them. Most of the major problems trombonists face can be solved by proper use of air.

Strive to Develop a Background in the Jazz Language

If your favorite artist on the trombone is Slide Hampton, strive to find out all you can about how he plays. Then, research his influences and then explore their playing. Once you have gone back far enough, you will then begin to create the kind of depth of background needed to perform a variety of styles. When you see the admiration and reverence such contemporary greats such as Wynton Marsalis have for the older music—for example, Duke Ellington's—you will understand the importance of this kind of study. The joy comes when the roots of your idols come out in your playing.

Study With the Four Greatest Private Teachers in the World

The four greatest private teachers are the *tape recorder, tuner, metronome*, and *mirror*. Use these tools in sectional rehearsals as well as in your private practice.

Tape Recorder

Use a tape recorder during practice to correct obvious errors that would normally be corrected in the first 30 minutes of your lesson, which enables you to have lessons on a higher musical level. Record yourself as you prepare for auditions so you learn to hear what the audience is hearing. In general, tape recording is a great way to maintain a very high level of performance and avoid sloppiness or carelessness that may begin to creep into your work.

Tuner

Keep a tuner on at all times where you can refer to it. When you play back your recorded session, watch the tuner while you listen. Remember that the one thing trombonists can do that no other instrument can is *always* play in tune. The trombone slide is the world's longest tuning slide!

Metronome

Practice with a metronome and constantly write down at what metromone marking you are practicing. Listen for evenness in technical passages. Try adding a click on the upbeats to create another rhythmical time standard. It is also useful to practice with the metronome on beats 2 and 4, like a hi-hat.

Mirror

Especially when you warm up, keep a mirror handy to help you observe your embouchure for correctness, observe unnecessary movement when you tongue, ensure that you are playing with good posture, and so on.

Develop the Proper Attitude Toward the Music

"Attitude is everything" and "You are what you think" are two sayings that are absolutely true in our profession. Keep an open mind about all types of music. Take the opportunity to play in as many diverse ensembles as possible, including rehearsal bands that may not perform on a regular basis. Everything you play enters your experience and could be used later in your career. Playing a Bach chorale in brass ensemble may not relate directly to jazz but may help you understand harmony better, develop your ear, or build up your chops. You might even use those sounds in a future solo. Everything is relative. Performing music that is not really jazz may make you appreciate those times when you get to select your own music and really get to solo. Learn to play with other musicians in all types of ensembles. When you play in a section, you may have to make many compromises when you adjust your tuning, for example, to the tired lead player, or play a chart with an interpretation with which you may not agree. The goal should be for the section to sound good. Save your individuality and ego for solos and other opportunities that are appropriate. Have a deep respect for those trombonists who came before you, and realize that we are where we are today because we are standing on their shoulders.

Study With the Masters

Study with the masters means to take lessons with all of the master teachers possible, for example, Alan Raph or Charlie Vernon. Accomplish this by studying the recordings of these master players. When you become a "professional listener," you begin to hear what the greats played, both in terms of licks and in terms of sound, vibrato, style, and phrasing. Learn to transcribe. Find transcription books of your favorite performers and play along with the masters on the original CDs.

Study Improvisation

Dr. Willie Hill, Shelly Berg, Hal Crook, Jamey Aebersold, and Jerry Coker all provide the materials it takes to help you learn how to be a very successful improviser. Study improvisation as you do your trombone: in a serious and logical manner. If you are a beginner, Shelly Berg's series *Chop-Monster* will get you started. Berg's *Goal Note Method* will teach you more advanced techniques, as will the Crook *Ready Aim Improvise* and the Coker *Elements of the Jazz Language*. Hal Crook's text has a great deal of helpful information regarding how to practice and what to practice. This is the most comprehensive of all the sources. Next you will learn the essential repertoire for a jazz musician, or the standard tunes, from Dr. Willie Hill's series *Approaching the Standards*. This three-volume book/CD set includes eight well-known standards per volume with parts for all instruments. Innovations include a brief history and background of the tune, a written-out solo, a "Licks & Tricks" section, and a play-along CD.

Another very useful tool for developing as an improviser is investigating your idol's influences. For example, Bill Watrous's influences include Clifford Brown, Charlie Parker, Carl Fontana, Vic Dickenson, and Dizzy Gillespie. Investigating Bill's influences will bring you to other great performers, some on instruments other than the trombone!

Hear Live Performances as Much as Possible

Attend as many live performances as you can. Keep in touch with our art form. I recently heard the Vanguard Jazz Orchestra live in concert. The leader of the group was lead trombonist John Mosca. I still remember his great solos and ability to lead the band from the Trombone 1 chair! Every member of that fine ensemble was an outstanding soloist. Attending many live performances can inspire us, excite us, and help keep us focused on our goals. In addition, it is necessary for you to be a live performer too. You are what you do, so make an effort to keep performing in all styles and groups as often as possible.

Have a Dream

I recently heard an outstanding clinician regret that he hadn't dreamed high enough. We all start as beginners on our instrument. The ones who make it are the ones who dream big and set the highest goals. Set these goals, work hard, and you will attain them.

DIRECTOR'S CHECKLIST FOR TROMBONE

Review the ten attributes of a successful trombonist.

- Become the greatest musician possible.

- Become the greatest trombonist possible.

- Become a musical athlete.

- Seek out the best equipment.

- Study with the four greatest private teachers in the world.

- Develop the proper attitude toward the music and to the study of music.

- Study with the masters.

- Study improvisation.

- Hear live performances as much as possible.

- Read this chapter ten times!

ELEVEN SUGGESTED TROMBONE RECORDINGS

1. Hal Crook: *ARAYANI 1997*. Ram Records RMCD 4522.
2. Carl Fontana and Frank Rosolino: *Bobby Knight's Great American Trombone Co*. 1996: Craig Recording/Jazz Mark JM 116.
3. Carl Fontana; Ian McDougall; Bill Watrous; Jiggs Whigham: *The Brass Connection*, A 5 Star Edition 1991: The Jazz Alliance TJA 10002.
4. Curtis Fuller: *Imagination by the Curtis Fuller Sextette*. 1959: Savoy Jazz Classics MG 1214.
5. Wycliffe Gordon: *Wycliffe Gordon & Ron Westray*. Bone Structure 1996: Atlantic Records 82936-2.
6. Conrad Herwig: *The Latin Side of John Coltrane*. Astor Place Recordings; 1996: TCD 4003.
7. J. J. Johnson: *Stan Getz & J. J. Johnson at the Opera House*. 1957: Verve 831 272-2.
8. Nils Landgren: *Nils Landgren Funk Unit - Live at Montreux*. 1998: ACT Records 9265-2.
9. Bob McChezney: *Bob McChezney: No Laughling Matter*. 2000: Summit Records DCD 261.
10. Frank Rosolino: *Fond Memories of Frank Rosolino*. 1996: Double Time Records DTRCD-113.
11. Bill Watrous: *A Time for Love,* 1993: GNP Crescendo Records GNP D222.

A SELECTED LIST OF IMPORTANT TROMBONISTS

Major soloists listed by style:
- **Dixieland/traditional:** Kid Ory, Miff Mole, Turk Murphy.
- **Swing:** Jack Teagarden, Lawrence Brown, Joe "Tricky Sam" Nanton, Tommy Dorsey, Trummy Young, Vic Dickenson, Bill Harris.
- **Bebop:** Bennie Green, J. J. Johnson, Kai Winding, Curtis Fuller, Jiggs Wigham.
- **West Coast/Cool:** Bob Brookmeyer, Jimmy Cleveland, Kai Winding.
- **Hard Bop:** Frank Rosolino, Carl Fontana, Slide Hampton, Bart van Lier, Jimmy Knepper, Bill Watrous.
- **Avant Garde:** Albert Mangelsdorff, Hal Crook, Roswell Rudd.
- **Contemporary:** John Allred, Bob McChezney, Bill Watrous, Ray Anderson, Andy Martin, Conrad Herwig, Steve Turre, Dave Bargeron, Wycliffe Gordon, Robin Eubanks, Jim Pugh, Mark Nightengale (has written jazz method books), Michael Davis (a talented arranger/composer), Nils Landgren (has a great funk band in Europe).
- **Latin Jazz:** Conrad Herwig, Steve Turre, Barry Rodgers, Jimmy Bosch, William Capeda, Wayne Wallace, Arturo Velazco, Luis Bonilla.

Major bass trombonists:
- **Paul Faulise:** NYC Studios.
- **Dick Hixson:** Elgart Bands (1950s and NYC Studios).
- **Dick Lieb:** NY Tonight Show; NYC Studios; Arranger; Kai Winding Septet.
- **Alan Raph:** Gerry Mulligan and NYC Studio; several solo recital albums.
- **George Roberts:** LA Studio (set the style for the modern studio bass bone).
- **Dave Taylor:** Bob Mintzer and NYC Studios; major solo recitalist/albums.
- **Bart Varsalona:** Stan Kenton.

Please refer to the Resource Guide Index.

Chapter 18

VOCAL JAZZ

by Jennifer Shelton Barnes

There are differing opinions as to whether the idiom of jazz had a vocal origin of "work songs" as predecessors to the blues or had an instrumental origin that vocalists began to imitate when people both played an instrument and sang (Louis Armstrong, for example).

Two things are certain though:
1. Vocalists have been expressing themselves in the jazz style for as long as instrumentalists.
2. Listeners continue to gravitate toward the wonderful, unique expression that a lyric delivery can provide, in addition to the rich harmonic and rhythmic traditions of the jazz language.

STARTING A VOCAL JAZZ PROGRAM

While instrumental jazz programs have flourished in educational institutions in recent years, vocal jazz programs have lagged behind in terms of the number of schools that offer such programs, as well as the overall sophistication levels of such programs. The reasons for that trend are many, which I won't endeavor to explain here. Rather, I will provide a basic overview of some issues that are unique to the study of jazz for vocalists, plus a few practical suggestions to get a novice director pointed in the right direction.

The foundational principle that is repeatedly proven in successful vocal jazz ensembles is that students benefit tremendously from being challenged to sing in the jazz idiom—particularly because of the aural strength required to sing it well. They excel in all areas of musicianship when given sound instruction in the jazz idiom.

Aural Development

Vocalists have certain advantages over instrumentalists in terms of learning to "speak" the language of jazz; however, there are many disadvantages as well. It is useful to be familiar with both in order to be effective in teaching jazz to vocalists.

Advantages of the vocal instrument

- No expense involved in purchase of instrument.
- Most people begin singing at an early age and are familiar with the sensation of singing.
- No need to learn special fingerings to produce tones.
- Not essential to know actual note names in order to sing pitches.
- Most acoustic voices do not produce as loud a sound as most instruments.
- Can practice almost anytime, anywhere, due to connection between brain and ear.

Disadvantages of the vocal instrument

- Must "hear" a pitch accurately in order to produce an accurate pitch.
- Unable to simply finger a note and have the correct pitch sound.
- Physical illness can render the voice temporarily or permanently damaged.
- When scat-singing, one must choose syllables.
- Most acoustic voices do not produce as loud a sound as most instruments.

By observing these characteristics, one can see that while aural training should be a priority for all musicians, it is virtually essential for vocal musicians. This fact is accentuated when the idiom of jazz is being taught due to the high level of harmonic and melodic dissonance that is generally present in jazz. This is especially true when compared to the Western European music that most students' ears are accustomed to hearing (or singing) if the student has been exposed to music study of any kind.

One example would be a young male vocalist who becomes interested in singing in a jazz choir after having experience in a concert choir. In the concert choir, he sang the bass vocal part (the lowest tessitura available in a choir), which requires him most often to sing roots of harmonic structures (chords) and occasional other parts (fifths or other passing tones). In addition, the vocal parts sung above his part usually have consonant intervals that do not challenge his ability to maintain his note (see Example 1).

As a bass/baritone in the jazz choir, he will suddenly be asked to sing the 7ths or 3rds of chords a majority of the time, with intervals such as augmented 4ths and major 7ths sounding above his part (see Example 2).

Example 1

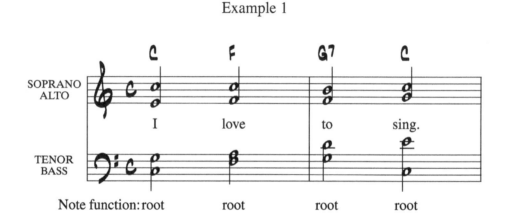

Example 2

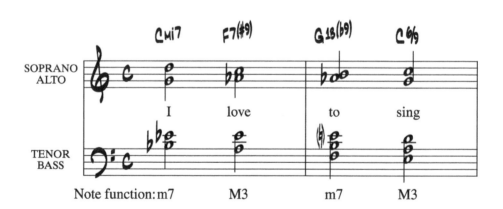

This new challenge will stretch and develop his aural strength, yet he will be frustrated until he becomes accustomed to the characteristic dissonances that sound odd or wrong to him. (For more information on how to develop aural strength, see the rehearsal techniques section on page 279.)

Listening: Why It's Essential and How to Do It

A common mistake many jazz instructors and directors make is to be so focused on preparing students to perform (learning repertoire for concerts, festivals, etc.) that they neglect the primary means by which those students will learn to excel in their stylistic development: *listening.*

Jazz is often called a language. The comparison is simple yet fundamentally sound: you can spend all day reading a book about speaking French and have no more idea about how to communicate in the

French language at the end of the day than you did at the beginning. The reason is obvious: learning a language should primarily be focused on absorption and imitation of the sounds of that language, whether informally (like an infant hearing his or her family communicate) or formally (by hearing an instructor speak the language). The same is true of jazz. Particularly, the critical rhythmic elements of jazz simply cannot be learned any other way. Those elements include but are not limited to time feel (whether swing, Latin, or other), articulation, and use of varieties of rhythms (particularly in improvisation).

Make Time in Rehearsals

The best way to get students listening to jazz is to make time in ensemble rehearsals for group listening and discussion so that your students begin to cross-reference what they hear with what they are trying to express themselves. It is especially important for vocalists to learn to listen to instrumental jazz and identify similarities between what they hear instruments doing and how they can produce similar sounds with their voices.

For example, many vocal arrangements have at least some sections that are written in a style imitative of big band style (sometimes called soli sections or shout choruses). A vocal jazz choir that has never heard a big band play (especially the traditional greats like the Count Basie Orchestra and the Duke Ellington Orchestra) will have a very difficult time executing those sections in a stylistically accurate way. It's possible that you may not have much experience listening to this kind of music yourself, but that shouldn't stop you from learning simultaneously with your students.

Recordings

Try to find recordings of the songs your ensemble is learning and recordings of the original performance of arrangements if available. You may want to begin your classroom listening by purchasing a basic jazz collection such as *The Smithsonian Collection of Classic Jazz*, or, more recently, Ken Burns' series called *Jazz*. See the discography at the end of the chapter for more listening suggestions.

Hear the Real Thing

You may also wish to seek opportunities to hear live jazz in the area in which you live. Students will benefit tremendously from seeing jazz performed live, even if the artists are not internationally touring or recording artists. Watching the interplay and improvisation in real time is an invaluable experience, compared to simply listening to CDs repeatedly.

Scat-Singing

Few subjects have as many differing opinions on their role, appropriateness, and how-to's as scat-singing. Again, my objective here is to give an introduction and a few practical tips for getting started with students.

One of the best things to keep in mind is everything that we just covered on *listening*; in no area of jazz for vocalists is this principle more important.

For purposes of clarity, I will refer to scat-singing from here forward as improvisation, meaning that the vocalist is spontaneously creating a new melody with some kind of nonsense syllables as opposed to lyrics.

Improvisation Basics

Beginning vocal improvisers (and instructors of same) should be made aware that skillful and effective improvisation is achieved the same basic way that instrumentalists achieve it. All jazz improvisers are pursuing the same artistic goals, some of which are:
- Good rhythmic feel or groove.
- Good note choices (correct and interesting notes).
- Creating an overall shape to your solo.
- Variety of rhythms.
- Full use of the instrument's range.

- Variety of dynamics.
- Use of space (stopping to breathe and listen).
- Use of repetition of a short idea for recognition.
- Variety of articulations or syllables for vocalists.

Because of this similarity, it will be useful to listen to both vocalists and instrumentalists who improvise; you will likely discover that those who are most effective generally employ many of those characteristics in their improvisation. One excellent way to improve improvisation skills is to tape-record a practice session and then have the student listen back and rate themselves in the aforementioned areas, being careful not to be overly critical, especially the first few times.

Effective Syllables

Many vocalists struggle tremendously with the question of what syllables to use. This is understandable since it is an issue that instrumentalists do not face and because most vocalists are used to singing words that are provided, not inventing their own. For most vocalists, the best approach is one that de-emphasizes the syllables so that the singer can focus instead on the melodic line that he or she is creating. Syllables that flow in pairs are effective, especially in swing feel because eighth notes are often sung in succession. Below are some of the most effective syllables:

Single notes	*Two-note pairings*	*Triplet pairings*
Bahp	Bah-daht	Bah-dih-luh
Doot	Doo-doot	Doo-dih-luh
Bip	Bay-bay	Bay-dih-lay
Zaht	Zah-daht	Zoo-dih-luh
Deet	Vah-vah	Dee-dn-dee
Yoot (end of a phrase)	Doo-dl	Did-dl-eh

One way to experiment with creating your own syllables is to practice using all of the consonants in the alphabet paired with various different vowel sounds. Try choosing two consonants paired with any vowel while improvising over the chord progression for the 12-bar blues (see Example 3). You will fairly automatically sing notes from the blues scale, freeing you from worrying about chord progressions for a moment. This is a fun exercise to do both individually and with a jazz choir; remind students (and perhaps yourself) that music-making should be fun, and this is sure to get students laughing (if not feeling a little silly while doing it).

Example 3

- Consonants of the alphabet (minus X, add Y):

    B C D F G H J K L M N P Q R S T V W Y Z
- Basic vowel sounds:

    AH, EH, A (like "dad"), AY, EE, IH, AW, UH, OH, OO
- Examples of consonant pairings (to be used with any and all vowels):

    1. W and L

    2. M and N

    3. R and D

Understanding Form and Harmony

In addition to working on developing a syllabic vocabulary, vocalists must be committed to developing an understanding of form and harmony in order to be able to sing over chord changes successfully. This is a process that takes years for all musicians, but vocalists would be especially well advised to develop a basic level of proficiency on the keyboard to aid in the visualization of chord structures.

Some musicians (and directors) may ask, "But isn't it true that there have been many great jazz musicians throughout history who didn't even know how to read music?" Although that statement bears some truth, there is no question that for the majority of aspiring musicians, improvising by ear will only take you so far. Beyond that point, you will find that you are continually getting lost, singing (or playing) notes that do not fit with the chords, and generally being frustrated that you cannot keep up with more harmonically complex chord progressions.

How to Learn a Song and Improvise Over It

Here are some suggestions on how to get your students started learning a song that they want to be able to improvise over:

1. Learn and memorize the melody and lyrics to the song.
2. Listen to as many recordings of the song as possible.
3. Improvise using the melody as a departure point.
4. Optional but highly recommended: Learn to play the root of each chord in your left hand while you play the correct quality of 3rd and 7th in your right hand in time (use a metronome) all the way through the song.
5. Optional but also highly recommended: Find an improvised solo on one of the recordings that you particularly enjoyed, and learn to sing along with the solo until you can match it exactly (including pitches, inflections, dynamics, vibrato, and tone color).
6. Practice singing through the roots of each chord (in time) until you're able to do it accurately *a cappella*.
7. Use a variety of patterns to do the same thing—triads, 7th chords, scalar patterns—and soon you'll be able to hear the chord progression in your head, with no external reinforcement needed. At this point you've begun to learn the changes and you're ready to begin working on saying something musical with your soloing.

The Importance of Lyrics

The one tool that vocalists have that instrumentalists do not is the lyric. A lyric is a very powerful way of connecting with listeners; we seek to make them feel what the song's lyricist indicated—whether the joy of new love or the pain of a broken heart.

Explore the Emotional Depth

Many vocalists (especially jazz choirs) fail to explore thoroughly the depth of the emotional content of the songs they sing, instead exclusively focusing on executing rhythms and vertical chord structures with accuracy. While those things should not be glossed over, the lyric gives an opportunity for connection that notes alone simply can't. It is up to a director to ensure that students understand and execute an emotionally appropriate delivery of the text they are singing.

I strongly suggest doing research on the songs you are teaching (whether solo or ensemble) to uncover the context in which the lyric was written. Very often, what are considered standard jazz tunes have their origin in the theater, and it's easy to find the source of the original song. Explaining this to your students can greatly assist them in taking ownership of the emotional content of the song.

Rehearsal Tips

In rehearsal, you might want to try the following exercise to get your students involved in the process of discovering their expressive potential. This is particularly effective when working on *a cappella* ballads sung in a rubato style (freely), but you can do the exercise with any song by treating it as if it were written in that style.

1. Have one of the lead sopranos (or all of them) sing two or four bars of melody as if they were singing it as a solo.
2. Then add one part at a time, trying to maintain the spirit of the solo version.

This may take weeks to really gel, but is well worth the effort, resulting in a much more expressive interpretation.

Another mistake that many directors make is allowing the students to get away with lackluster, unexpressive deliveries of text in rehearsal, assuming that the students will somehow come alive in performance. This almost *never* occurs! The students will be distracted and usually *less* emotionally connected in performance, not more. Therefore, it is essential that directors insist that the students' faces reflect the appropriate mood of the song, even in everyday rehearsals. (Sometimes I have to threaten to start a song over every time I see a disconnected face; we end up starting over three or four times before they actually get it.)

Amplification

The subject of amplification is another with potential for a variety of opinions. The basic principle is that vocal jazz choirs usually need to be amplified because of two basic reasons:

1. There is accompaniment of at least piano, but the majority of the time it is piano, bass, and drums.
2. When performing unaccompanied *(a cappella),* the desire for a relaxed, conversational tone production negates the type of projection required for a jazz choir to be heard adequately in most performance venues.

Microphones, Monitors, Speakers

The best way for a jazz choir of 16 voices or less to be amplified is through a sound system that uses one microphone per person (for larger choirs, group mikes may be used) in addition to monitor speakers (for singers and rhythm sections to hear themselves and each other) and main speakers. Sound systems may also be expanded to include special effects, equalizers, and recording capabilities. The best way to find out what will work for you and your budget is to consult with a professional audio technician in your area.

When using the one-on-a-mike method of amplification, the music industry standard microphone has become the Shure SM-58 due to its combination of durability, performance, and affordability. There are other mikes that will perform comparably; again, the best way to find what's right for you is to experiment under the guidance of an expert.

What students need to be aware of is that most microphones don't work like the ones they see on TV or in live performance used by solo "stars." Most mikes used for amplifying ensembles, and particularly the SM-58, are designed to be used in very close proximity to the mouth. Exceptions can be made for extremely high notes or to achieve effects like dynamic extremes. Other than that, vocalists should get accustomed to having the mikes no more than one inch from the lips, with a slight downward tilt so as not to obstruct the mouth visually. Anything other than that distance will compromise the quality of sound that is amplified.

Rehearsal Techniques

Conducting efficient rehearsals is a goal to which most directors aspire. In the idiom of vocal jazz, most good principles of rehearsal technique will be effective, but some need slight modification to achieve the best results. Here are a few general suggestions:

- When first reading a new arrangement, use syllables only, adding lyrics after some confidence in notes and rhythms is developed.
- Take smaller sections and work out rhythms without notes; be sure to emphasize reading rhythms (including rests) as well as notes.
- Play along with each vocal part on the piano, not playing for them (at least at first). Because they can, vocalists often will tend to want to learn by rote instead of reading.
- On challenging phrases, build parts by starting with the top or bottom part alone, adding one at a time from bottom part up or top part down.
- For the most challenging chords, be sure to sing to the chord and hold it once you arrive, making sure that the chord is in tune and solid. If not, go to the previous chord and hold it; then move back and forth between the chords until they sound accurately and the students hear the chord change.
- For a break from singing, take the time to analyze some of the chords that are particularly difficult so the students understand why.
- To really ensure that they are getting it, break down small phrases and have them sing *a cappella* to build their confidence.
- Break down your group into smaller groups and have them perform challenging assigned passages for each other from time to time. It helps them to know where they're not as strong as they thought, and they usually have good, constructive comments for each other if you encourage that.
- Practice at a slower rehearsal tempo for accuracy, but as soon as possible, sing through at least sections of the piece at performance tempo so the students start to feel the faster tempo.
- Contrast between very slow accurate rehearsing and performance tempo, reinforcing that at the fast tempo the students should focus more on the feel of the tempo than the accuracy of each individual note. This is generally more effective than simply gradually speeding up the tempo from slow to fast, when time feel will be sluggishly compromised.
- When rehearsing *a cappella* rubato arrangements, work at a slow but steady tempo in the earliest note-pounding stage, but as soon as possible (usually sooner than you think), insist that the students begin to sing the phrases in a conversational tempo. This is one of the most difficult skills for groups to develop. (See the section on The Importance of Lyrics.)
- Even if for only four bars at a time, get away from that piano as soon as possible!

Listening Suggestions

There are many approaches to developing listening libraries. What follows are two lists that may be helpful to a director who would like to set attainable goals for aural recognition of historically important figures in jazz.

30 JAZZ ARTISTS YOUR VOCAL JAZZ STUDENTS SHOULD KNOW

NAME	INSTRUMENT(S)
1. Louis Armstrong	Cornet, trumpet, voice
2. Duke Ellington	Piano, big band
3. Count Basie	Piano, big band
4. Billie Holiday	Voice
5. Charlie Parker	Alto saxophone
6. Ella Fitzgerald	Voice
7. Thelonious Monk	Piano
8. Dizzy Gillespie	Trumpet
9. Sonny Rollins	Tenor saxophone
10. Art Blakey	Drums
11. Miles Davis	Trumpet
12. Bill Evans	Piano
13. John Coltrane	Tenor saxophone
14. Clifford Brown	Trumpet
15. Jon Hendricks	Voice
16. J.J. Johnson	Trombone
17. Milt Jackson & Modern Jazz Quartet	Vibes, small group
18. Sarah Vaughan	Voice
19. Lambert, Hendricks & Ross	Vocal group
20. Chet Baker	Trumpet, voice
21. Stan Getz	Tenor saxophone
22. Carmen McRae	Voice
23. Antonio Carlos Jobim	Guitar, piano, voice
24. The Singers Unlimited	Vocal group
25. Herbie Hancock	Piano, keyboard
26. The Manhattan Transfer	Vocal group
27. Bobby McFerrin	Voice
28. Take 6	Vocal group
29. The Real Group	Vocal group
30. The New York Voices	Vocal group

A SELECTED LIST OF VOCAL JAZZ ARTISTS

Female Vocalists	Male Vocalists	Vocal Groups
Karrin Allyson	Louis Armstrong	The Bobs
Leny Andrade	Chet Baker	Boca Livre
Dee Dee Bridgewater	Tony Bennett	Les Doubles Six
Betty Carter	George Benson	The Four Freshmen
Rosemary Clooney	Freddy Cole	The Hi-Lo's!
Natalie Cole	Nat King Cole	Ladysmith Black Mambazo
Madeline Eastman	Harry Connick Jr.	Lambert, Hendricks & Ross
Ella Fitzgerald	Bob Dorough	The Manhattan Transfer
Nnenna Freelon	Kurt Elling	M-Pact
Astrud Gilberto	Giacomo Gates	The New York Voices
Billie Holiday	João Gilberto	Rare Silk
Shirley Horn	Miles Griffith	The Real Group
Nancy King	Johnny Hartman	The Ritz
Diana Krall	Jon Hendricks	The Singers Unlimited
Cleo Laine	Al Jarreau	The Swingle Singers
Abbey Lincoln	Eddie Jefferson	Vocal Sampling
Carmen McRae	Kevin Mahogany	Voice Trek
Jane Monheit	Bobby McFerrin	Take 6
Anita O'Day	Mark Murphy	Toxic Audio
Dianne Reeves	Kenny Rankin	Vox One
Diane Schuur	Frank Sinatra	Zap Mama
Janis Siegel	Mel Torme	
Sarah Vaughan	Joe Williams	
Dinah Washington		
Cassandra Wilson		
Nancy Wilson		

TEN SUGGESTED RECORDINGS OF JAZZ VOCAL ARTISTS

1. Ella Fitzgerald, *Ella Fitzgerald: Jazz Masters 6* (Verve 314 519 822-2).
2. Sarah Vaughan, *Live in Japan* (Mainstream Records MFCD 2-844-1).
3. *Count Basie & Joe Williams (Compact Jazz Series)* (Verve 835 329-2).
4. *Mel Torme: The Concord Jazz Heritage Series* (Concord Jazz CCD-4811-2).

5. *Astrud Gilberto (Compact Jazz Series)* (Verve 831 369-2).
6. The Singers Unlimited, *Magic Voices* (MPS 539 130-2) (seven-CD compilation set).
7. The Manhattan Transfer, *Extensions* (Atlantic CD 19258).
8. Take 6, *Join the Band* (Reprise 45497-2).
9. The Real Group, *Unreal!* (Town Crier TCD 519).
10. The New York Voices, *Sing! Sing! Sing!* (Concord Jazz CCD 4961-2).

VOCAL JAZZ RESOURCES

Books

• *Approaching the Standards for Jazz Vocalists* by Dr. Ron McCurdy and
  Dr. Willie L. Hill, Jr.: Warner Bros. Publications.
  www.warnerbrospublications.com.
• *Guide for Jazz and Scat Vocalists* by Denis DiBlasio: Jamey Aebersold Jazz.
  www.jazzbooks.com.
• *Vocal Improvisation* by Michele Weir: Advance Music.
  www.advancemusic.com.

Web Sites

• The Vocal Jazz Resource: www.jazzvocal.com.
  Information and links to lots of sites and people pertaining to vocal jazz for professionals,
  students, and educators. Outstanding!
• International Association for Jazz Education: www.iaje.org.
  Great resource for materials and information about the famous annual conference that vocal
  jazz directors should check out. The site also features a section where you can
  e-mail your questions about vocal jazz to Resource Team Members who'll respond
  specifically to you.
• Primarily A Cappella: www.singers.com.
  Fantastic resource for recordings by vocal groups (mostly *a cappella,* as the name indicates)
  that are hard to find, plus lots of other information related to vocal jazz.
• UNC Jazz Press: www.arts.unco.edu/UNCJazz/main.html
  Web Site for one of the largest current publishers of all levels of printed vocal jazz
  arrangements. Many sound clips and first pages available for viewing on this site.

Jazz Vocal Camps

1. Phil Mattson Vocal Jazz/Choral Music Workshops. Contact Phil Mattson at
   mattson@swcc.cc.ia.us.
2. Jamey Aebersold Jazz Camps. Contact Jamey Aebersold at www.jazzbooks.com.
3. Stanford Jazz Workshop Vocal Program. Contact Madeline Eastman at
   www.madelineeastman.com.
4. University of North Texas Vocal Jazz Camp. Contact Paris Rutherford at
   www.pruth2@gte.net.

DIRECTOR'S CHECKLIST FOR VOCAL JAZZ

• Develop a daily listening routine to hear professional jazz vocalists.

• Work to develop usable scat syllables.

• Establish a routine that will enable you to make a foundation of jazz sounds with your voice.

• Learn and understand the importance of the lyrics to standard jazz tunes.

• Work toward understanding and using microphones.

• Establish a series of rehearsal techniques both for the group and individual.

• Buy the ten suggested vocal recordings or similar to start your vocal jazz library.

• Study with a qualified teacher whenever possible.

• Know the historically important people in jazz and what they sound like.

Please refer to the Resource Guide Index.

Chapter 19

JAZZ FESTIVALS AND TOURS

by J. Richard Dunscomb

Educational jazz festivals are prevalent throughout much of North America. Jazz ensembles, combos, and vocal jazz groups are participating in record numbers. This participation is a positive indication that the directors and students realize the value of the judges' evaluations, the value of the clinicians' comments, and the value of hearing other groups perform.

> The words "adjudicator" and "judge" are used interchangeably at festivals. Most of us have had judges along the way that made only negative comments that were not helpful to us. Just as there are good bands and others, good directors and others, there are good judges and others. Adjudication commentary, if and when pointing out faults, should always include solutions and specific resolutions that can be put into practice.

FESTIVAL BASICS

What exactly happens at educational jazz festivals? What is the difference between competitive and non-competitive festivals? How do you prepare your ensemble to perform at jazz festivals? What are adjudicators listening to? How do you manage the travel logistics?

The authors have participated extensively in both competitive and non-competitive festivals as directors, adjudicators, and clinicians. In this chapter we will share our observations and thoughts about competitive and non-competitive events. We also will outline what it takes to get ready, both from a musical and organizational perspective.

Setting Your Festival Goals

If you took the time to write your jazz program philosophy and mission statement as suggested in Chapter 4, it will be easy to align your festival goals with your educational goals.

Ideally your festival goals will include striving to play the music as well as possible, with professional standards. In our opinion, the real winners at any festival are those groups who partake in a wide range of jazz music, from traditional to contemporary, and are able to apply the musicianship they've gained from one chart to the next.

If you decide to participate in a competitive event, avoid the win-at-all-costs attitude. Directors who spend an entire year preparing three or four contest charts are only kidding themselves that it is an educational experience for their students.

If participating in any type of festival results in your losing sight of your educational goals, then festivals are probably not for you or your ensemble.

What to Expect

You submitted an application to a jazz festival committee, and your group was accepted to participate. Congratulations!

Now you're riding on a bus with your jazz ensemble, instruments, amplifiers, and a large case of music folders. You're looking forward to the opportunity to hear other groups and receive commentary about your ensemble from professional adjudicators, clinicians, and other jazz artists.

When you arrive at the festival venue, your bus pulls alongside a number of others, also filled with groups who, like yours, are eager to perform their music in front of a live audience. You jump into command mode, find the festival organizer and get your instructions, unload your students and their gear, and are guided to a warm-up room where students may store their instrument cases and other personal items.

Time to Perform

You preview the schedule of events, hustle your students into the auditorium, and listen attentively to a number of other ensembles. As the director, you notice where the adjudicators are seated. You preview the stage, lighting, and microphone set-up and observe the sound volume in the hall. You watch how each group enters and exits the stage. Mostly, you enjoy the music.

Soon it is your turn to exit the auditorium and warm up your band, and before you know it, you're walking out on stage! Ideally you feel relaxed, and your three or four charts seem to go by quickly. You're proud of your ensemble's performance, and you tell them so.

Clinics

Next, your group is led into a rehearsal room for a jazz clinic. A clinician greets you and your ensemble, asks to hear a piece your ensemble is working on, and then proceeds to hold a 15- to 30-minute clinic while you observe and take notes. Afterward, the clinician may meet with you to offer constructive observations and suggestions.

Next, your group returns to the auditorium to listen to additional groups. During your students' lunch hour, you may have the option to participate in a directors' clinic. Some festivals also provide a time slot for a student-focused clinic involving all festival participants.

Evaluation

If the festival is competitive, a slate of semifinalists or finalists is announced after all groups have performed. Adjudicator evaluation forms with comments and a competition ranking are distributed to all participating directors. The finalists may perform at an evening concert.

If the festival is non-competitive (where all groups are considered winners), adjudicator evaluation forms with comments are distributed to participating directors after all groups have performed. An evening concert featuring guest soloists with a professional combo or big band may be scheduled. This might be the first opportunity for some of your students to hear a professional jazz group, and it will certainly make a lasting impression.

Scholarship Opportunities

In either case, some of the larger festivals award scholarships of various sizes from jazz camps, community colleges, or universities to outstanding individual musicians at the end of the festival. Scholarship opportunities are a positive reason to participate in a festival, especially for those students who have decided to pursue a music career.

Understanding the Adjudicator's Job

Viewing the festival process from an adjudicator's perspective is helpful as you prepare your ensemble for festival performance. In addition to the categories listed on the adjudication evaluation sheet (see Example 1), there are many other positive ways to help you prepare your ensemble for festival performance that are listed in the following excerpt from *Adjudicating a Jazz Festival* by Dr. Gordon Vernick. Put this list beside you at your next rehearsal and look at and listen to your ensemble with an adjudicator's eyes and ears. In addition, it's always a good idea to invite other musicians to your rehearsals to make pre-festival evaluations.

ADJUDICATOR'S CHECKLIST

- Note the set-up of the band. How's the rhythm section placed?
- Are the musicians playing into the stands?
- Is the director needlessly conducting?
- How does the conductor count off the tempos?
- Does the band use acoustic, electric, or keyboard bass?
- Is the music of high value/quality? Is it beyond the capabilities of the players?
- Are the saxes putting enough air into their instruments?
- Do the saxes project their sound? What type of equipment are they playing?
- Note the intonation of sax unisons.
- Does the lead alto sax dominate the section?
- Does the lead trumpet dominate the ensemble passages?
- Same sax comments above for brass.
- Are the electric instruments too loud? Is the bass too heavy?
- Do the brass play with a loud, uncentered sound or with a controlled, focused sound?
- Do the saxes slur excessively, or do they use good jazz articulation?
- Do the lines swing?
- Is the band accenting the upbeats in the swing style or are they heavily downbeat-oriented?
- Is there doubling (more than one on a part) in any of the sections?
- Are there any parts missing?
- Do the saxes stand on their solis?
- Note the hand position of the bassist (if possible).
- Note position of amplifiers.
- Note the pianist's chord voicings. Is he or she using sustain pedal?
- Are the guitarist and pianist both comping at the same time? Do they overplay? Are they getting in each other's way?
- Do the band and rhythm section play with a good sense of time, or does the rhythm section tend to accompany the band?
- Is the rhythm section playing too busily?
- Do the members of the rhythm section play aggressively or timidly?
- Is auxiliary percussion being used effectively or just to give players something to do?
- Are the charts programmed well? Does the set progress logically and contain stylistic variation?
- Is the baritone sax player lined up with the bass trombonist? Are all of the lead players lined up?
- Does the drummer have the hi-hat positioned so that it is comfortable and easy to reach?
- Are the drums well tuned for a jazz sound or deadened for a rock sound?
- Does the pianist comp percussively?
- Does the guitar play with too much treble?
- Does the band rush ends of phrases? How about loud phrases versus soft phrases?
- Does the band play with a wide dynamic range?
- Does the band (and each section) execute phrases clearly and with good definition?
- How are the attacks? Do long notes have direction? How are the releases?
- How are the soloists? Are they improvising? Are they playing written-out memorized solos?
- Are they making the chord changes? Do they display any guidance? Have they done any listening?
- Are forte pianos and crescendos overused?
- Are brass players attempting to play beyond their range capabilities? Are they pinching? Are they playing sharp?
- What is the quality of teaching in the band being adjudicated?

Wow! That is a lot to think about. However, these points are just some of the things that go through a judge's mind at festival time.

Keep in mind that adjudicators have been hearing and judging bands for a long time, not just the day of the festival. They will hear many, many bands throughout the day of the festival. By focusing on the elements listed above, you will allow the judges to relax and enjoy your group's performance.

Programming Considerations

Music selection, programming order, and the quality of your soloists' improvisations will definitely affect the adjudicator's impression of your ensemble.

Selecting the Music

Selecting charts within the capability of your group is absolutely necessary. It is a turn-off for festival adjudicators to hear a group perform charts that are either too easy or too hard. The music should be such that it allows the musicians to reach an attainable goal.

Be sure that you select high-quality jazz literature. Do not use the latest pop hits or second-rate arrangements. Pick the best-quality music your students can handle. Chapter 15 contains listings of festival-appropriate music sorted by grade level and four style categories.

Programming Order

Plan to program three or four charts in varying styles, depending on the allotted performance time at the festival.

If programming three charts:
- The opener should be one that the ensemble is very confident with and can serve as a springboard for the remainder of the program. (This is usually a medium or medium up-tempo swing chart.)
- The second/middle selection is often a ballad or a slow swing chart.
- The third/closing number is often a Latin or rock-influenced chart.

If there is enough time allotted to program a fourth title, choose a style that contrasts with the others. Regardless of whether you are programming three or four charts, the style of the closing number needs to be one that presents your ensemble and the soloists in the best light. The last selection is what may linger in the memory of the adjudicators and will therefore reflect an overall opinion of the performance, so make it a positive memory.

Soloists

Another important yet often overlooked aspect of music selection involves checking out the chord changes in the solo sections of each chart. Be sure the chord progressions are within the foreseeable grasp of your soloists.

Soloists should be well prepared. They should be ready to perform at a level commensurate with the ensemble quality. If you do not consider yourself a strong improviser, invite a local jazz artist to work with your group for one or two rehearsals.

Try to avoid using the same soloist on every number. The judges will be pleasantly impressed with hearing multiple soloists, as long as they all sound comfortable with the chord changes and styles. One way to ensure this is to use music with shorter solo sections that match up with the students' abilities.

Festival Evaluation Forms

Posting a blank copy of the festival's adjudication form in the rehearsal room can enhance your ensemble's understanding of the festival evaluation process prior to the event. This will allow your students to see what the judges will work from at the festival. You may also use it to underscore the musical points you make in rehearsals.

Here are samples of forms that are used by the IAJE festivals. The authors believe that whatever forms are used, they should have a description of the terms used. Example 1 is the front of the form, and Example 2 is the back of the form.

Jazz Performance

Prepared by the International Association for Jazz Education

RATING

Use no plus or minus
signs in final rating

Event _____ Class _____ Date _____ 20 _____

Name of Organization _____ No. of Players _____

School _____ Director _____ School _____

City _____ State _____ District _____ Enrollment _____

ARTISTIC MERIT 60 POINTS		Points Awarded
Improvisation	25	
Style/ Interpretation	15	
Programming/ Presentation	10	
Musicality	10	
Total Points Awarded		

TECHNICAL MERIT 40 POINTS		
Time & Rhythm	15	
Ensemble	10	
Intonation	10	
Technique/Diction/ Articulation	5	
Total Points Awarded		
GRAND TOTAL OF POINTS		

COMMENTS
Use reverse side for additional comments

Recommended Division Rating Criteria: <u>90 and above – I;
75-89 – II; below 75 – III</u>. The numerical system is intended to serve only as a guide. Final ratings should be determined by common sense and appropriate musical judgments.

_____
Adjudicator Signature

Adjudicator's private comments for _____ to be detached by adjudicator
and   (Name of Director)

sealed in attached envelope furnished by Festival Chairperson.

Choice of material   _____
Program order   _____
Stage presence
 & communication   _____
Other _____

<u>Rating Criteria</u>
A - Excellent
B - Good
C - Fair
D - Poor

Use reverse side for additional comments

IMPROVISATION: Evaluation based on soloists' awareness of stylistic and harmonic content, ability to communicate ideas, and the ability to make creative, personal, musical statements.

STYLE/INTERPRETATION: Evaluation based on group's (conductor's) awareness of what entails the correct stylistic performance and interpretation of the chosen composition.

PROGRAMMING/PRESENTATION: Evaluation based on the appropriateness of the music relative to the group's abilities (technical and artistic) and how the music is presented (amount and type of improvisation, staging, microphone use, etc.)

MUSICALITY: Evaluation based on emotional communication, to the extent that technique is used to create an expressive and meaningful performance, for performers and audience.

TIME & RHYTHM: Evaluation based on the performance of the tempo (beat) and the figures (rhythms) relative to one another and to the rhythmic concept of the composition. (Is it correct and effective?)

ENSEMBLE: Evaluation based on the ability of the group to consistency perform the music in a fundamentally correct manner (phrasing, accents, dynamics, balance, etc.).

INTONATION: Evaluation based on the ability to perform in tune, within and between each section.

TECHNIQUE/DICTION/ARTICULATION: Evaluation based on the ability of the group to perform clean, clear, articulate musical phrases.

Prepared by the International Association for Jazz Education
P.O. Box 724
Manhattan, KS 06502
© 1989

Additional Comments

(Private comments continued)

Signature of Adjudicator _____

The wording in Example 2 clarifies how each category on the jazz performance sheet is to be judged. It is the duty of adjudicators and directors to understand it. As a result, everyone will be on the same track as they work toward a fair and impartial adjudication.

Enjoy the Experience

Understanding the adjudication process will make the festival experience more enjoyable and beneficial to you and your ensemble. Take the festival comments from each individual judge as the feelings and opinions of one person. Don't get too down and let it create a bad experience for you and your students. Learn from the collective comments and make it a positive learning situation for everyone in the jazz ensemble.

TRIPS AND EXTENDED TOURS

Trips or tours can take many forms and will create lasting experiences and memories for you and your students. A trip can be as simple as a recruiting trip to an elementary or middle school in your district. Conversely, it could be as involved as a trip to a major jazz festival outside the country in which you reside. The authors have taken ensembles on tours that range from the most simple to the most complex. Whatever the event, the intent should be educationally sound with a goal of improving your students' understanding of jazz.

Trips or tours can be tremendously rewarding, or they can be nightmares. Proper planning and follow-through can alleviate many of the anticipated problems. Be sure to share the responsibilities with others. Here are some tips culled from many trips that the authors have taken with many different types of jazz ensembles.

Short Day Trip

Planning a trip in your school district is simple. It can be accomplished quite easily with proper advance time and careful planning by you alone. This is virtually a must for recruiting future participants in your jazz program. The following tips are items to check into when planning this type of trip.

DIRECTOR'S CHECKLIST: SHORT DAY TRIP

- Obtain permission of the principal or administrator of the school you will visit.
- Obtain permission of your school's principal or administrator.
- To attend, each student needs a written permission slip signed by a parent or guardian.
- Schedule a bus well in advance.
- Make a checklist of musical needs (music, music stands, sound system, etc.).
- Check safety measures to transport instruments (proper cases, instruments properly padded in the cases).
- Visit the site of the performance in advance.
- Create posters announcing the performance.
- Make a schedule for the day and give it to the students.

Overnight Trip Outside the School District

Planning an overnight trip outside the school district is not as simple as a short day trip and will generally require the assistance of experts. Enlisting the aid of an interested and knowledgeable parent will allow you to designate some of the paperwork and phone calls involved.

Depending on the length and magnitude of the trip, it is a good idea to involve an experienced travel agent. Always try to find an agency that has experience taking music groups on tours. There are many agencies that specialize in music travel. Ask for the name of groups they have assisted before and phone those directors to see how their trips were.

Traveling to jazz festivals or other events that involve overnight lodging require a great deal of advance planning. Here are some things to do when planning such a trip.

DIRECTOR'S CHECKLIST: OVERNIGHT TRIP

- Set rules and consequences for breaking those rules.
- Obtain permission from your principal or administrator to make the trip.
- Contact a travel agent with experience in music travel.
- Recruit or appoint an adult volunteer or colleague to help with paperwork.
- Arrange for the bus.
- Arrange for the hotel.
- Arrange for meals.
- Provide cost estimates to all concerned.
- Consider a payment timetable if necessary.
- Consider fundraising events if necessary.
- Make an itinerary for each day and give it to the students. Include specifics for each day, including the day they perform—it should involve listening to other groups, clinics, etc.
- Make it an educational experience and spell that out to all involved.
- Have travel cases for all musical instruments.
- Check with the festival to see if they provide music stands, back-line equipment, etc.
- Check with festival hosts regarding recordings of the performance.
- Assign students to help with loading and unloading the bus.
- Appoint someone to be responsible for the music.
- If possible, visit the site beforehand.

International Travel

Overseas travel is much more involved. The above checklists apply, as well as several other considerations. With the popularity of international jazz festivals, many educational groups are experiencing new travel opportunities. Most international festivals are quite well organized and roll out the red carpet for participating groups. Most require a recorded application and accept only the top performing ensembles. This adds much prestige to being selected for such an event. At the same time, it is a good idea to check with other groups that have attended in the past year. Directors are generally willing to share the information and will also provide tips that worked for them.

DIRECTOR'S CHEKCLIST: INTERNATIONAL TRAVEL

- Obtain permission in writing from parents, school administrators, etc. This should also include medical concerns.
- Have meetings with the students and parents to discuss the detailed plans.
- Determine the number of parents/chaperones needed.
- Set rules for the trip and consequences for breaking those rules.
- Select a travel agent with much experience in international travel, particularly one that has taken instrumental groups on similar tours.
- Contact a director who has taken his or her group to this event in the past year or two. You can learn a lot about the event, what to expect, etc.
- Arrange the air travel with a travel agent.
- Arrange the hotel with a travel agent.
- Arrange the meals with a travel agent.
- Provide instructions on how/when to apply for a passport and visa if required. Include passport cost.
- Be sure you know what the festival provides (music stands, back-line equipment, etc.) or does not provide.
- Get everything in writing—EVERYTHING!
- Recruit or appoint an adult volunteer or colleague to help with paperwork.

- Make an itinerary for each day and give it to the students. Include specifics for each day, including the day they perform—it should involve listening to other groups, clinics, etc.
- Make it an educational experience and spell that out to all involved.
- Have travel cases for all musical instrument. Road cases are expensive but necessary.
- Assign students to help with loading and unloading the bus.
- Assign someone to be responsible for the music.
- You may need a converter. Electrical current may be different.
- If you plan to perform at other venues on tour, make sure you have all of the necessary equipment: stands, amps, keyboard, power supply in the correct voltage, sound, etc.
- If possible, visit the festival a year in advance of the trip.

A list of educational jazz festivals is published each year in the *Jazz Educators Journal* (November issue) as well as *DownBeat* and *Jazz Times* magazines.

Chapter 20

INTERNATIONAL ASSOCIATION FOR JAZZ EDUCATION

by Bill McFarlin

With a mission to ensure the continued growth and development of jazz through education and outreach, the International Association for Jazz Education (IAJE) serves 8,000 members in 40 countries. IAJE can serve as an invaluable resource to music educators for professional development, curriculum ideas, peer networking, student opportunities, and research. Several of IAJE's programs are outlined below with suggestions on how they can be used to your maximum benefit.

Jazz Educators Journal

The *Jazz Educators Journal* is an important source for news and information in the field of jazz education. Published six times a year, the magazine is distributed to all IAJE members, jazz industry representatives, and more than 300 libraries. Each issue includes information on top jazz artists, reviews, transcriptions, industry news, and articles on improvisation, composition, arranging, music business, and more. Articles can be used in the classroom or for personal growth.

IAJE Annual Conference

The IAJE Conference is the largest annual gathering of the global jazz community, with upwards of 7,000 attendees from 30 countries. The conference features more than 100 performances by internationally recognized artists and students on nine fully produced venues. In addition, there are more than 50 clinics, workshops, panel sessions, video and technology presentations, research paper presentations, and a 50,000-square-foot music industry exposition. The conference is traditionally held in early January in rotating North American cities and always includes a dedicated teacher training track. College credit and continuing education units are available to those attending. The conference can also be a tremendous experience for your students. Log on to www.iaje.org for an updated list of conference dates.

Teacher Training Institutes

Teacher Training Institutes are two-and-a-half-day intensive workshops presented in partnership by IAJE and the National Association for Music Education (MENC). Designed for band, string, vocal, and general music and independent music teachers who desire to increase their understanding of and competency in jazz education, the institute is also open to college students currently enrolled in a music education program. This program can be particularly helpful for music educators who have had little or no exposure to jazz pedagogy. College credit and continuing education units are available.

Artist Outreach Network

This two-tiered program includes an Artist Outreach Network Listing Service and an Artist Outreach Network Grants Program. You can list your school or institution on the network or search the network for artists and clinicians who may be traveling to your area. The grants program can be a resource for funding artists to do a workshop with your students.

IAJE-Approved Festivals

If you are considering sponsoring an educational jazz festival at your school, it is advisable to become an IAJE-approved festival. To be accepted as an IAJE-approved festival, festival directors must be IAJE members, complete a required approved festival application, and meet a minimum set of festival standards and guidelines. Benefits of being an IAJE-approved festival include a festival listing in the *Jazz Educators Journal* and two $150 student scholarships.

Talent Recognition Programs

Through a unique collaboration by IAJE, the National Foundation for Advancement in the Arts (NFAA), and the Herb Alpert Jazz Endowment, five outstanding high school jazz students are selected each year as recipients of the annual Clifford Brown/Stan Getz Fellowship (also known as the Young Talent All-Stars). Winners receive an all-expense-paid trip to the IAJE Annual Conference for private master classes and rehearsals culminating in a special conference performance, an additional all-expense-paid NFAA week of master classes in Miami, Florida, and eligibility for selection as a Presidential Arts Scholar. Past recipients of this fellowship program include a number of top jazz artists including Dianne Reeves, Roy Hargrove, Harry Connick Jr., and Geoff Keezer. If you have a student with exceptional talent, this is a great opportunity. The program also awards $500 to $3,000 cash scholarships to each participant. Application forms are available at www.iaje.org.

Sisters in Jazz

The purpose of the IAJE Sisters in Jazz program is to encourage and promote the participation of young women in the art of jazz music both educationally and professionally. The program provides local and regional mentoring programs, mentoring opportunities for young women in jazz through apprenticeship with established women jazz artists, and an international collegiate competition. Winners of the collegiate competition must be currently enrolled college music students who are selected by competitive audition. Winners receive an all-expense-paid trip to perform at the IAJE Annual Conference and participate in mentoring master classes with established women jazz artists. Application forms are available at www.iaje.org.

IAJE Web Site

The IAJE Web site provides access to a variety of resources, including an extensive list of links, selected articles from the *Jazz Educators Journal,* an online community in which you can interact with other jazz educators from around the world, and information on various IAJE programs. One of the most useful areas on the IAJE site is the IAJE Resource Team. Resource Team members are highly respected authorities from their areas of expertise in the jazz field and will respond to specific questions online. An archive of past questions and answers is also featured on the site. To access the site, log on to www.iaje.org. Portions of the site are available only to IAJE members, but there is also very useful information in the non-member area.

Become a Member of IAJE

Membership can be registered by telephone, by mail, or through the Web site.
For more information, write: IAJE, P.O. Box 724, Manhattan, KS 66502, USA.
Tel: (785) 776-8744; Fax: (785) 776-6190; E-mail: info@iaje.org; Web site: www.iaje.org.

Highlights in the Public School Jazz Education Movement

by J. Richard Dunscomb and Marcia F. Dunscomb

1920s and 1930s

As jazz music began to develop as an art from at the turn of the century, there were no materials or methods for teaching and learning jazz. A musician wanting to play this style of music learned by listening to the early masters, either in live performance or on recordings. The first recordings of jazz began around 1917. Thus, the first classrooms for jazz were jazz clubs.

Even though jazz was still regarded as pop music, and therefore thought of as inferior to classical music by some educators in the 1930s, there were a few noteworthy instances of foresight by a few important individuals. For example, Arturo Toscanini, when forming the NBC Symphony, thought it important to hire several brass players with jazz experience.

During the 1930s, *DownBeat* magazine began publishing transcriptions of jazz solos, *Metronome* magazine began to include articles on jazz and swing, and many colleges and universities had student dance bands playing swing music for school events.

1940s

During the 1940s most high school and university jazz ensembles were student-led and met outside of scheduled class time. During this decade, Armed Service Radio began to broadcast jazz and swing, and Leonard Feather instituted a lecture series on jazz at the New School for Social Research in New York City. Noted conductor Leopold Stokowski stated that jazz was a vitally important part of our folk music with no traditions or limitations. He said it would go on developing as long as musicians gave free rein to their imaginations. At the same time, other noted classical professionals were issuing warnings against allowing youngsters to hear and study jazz, saying it was music of the devil.

By the end of the forties, only a handful of colleges were offering classes in jazz, including Berklee School of Music, Los Angeles City College, California State Polytechnic, North Texas State College, Alabama State University, Tennessee State University, and others. A number of jazz publications began to appear, including *30 Studies in Swing* by David Gornston, *Jam at Home* by Nick Fatool, *Special Arrangements for Small Orchestra* by Artie Shaw, and *How to Play Bebop* by Dr. Billy Taylor.

1950s

In the 1950s, about 30 more colleges added jazz classes to their schedule but most were non-credit courses. Many of these classes were focused on improvisation, arranging, and jazz history. In 1953 the first high school jazz festival took place in Brownsville, Texas. The first charts written specifically for school bands were published in 1954. Early composers/arrangers included Sammy Nestico, Marshall Brown, Neal Hefti, Clem DeRosa, John LaPorta, and Ralph Mutchler. High school and university jazz ensembles were often called stage bands due to the negative perception some school administrators associated with the word jazz.

By 1955, a few jazz clinics and festivals began to be presented around the country, and in 1959 the National Stage Band Camp was organized by Ken Morris. Faculty for this camp, which was held on the campus of Indiana University, included Stan Kenton, Russ Garcia, Shelly Manne, Laurindo Almeida, Don Jacoby, Eddie Safranski, Ray Santisi, Matt Betton, and Gene Hall.

During this time we began to see more college and university bands plus a few high school big bands led by the school band director. Many of these band directors had experience in one of the many professional big bands or military service bands. By the late 1950s, the music industry began to hire jazz professionals as clinicians and composer/arrangers for charts written with the limitations of a school jazz band in mind. In 1958 Leonard Feather and Marshall Stearns co-wrote "The Subject Was Jazz," a TV series that aired for 13 weeks.

1960s

During the 1960s, jazz education began to expand slowly. It is estimated that in the early sixties there were only 5,000 school jazz ensembles, a number that increased to 15,000 by the end of the decade. The first Stan Kenton Summer Jazz Clinic was presented on 1961. School jazz began to be promoted by instrument manufacturers and music publishers. Many professional jazz artists began to be involved in jazz education activities.

Where many people once thought jazz was an innate skill that could not be taught, it was now recognized that, by analysis of performances of the masters, rules for learning improvisation and theory principals could be established. The first jazz education materials began to appear during the sixties. By 1970 many jazz methods began to be available.

By the end of the sixties there were more than 275 colleges offering some courses in jazz, with more than 125 offering those classes for credit. The dozen or so high school jazz festivals being presented in the early sixties had grown to more than 75 by the end of the decade. Several college jazz festivals were established during this time, including Notre Dame; Villanova; Mobile, Alabama; California State University–Northridge; Elmhurst College; Quinnipiac College; and the University of Utah. In 1964 Dr. Billy Taylor started Jazz Mobile (a mobile stage on a trailer that would showcase jazz artists throughout the city) in New York City.

The first formal jazz seminar sponsored by MENC was presented in Atlantic City. Clinicians included Dr. Billy Taylor, Dr. Ralph Pace, Dr. Gene Hall, and Charles Suber. In 1968 the first meeting of the National Association of Jazz Educators (NAJE) was formed as an auxiliary organization of MENC. Founding members included Matt Betton, Dr. M. E. Hall, Dr. Bill Lee, Dr. Jack Wheaton, and John T. Roberts.

The one-person jazz faculty flourished. Some of the leaders of the early university jazz faculty included Leon Breeden, Buddy Baker, Jerry Coker, David Baker, Roger Schueler, Evan Solat, John Garvy, Bob McDonald, Dick Carlson, Ralph Mutchler, Ladd McIntosh, and Bill Dobbins.

Some of the earliest professional jazz clinicians visiting university campuses were Dizzy Gillespie, Doc Severinsen, Marvin Stamm, Clark Terry, Buddy Baker, David Baker, Urbie Green, Frank Rosolino, Rich Matteson, Phil Wilson, Cannonball Adderley, Jerry Coker, Buddy DeFranco, Sam Donahue, Paul Horn, John LaPorta, Charlie Mariano, Jack Peterson, Howie Roberts, Sal Salvador, Johnny Smith, Dan Hearle, Marian McPartland, Ray Santisi, Dr. Billy Taylor, Ray Brown, Carl Kaye, Mike Moore, Eddie Safranski, Louie Bellson, Roy Burns, Alan Dawson, Jack DeJohnette, Clem DeRosa, Elvin Jones, Joe Morello, Charlie Perry, Ed Thigpen, Manny Albam, Don Ellis, Maynard Ferguson, Woody Herman, Quincy Jones, Thad Jones, Stan Kenton, Chuck Mangione, Oliver Nelson, and Johnny Richards.

1970s

During the 1970s jazz education began to gain significant ground. By 1976, there were more than 500,000 student musicians participating in jazz ensembles in their high schools and colleges throughout the country. Approximately 400 universities were offering jazz ensemble as a credit class. A number of universities were even offering post-graduate jazz programs, including Indiana University, North Texas State University, Wesleyan, Eastman School of Music, University of Northern Colorado, University of Illinois, New England Conservatory of Music, and the University of Miami. Professional leaders such as Buddy Rich, Woody Herman, Stan Kenton, Maynard Ferguson, and Bill Watrous began to recruit their sidemen directly from these campuses.

During the 1970s, a number of universities bestowed honorary degrees and artist-in-residence positions to jazz greats such as Duke Ellington, Benny Carter, Gerry Mulligan, Herbie Hancock, Oliver Nelson, Quincy Jones, and Eubie Blake. Dr. Herb Wong established a jazz improvisation program at Washing Elementary School (the lab school for the University of California–Berkeley). In Grades K–6, he was able to prove that learning improvisation skills on conventional music instruments enabled students to improve their academic skills such as reading and mathematics.

In 1972 the first combo/improvisation clinics were presented. Around the same time, many awards for jazz were presented, including more than $500,000 in National Endowment for the Arts grants. Use of the term *stage band* slowly began to be replaced by *jazz band, jazz orchestra,* or *jazz ensemble*. The Canadian Stage Band Festival (MusicFest Canada) grew from 18 groups in 1973 to more than 8,000 students participating by 1987.

The first NAJE national conference took place in Chicago in December 1974 with fewer than 100 participants. In 1976, the first K–12 Curriculum Committee was established by IAJE to survey trends of jazz education in the public schools.

1980s

By 1980 more than 500 colleges were offering jazz-related courses for credit. More than 70% of the 30,000 junior and senior high schools had at least one jazz ensemble. Many educators in the mainstream of music education began to appreciate jazz and approve of its inclusion in classroom curricula. By 1982, 72 colleges/universities offered degrees in music with some sort of major or minor in jazz studies.

Dr. Billy Taylor became a regular on the CBS "Sunday Morning" television show in 1981. New publications with an emphasis on jazz, such as *Jazziz* and *Jazz Times,* emerged and thrived during the eighties until the present. By the mid 1980s, many middle schools had jazz ensembles.

In 1987 Representative John Conyers, Jr., of Michigan was able to persuade the House of Representatives to pass a resolution designating jazz "a rare and valuable national American treasure."

With a name change in 1989 to the International Association of Jazz Educators (IAJE), annual participation at conferences now exceeded 7,000.

1990s to Present

By the early 1990s, there was no longer any doubt about the validity of jazz as America's original art form or the importance of its place in music education. Today students can earn a bachelor's or master's degree in jazz studies at more than 100 American colleges or universities. A doctorate in jazz studies can be earned at many universities, including the University of Miami, the University of Northern Colorado at Greeley, New York University, and the University of Southern California. Jazz degree programs are now established around the globe in England, Europe, Australia, South Africa, and Canada.

In 2000, the Ken Burns series titled *Jazz* was aired on public television. This series presented 19 hours of jazz history in prime time. Membership in IAJE has grown to almost 10,000 members from around the world, with almost 8,000 attending the conference annually. The National Endowment for the Arts supported and presented annual awards of $20,000 to each of three "Jazz Masters" at the IAJE conference. TV and radio have begun to incorporate jazz tunes and sounds in many commercials. BET on Jazz (BET) gave IAJE a grant for $500,000 to support educational programs.

IAJE changed its name in 2002 to the International Association for Jazz Education.

The volume of educational jazz materials has exploded. Today there are many charts, play-along materials, method books, classroom series, biographies, jazz history texts, and more available to anyone wanting to learn more about jazz. Historians consider jazz to be among America's most significant contributions to the world of music.

Chapter 21

USING TECHNOLOGY TO TEACH JAZZ

by Kimberly McCord, D.M.E.

Technology is a powerful tool for jazz educators. With computer software, we may improvise chorus after chorus with a patient and steady rhythm section that will never tire of our mistakes as we learn. We can slow or quicken the tempo without changing the pitch. We can access information via the Internet on everything from jazz history to finding Web sites that enable our students to e-mail jazz artists and ask questions. In the not-too-distant future we will have the power to jam online with a drummer from New York, a bass player from Moscow, and a pianist from rural Wyoming. MIDI (Music Instrument Digital Interface) will continue to provide a way to create and record our compositions, improvisations, and accompaniments.

TECHNOLOGY BASICS

This chapter is organized into five sections for easy reference:
1. Overview of computer-related hardware items.
2. MIDI software applications for improvisation.
3. MIDI software for specific instruments or specific jazz styles.
4. Software for studying the history and appreciation of jazz.
5. Internet resources for jazz educators and their students.

Overview of Computer-Related Hardware Items

As you begin to research various computer software options for teaching jazz, you may encounter unfamiliar terminology. The following descriptions provide a basic overview of common terms.

Computer Platforms, Speed, and Memory

Music software is generally available for either Macintosh or Windows (PC) operating systems. The processing (CPU) speed, memory (RAM), and storage space (hard drive size) requirements vary considerably among programs. In many cases older computers will be sufficient, but newer programs or upgrades will require newer computers with higher specifications.

MIDI

MIDI is a digital interface developed by keyboard instrument manufacturers to enable all brands to communicate with each other, as well as computers.

General MIDI Sound Generation

General MIDI is a term that refers to a predetermined set of 128 MIDI sounds (flute, trumpet, saxophone, organ, piano, etc.). Music created with General MIDI presets will sound identical on all brands of hardware or software. You many access General MIDI sounds in two ways:
1. Through the internal sound generation of the computer (internal sound card for Windows and QuickTime Musical Instruments for Macintosh). This accessibility is sufficient for playback of software files for listening activities.

2. By connecting your computer to a General MIDI keyboard using a MIDI interface. You will need a General MIDI keyboard if you want your students to play or record from a keyboard or other MIDI instrument.

CD-ROM or DVD-ROM Drive

Computers are equipped with certain drives such as a CD-ROM or DVD-ROM drive. You may use CD-ROM software or play regular audio CDs in the CD-ROM drive. You may use DVD software, CD-ROM software, and audio CDs with a DVD-ROM drive. (ROM means "read only memory.")

CD-ROM Burner

A CD-ROM burner is a CD-ROM drive that can write (burn) software files onto CD-R disks.

Powered Speakers or Headphones

The sound from either a computer and/or keyboard must be amplified to be heard. Therefore, the sound out of a computer and/or keyboard must be connected to powered speakers or powered headphones. The sound out of computers and keyboards may be connected to most classroom stereos and amplified for groups to hear.

When both the sound of the computer and the sound of the keyboard must be heard simultaneously (as when using sequencing software with digital audio), a simple audio mixer will suffice in most cases.

Internet-Capable

The computer will need to have an Internet connection, either a dedicated network connection, a modem connection, or some kind of high-speed access such as DSL or broadband.

Computer Display Projector

These devices allow larger groups to view the screen you are displaying on the computer monitor. This is usually done by connecting the "video out" of the computer to a one of the following:
- Large-screen TV using a scan converter box.
- An LCD panel on an overhead projector.
- An LCD projector.

Microphone

Some computers have internal, built-in microphones. Others need to have an external microphone connected to the "audio in" of the computer. Basic-level microphones generally are suitable for most programs requiring microphones. Some manufacturers package a microphone with their product if they have particular microphone specifications.

"Video-In" Capability

Video-in capability means the computer will need to have a digital video card that can digitize the video output of video cameras or VCRs. The video output from cameras or VCRs may be connected by NTSC (composite) video or by S-video. NTSC video output is available on all video equipment and uses common RCA-style (stereo) connectors.

MIDI SOFTWARE RECOMMENDATIONS

The software recommendations in this chapter are most often available for both Windows and Macintosh platforms and are readily available through school music vendors or by downloading from the World Wide Web.

Many music software programs may be configured to play sound using the internal General MIDI sound generation capability of the computer or to play sound by connecting to a MIDI keyboard or sound module. When software does not specifically call for MIDI keyboards, it should be configured to use the internal General MIDI sound generation. On Windows computers, use the internal sound card. On Macintosh computers, have the *QuickTime Musical Instruments* system software installed.

MIDI Software Applications for Improvisation

The development of MIDI in the 1980s enabled a huge step forward for creating accompaniment files and studying improvisation. There are a number of programs designed specifically to encourage musicians to learn how to improvise jazz, such as *Band-in-a-Box, MiBac Jazz, SmartMusic Studio,* and *MIDI Jazz Improvisation.* See the Resource Guide for a listing.

Band-in-a-Box

One of the most popular software programs is PG Music's *Band-in-a-Box*. Let's take a look at how its features are useful for teaching improvisation.

- *Band-in-a-Box (BIAB)* allows the user to type in chords to any song and generate a rhythm section accompaniment in a variety of styles with the click of a button. Available styles range from the late 1930s Basie rhythm section to a Miles Davis funk-era rhythm section. Accompaniments can include up to five instruments such as bass, drums, piano, guitar, and strings. Tempos and keys can all be adapted for different skill levels.
- *BIAB* offers a multisensory learning environment that visual learners will especially appreciate. For example, *BIAB* displays a small piano keyboard at the top of the screen that highlights the keys as the music plays. This is a powerful tool to help pianists visualize voicing chords. The program has a drum window that displays pictures of percussion instruments and a full drum set. As the music plays, the percussion sounds animate in time to the music. A guitar fingerboard can be accessed that will show guitar chord voicings, fingerings of melody lines, and names of notes.
- *BIAB* is great for singers and includes an option to add a melody line complete with scrolling lyrics that highlight each word in time to the music. The student can view *BIAB* in the standard window, which displays chord changes that highlight as the music plays. By clicking the notation button, the student can see in standard notation any of the parts entered into *BIAB*. And, as in any of the features, the notation highlights and scrolls as the music plays. Drums do not translate into notation well; *BIAB* assigns pitches to each sound, which makes the drum part unreadable.
- In Version 7 and higher, a new feature has been added called automatic soloing. After clicking on the solo button, the user will see a window that displays a list of individual musicians or small groups. *BIAB* has been programmed to generate solos in the style of a number of jazz musicians, including Miles Davis, Django Reinhardt, Jaco Pastorius, Louis Armstrong, Benny Goodman, Gary Burton, Coleman Hawkins, Dizzy Gillespie, Charlie Parker, and Pat Metheny. This feature is helpful to create a file that will trade fours with the student and for the student to study ideas particular musicians might play over certain tunes and styles. Each time the solo button is clicked, a completely new solo is generated. Solos can be printed out or viewed with notes highlighting as the music plays.
- Jazz educators can create their own playback files that students can practice improvising, either with the computer MIDI set-up or recorded to tape or CD to practice at home. Since the selections may be slowed down, you can create a practice tape of the same file recorded in a series of different tempos that gradually work up to a performance tempo.
- Rhythm section players can practice with the accompaniments as well. The teacher or student can mute rhythm section instruments to create music-minus-one-style files for practicing.
- There is a large assortment of *BIAB* MIDI songs that may be purchased, ranging from the jazz standards to something as simple as a B-flat blues.

SmartMusic Studio®

- Coda Music Technology's program, *SmartMusic Studio,* also offers jazz accompaniments including the Aebersold Volumes 2, 12, 25, and 31. The program uses General MIDI sounds through your MIDI instrument or can be used with a PC sound card or Macintosh *QuickTime Musical Instruments* built into the system's software. SmartMusic Studio offers the sophisticated ability to follow a soloist's or vocalist's every tempo nuance through a special microphone hook-up, if desired, which is particularly effective on ballads. *SmartMusic Studio* listens to the soloist and adjusts the tempo as he or she plays or sings with the accompaniment.

MiBac Jazz

MiBac Jazz (MiBac) is a jazz accompaniment program that enables the user to create custom play-alongs with features like voicing piano chords in open or closed voicings and lists of all chords related to any triad that can be automatically inputted into the tune and played back. MiBac also uses MIDI but can be configured to play back without MIDI using a sound card or QuickTime.

MIDI Jazz Improvisation

Electronic Courseware Systems' *MIDI Jazz Improvisation* in two volumes is another teaching tool to train beginning and intermediate improvisers. Essentially each volume comes with several MIDI files that can be played back in any sequencer program.

- The MIDI files in Level 1 introduce the student to II-V-I progressions, slow blues in B-flat, medium blues in F, fast blues in C, minor blues, and an original sample tune. Level 2 exercises include samba, ballad with II-V progressions, and 12-bar blues with substitutions, blues with bridge, funk/rock improvisation, and complex II-V-I progressions.
- Both volumes come with a book with notated printouts for C, B-flat, E-flat, and bass clef instruments. Melodies, scale studies, riffs, and solos are written out for each part to be used with each MIDI file.
- The MIDI sequencer files enable the student to practice scales, riffs, solos, and melodies with or without rhythm section tracks by muting tracks they aren't using. As with any sequencing program, you may adjust the tempo.

The Jazz Soloist

- PG Music, the makers of Band-in-a-Box, have a number of other programs based on *BIAB,* including *The Jazz Soloist. The Jazz Soloist* is packaged in three volumes, with 50 pieces in each volume. The program is designed to teach how to analyze and play jazz solos and improve sight-reading. Jazz solos played by different musicians have been entered into the program and can be displayed in notation. Students can practice sight-reading the solos or create original solos to the MIDI tunes.

MIDI Software for Specific Instruments or Specific Jazz Styles

- PG Music's software *The Modern Jazz Pianist* features pianists like Renee Rosnes and Miles Black performing in a variety of jazz styles including those by Herbie Hancock, Fred Hersch, Cedar Walton, Mulgrew Miller, and others. The program includes an onscreen piano keyboard that displays what the pianist is playing and may be slowed down for easier study.
- Additional and similar PG Music programs are *The New Orleans Pianist, Oscar Peterson* (for Windows only), *The Blues Pianist, The Latin Pianist, Jazz Piano Masterclass Featuring Miles Black, Jazz Guitar Masterclass, The Blues Guitarist,* and *The Jazz Saxophonist.*
- *Transkriber* is a software program that enables the user to record whole tunes or sections and has built-in features to slow down the music for easier transcribing. The program has optional controls to loop files, balance of left and right stereo channels, voice eliminator, pitch adjust,

and pitch reference. The pitch reference is handy because it can be used to hear any chromatic pitch, which helps with figuring out the key, chord roots, or individual notes while transcribing.

Software for Studying the History and Appreciation of Jazz

- Dick Hyman's *Century of Jazz Piano* (JSS Music) is packaged with two CD-ROMs and is both an introduction to the history of jazz piano and a tool to study piano styles of some 70 different jazz pianists from James P. Johnson to Bill Evans. The program features an interactive interface that allows the user to investigate pianists from different eras and read, view, and listen to Dick Hyman playing classic pieces in the style of each pianist. The Hyman recordings are MIDI files that can be printed out or played back through MIDI equipment or through the PC sound card or *QuickTime*.
- *History of Jazz* from CLEARVUE/eav seems to be based on the filmstrips narrated by Billy Taylor produced in the late 1960s. The program has minimal interactivity for the student and can be played from beginning to end with screens and narration, or the student can select a particular unit to view. Text is displayed as Taylor reads with blue text hyperlinked to an online glossary and green text hyperlinked to short biographies on musicians, groups, and jazz styles.
- *The Instrumental History of Jazz* (available through MENC) is an interactive CD-ROM that includes much multimedia information including video, music, and text. The program is comprehensive and lists styles from ragtime to mainstream jazz and beyond. The program includes a booklet with a discography, videography, and bibliography and lists of 30 must-have CDs and box sets.

RESOURCES

INTERNET RESOURCES FOR JAZZ EDUCATORS AND THEIR STUDENTS

- DownBeat Education: www.downbeat.com. Great links to other jazz sites, good sources for interviews, and research on jazz and jazz musicians.
- Duke Ellington Centennial Celebration: www.dellington.org. Wonderful Web site designed to be used in the classroom. Lots of photos, recordings, and interactive material for kids.
- ejazz.fm: www.ejazz.fm. Internet-based radio station. A source for hearing jazz anywhere in the world.
- GMN Global Music Network: www.gmn.com. Another great source for hearing and seeing video of jazz concerts.
- IAJE: www.iaje.org. The International Association of Jazz Educators. Join IAJE to learn more about teaching jazz. Great resources online but even better resources at the annual conference. Teacher Training Institutes offered in the summer for instrumental, vocal, general music, private piano teachers, and string areas. **A place for beginners in jazz and improvisation to learn how to teach it!**
- Jazz at Lincoln Center: www.jazzatlincolncenter.org. A great resource for teachers. Many educational programs are available. Check out the new jazz curriculum, *Jazz for Young People Curriculum*.
- Jazz Corner: www.jazzcorner.com. A Web site that offers links to jazz musicians. Many women artists are also listed. Students can interact through e-mail with jazz musicians.
- Jazz in America: www.jazzinamerica.com. Jazz Curriculum project for music and social studies teachers. Eleventh grade is online now. Eighth grade will soon be online, and next year fifth grade.
- Jazz Portal: www.jazzonweb.com. More links to jazz artists.
- Jazz Roots: www.jass.com. Great Web site for researching and learning about early jazz history. Many period photos.
- Jazze.com: www.jazze.com. More Web-based radio and additional links to the jazz world.

- Ken Burns Jazz: www.pbs.org/jazz. The Ken Burns site for the recently released PBS film. Possibly the best site for elementary students. An entire area is devoted to lessons for children. Lots of recorded examples and photos. Very interactive and integrates with language arts, social studies, and other school subjects.
- Kennedy Center Jazz: www.kennedy-center.org/programs/jazz. Education links to jazz programs offered by the Kennedy Center. Includes touring programs.
- Memphis Music: www.memphisguide.com/music2. Find out about the important role Memphis had in the development of the blues.
- Swinging Through Time: The Graystone Museum and the Story of Detroit Jazz. www.ipl.org/exhibit/detjazz. Learn about the many musicians from Detroit who were important contributors to jazz.
- The Golden Age of Jazz: www.jazzphotos.com. Photographer William Gottlieb's Web site. Many of his famous photos are displayed here and lots of interesting history of jazz.
- The Verve Music Group: www.vervemusicgroup.com/jazzed. Another great Web site for jazz education. Many interactive areas and lessons.
- MENC Opportunity-to-Learn Music Technology Standards. www.menc.org.

SOURCES

1. *Dick Hyman's Century of Jazz Piano,* JSS Music. www.jssmusic.com.
2. *History of Jazz*, CLEARVUE/eav, 6465 North Avondale Chicago, IL 60631. 1-800-253-2788. www.clearvue.com.
3. *The Instrumental History of Jazz* by Willie Hill, N2K.
4. *MiBac* Music Software, P.O. Box 468 Northfield, MN 55057. www.mibac.com.
5. *MIDI Jazz Improvisation*, Level I and Level II, by Tom Rudolph and Roger Morgan. Published by Electronic Courseware Systems, Inc., 1713 S. State Street, Champaign, IL 61820. 217-359-7099. www.ecsmedia.com.
6. PG Music, 266 Elmwood Ave., Suite 111, Buffalo, NY 14222. (250) 475-2874. www.pgmusic.com.
7. *SmartMusic,* by Coda Music Technology, 6210 Bury Drive, Eden Prarie, MN 55346-1718. 1-800-843-2066. www.codamusic.com.
8. *Transkriber,* by Reed Kotler Systems, Inc. www.reedkotler.com.

Please refer to the Resource Guide Index.

Chapter 22

VIDEO CONTENTS

Middle School Level Rehearsal Techniques by Dr. Willie L. Hill, Jr.

Hammocks Middle School, Miami, FL. Steve Kirkland, director

1. **Opening comments:** Dr. Willie L. Hill, Jr.
2. **Swing:** "Do Nothin' 'Til You Hear From Me"

    Topics include: Set-up, subdivision, and dynamics
3. **Ballad:** "'Round Midnight"

    Topics include: Straight eighth notes, phrasing, and vibrato
4. **Latin:** "Mambo Hot"

    Topics include: Latin groove, rhythm, and syncopation
5. **Bluesy swing:** "St. James Infirmary"

    Topics include: Triplet feel, mutes, and unison

High School Level Rehearsal Techniques by J. Richard Dunscomb

Northwestern High School, Miami, FL. Chris Dorsey, director

1. **Opening comments:** J. Richard Dunscomb
2. **Swing:** "Sonny's Place"

    Topics include: Metronome, shaping, and concept
3. **Latin:** "Puffy Taco"

    Topics include: Clave, the Latin feel, and ensemble clapping

College Level Rehearsal Techniques by Bob Mintzer

Florida International University, Miami, FL. J. Richard Dunscomb, director

1. **Opening comments:** Bob Mintzer
2. **Swing:** "Cute"

    Topics include: Lead players, groove, and shaping lines
3. **Latin:** "El Cabrojeno"

    Topics include: Precision, the horizontal groove, and pacing of solos
4. **Swing:** "One O'Clock Jump"

    Topics include: Jazz vocabulary, attack, and team concept

Teaching Jazz Improvisation Techniques by Dr. Willie L. Hill, Jr.

Centerville High School Jazz Camp, Centerville High School, Centerville, VA.

David Detwiler, director

1. **Jazz-rock:** "Cantaloupe Island"

    Topics include: Playing the head, internalizing, and solo style

2. **Swing:** "Billie's Bounce"

    Topics include: Melodic, rhythmic, and harmonic vocabulary; key elements; call-and-response

Rhythm Section Techniques. Excerpts From *The Contemporary Rhythm Section*

by Steve Houghton, Tom Rainer, Paul Vaipiano, and Tom Warrington

1. **Set-up:** Drums, bass, piano, guitar, and percussion
2. **Medium swing concept**
3. **Latin feel**
4. **Ballad concept**
5. **Roundtable discussion**

Audio Examples

1. **Swing articulation:** "Just Friends" (vocal) (01:03)
2. **Swing articulation:** "Just Friends" (instrumental) (01:02)
3. **Mambo example:** "Mambo Hot" (00:49)
4. **Mambo example:** "Mambo Beat" (00:54)
5. **Salsa example:** "Mondongo" (01:19)
6. **Merengue example:** "Mr. Papi" (00:55)
7. **Samba example:** "Gentle Rain" (00:51)
8. **Afro-Cuban example:** "Miami Spice" (01:15)

Credits

VIDEO PRODUCTION

Video Director: Dave Olive, Vertical Hold Inc.
Video Production
Tampa, FL

Middle School Level Rehearsal Techniques: Directed by Dr. Willie L. Hill, Jr.
Hammocks Middle School, Miami, FL. Steve Kirkland, director

High School Level Rehearsal Techniques: Directed by J. Richard Dunscomb
Northwestern High School, Miami, FL. Chris Dorsey, director

Collegiate Level Rehearsal Techniques: Directed by Bob Mintzer
Florida International University, Miami, FL. J. Richard Dunscomb, director

Jazz Improvisation Teaching Techniques: Directed by Dr. Willie L. Hill, Jr.
Centerville High School Jazz Camp, Centerville, VA. David Detwiler, director

MUSIC PERFORMED

BILLIE'S BOUNCE

CHARLIE PARKER
© (Renewed 1973) ATLANTIC MUSIC CORP.
This Edition © 1999 ATLANTIC MUSIC CORP.
All Rights Reserved Used by Permission

CANTALOUPE ISLAND

HERBIE HANCOCK
© 1973 HANCOCK MUSIC (BMI)
All Rights Reserved Used by Permission

THE CONTEMPORARY RHYTHM SECTION - COMPLETE

By STEVE HOUGHTON, TOM RAINER, PAUL VAIPIANO and TOM WARRINGTON
© 1994 WARNER BROS. PUBLICATIONS U.S. INC.
All Rights Reserved

CUTE

Music by NEAL HEFTI
Arranged by BOB MINTZER
© 1958 WB MUSIC CORP. (Renewed)
This Arrangement © 2000 WB MUSIC CORP.
All Rights Reserved Including Public Performance

DO NOTHIN' 'TIL YOU HEAR FROM ME

Music by DUKE ELLINGTON
Lyric by BOB RUSSELL
Arranged by JOE JACKSON
© 1943 (Renewed 1971) FAMOUS MUSIC CORPORATION and
HARRISON MUSIC CORP. in the USA
All Rights outside the USA Administered by EMI ROBBINS CATALOG INC. (Publishing)
and WARNER BROS. PUBLICATIONS U.S. INC. (Print)
All Rights Reserved

EL CABOROJENO

BOB MINTZER
© 1998 by MINTZER MUSIC CO.
Used by Permission   All Rights Reserved - International Copyright Secured -
Made in USA
Sole Selling Agent KENDOR MUSIC, INC. Delavan, NY 14042 USA

GENTLE RAIN

LUIZ BONFA
© 1965 (Renewed 1993) EMI UNART CATALOG INC.
All Rights Controlled by EMI UNART CATALOG INC. (Publishing) and
WARNER BROS. PUBLICATIONS U.S. INC (Print)
All Rights Reserved

JUST FRIENDS

Music by JOHN KLENNER
Lyric by SAM M. LEWIS
Arranged by JOE JACKSON
© 1931 (Renewed 1959) METRO-GOLDWYN-MAYER, INC.
All Rights Controlled by EMI ROBBINS CATALOG INC. (Publishing) and
WARNER BROS. PUBLICATIONS U.S. INC.(Print)
This arrangement © 2000 EMI ROBBINS CATALOG INC.
All Rights Reserved Including Public Performance

KING OF THE TIMBALES - A TRIBUTE TO TITO PUENTE

Music by TITO PUENTE
Arranged by VICTOR LOPEZ
"Mambo Beat" © 1957 (Renewed 1985)
This arrangement © 2000 EMI LONGITUDE MUSIC (BMI)
All Rights Reserved Including Public Performance

MAMBO HOT

VICTOR LOPEZ
© 2000 BELWIN-MILLS PUBLISHING CORP. (ASCAP)
All Rights Administered by WARNER BROS. PUBLICATIONS U.S. INC.
All Rights Reserved Including Public Performance

MIAMI SPICE

VICTOR LOPEZ
© 2000 BELWIN-MILLS PUBLISHING CORP. (ASCAP)
All Rights Administered by WARNER BROS. PUBLICATIONS U.S. INC.
All Rights Reserved Including Public Performance

MONDONGO

VICTOR LOPEZ

MR. PAPI

VICTOR LOPEZ

ONE O'CLOCK JUMP

Music by COUNT BASIE
Arranged by BOB MINTZER

PUFFY TACO

VICTOR LOPEZ

'ROUND MIDNIGHT

Words by BERNIE HANIGHEN
Music by COOTIE WILLIAMS and THELONIOUS MONK
Arranged by VICTOR LOPEZ

SONNY'S PLACE

CARL STROMMEN

ST. JAMES INFIRMARY

Words and Music by JOE PRIMROSE
Arranged by TOM DAVIS
© 1929 EMI MILLS MUSIC, INC.
Copyright Renewed
Rights Throughout the World Controlled by EMI MILLS MUSIC, INC. (Publishing)
and WARNER BROS. PUBLICATIONS U.S. INC. (Print)
This arrangement © 2000 EMI MILLS MUSIC, INC.
All Rights Reserved Including Public Performance

Chapter 23

FREQUENTLY ASKED QUESTIONS

by J. Richard Dunscomb

- My band just doesn't swing—what can I do? p. 62, 64–66

- What charts can I play for my upcoming concert/festival? p. 165–181

- How can I incorporate an improvisation component into my jazz program? p. 36, 39, 40, 41

- What CDs should I use first to start a listening library? p. 28, 214

- How can I improve the sound of my individual sections? p. 186–188, 236, 238, 244, 260

- I want to do some Latin charts—what are some good titles? p. 168, 171, 174, 176, 177

- Which students should play which parts? p. 134

- The wind sections are not balanced—what can I do? p. 129, 236, 237, 244, 260

- What does a merengue sound like? p. 93, Video

- What's the best set-up for rehearsal? p. 131

- Should I start a combo? p. 119

- What music should I use for auditions? p. 132

- What size cymbals should my drummer use? p. 217, 218

- Where can I observe a jazz improvisation rehearsal? p. 304, Video

- What mouthpieces and reeds should I use for my sax section? p. 240

- Where can I find help with a budget for the jazz ensemble? p. 55

- How can I get some help with my rhythm section? p. 159, 186, 305, Video

- Where can I find help about taking a trip? p. 290

- What are some tips for playing the flugelhorn? p. 251

- Where can I find out about jazz history? p. 16–27

- How do I rehearse a ballad? p. 304, Video

- What videos and CDs will help my students? p. 214, 362–370

- Block scheduling is coming to my school next year—what will happen to my band program? p. 43, 53

- Who can I recommend my students listen to on their own instrument? p. 312

- How can I find music that will really fit my jazz ensemble? p. 163

- What can I expect from a festival? p. 284

- How can I get people to help with my group without paying big bucks for it? p. 159

- Who are some of the most important people in big band history? p. 138–147

- What should I buy with the extra money my band boosters raised? p. 55–57

- Where can I find help justifying jazz in my program? p. 8, 11

- My band just doesn't sound right—what am I doing wrong? p. 29, 63, 154, 304, Video

- What kind of conceptual approach should my wind instrument use in jazz ensemble that is different from my concert band? p. 28, 62, 64, 65, 67

- What's this about having the band sing? p. 156, 273

- Why should I join IAJE? p. 293, 294

- What is jazz vocabulary? p. 97

- What should my students listen for when they listen to jazz? p. 30, 154

- How should I conduct the jazz ensemble differently? p. 157

- How should I set up the jazz ensemble? p. 130, 131

- How can I identify the different types of Latin jazz? p. 80–88, 305, Video

- How can I best teach the swing style? p. 62, 304, Video

- Where should I start with jazz articulations? p. 64, 67

- My band is ready musically for festival—what else can I do to prepare them? p. 286, 287

- What are the judges listening for at a festival? p. 286

- What is the jazz sound and how can my band get it? p. 29, 154

- How can my rhythm section sound authentic in the Latin style? p. 80, 89, 305, Video

- Where can I get help about Latin styles? p. 84, 93, 305, 334, Video

- My bass player gets a horrible sound—what's the solution? p. 211

- My student's drum set doesn't sound like a jazz drum set—what can I do? p. 216–218

- How can I get my piano and guitar to understand how to comp? p. 198, 228, Video

- Where do I go to get help with voicings for piano and guitar? p. 193, 228

- What is comping? p. 189, 305, Video

- How can I explain to my bass player how to play a walking bass line? p. 207, 305, Video

APPENDIX A
LIST OF JAZZ PROS

The purpose of this list is to provide models for each instrument or voice. Although no list can be complete, we have attempted to include both contemporary and traditional performers. With the Internet, finding recordings of each will be relatively easy.

SOPRANO SAXOPHONE
Sidney Bechet
Jane Ira Bloom
John Coltrane
Jan Gabarek
Steve Lacy
David Liebman
Branford Marsalis
Wayne Shorter
Grover Washington

ALTO SAXOPHONE
Cannonball Adderley
Benny Carter
Ornette Coleman
Hank Crawford
Paquito D'Rivera
Paul Desmond
Eric Dolphy
Gary Foster
Kenny Garrett
Bunky Green
Johnny Hodges
Lee Konitz
Eric Marienthal
Jackie McLean
Lanny Morgan
Oliver Nelson
Charlie Parker
Art Pepper
Houston Person
Vi Redd
David Sanborn
Sonny Stitt
Bobby Watson
Phil Woods

TENOR SAXOPHONE
Eric Alexander
Bob Berg
Michael Brecker
Don Byas
Ed Calle
George Carzone
Pete Christlieb
George Coleman
John Coltrane
Eddie "Lockjaw" Davis
Joe Farrell
Frank Foster
Von Freeman
Stan Getz
Benny Golson
Dexter Gordon
Johnny Griffin
Billy Harper
Coleman Hawkins
Jimmy Heath
Joe Henderson
Greg Herbert
L'Ana Hyams
Dave Liebman
Joe Lovano
Branford Marsalis
Don Menza
Bob Mintzer
Hank Mobley
James Moody
Joshua Redman
Sonny Rollins
David Sanchez
Tom Scott
Wayne Shorter
Zoot Sims
Stanley Turrentine
Ben Webster
Lester Young

BARITONE SAXOPHONE
Pepper Adams
Nick Brignola
Harry Carney
James Carter
Serge Chaloff
Ronny Cuber
Gerry Mulligan
Gary Smulyan

CLARINET
Paquito D'Rivera
Eddie Daniels
Buddy DeFranco
Johnny Dodds
Pete Fountain
Benny Goodman
Jimmy Guiffre
Pee Wee Russell
Artie Shaw

FLUTE
Jose Fajardo
Joe Farrell
Raashan Roland Kirk
Hubert Laws
Herbie Mann
James Moody
James Newton
Joaquim Oliveros
Ali Ryerson
Lew Tabakin
Nestor Torres
Dave Valentin
Orlando "Maraca" Valle
Frank Wess

TRUMPET
Nat Adderley
Louis Armstrong
Chet Baker
Guido Basso
Bix Beiderbecke
Terrance Blanchard
Randy Brecker
Clifford Brown
Clora Bryant
Don Cherry
Miles Davis
Kenny Dorham
Dave Douglas
Harry "Sweets" Edison

Roy Eldridge
Jon Faddis
Maynard Ferguson
Dizzy Gillespie
Tim Haggans
Roy Hargrove
Tom Harrell
Freddie Hubbard
Dolly Hutchinson
Ingrid Jensen
Thad Jones
Wynton Marsalis
Lee Morgan
Fats Navarro
Joe "King" Oliver
Nicholas Payton
Claudio Roditi
Red Rodney
Arturo Sandoval
Woody Shaw
Bobby Shew
Valaida Snow
Marvin Stamm
Byron Stripling
Clark Terry
Cootie Williams

TROMBONE
John Fedchock
Carl Fontana
Curtis Fuller
Urbie Green
Slide Hampton
Conrad Herwig
J. J. Johnson
Melba Liston
Albert Mangelsdorf
James Morrison
"Tricky Sam" Nanton
Edward "Kid" Ory
Bill Reichenbach
Frank Rosolino
Jack Teagarden
Steve Turre
Papo Vazquez
Bill Watrous
Phil Wilson
Jiggs Whigham
Kai Winding

VALVE TROMBONE/EUPHONIUM
Ashley Alexander
Bob Brookmeyer
Rich Matteson
Rob McConnell
Juan Tizol

TUBA
Bill Barber
Howard Johnson
Rich Matteson

PIANO
Toshiko Akiyoshi
Monty Alexander
Lovie Austin
Count Basie
Shelly Berg
Joann Brackeen
Dave Brubeck
Michel Camilo
Nat "King" Cole
Chick Corea
Dorothy Donnegan
Duke Ellington
Bill Evans
Tommy Flanagan
Red Garland
Benny Green
Herbie Hancock
Lil Hardin-Armstrong
Barry Harris
Earl Hines
Bob James
Keith Jarrett
Hank Jones
Wynton Kelly
Kenny Kirkland
Ramsey Lewis
Jim McNeely
Marian McPartland
Brad Meldau
Mulgrew Miller
Thelonious Monk
Danilo Perez
Oscar Peterson
Michel Petrucciani
Bud Powell
Marcus Roberts
Gonzalo Rubalcaba
Emiliano Salvador

Maria Schneider
George Shearing
Horace Silver
Art Tatum
Billy Taylor
Bobby Timmons
McCoy Tyner
Chucho Valdes
Fats Waller
Cedar Walton
Mary Lou Williams
Joe Zawinul

ORGAN
Joey DeFrancesco
Charles Earland
Larry Goldings
Groove Holmes
Jack McDuff
Jimmy McGriff
Jimmy Smith
Lonnie Smith
Larry Young

GUITAR
John Abercrombie
George Benson
Kenny Burrell
Charlie Byrd
Charlie Christian
Al DiMeola
Herb Ellis
Tal Farlow
Freddie Green
Jim Hall
Stanley Jordan
Barney Kessel
Russell Malone
Pat Martino
John McLaughlin
Pat Metheny
Wes Montgomery
Mary Osborne
Joe Pass
Bucky Pizzarelli
John Pizzarelli
Jimmy Rainey
Django Reinhardt
Emily Remler
John Scofield
Mike Stern

BASS
Jimmy Blanton
Ray Brown
Ron Carter
Paul Chambers
Stanley Clarke
John Clayton
Richard Davis
Jimmy Garrison
Eddie Gomez
Charlie Haden
Percy Heath
Milt Hinton
Dave Holland
Marc Johnson
Sam Jones
Scott LaFaro
Christian McBride
Marcus Miller
Charlie Mingus
George Mraz
Walter Page
Jaco Pastorius
John Patitucci
Gary Peacock
Niels Henning Orsted Pedersen
Oscar Pettiford
Elisa Pruett
Rufus Reid
Slam Stewart
Miroslav Vitous
Tom Warrington
Buster Williams
Victor Wooten

DRUMS
Louie Bellson
Ignacio Berroa
Cindy Blackman
Art Blakey
Terry Lynn Carrington
Sid Catlett
Kenny Clarke
Jimmy Cobb
Billy Cobham
Vinnie Colaiuta
Jack DeJohnette
Baby Dodds
Peter Erskine
Al Foster
Steve Gadd

Sonny Greer
Louis Hayes
Roy Haynes
Albert Heath
Horacio "El Negro" Hernandez
Billy Higgins
Steve Houghton
Elvin Jones
Harold Jones
Jo Jones
Philly Joe Jones
Gene Krupa
Mel Lewis
Victor Lewis
Shelly Manne
Joe Morello
Paul Motian
Alphonse Mouzon
Ndugo (Chancellor)
Adam Nussbaum
Sonny Payne
Buddy Rich
Max Roach
Zutty Singleton
Ed Soph
Ed Thigpen
Chick Webb
Dave Weckl
Lenny White
Tony Williams
Sam Woodyard

VIBRAPHONE
Gary Burton
Terry Gibbs
Lionel Hampton
Bobby Hutcherson
Marjorie Hyams
Milt Jackson
Mike Mainieri
Red Norvo
Tito Puente
Cal Tjador

PERCUSSION
Alex Acuna
Don Alias
Ray Barretto
Candido Camero
Changuito (Jose Luis Quintana)
Luis Conte

Paulino de Costa
Sheila E
Trilok Gurta
Giovanni Hidalgo
Airto Moreira
Ndugo (Chancellor)
Tito Puente
Bobby Sanabria
Mongo Santamaria
Nana Vasconcelos

MISCELLANEOUS INSTRUMENTS
Regina Carter - violin
Bela Fleck - banjo
Stephane Grappelli - violin
Ron McCorby - whistler
Jean Luc Ponty - violin
Toots Thielemans - harmonica
Joe Venuti - violin

FEMALE VOCALISTS
Karrin Allyson
Leny Andrade
Carmen Bradford
Dee Dee Bridgewater
Betty Carter
June Christy
Rosemary Clooney
Natalie Cole
Madeline Eastman
Ella Fitzgerald
Nnenna Freelon
Astrud Gilberto
Billie Holiday
Shirley Horn
Nancy King
Diana Krall
Cleo Laine
Peggy Lee
Abbey Lincoln
Carmen McRae
Jane Monheit
Barbara Morrison
Anita O'Day
Dianne Reeves
Vanesa Rubin
Diane Schuur
Janis Siegel
Bessie Smith
Tierney Sutton
Sarah Vaughan
Dinah Washington

Cassandra Wilson
Nancy Wilson

MALE VOCALISTS
Ernie Andrews
Louis Armstrong
Chet Baker
Tony Bennett
George Benson
Ray Charles
Freddy Cole
Nat King Cole
Harry Connick Jr.
Bob Dorough
Kurt Elling
Giacomo Gates
Joao Gilberto
Miles Griffith
Johnny Hartman
Jon Hendricks
Al Jarreau
Eddie Jefferson
Kevin Mahogany
Bobby McFerrin
Mark Murphy
Kenny Rankin
Frank Sinatra
Mel Torme
Joe Williams

VOCAL GROUPS
The Bobs
Boca Livre
The Four Freshmen
The Hi-Lo's
Ladysmith Black Mambazo
Lambert, Hendricks & Ross
Les Doubles Six
M-Pact
Manhattan Transfer
New York Voices
Rare Silk
Real Group
The Ritz
Singers Unlimited
The Swingle Singers
Vocal Sampling
Voice Trek
Take 6
Toxic Audio
Vox One
Zap Mama

RESOURCE GUIDE INDEX

Section I: Jazz Materials

Section II: Individual Instruments

Section III: Software/Web Sites

Section IV: DVDs/Videos

RESOURCE GUIDE

SECTION I: JAZZ MATERIALS

Reference Books

Adolfo, Antonio, *Brazilian Music Workshop*, JA Jazz. Book/CD.

Aebersold, Jamey, *Combo Rehearsal Guidelines*, JA Jazz. Educator level.

Althouse, Jay, *Copyright: The Complete Guide for Music Educators*, Music in Action.

Baker, David N., *How to Play Bebop*, Volume 1: *The Bebop Scales and Other Scales in Common Use*, Tichenor Publishing.

Baker, David N., *How to Play Bebop*, Volume 2, Alfred Publishing.

Baker, David N., *Jazz Improvisation: A Comprehensive Study for All Players*, Alfred Publishing.

Baker, David N., *Jazz Improvisation: A Comprehensive Study for All Players*, Maher Publications, 1969.

Baker, David N., *Jazz Pedagogy*, Alfred Publishing. Educator level.

Baker, David N., *Practicing Jazz: A Creative Approach*, JA Jazz.

Bash, Lee, "An Index of the NAJE Educator and Jazz Educators Journal 1969–1985," Volumes I–XVII, IAJE. 1985. Educator level.

Berry, John, *The Jazz Ensemble Director's Handbook*, Hal Leonard Publications. Educator level.

Coker, Jerry, *How to Listen to Jazz* (Revised), Prentice Hall Press.

Coker, Jerry, *How to Practice Jazz*, JA Jazz. All levels.

Coker, Jerry, *Improvising Jazz*, Simon & Schuster, Inc.

Coker, Jerry, *The Jazz Idiom*, Prentice Hall Press, 1975. All levels.

Coker, Jerry, *Listening to Jazz*, Prentice Hall Press, 1978.

Coker, Jerry, *The Teaching of Jazz*, JA Jazz.

Dahl, Linda, *Stormy Weather: The Music and Lives of a Century of Jazz Women*, Pantheon Books, 1984. Enhanced CD format.

Feather, Leonard, *The Book of Jazz*, Horizon, 1976.

Galper, Hal, *The Touring Musician*, Watson-Guptill Publishers.

Haerle, Dan, *The Jazz Language*, Warner Bros. Publications.

Henry, Robert, *The Jazz Ensemble: A Guide to Technique*, Prentice Hall Press. Educator level.

Hill, Willie, *The Instrumental History of Jazz*, N2K Inc., 1997.

Johnson, Conrad O., *Improvisational Rehearsal Techniques for Stage Band*, Conrad Johnson Music Publishers. Educator level.

Kernfeld, Barry, *The New Grove Dictionary of Jazz*, St. Martin's Press.

Kuzmich, John, Jr. and Lee Bash, *Complete Guide to Combo Jazz Instruction*, Warner Bros. Publications. Educator level.

Kuzmich, John, Jr. and Lee Bash, *Complete Guide to Instrumental Jazz Instruction*, Warner Bros. Publications. Educator level.

Kuzmich, John, Jr. and Lee Bash, *Complete Guide to Teaching Improvisation*, Warner Bros. Publications. Educator level.

Lawn, Rick, *The Jazz Ensemble Director's Manual*, CL Barnhouse Music Publishing Co. Educator level.

Leder, Jan, *Women in Jazz: A Discography of Instrumentalists*, Greenwood Publishing Group, Inc., 1968.

Lees, Gene, *Cats of Any Color*, Da Capo Press.

Leibman, David, *The Art of Recording*, JA Jazz.

Marsalis, Wynton, *Jazz for Young People Curriculum*, Warner Bros. Publications.

Mehegan, John, *Jazz Improvisation 1: Tonal and Rhythmic Principles*, Music Sales Corporation.

Mehegan, John, *Jazz Improvisation 2: Jazz Rhythm and the Improvised Line*, Music Sales Corporation.

Mehegan, John, *Jazz Improvisation 3: Swing and Early Progressive Piano Styles*, Music Sales Corporation.

MENC, *Teaching Jazz: A Course of Study*, (IAJE).

Porter, Lewis, *Jazz: A Century of Change*, G. Schirmer, Inc.

Rinaldo, John, *Jazz Beginnings*, J & J Publishers, 5236 Argus Drive, Los Angeles, CA 90041.

Rowlyk, Terry, *Jazz for the Music Educator*, JA Jazz.

Schemel and Krasilovsky, *The Business of Music*, Watson-Guptill Publishers.

Schueler, Roger, *So, You Want to Lead a Jazz Band?*, Houston Publishing, Inc.

Schuller, Gunther, *Early Jazz: Its Roots and Musical Development*, Oxford University Press, 1960.

Stark, Scott Hunter, *Live Sound Reinforcement*, www.Artistpro.com, LLC.

Taylor, Billy, *Jazz Piano: A Jazz History*, William C. Brown, 1983.

Tracy, Mike, *Jazz Piano Voicing for the Non-Pianist*, JA Jazz.

Werner, Kenny, *Effortless Mastery*, JA Jazz.

Wiskirchen, Rev. George, C.S.C., *Developmental Techniques for the School Dance Band Musician*, Berklee Press.

Jazz History and Biographical Materials

Armstrong, Louis, *Louis Armstrong: In His Own Words*, Oxford University Press.

Armstrong, Louis, *Satchmo: My Life in New Orleans*, Da Capo Press.

Britt, Stan, and Brian Case, *The Illustrated Encyclopedia of Jazz*, Crown Publishing Group.

Brown, Charles, *The Jazz Experience*, Brown and Benchmark.

Burns, Ken, *Jazz: A Film by Ken Burns*, PBS Home Video.

Burns, Ken, and Geoffrey C. Ward, *Jazz: A History of America's Music*, Alfred Knopf.

Carner, Gary, *Miles Davis Companion*, Music Sales Corporation.

Carr, Ian, *Miles Davis: A Biography*, Avalon New York.

Carr, Ian; Digby Fairweather; and Brian Priestley, *Jazz: The Essential Companion*, Prentice Hall Press.

Chambers, Jack, *Milestones, The Music and Times of Miles Davis*, Da Capo Press.

Dahl, Linda, *Stormy Weather: The Music and Lives of a Century of Jazz Women*, Pantheon Books.

Dance, Stanley, *The World of Count Basie,* Simon & Schuster, Inc.

Dance, Stanley, *The World of Duke Ellington,* Da Capo Press.

Dance, Stanley, *The World of Earl Hines,* Da Capo Press.

Dance, Stanley, *The World of Swing,* Da Capo Press.

Davis, Francis, *Bebop and Nothingness,* Music Sales Corporation.

DeValk, Jeroen, *Chet Baker,* Berkeley Hill Books.

Dunscomb, Marcia, *Evolution of Jazz,* McGraw-Hill Primis Custom Publishing.

Early, Gerald, *Miles Davis and American Culture,* Missouri Historical Society Press.

Ellington, Duke, *Music Is My Mistress,* Da Capo Press.

Ellington, Mercer, *Duke Ellington in Person,* Houghton Mifflin Co., 1978, Da Capo Press (paperback).

Elliston, Ralph, *Living With Music: Jazz Writings,* Random House, Inc.

Feather, Leonard, *Biographical Encyclopedia of Jazz*, Oxford University Press.

Feather, Leonard, *The Encyclopedia of Jazz in the Seventies,* Da Capo Press.

Feather, Leonard, *The Encyclopedia of Jazz in the Sixties,* Da Capo Press.

Feather, Leonard, *From Satchmo to Miles,* Da Capo Press.

Feather, Leonard, *The New Encyclopedia of Jazz,* Da Capo Press.

Fisher, Larry, *Jazz Connections: Miles Davis and David Liebman,* Edwin Mellen Press.

Fordham, John, and Sonny Rollins, *Jazz: The Essential Companion for Every Jazz Fan,* Barnes & Noble Books.

Gillespie, Dizzy, *To Be or Not to Bop,* Doubleday, 1979.

Gioia, Ted, *The History of Jazz,* Oxford University Press.

Gitler, Ira, *Jazz Masters of the Forties,* Macmillan Publishers, 1966, reprinted by Da Capo Press.

Goldberg, Joe, *Jazz Masters of the Fifties,* Macmillan Publishers, 1965, reprinted by Da Capo Press.

Gridley, Mark, *How to Teach Jazz History: A Teacher's Manual,* IAJE.

Gridley, Mark, *Jazz Styles: History and Analysis,* Prentice Hall Press.

Hasse, John Edward, *Beyond Category: The Life and Genius of Duke Ellington,* Da Capo Press.

Hasse, John Edward, *Jazz: The First Century,* William Morrow & Co.

Hill, Willie, *The Instrumental History of Jazz,* N2KE-10004, 1997. An enhanced two CD set.

Hischke, Jon J.; David Sharp; and Randall Snyder, *An Outline History of American Jazz,* Kendall/Hunt.

Hodeir, Andre, *Jazz: Its Evolution and Essence*, Da Capo Press.

Kahn, Ashley, *The Making of* Kind of Blue, Da Capo Press.

Kirchner, Bill, *A Miles Davis Reader,* Smithsonian Institution Press.

Kirchner, Bill, *Oxford Companion to Jazz,* Oxford University Press.

Lawrence, A. H., *Duke Ellington and His World,* Routledge Press.

Leder, Jan, *Women in Jazz: A Discography of Instrumentalists,* Greenwood Publishing Group, Inc.

Lees, Gene, *Cats of Any Color,* Oxford University Press.

Lees, Gene, and John Reeves, *Jazz Lives: 100 Portraits in Jazz,* Firefly Books.

Leibman, David, *In Conversation With Lieb,* JA Jazz.

Lyons, Len, *The Lives and Music of the Jazz Masters,* William Morrow & Co.

Meadows, Eddie, *Jazz Reference and Research Materials: A Bibliography,* Garland Publishing.

Megill, Donald D., and Richard S. Demory, *Introduction to Jazz History,* Prentice Hall Press.

Merriweather, D., *Mister, I Am The Band, Buddy Rich: His Life and Travels*, Hal Leonard Publications.

Milkowski, Bill, *Jaco: The World's Greatest Bass Player*, BackBeat Books.

Porter, Lewis, *Jazz: A Century of Change*, Simon & Schuster, Inc.

Porter, Lewis, *John Coltrane: His Life and Music*, University of Michigan Press.

Reisner, Robert, *Bird: The Legend of Charlie Parker*, Citadel, 1962, reprinted by Da Capo Press.

Russell, Ross, *Bird Lives: The High Life and Hard Times of Charlie Parker*, Charterhouse, 1973.

Schiedt, Duncan, *Twelve Lives in Jazz*, JA Jazz.

Schuller, Gunther, *Early Jazz: Its Roots and Musical Development*, Oxford University Press.

Schuller, Gunther, *The Swing Era: The Development of Jazz 1930–1945*, Oxford University Press.

Shapiro, Nat, and Nat Hentoff, *Jazz Makers*, Greenwood Publishing Group, Inc. and Da Capo Press.

Simon, George T., *The Big Band*, Music Sales Corporation.

Tanner, Paul; David W. Megill; and Maurice Gerow, *Jazz*, McGraw-Hill.

Taylor, Billy, *Jazz Piano: A Jazz History*, William C. Brown.

Tesser, Neil, *The Playboy Guide to Jazz*, Penguin Putnam, Inc.

Tinger, Paul, *Miles Beyond: Miles Davis 1971–1991*, Watson-Guptill Publishers.

Tirro, Frank, *Jazz: A History*, WW Norton & Co.

Torme, Mel, *Traps, The Drum Wonder: The Life of Buddy Rich*, Hal Leonard Publications.

Troupe, Quincy, *Miles: The Autobiography*, Simon & Schuster, Inc.

Ulman, Michael, *Jazz Lives*, Penguin Putnam, Inc.

Walser, Robert, *Keeping Time: Readings in Jazz History*, Oxford University Press.

Wheaton, Jack, *All That Jazz*, Scarecrow Press, Inc.

Williams, Martin, *The Art of Jazz: Ragtime to Bebop*, Da Capo Press.

Williams, Martin, *Jazz Masters of New Orleans*, Macmillan Publishers, Collier and Da Capo Press, 1970.

Williams, Martin, *Smithsonian Collection of Classic Jazz*, New York: WW Norton & Co.

Woideck, Carl, *The Charlie Parker Companion*, Music Sales Corporation.

Yanow, Scott, *All Music Guide to Jazz*, BackBeat Books.

Yanow, Scott, *Bebop*, BackBeat Books.

Yanow, Scott, *Bebop and Nothingness*, JA Jazz.

Yanow, Scott, *Trumpet Kings*, BackBeat Books.

Band Methods/Materials

Beach, Doug, *Essential Rhythms of Jazz*, Kendor Music, Inc.

Bencriscutto, Frank, and Hal Freese, *Total Musicianship*, Neil A. Kjos.

Berg, Shelly, *Chop Monster*, J Fraser Collection.

DiBlasio, Denis, *The Denis DiBlasio Jazz Ensemble Book*, Kendor Music, Inc.

Hunt, Clyde E., *Call & Response Jazz*, B♭ Music Production.

Hunt, Clyde E., *Cedar Grove Swing*, B♭ Music Production.

La Porta, John, *Developing the School Jazz Ensemble*, Berklee Press.

New Music Reviews in "The Instrumentalist, BD Guide," *Jazz Educators Journal*.

Rickson, Roger, *Comprehensive Guide to Jazz Ensemble Literature*.

Rinaldo, Johnny, *Jazz Beginning,* J & J Publishers, 5236 Argus Drive, Los Angeles, CA 90041.

Sorenson, Dean, and Bruce Pearson, *Standard of Excellence Jazz Ensemble Method,* Kjos Music. Beginner.

Steinel, Mike, *Essential Elements for Jazz Ensemble,* Hal Leonard Publications. Beginner.

Strommen, Carl, and Sandy Feldstein, *The Sound of Jazz,* Alfred Publishing. Beginner.

Jazz Ensemble Warm-up Materials

Beach, Doug, *Threshold Series: Rock Rhythms and Swing Rhythm,* Kjos Music. Beginner/Intermediate.

Berry, John, *Jazz Ensemble Warm-ups,* Hal Leonard Publications. Beginner.

Clark, Andy, *Five Minutes a Day,* CL Barnhouse Music Publishing Co.

Edmondson, John, *Jazz Warm-up,* Hal Leonard Publications.

Jennings, Paul, *Blues Warm-up Workout,* Hal Leonard Publications.

Jennings, Paul, *Modal Warm-up Workout,* Hal Leonard Publications.

Lewis, Mike, and Jack Bullock, *Daily Warm-up Exercises for Jazz Ensemble,* Volumes 1/2, Warner Bros. Publications. Beginner.

Metcalf, Greg, *Big Band Warm-up,* Barry.

Owen, Steve, *Jazz Builder Step 1*, Matrix Publishing.

Sweeney, Mike, *Instant Warm-up,* Hal Leonard Publications.

Jazz Combo Materials

Aebersold, Jamey, *Combo Rehearsal Guidelines,* JA Jazz.

Baker, David N., *Arranging and Composing for the Small Ensemble: Jazz, R&B, Jazz Rock,* Alfred Publishing.

Houghton, Steve, *A Guide for the Modern Jazz Rhythm Section,* CL Barnhouse Music Pub. Co.

Kuzmich, John, Jr., and Lee Bash, *Complete Guide to Improvisation Instruction,* Warner Bros. Publications.

Kuzmich, John, Jr., and Lee Bash, *Complete Guide to Combo Jazz Instruction,* Warner Bros. Publications.

Kuzmich, John, Jr., The Great Combo Treasure Hunt, *Jazz Educators Journal,* Winter, 1989.

Rinaldo, John, *Jazz Beginnings,* J & J Publishers, 5236 Argus Drive, Los Angeles, CA 90041.

Sherman, Hal, *The Rhythm Section,* Hal Leonard Publications. All levels.

Silver, Horace, *The Art of Small Jazz Combo Playing,* Hal Leonard Publications.

Improvisation Materials

Aebersold, Jamey, *Jazz Catalog,* an extensive catalog, JA Jazz.

Aebersold, Jamey, *Video: Anyone Can Improvise,* JA Jazz. Beginner/Intermediate.

Allard, Joe, *Advanced Rhythms,* JA Jazz.

Allen, Eddie, *The Bb Blues,* JA Jazz. Beginner.

Amadie, Jimmy, *Harmonic Foundation for Jazz & Popular Music,* Thornton Publications.

Amadie, Jimmy, *Jazz Improv: How to Play It,* Thornton Publications. Intermediate/Advanced.

Baker, David N., *Advanced Improvisation*, Vol. 2, JA Jazz.

Baker, David N., *Bebop Jazz Solos,* correlated with JA Vol. 10 and 13, JA Jazz.

Baker, David N., *The Blues: How to Play,* JA Jazz.

Baker, David N., *Improvisational Patterns: The Bebop Era,* Vol.1, Charles Colin Music Publications.

Baker, David N., *Jazz Expressions and Explorations,* JA Jazz.

Baker, David N., *Jazz Improvisation,* Alfred Publishing. Advanced.

Baker, David N., *Jazz Improvisation: A Comprehensive Method,* Tichenor Publishing.

Baker, David N., *Jazz Solos,* written-out solos for JA Vols. 5 and 6, JA Jazz.

Baker, David N., *Modern Concepts in Improvisation,* JA Jazz.

Baker, David N., *Practicing Jazz: A Creative Approach,* JA Jazz.

Berg, Shelton, *Chop-Monster Series,* Books 1 and 2, J. Fraser Collection. Book/CD.

Berg, Shelton, *Jazz Improvisation: The Goal Note Method,* Kendor Music, Inc. Intermediate/Advanced.

Bergonzi, Jerry, *The Jazz Line,* JA Jazz.

Bergonzi, Jerry, *Melodic Rhythms,* JA Jazz.

Bergonzi, Jerry, *Pentatonics: Inside Improv,* Vol. 2, JA Jazz.

Bergonzi, Jerry, *Thesaurus of Intervallic Melodies,* JA Jazz.

Berle, Arnie, *Complete Handbook for Jazz Improvisation,* Music Sales Corporation.

Berle, Arnie, *How to Create and Develop a Jazz Sax Solo,* Mel Bay Publications, Inc.

Berle, Arnie, *Improvising for the Contemporary Musician,* Music Sales Corporation.

Berliner, Paul, *Thinking in Jazz,* JA Jazz.

Blake and Harmon, *Strings: Jazz Improv Made Easy,* JA Jazz.

Boer and Lutz, *The Swinging Beginning,* JA Jazz. Book/CD.

Bouchard, George, *Intermediate Jazz Improvisation,* JA Jazz.

Campbell, Gary, *Connecting Jazz Theory,* Hal Leonard Publications.

Campbell, Gary, *Expansions,* Hal Leonard Publications.

Campbell, Gary, *Triad Pairs for Jazz,* Warner Bros. Publications.

Coker, Jerry, *A Complete Method for Jazz Improvisation,* Warner Bros. Publications. Intermediate/Advanced.

Coker, Jerry, *Drones for Improvisation,* Warner Bros. Publications.

Coker, Jerry, *Elements of the Jazz Language for the Developing Improviser,* Warner Bros. Publications. All levels.

Coker, Jerry, *Improvising Jazz,* Prentice Hall Press. All levels.

Coker, Jerry, *The Jazz Ballad,* JA Jazz.

Coker, Jerry; Jimmy Casale; Gary Campbell; and Jerry Greene, *Patterns for Jazz,* Warner Bros. Publications.

Coker, Jerry, and Vincent Knapp, *Hearing the Changes,* JA Jazz.

Colin and Bower, *Rhythms Complete,* JA Jazz.

Corpolongo, Rich, *217 Sequences for the Contemporary Musician,* JA Jazz.

Crook, Hal, *How to Improvise,* JA Jazz.

Crook, Hal, *Ready, Aim, Improvise,* JA Jazz.

DeCosmo, Emile, *The Polytonal Rhythm Series,* JA Jazz.

DeCosmo, Emile, *The Woodshedding Source Book*, Hal Leonard Publications.

DeFranceso, Joey, *Concepts for Improvisation*, Hal Leonard Publications.

DiBlasio, Denis, *Basic Workout Drills for Creative Jazz Improvisation*, Houston Publishing, Inc.

DiBlasio, Denis, *DiBlasio's Bop Shop: Getting Started in Improvisation*, Kendor Music, Inc.

DiBlasio, Denis, *Guide for Jazz and Scat Vocalists*, JA Jazz. Book/CD.

DiBlasio, Denis, and Steve Weist, *DiBlasio's Bop Shop: The Sequel: Conception and Ear Training for Beginning Improvisation*, Kendor Music, Inc.

Green, Bunky, *Inside/Outside*, JA Jazz.

Haerle, Dan, *The Jazz Language*, Warner Bros. Publications. All levels.

Haerle, Dan, *The Jazz Sound*, Hal Leonard Publications. Intermediate/Advanced.

Haerle, Dan, *Scales for Jazz Improvisation*, Warner Bros. Publications.

Harbison, Pat, *20 Authentic Bebop Solos*, JA Jazz.

Harrison, Wendell, *The Bebopper's Method Book #1*, Wenha Music.

Harrison, Wendell, *The Bebopper's Method Book #2*, Wenha Music.

Higgins, Dan, *120 Blues Choruses*, JA Jazz.

Higgins, Dan, *Jazz Etude Book*, JA Jazz.

Higgins, Dan, *V7-I Progression in Solo Form*, JA Jazz.

Hill, Dr. Willie L., Jr., *Approaching the Standards*, Warner Bros. Publications, 2000. 3 Volumes. Books/CDs.

Johnson, J.J., *J.J. Johnson Trombone Solos*, JA Jazz.

Kynaston, Trent P,. and Robert J. Ricci, *Jazz Improvisation*, Prentice Hall Press. Intermediate/Advanced.

La Porta, John, *A Guide to Jazz Improvisation*, Berklee Press. Book/CD.

Lateef, Yusef, *123 Duets*, Fana Music.

Lateef, Yusef, *How to Perform Autophysiopsychic Music*, Fana Music.

Leibman, David, and Gunnar Mossblad, *Improvisation Concepts and Techniques*, JA Jazz. Book/CD.

Leibman, David, *Chromaticism/Non-Diatonic Scales*, JA Jazz.

Leibman, David, *Ten Compositions in a Chromatic Style*, JA Jazz.

Lenten, Van, *Creative Jazz Exercises*, JA Jazz.

Liebman, David, *A Chromatic Approach to Jazz Harmony and Melody*, Advance Music. Advanced.

Liebman, David, *David Liebman Plays: Stereo CD*, JA Jazz.

Liebman, David, *David Liebman Scale Syllabus Solos*, JA Jazz.

Liebman, David, *David Liebman Tenor Solos*, JA Jazz.

Ligon, Bert, *Comprehensive Technique for Jazz Musicians*, Hal Leonard Publications.

Ligon, Bert, *Connecting Chords With Linear Harmony*, JA Jazz.

Matteson, Rich, and Jack Peterson, *Flexibility and Improv Patterns*, JA Jazz.

Mehegan, John, *Improvising Jazz Piano*, Music Sales Corporation.

Mehegan, John, *Jazz Improvisation 1: Tonal and Rhythmic Principles*, Music Sales Corporation.

Mehegan, John, *Jazz Improvisation 2: Jazz Rhythm and the Improvised Line*, Music Sales Corporation.

Mintzer, Bob, *14 Blues & Funk Etudes*, Warner Bros. Publications. Book/CD.

Mintzer, Bob, *15 Easy Jazz, Blues & Funk Etudes*, Warner Bros. Publications. Book/CD.

Mintzer, Bob, *15 Jazz & Funk Etudes*, Warner Bros. Publications. Book/CD.

Mirigian, David, *For Players Only*, scales and scale patterns, JA Jazz.

Mirigian, David, *Jazz Pattern Books*, JA Jazz.

Niehaus, Lennie, *Lennie Niehaus Plays the Blues in All 12 Keys*, JA Jazz.

Nelson, Oliver, *Patterns for Improvisation*, JA Jazz.

Pozzi, Dave, *An Approach to Jazz Improvisation*, Musicians Institute.

Quigley, Greg, and Vince Genova, *The Jazzworx! Improv Method*, Kendor Music, Inc.

Racina, John, *Blues Etudes, Patterns and More*, JA Jazz.

Racina, John, *Blues Riffs*, Vol. 1, JA Jazz.

Racina, John, *Jazz Etudes to "Rhythm" Changes*, JA Jazz.

Reeves, Scott D., *Creative Beginnings: Intro to the Jazz Idiom*, Prentice Hall Press.

Reeves, Scott D., *Creative Jazz Improvisation*, Prentice Hall Press. Intermediate/Advanced.

Ricker, Ramon, and Walt Weiskopf, *The Augmented Scale in Jazz*, JA Jazz.

Ricker, Ramon, and Walt Weiskopf, *Coltrane: A Player's Guide to His Harmony*, JA Jazz.

Ricker, Ramon, *New Concepts in Linear Improvisation*, Warner Bros. Publications. Intermediate/ Advanced.

Rinaldo, Johnny, *Jazz Beginnings*, J & J Publishers, 5236 Argus Drive, Los Angeles, CA 90041.

Riposo, Joe, *Jazz Improvisation: A Whole-Brain Approach*, JA Jazz.

Roldinger, *Jazz Improvisation & Pentatonic*, JA Jazz.

Russell, George, *The Lydian Chromatic Concept*, www.georgerussell.com., Concept Publications.

Shneidman, Jack, *1001 Jazz Licks*, Cherry Lane Music. Beginner/Intermediate.

Shneidman, Jack, *A Complete Vocabulary for the Improvising Musician*, Cherry Lane Music.

Slonimski, Nicolas, *Thesaurus of Scales and Melodic Patterns*, JA Jazz.

Snidero, Jim, *Jazz Conception*, Advance Music. Book/CD.

Spera, Dominic, *Blues and the Basics*, Hal Leonard Publications. Book/cassette.

Spera, Dominic, *Making the Changes*, Hal Leonard Publications. Book/cassette.

Steinel, Mike, *Building a Jazz Vocabulary*, Hal Leonard Publications.

Swayzee, Tom, Jr., *Scales & Etudes for Modern Musicians*, Franton Music. Book/cassette.

Thomas, Willie, *Fundamental Fun*, Warner Bros. Publications.

Thomas, Willie, *Jazz Anyone...?*, Warner Bros. Publications. Book/cassette.

Van Lenten, Lance, *Creative Jazz Exercises, Volumes 1 and 2*, Charles Colin Music Publications.

Weiskopf, Walt, *Around the Horn*, JA Jazz.

Weiskopf, Walt, *Intervallic Improvisation—The Modern Sound: A Player's Guide*, JA Jazz.

Ear Training

Aebersold, Jamey, *Advanced Ear Training for Jazz Musicians*, JA Jazz. Advanced.

Aebersold, Jamey, *Chromatic Pitch Pipe*, JA Jazz.

Aebersold, Jamey, *Jamey Aebersold Ear Training*, JA Jazz. Two CDs/cassettes. All levels.

Aebersold, Jamey, *Jazz Ear Training*, JA Jazz. Beginner/Advanced.

Baker, David N., *A New Approach to Ear Training for Jazz Musicians*, Warner Bros. Publications. Five volumes. Intermediate/Advanced.

Coker, Jerry, *Listening to Jazz*, Prentice Hall Press.

DiBlasio, Denis, and Steve Weist, *DiBlasio's Bop Shop: The Sequel: Conception and Ear Training for Beginning Improvisation*, Kendor Music, Inc.

Donelian, Armen, *Training the Ear*, JA Jazz.

LaPorta, John, *Jazz Ear Training*, Kendor Music, Inc. Intermediate/Advanced.

Mason, Thom, *The Art of Hearing*, Hal Leonard Publications.

Mason, Thom, *Ear Training for Improvisers*, Alfred Publishing. Intermediate.

Mixon, Donavan, *Performance Ear Training*, JA Jazz.

Pickens, Harry, *Ear Training for the Jazz Musician*, JA Jazz.

Play-Along

Aebersold, Jamey, *A New Approach to Jazz Improvisation*, JA Jazz. 90+ volumes.

Charles Mingus: More Than a Play-A-Long, Hal Leonard Publications. Book/two CDs.

Chet Baker Play-Along, JA Jazz. Book/CD.

Chick Corea Play-Along Collection, Warner Bros. Publications. Book/CD.

Crook, Hal, *Creative Comping for Improv*, three volumes, JA Jazz.

Gerry Mulligan Play-A-Long, Hal Leonard Publications.

Haerle, Dan; Jack Petersen; and Rich Matteson, *Jazz Tunes for Improvisation*, Warner Bros. Publications.

Hill, Willie L., Jr., *Approaching the Standards*, Volumes 1, 2, and 3, Warner Bros. Publications, 2000. Book/CDs.

Houghton, Steve, and Tom Warrington, *Blues Master Tracks*, JA Jazz. Book/CD.

Jazz Workshop Series, Advance Music. All levels.

LaPorta, John, *10 Easy Jazz Duets*, Warner Bros. Publications. Book/CD.

Mantooth, Frank, *Cole Porter Classics*, Hal Leonard Publications.

Mantooth, Frank, *Essential Jazz Standards*, Hal Leonard Publications.

Mantooth, Frank, *Jazz Classic Standards*, Hal Leonard Publications.

Mantooth, Frank, *Jazz Favorites*, Hal Leonard Publications.

Mantooth, Frank, *Jazz Gems*, Hal Leonard Publications.

Mantooth, Frank, *Patterns for Improv—From the Beginning*, Hal Leonard Publications.

Mantooth, Frank, *Patterns for Improv—Movin' On to the Blues*, Hal Leonard Publications.

Mintzer, Bob, *14 Blues and Funk Etudes*, Warner Bros. Publications. Book/CD.

Mintzer, Bob, *15 Easy Jazz, Blues, and Funk Etudes*, Warner Bros. Publications. Book/CD.

Mintzer, Bob, *15 Jazz and Funk Etudes*, Warner Bros. Publications. Book/CD.

Muy Caliente, JA Jazz. Book/CD.

Play the Duke, JA Jazz. Book/CD.

Ricker, Ray, *Ray Ricker Improv Series*, three volumes, JA Jazz. Book/CD.

Sher, Chuck, *Play-A-Long Cassettes for the New Real Book*, Sher Music. All levels.

Snidero, Jim, *Easy Jazz Conceptions*, Advance Music. Book/CD.

Snidero, Jim, *Jazz Conception*, Advance Music. Book/CD.

Spera, Dominic, *Blues and the Basics,* Hal Leonard Publications. Book/cassette.

Spera, Dominic, *Making the Changes,* Hal Leonard Publications. Book/cassette.

Swayzee, Tom, Jr., *Scales and Etudes for Modern Musicians,* Franton Music. Book/cassette.

Taylor, Mark, *Jazz Play Along Series: Volumes 1, 2 and 3,* Hal Leonard Publications.

Thomas, Willie, *Fundamental Fun,* Warner Bros. Publications. Book/cassette.

Thomas, Willie, *Jazz Anyone...?,* Warner Bros. Publications. Book/cassettes.

Rhythm Pattern Materials

Baker, David N., *Modal and Contemporary Patterns* (treble clef), Charles Colin Music Publications. Intermediate/Advanced.

Baker, David N., *Modal and Contemporary Patterns* (bass clef), Charles Colin Music Publications. Intermediate/Advanced.

Baker, David N., *Improvisation Patterns: The Blues,* Charles Colin Music Publications. Intermediate/ Advanced.

Campbell, Gary, *Expansions,* Houston Publishing, Inc. Intermediate/Advanced.

Campbell, Gary, *Triad Pairs for Jazz,* Warner Bros. Publications.

Coker, Jerry; Jimmy Casale; Gary Campbell; Jerry Greene, *Patterns for Jazz,* Warner Bros. Publications.

Sight-Reading Materials

Coker, Jerry, *Figured Reading Series,* Warner Bros. Publications.

DeCosmo, Emile, *The Woodshedding Source Book—The Ultimate Practice Manual,* Hal Leonard Publications.

Fischer, Lou, *Stylistic Etudes in the Jazz Idiom,* Hal Leonard Publications. Intermediate.

Montgomery, Bob, and Willie Hill, Jr., *Learning to Sight Read Jazz,* Scarecrow Press, Inc., 1994.

Rizzo, Jacques, *Reading Jazz,* Warner Bros. Publications.

Fake Books

101 Montunos, Sher Music.

50 Essential Bebop Heads, Hal Leonard Publications.

African Percussion, Sher Music.

The Antonio Carlos Jobim Anthology, Hal Leonard Publications.

Beatles Fake Book, Hal Leonard Publications.

Best Fake Book Ever, 2nd Edition, Hal Leonard Publications.

Best of the Brecker Brothers, Hal Leonard Publications.

Bill Evans Fake Book, Hal Leonard Publications.

Billie Holiday Anthology, Music Sales Corporation.

Blues Fake Book, Hal Leonard Publications.

Brazilian Guitar, Sher Music.

Chicago Fakebook, Hal Leonard Publications.

Choice Jazz Standards, Hal Leonard Publications.

Concepts for Bass Soloing, Sher Music.

Definitive Jazz Collection, Hal Leonard Publications.

Disney Fake Book, Hal Leonard Publications.

Esterowitz, Michael, *How to Play From a Fake Book*, Warner Bros. Publications.

Great Jazz Classics, Hal Leonard Publications.

Greatest Legal Fake Book of All Time, Warner Bros. Publications.

Hyman, Dick, *All the Right Changes*, Ekay Music.

Hyman, Dick, *Professional Chord Changes and Substitutions for 100 Tunes*, Ekay Music.

Jazz Bible Series, Hal Leonard Publications.

Jazz Etudes to Rhythm Changes, JA Jazz.

Jazz of the '50s, Hal Leonard Publications.

Jewish Fake Book, Hal Leonard Publications.

Just Blues Real Book, Warner Bros. Publications.

Just Jazz Real Book, Warner Bros. Publications.

Just Standards Real Book, Warner Bros. Publications.

Latin Bass Book, Sher Music.

Latin Fakebook, Sher Music.

Latin Real Book, Sher Music.

Levine, Mark, *Jazz Piano Book*, Sher Music.

Mantooth, Frank, *Best Known Chord Changes*, Hal Leonard Publications.

Mantooth, Frank, *The Best Chord Changes for the Most Requested Standards*, Hal Leonard Publications.

Mantooth, Frank, *The Best Chord Changes for the World's Greatest Standards*, Hal Leonard Publications.

Muy Caliente!, Sher Music.

Neely, Blake, *How to Play From a Fake Book*, Hal Leonard Publications.

New Real Book, Vol. 1, Sher Music.

New Real Book, Vol. 2, Sher Music.

New Real Book, Vol. 3, Sher Music.

Pat Metheny Songbook, Hal Leonard Publications.

Pocket Changes, Jeffersonville, IN.

Professional Pianist Fake Book, Hal Leonard Publications.

Professional Singer Pop/Rock Fake Book, Hal Leonard Publications.

R&B Fake Book, Hal Leonard Publications.

Ragtime & Early Jazz 1900–1935, Hal Leonard Publications.

Real Jazz Book, Hal Leonard Publications.

Real Jazz Standards Fake Book, Hal Leonard Publications.

Real Little Ultimate Fake Book, Hal Leonard Publications.

Salsa Guide Book, Sher Music.

Standards Real Book, Sher Music.

Straight Ahead Jazz Fakebook, Music Sales Corporation.

Swing Era 1936–1947, Hal Leonard Publications.

TV Fake Book, Hal Leonard Publications.

Ultimate Fake Book, 3rd Edition, Hal Leonard Publications.

Various Styles Fake Book, Country, Rock, Pop, R&B, etc., Hal Leonard Publications.

World's Greatest Fake Book, Jazz/Fusion, Sher Music.

World's Greatest Fake Book, Sher Music.

World's Greatest Fake Book, Warner Bros. Publications.

Yellowjackets Song Book, Sher Music.

Transcribing Aids

Doky, Niels Lan, *Jazz Transcriptions,* JA Jazz.

Liebman, David, *Improviser's Transcription Guide,* JA Jazz.

Listen and Learn Transcriber, JA Jazz. Software.

Slow Gold Transcribing Software, JA Jazz.

TR-400 Digital Transcribing Box, www.reedkotler.com. Software.

Jazz Theory

Baker, James, *Music Theory in Concept and Practice,* University of Rochester Press.

Berle, Arnie, *Theory and Harmony for the Contemporary Musician,* Music Sales Corporation.

Boling, Mark E., *The Jazz Theory Workbook,* Advance Music. All levels.

Campbell, Gary, *Triad Pairs for Jazz,* Warner Bros. Publications.

Campbell, Gary, *Connecting Jazz Theory,* Hal Leonard Publications.

Colin, Charles, *Encyclopedia of Scales,* Charles Colin Music Publications.

D'Amante, Elvo S., *All About Chords,* Encore Music Publishing.

Delamont, Gordon, *Modern Harmonic Technique,* Vols. 1 & 2, Kendor Music, Inc.

Grantham, Jim, *Jazz Master Workout Workbook,* Nightbird Music.

Grove, Dick, *Basic Harmony & Theory Applied to Improvisation,* Vol. 1, Alfred Publishing. Beginner/Intermediate.

Grove, Dick, *Basic Harmony & Theory Applied to Improvisation,* Vol. 2, Alfred Publishing. Intermediate.

Grove, Dick, *Basic Harmony & Theory Applied to Improvisation,* Vol. 3, Alfred Publishing. Intermediate/Advanced.

Grove, Dick, *Fundamentals of Modal Harmony,* Alfred Publishing.

Grove, Dick, *Fundamentals of Modern Harmony,* Book 1, Part 1, Alfred Publishing. Beginner/Intermediate.

Grove, Dick, *Fundamentals of Modern Harmony,* Book 1, Part 2, Alfred Publishing. Beginner/Intermediate.

Grove, Dick, *Fundamentals of Modern Harmony,* Book 2, Part 1, Alfred Publishing. Beginner/Intermediate.

Grove, Dick, *Fundamentals of Modern Harmony,* Book 2, Part 2, Alfred Publishing. Beginner/ Intermediate.

Haerle, Dan, *The Jazz Language,* Warner Bros. Publications.

Haerle, Dan, *The Jazz Sound,* JA Jazz.

Jaffe, Andy, *Jazz Harmony,* Cherry Lane Music.

Keller, Gary, *The Jazz Chord/Scale Handbook,* JA Jazz.

Lawn, Richard, and Jeffrey Hellmer, *Jazz Theory and Practice,* Alfred Publishing.

Levine, Mark, *The Jazz Theory Book,* Sher Music.

Nettles and Graf, *The Chord Scale Theory and Jazz Harmony,* JA Jazz.

Rizzo, Phil, *Theory Method and Workbook,* National Stage Band, 1962.

Rizzo, Phil, *Theory Text,* Jazz Education Press.

Rizzo, Phil, *Workbook,* Jazz Education Press.

Roseman, Ed, *Eddy's Music Theory for Practical People,* Musical Edventures.

Stanton, Ken, *Jazz Theory: A Creative Approach,* Taplinger Publishing Co.

Jazz Arranging/Composition

Alexander, Van, *First Chart,* Criterion Music.

Baker, David N., *Arranging and Composition for the Small Ensemble,* Alfred Publishing.

Coker, Jerry, *A Guide to Composition and Arranging,* JA Jazz.

Delamont, Gordon, *Modern Arranging Technique,* Kendor Music, Inc.

Delamont, Gordon, *Modern Contrapuntal Technique,* Kendor Music, Inc.

Dobbins, Bill, *Jazz Arranging and Composing: A Linear Approach,* Advance Music. All levels.

Garcia, Russell, *The Professional Arranger/Composer,* Book 1, Criterion Music, 1954.

Garcia, Russell, *The Professional Arranger/Composer,* Book 2, Criterion Music, 1954.

Goldstein, Gil, *Jazz Composer's Companion,* Music Sales Corporation.

Grove, Dick, *Arranging Concepts Complete,* Alfred Publishing.

Mancini, Henry, *Sounds and Scores,* Warner Bros. Publications.

Marohnic, Chuck, *How to Create Jazz Chord Progressions,* Warner Bros. Publications.

Miller, Ron, *Modal, Jazz Composition and Harmony,* JA Jazz.

Miller, Ron, *Modal, Jazz Composition and Harmony,* Vol. 2, JA Jazz.

Naus, Wayne, *Beyond Functional Harmony,* JA Jazz.

Nestico, Sammy, *The Complete Arranger,* Kendor Music, Inc. Book/CD.

Pease, Ted, *Modern Jazz Voicings,* Hal Leonard Publications.

Riddle, , *Arranged by Nelson Riddle,* Warner Bros. Publications.

Russo, William, *Composing for the Jazz Orchestra,* University of Chicago Press.

Russo, William, *Jazz Composition and Orchestration,* University of Chicago Press.

Sebesky, Don, *The Contemporary Arranger,* Alfred Publishing.

Sturm, Fred, *Changes Over Time: The Evolution of Jazz Arranging,* JA Jazz. Book/CD.

Wright, Rayburn, *Inside the Score,* Kendor Music, Inc. Advanced.

Notation Materials

Brandt, Carl and Clint Roemer, *Standardized Chord Symbol Notation,* Roerick Music.

Casale, Sammy, *The Art of Music Copying and Basic Notation,* Mel Bay Publications, Inc.

Purse, Bill, *A Finale Primer,* BackBeat Books.

Roemer, Clinton, *The Art of Music Copying,* Roerick Music.

Rosencrans, Glen, *A Music Notation Primer,* Music Sales Corporation.

SECTION II:
INDIVIDUAL INSTRUMENT BOOKS

Drums

Methods/Technique

Bellson, Louie, *The Musical Drummer,* Warner Bros. Publications. Book/CD.

Bellson, Louie, *Their Time Was the Greatest,* Warner Bros. Publications.

Berroa, Ignacio, *Groovin' in Clave,* Playin' Time Productions. Book/CD.

Blakey, Art, *Jazz Messages*, Warner Bros. Publications. Book/CD.

Bradfield, Martin, *Drumming: The Forest and the Trees,* JA Jazz.

Carter, Allen, *The Developing Drummer,* AC Muzik. CD-ROM.

Chaffee, Gary, *Patterns: Rhythm & Meter,* Warner Bros. Publications.

Chaffee, Gary, *Patterns: Sticking,* Warner Bros. Publications.

Chaffee, Gary, *Patterns: Techniques,* Warner Bros. Publications.

Chaffee, Gary, *Patterns: Time Function,* Warner Bros. Publications.

Chambers, Dennis, *In the Pocket,* Warner Bros. Publications. Book/CD.

Chambers, Dennis, *Serious Moves,* Warner Bros. Publications. Book/CD.

Cohan, Jon, *Zildjian: A History of the Legendary Cymbal Makers,* JA Jazz.

Dahlgren, Marvin, and Elliot Fine, *Four-Way Coordination,* Warner Bros. Publications.

Davis, Mike, *Basic Beats,* Warner Bros. Publications, 1974.

Davis, Steve, *"Killer Joe" Drum Styles & Analysis,* JA Jazz. Book/CD.

Davis, Steve, *"Maiden Voyage" Drum Styles and Analysis,* JA Jazz. Book/CD.

Davis, Steve, *Drummers: Masters of Time,* JA Jazz. Book/CD.

Davis, Steve, *Standard Time,* JA Jazz. Book/play-along CD.

Davis, Steve, *Standard Time for the Working Drummer,* JA Jazz. Book/CD.

Dawson, Alan, *The Drummer's Complete Vocabulary,* Warner Bros. Publications.

Dowd, Charles, *Jazz, Rock & Latin Sourcebook,* JA Jazz, Warner Bros. Publications. Book/CD.

Erskine, Peter, *Drum Concepts and Techniques,* Hal Leonard Publications.

Gadd, Steve, *Up Close,* Warner Bros. Publications. Book/CD

Goines and Ameen, *Afro-Cuban Grooves for Bass and Drums – Funkifying the Clave,* Warner Bros. Publications. Book/CD.

Hakim, Omar, *Express Yourself,* Warner Bros. Publications. Book/CD.

Hammond, Doug, *Percussion and Rhythm Workshop,* JA Jazz.

Hart, Billy, *Jazz Drumming,* JA Jazz. Book/CD.

Hartigan, Royal, *West African Rhythms for Drumset,* Warner Bros. Publications. Book/CD.

Houghton, Steve, *Big Band Drumming,* JA Jazz.

Houghton, Steve, *The Drum Set Performer,* Warner Bros. Publications. Book/CD.

Houghton, Steve, *The Drumset Soloist,* Warner Bros. Publications. Book/CD.

Houghton, Steve, *A Guide for the Modern Rhythm Section,* Warner Bros. Publications.

Houghton, Steve, *Studio and Big-Band Drumming,* CL Barnhouse Music Publishing Co.

Houghton, Steve and Tom Warrington, *Essential Styles for the Drummer and Bassist,* Vols. 1 and 2, Alfred Publishing.

Houllif, Murray, *Contemporary Drumset Solos,* Alfred Publishing.

Houllif, Murray, *Fantastic Fills for Drumset,* Alfred Publishing.

Houllif, Murray, *Today's Sounds for Drumset,* Alfred Publishing.

Krupa, Gene, *Gene Krupa Drum Method,* Warner Bros. Publications.

Latham, Rick, *Contemporary Drumset Techniques,* Warner Bros. Publications.

Malabe, Frank, and Bob Weiner, *Afro-Cuban Rhythms for Drumset,* Warner Bros. Publications. Book/CD.

Mattingly, Rick, *The Drummer's Time,* Hal Leonard Publications.

Maturano, Phil, *Latin Soloing for Drumset,* Hal Leonard Publications.

Miller, Russ, *The Drum Set Crash Course,* Warner Bros. Publications. Book/CD.

Miller, Russ, *Transitions,* Warner Bros. Publications. Book/CD.

Morgenstein, Roger, *Drum Set Warm Ups,* Hal Leonard Publications.

Morgenstein, Roger, and Rick Mattingly, *The Drumset Musician,* Hal Leonard Publications. Book/CD.

Myers, Ken, *The Solid Time Tool Kit,* Mel Bay Publications, Inc. Book/CD.

Perry, Charles, *Introduction to the Drumset,* Vols. 1 & 2, Warner Bros. Publications.

Pickering, John, *The Drummer's Cookbook,* Mel Bay Publications, Inc.

Prins, Jan, *Hi-Hat Integration,* JA Jazz.

Ramsey, John, *Art Blakey's Jazz Messages,* Warner Bros. Publications. Book/CD.

Reed, Ted, *Bass Drum Technique,* JA Jazz.

Reed, Ted, *Bongo and Conga Drum Technique,* JA Jazz.

Reed, Ted, *Drums Solos and Fills, Books 1 and 2,* JA Jazz.

Reed, Ted, *Latin Rhythms,* JA Jazz.

Reed, Ted, *Syncopation,* Vols. 1 and 2, JA Jazz.

Rich, Buddy, *Jazz Legend,* Warner Bros. Publications.

Riley, John, *The Art of Bop Drumming,* Warner Bros. Publications. Book/CD.

Riley, John, *Beyond Bop Drumming,* Warner Bros. Publications. Book/CD.

Snidero, Jim, *Jazz Conception for Drums,* Advanced Music. Book/CD.

Soph, Ed, *Essential Techniques for Drum Set,* JA Jazz.

Spagnardi, Ron, *Greatest Jazz Drummers,* Modern Drummer Publications.

Spagnardi, Ron, *The Big Band Drummer,* Hal Leonard Publications.

Thompson, Rich, *Jazz Solos for Drum Set,* Vol. 1, Kendor Music, Inc.

Weckl, Dave, *Back to Basics,* Warner Bros. Publications. Book/CD.

Weckl, Dave, *Contemporary Drummer + One,* Warner Bros. Publications.

Weckl, Dave, *Ultimate Play-Along for Drums,* Vols. 1 and 2, Warner Bros. Publications. Book/CD.

Brushes

Bellson, Louie, and Dave Black, *Contemporary Brush Techniques,* Alfred Publishing.

Hazilla, Jon, *Mastering the Art of Brushes,* Hal Leonard Publications.

Thigpen, Ed, *The Essence of Brushes,* Warner Bros. Publications.

Thigpen, Ed, *The Sound of Brushes,* Warner Bros. Publications. Book/CD.

Drum Transcriptions

Davis, Steve, *Drummers: Masters of Time,* JA Jazz.

Drum Standards: Classic Jazz Masters Series, Hal Leonard Publications.

Auxiliary Percussion

Blanc, Serge, *African Percussion: The Djembe Book,* Warner Bros. Publications. Book/CD.

Bouroon, Christian, *African Rhythms for Drumset,* JA Jazz.

Da Fonseca, Duduka, and Bob Weiner, *Brazilian Rhythms for Drumset,* Warner Bros. Publications. Book/CD.

Dworsky, Alan, and Betsy Sansby, *Conga Drumming: A Beginner's Guide to Playing With Time,* Warner Bros. Publications. Book/CD.

Evans, Bob, *Authentic Bongo Rhythms (revised),* Warner Bros. Publications.

Evans, Bob, *Authentic Conga Rhythms (revised),* Warner Bros. Publications.

Gajate-Garcia, Richie, *Play Congas Now,* Warner Bros. Publications.

Garibaldi, David, *Tiempo,* Warner Bros. Publications.

Garibaldi, David, *Timbafunk,* Warner Bros. Publications.

Hernandez, Horacio "El Negro," *Conversations in Clave,* Warner Bros. Publications. Book/CD.

Morales, Humberto, and Henry Adler, *How to Play Latin American Rhythm Instruments,* Warner Bros. Publications.

Puente, Tito, *Tito Puente: Drumming with the Mambo King,* Hudson Music. Book/CD.

Quintana, Jose Luis, *Changuito: A Master's Approach to Timbales,* Warner Bros. Publications. Book/CD.

Sulsbruck, Birge, *Latin American Percussion,* Music Sales Corporation.

Uribe, Ed, *The Essence of Afro-Cuban Percussion and Drum Set,* Warner Bros. Publications.

Uribe, Ed, *The Essence of Brazilian Percussion and Drum Set,* Warner Bros. Publications.

Piano

Piano Methods

Campos, Carlos, *Afro Cuban Music for Piano*, ADG Productions.

Campos, Carlos, *Latin Jazz Piano*, Vol. 1, Hal Leonard Publications. Book/CD.

Campos, Carlos, *Salsa: Afro Cuban Montunos for Piano*, ADG Productions.

Coker, Jerry, *Elements of the Jazz Language for the Developing Improviser*, Warner Bros. Publications.

Coker, Jerry, *How to Practice Jazz*, JA Jazz.

Coker, Jerry, *Improvising Jazz*, Simon & Schuster, Inc., 1964.

Coker, Jerry, *Jazz Keyboard for the Pianist or Non-Pianist*, Warner Bros. Publications .

Deneff, Peter, *Jazz Hanon*, Hal Leonard Publications.

Deneff, Peter, *Salsa Hanon*, Hal Leonard Publications.

Denke, Debbie, *The Aspiring Jazz Pianist*, Hal Leonard Publications.

Dobbins, Bill, *The Contemporary Jazz Pianist*, Books 1– 4, Advance Music.

Dobbins, Bill, *A Creative Approach to Jazz Piano Harmony*, Advance Music.

Gardner, Jeff, *Jazz Piano: Creative Concepts and Techniques*, JA Jazz.

Haerle, Dan, *The Jazz Language*, Warner Bros. Publications, 1980.

Haerle, Dan, *The Jazz Sound*, Hal Leonard Publications.

Haerle, Dan, *Technique Development in Fourths*, Warner Bros. Publications.

Harris, Gene, *Gene Harris Collection*, JA Jazz.

Hyman, Dick, *Century of Jazz Piano*, Ekay Music, Inc. CD-ROM.

Lawn, Richard, and Jeffrey Hellmer, *Jazz: Theory and Practice*, Alfred Publishers.

Lee, Bill, *The Complete Jazz Piano Method*, Book 1, Warner Bros. Publications.

Levine, Mark, *The Jazz Piano Book*, Sher Music Co.

Mauleon, Rebecca, *The Salsa Guidebook*, Sher Music Co.

Mauleon-Sanatana, Rebecca, *101 Montunos*, Sher Music Co.

McNeely, Jim, *The Art of Comping*, JA Jazz.

Novello, John, *The Contemporary Keyboardist*, *Revised*, Hal Leonard Publications.

Novello, John, *Stylistic Etudes for Piano*, Hal Leonard Publications.

Orta, Mike, *Jazz Piano Etude Book*, Warner Bros. Publications. Book/CD.

Smith, Paul T., *Jazz Studies for Piano*, JA Jazz.

Soul, Xavier, *Cookin' With Salsa*, JA Jazz. Book and CD-ROM.

Piano Chord/Scale/Improvisation

Amadie, Jimmy, *Harmonic Foundation for Jazz and Popular Music*, Thornton Publications.

Amadie, Jimmy, *Jazz Improvement: How to Play It and Teach It*, Thornton Publications.

Baker, David, *Jazz Improvisation: A Comprehensive Method of Study for All Musicians*, Alfred Publishing.

Berg, Shelton, *Jazz Improvisation: The Goal Note Method*, Kendor Music, Inc.

Boyd, Bill, *Exploring Basic Blues for Keyboards*, Hal Leonard Publications.

Boyd, Bill, *Exploring Traditional Scales and Chords for Jazz Keyboard*, Hal Leonard Publications.

Burns, Jeff, *Pentatonic Scales for the Jazz-Rock Keyboardist*, Hal Leonard Publications.

Champagne, Champ, *The Real Chord Changes & Substitutions*, Books 1–4, Hal Leonard Publications.

Coker, Jerry, *Patterns for Jazz*, Warner Bros. Publications.

DeFrancesco, Joey, *Concepts for Improvisation*, Hal Leonard Publications.

Dobbins, Bill, *A Creative Approach to Jazz Piano Harmony*, Advance Music.

Feldman, Frank, *Great Jazz Riffs for Piano*, Hal Leonard Publications. Book/CD.

Fischer, Claire, *Harmonic Exercises for Piano*, JA Jazz.

Haerle, Dan, *Jazz Improvisation for Keyboard Players: The Complete Edition*, Warner Bros. Publications.

Haerle, Dan, *Scales for Jazz Improvisation*, Warner Bros. Publications, 1975.

Haerle, Dan, *Technique Development in Fourths*, Warner Bros. Publications.

Haerle, Dan, *Jazz Tunes for Improvising*, Warner Bros. Publications.

Hyman, Dick, *All the Right Changes*, Book #2, Ekay Music, Inc.

Hyman, Dick, *Professional Chord Changes & Substitutions for 100 Tunes Every Musician Should Know*, Ekay Music, Inc.

Kerper, Mitch, *Jazz Riffs for Piano*, Music Sales Corporation.

Laverne, Andy, *Handbook of Chord Substitutions*, Warner Bros. Publications.

Laverne, Andy, *Tons of Runs for the Contemporary Pianist*, Warner Bros. Publications.

Long, Jack, *The Encyclopedia of Jazz Chords*, Music Sales Corporation.

Mann, Martan, *Jazz Improvisation for the Classical Pianist*, Music Sales Corporation.

Mantooth, Frank, *The Best Chord Changes for the Most Requested Standards*, Hal Leonard Publications.

Mantooth, Frank, *The Best Chord Changes for The World's Greatest Standards*, Hal Leonard Publications.

Mantooth, Frank, *Voicings for Jazz Keyboard*, Hal Leonard Publications.

Marohnic, Chuck, *How to Create Jazz Chord Progressions*, Warner Bros. Publications, 1979.

Mehegan, John, *Contemporary Piano Styles*, Music Sales Corporation.

Mehegan, John, *Improvising Jazz Piano*, Music Sales Corporation.

Mehegan, John, *Jazz Rhythm and the Improvised Line*, Music Sales Corporation.

Mehegan, John, *John Mehegan Jazz Series*, Music Sales Corporation.

Mehegan, John, *Swing and Early Progressive Piano Styles*, Music Sales Corporation.

Reeves, Scott, *Creative Beginnings: An Introduction to Jazz Improv*, Prentice Hall Press. CD-ROM.

Reeves, Scott, *Creative Jazz Improvisation*, 3rd Edition, Prentice Hall Press.

Snidero, Jim, *Jazz Conception for Piano Comping*, JA Jazz. Book/CD.

Snidero, Jim, *Jazz Conception for Piano*, Advance Music.

Steinel, Mike, *Building a Jazz Vocabulary*, Hal Leonard Publications.

Piano Voicing

Aebersold, Jamey, *Piano Voicings for all Musicians*, Vol. 1, JA Jazz.

Aebersold, Jamey, *Transcribed Piano Voicings*, JA Jazz.

Aebersold, Jamey, *Volume 70: "Killer Joe" Transcribed Piano Comping*, JA Jazz.

Boyd, Bill, *Traditional Scales and Chords for Jazz Keyboard,* Hal Leonard Publications.

Boyd, Bill, *An Introduction to Jazz Chord Voicings for Keyboard,* Hal Leonard Publications.

Boyd, Bill, *Exploring Basic Blues for Keyboard,* Hal Leonard Publications.

Boyd, Bill, *Intermediate Jazz Chord Voicing for Keyboard,* Hal Leonard Publications.

Coker, Jerry, *Jazz Keyboard for the Pianist or Non-Pianist,* Warner Bros. Publications.

DeGreg, Phil, *Jazz Keyboard Harmony,* Jamey Aebersold Jazz, Inc.

Galper, Hal, *Volume 55: Jerome Kern,* JA Jazz.

Gillespie, Luke, *Stylistic II/V7/I Voicings for Jazz Keyboard,* JA Jazz.

Haerle, Dan, *Jazz Piano Voicing Skills,* Warner Bros. Publications.

Haerle, Dan, *Jazz/Rock Voicings for the Contemporary Keyboard Player,* Warner Bros. Publications.

Harris, Matt, and Jeff Jarvis, *The Chord Voicing Handbook,* Kendor Music, Inc.

Hughes, Fred, *Left Hand Voicings and Chord Theory,* Warner Bros. Publications.

Mann, Martan, *Jazz Improvisation for the Classical Pianist,* Music Sales Corporation.

Mantooth, Frank, *The Best Chord Changes for the Most Requested Standards,* Hal Leonard Publications.

Mantooth, Frank, *The Best Chord Changes for the World's Greatest Standards,* Hal Leonard Publications.

Mantooth, Frank, *Voicings for Jazz Keyboard,* Hal Leonard Publications.

Marohnic, Chuck, *How to Create Jazz Chord Progressions,* Warner Bros. Publications.

McNeeley, Jim, *The Art of Comping,* Advance Music.

Pease and Pullig, *Modern Jazz Voicings,* JA Jazz.

Tracy, Mike, *Jazz Piano Voicings for the Non-Pianist,* JA Jazz.

Valerio, John, *Jazz Piano Concepts and Techniques,* Hal Leonard Publications.

Various Stylistic II/V7/I Voicings for Jazz Keyboard, Hal Leonard Publications.

Piano Arrangements/Transcriptions

20th Century Jazz Standards, JA Jazz.

Barron, Kenny, *Kenny Barron: The Collection,* JA Jazz.

Basie, Count, *The Best of Count Basie,* Warner Bros. Publications.

Basie, Count, *The Piano Style of Count Basie,* Warner Bros. Publications.

Benoit, David, *Anthology,* Warner Bros. Publications.

Benoit, David, *Anthology 2,* Warner Bros. Publications.

Brimhall, John, *Duke Ellington,* Warner Bros. Publications.

Brubeck, Dave, *At the Piano,* Warner Bros. Publications.

Brubeck, Dave, *Blue Rondo,* Warner Bros. Publications.

Brubeck, Dave, *A Dave Brubeck Christmas,* Warner Bros. Publications.

Brubeck, Dave, *Chromatic Fantasy,* Warner Bros. Publications.

Brubeck, Dave, *Dave's Diary,* Warner Bros. Publications.

Brubeck, Dave, *Glances,* Warner Bros. Publications.

Brubeck, Dave, *The Genius Continues...,* Warner Bros. Publications.

Brubeck, Dave, *The Genius of Dave Brubeck,* Warner Bros. Publications.

Brubeck, Dave, *Nocturnes,* Warner Bros. Publications.

Brubeck, Dave, *Two Part Adventures*, Warner Bros. Publications.

Brubeck, Dave, *Young Lions, Old Tigers*, Warner Bros. Publications.

Carmichael, Hoagy, *Hoagy Carmichael Collection*, JA Jazz.

Corea, Chick, *Chick Corea Piano Improvisations*, Vol. 1, JA Jazz.

Corea, Chick, *The Jazz Solos of Chick Corea*, JA Jazz.

Dobbins, Bill, *Chick Corea Solo Book: Now He Sings, Now He Sobs*, JA Jazz.

Dobbins, Bill, *Herbie Hancock Classic Jazz Solos and Tunes*, JA Jazz.

Evans, Bill, *The Artistry of Bill Evans*, JA Jazz.

Evans, Bill, *Bill Evans Artistry*, Vol. 1, Warner Bros. Publications.

Evans, Bill, *Bill Evans Artistry*, Vol. 2, Warner Bros. Publications.

Evans, Bill, *Bill Evans Plays Standards*, JA Jazz.

Evans, Bill, *Piano Solos*, JA Jazz.

Fischer, Claire, *Alone Together/Just Me*, JA Jazz.

Fischer, Claire, *Claire Fischer Songbook*, JA Jazz.

Haerle, Dan, *Dan Haerle's Transcribed Piano Comping of Volume 41: Body and Soul*, JA Jazz.

Haerle, Dan, and Mark Levine, *Volume 60 Freddie Hubbard*, JA Jazz.

Harris, Gene, *Collection*, JA Jazz.

Harris, Matt, *Jazz Solos for Piano, Vol. 1*, Kendor Music, Inc.

Hefti, Neal, *Anthology*, Warner Bros. Publications.

Hyman, Dick, *In the Style of the Great Piano Solos*, Warner Bros. Publications.

Hyman, Dick, *Piano Pro*, Warner Bros. Publications.

Jamal, Ahmad, *Ahmad Jamal: The Collection*, Hal Leonard Publications.

Jazz Ballads, JA Jazz.

Jazz Latina: 32 Latin Jazz Standards, Hal Leonard Publications.

Jazz Latina: Latin Jazz Standards, Hal Leonard Publications.

Jobim, Antonio Carlos, *Antonio Carlos Jobim Anthology*, Hal Leonard Publications.

Jobim, Antonio Carlos, *The Best of the Bossa Novas*, Hal Leonard Publications.

Jobim, Antonio Carlos, *The Jobim Collection*, Hal Leonard Publications.

Levine, Mark, *Transcribed Piano Voicings From* Vol. 1, JA Jazz.

Levine, Mark, *Volume 50: Magic of Miles*, JA Jazz.

Levine, Mark, *Volume 64: Salsa/Latin Jazz*, JA Jazz.

Levine, Mark, and Dan Haerle, *Volume 60: Freddie Hubbard Transcribed Piano Comping*, JA Jazz.

Mann, Martan, *Improvising Blues Piano*, Music Sales Corporation.

McPartland, Marian, *The Artistry of Marian McPartland*, Warner Bros. Publications.

McPartland, Marian, *Marian McPartland Piano Jazz*, Vols. 1 and 2, Warner Bros. Publications.

McPartland, Marian, *Willow Creek and Other Ballads*, Warner Bros. Publications.

Monk, Thelonious, *Thelonious Monk for Easy Solo Piano*, Hal Leonard Publications.

Monk, Thelonious, *Thelonious Monk for Intermediate Solo Piano*, Hal Leonard Publications.

Monk, Thelonious, *Thelonious Monk – Originals and Standards*, Gerard and Sarzin.

Parker, Charlie, *Charlie Parker for Piano* Book 1, Warner Bros. Publications.

Parker, Charlie, *Charlie Parker for Piano* Book 2, Warner Bros. Publications.

Parker, Charlie, *Charlie Parker for Piano*, Music Sales Corporation.

Peterson, Oscar, *Oscar Peterson Solos*, JA Jazz.

Play Like a Pro, JA Jazz.

Powell, Bud, *Bud Powell Classics*, Hal Leonard Publications.

Powell, Bud, *Bud Powell for Piano*, Music Sales Corporation.

Powell, Bud, *Originals and Standards*, Gerard and Sarzin.

Previn, Andre, *Andre Previn Collection*, JA Jazz.

Priestly, Brian, *Jazz Piano Solos*, JA Jazz.

Roberts, Marcus, *Gershwin for Lovers*, Warner Bros. Publications.

Scivales, Riccardo, *Tatum – The Right Hand*, Warner Bros. Publications.

Silver, Horace, *The Horace Silver Collection*, Hal Leonard Publications.

Strayhorn, Billy, *An American Master*, Cherry Lane Music.

Taylor, Billy, *Billy Taylor: The Collection*, Hal Leonard Publications.

Tyner, McCoy, *McCoy Tyner Piano Solos*, Hal Leonard Publications.

Waller, Thomas "Fats," *The Genius of Fats Waller*, Warner Bros. Publications.

Wilson, Teddy, *Collection*, JA Jazz.

Guitar

Guitar Methods

Almeida, Laurindo, *Laurindo Almeida Guitar Method*, Alfred Publishing. Intermediate.

Anderson, Tom, *Playing Guitar in the Jazz Band*, Hal Leonard Publications.

Bruner, Tom, *The Arranger/Composer's Complete Guide to the Guitar*, Mel Bay Publications, Inc.

Buckingham, Bruce, *Latin Guitar: The Essential Brazilian & Afro Cuban Rhythm Guide*, Hal Leonard Publications.

Carcassi and Block, *Classic Guitar Method*, Alfred Publishing. Intermediate/Advanced.

Christiansen, Mike, *Mel Bay's Complete Guitar Scale Dictionary*, Mel Bay Publications, Inc.

Christiansen, Mike, *Mel Bay's Complete Jazz Guitar Method*, Mel Bay Publications, Inc.

Christiansen, Mike and Corey, *Modern Swing Guitar*, Mel Bay Publishing. Book/CD.

Coryell, Larry, *Jazz Guitar*, BackBeat Books. Book/CD.

D'Auberge, Alfred, *Basic Guitar Method*, Alfred Publishing. Beginner.

D'Auberge and Manus, *New Electric Guitar Course*, Alfred Publishing. Beginner.

Deyner, Ralph, *The Guitar Handbook*, Knopf Publishers.

Diorio, Joe, *Fusion Guitar*, Warner Bros. Publications. Book/CD.

Diorio, Joe, *Giant Steps*, Warner Bros. Publications.

Ellis, Herb, *All the Shapes You Are*, Warner Bros. Publications. Book/CD.

Ellis, Herb, *The Herb Ellis Jazz Guitar Method: Swing Blues*, Warner Bros. Publications. Book/CD.

Ellis, Herb, *Rhythm Shapes*, Warner Bros. Publications.

Eschete, Ron, *Chord-Melody Phrases for Guitar*, Hal Leonard Publications. Book/CD.

Ferguson, Jim, *All Blues Scales for Jazz Guitar*, Mel Bay Publications, Inc. Book/CD.

Forman, Bruce, *Jazz Band Rhythm Guitar*, Mel Bay Publications, Inc.

Galbraith, Barry, *Guitar Comping Play-A-Long*, JA Jazz.

Galbraith, Barry, *Play-A-Long With Bach*, JA Jazz.

Gambale, Frank, *The Frank Gambale Technique Books*, 1 and 2, Warner Bros. Publications. Book/CD.
  Intermediate/Advanced.

Grassel, Jack, *Guitar Seeds*, Warner Bros. Publications.

Grassel, Jack, *The Guitarist's Guide to the Jazz Ensemble*, Hal Leonard Publications.

Grassel, Jack, *Jazz Rhythm Guitar*, Hal Leonard Publications. Book/CD.

Grassel, Jack, *Jazz Rhythm Guitar: The Complete Guide*, Hal Leonard Publications.

Green, Andrew, *Jazz Guitar Technique*, Microphonic Press.

Hall, Jim, *Exploring Jazz Guitar*, Hal Leonard Publications.

Holdsworth, Allan, *Just for the Curious*, Warner Bros. Publications. Book/CD.

Ingram, Adrian, *Jazz Masters: Cool Blues & Hot Jazz Guitar*, Warner Bros. Publications. Book/CD.

Jazz Guitar Bible, Hal Leonard Publications.

Jazz Guitar Standards: Artist Transcriptions, Hal Leonard Publications.

Johnson, Charlton, *Swing and Big Band Guitar* (Freddie Green style), Hal Leonard Publications.

Latarski, Don, *Don Latarski Guitar Books, six books*, Warner Bros. Publications.

Leavitt, William G., *A Modern Method for Guitar*, Books 1, 2, and 3, Hal Leonard Publications.
  Beginner/Intermediate/Advanced.

Marshall, D., *Learn to Play Brazilian Guitar*, Mel Bay Publications, Inc. Book/CD.

Munro, Doug, *Jazz Guitar: Bebop and Beyond*, Warner Bros. Publications. Book/CD.

Munro, Doug, *Jazz Guitar: Swing to Bebop*, Warner Bros. Publications.

Pass, Joe, *Joe Pass: The Guitar Method*, Hal Leonard Publications.

Pass, Joe, *Joe Pass Guitar Style*, Alfred Publishing. Advanced level.

Roberts, Howard, and Garry Hagberg, *Guitar Compendium*, Vols. 1, 2, 3, Advance Music.

Snidero, Jim, *Jazz Conception for Guitar*, Advance Music. Book/CD.

Sokolow, Fred, *Antonio Carlos Jobim for Guitar*, Hal Leonard Publications.

Sokolow, Fred, *Great Jazz Standards Anthology for Guitar*, Warner Bros. Publications.

Stewart, Jimmy, *The Evolution of Jazz Guitar*, Mel Bay Publications, Inc., 1988. Intermediate.

Van Eps, George, *Harmonic Mechanisms for Guitar*, Vols. 1, 2 and 3, Mel Bay Publications, Inc.

Guitar Chord/Scale/Improvisation

Arakawa, Yoichi, *Great Jazz Riffs for Guitar*, Cherry Lane Music. Book/CD.

Bay, William, *Deluxe Encyclopedia of Guitar Chords*, Mel Bay Publications, Inc.

Belkadi, Jean Marc, *Jazz-Rock: Triad Improvising for Guitar*, Hal Leonard Publications. Book/CD.

Bell, Joe, and Peter Pickow, *Improvising Jazz Guitar*, Music Sales Corporation.

Berle, Arnie, *Chords & Progressions for Jazz & Popular Guitar*, Omnibus Press. Beginner/Intermediate.

Berle, Arnie, *Modern Chords and Progressions for Guitar*, Music Sales Corporation.
  Beginner/Intermediate.

Campos, Carlos, *Salsa, Afro-Cuban Montunos for Guitar*, A.D.G. Productions. Book/CD.

Christiansen, Corey, *BeBop Blues*, Mel Bay Publications, Inc. Book/CD.

Coryell, Larry, *Creative Comping, Soloing and Improv*, BackBeat Books.

De Cosmo, Emile, *The Polytonal Guitar*, North Bergen: Edc.

De Mause, Alan, *101 Jazz Guitar Licks*, Mel Bay Publications, Inc. Book/CD.

Di Meola, Al and Bob Aslanian *A Guide to Chords, Scales & Arpeggios*, 21st Century Publications. Intermediate.

Diorio, Joe, *Giant Steps*, Warner Bros. Publications. Book/CD.

Elden, Lucky, *Jazz Guitar Lines*, Warner Bros. Publications. Book/CD.

Ellis, Herb, *The Herb Ellis Jazz Guitar Method*, Warner Bros. Publications.

Fowler, William L., *Advanced Chord Progressions*, Book 4, Fowler Music Enterprises, 1984. Advanced.

Galbraith, Barry, *Daily Exercises in Melodic and Harmonic Minor Modes*, Jazzwise.

Galbraith, Barry, *The Fingerboard Workbook*, covers scales and arpeggios, Weybridge Productions, 1979.

Galbraith, Barry, *Guitar Comping Play-A-Long*, Aebersold Publications. Book/CD.

Galbraith, Barry, *Guitar Improvisation*, Aebersold Publications. Book/CD.

Galbraith, Barry, *Play-A-Long With Bach*, Aebersold Publications. Book/CD.

Gambale, Frank, *Improvisation Made Easier*, Warner Bros. Publications. Book/CDs.

Grassel, Jack, *Monster Chops*, JA Jazz.

Grassel, Jack, *Super Ax*, JA Jazz.

Greene, Ted, *Chord Chemistry*, Warner Bros. Publications. Intermediate/Advanced.

Greene, Ted, *Jazz Guitar Single Note Soloing*, Vol. 1, Warner Bros. Publications.

Greene, Ted, *Jazz Guitar Single Note Soloing*, Vol. 2, Warner Bros. Publications.

Greene, Ted, *Modern Chord Progressions*, Warner Bros. Publications, 1976. Intermediate/Advanced.

Khan, Steve, *Contemporary Chord Khancepts*, Warner Bros. Publications. Book and 2 CDs.

Latarski, Don, *Practical Theory for Guitar*, Warner Bros. Publications. Book/CD.

Latarski, Don, *The Ultimate Guitar Chord Book Series: Jazz Chords*, Warner Bros. Publications.

Leavitt, William, *Melodic Rhythms for Guitar*, Hal Leonard Publications.

Marshall, Wolf, *Jazz Guitar*, Hal Leonard Publications.

Martino, Pat, *Creative Force*, Part 1, Warner Bros. Publications. Book/CD.

Martino, Pat, *Jazz*, Hal Leonard Publications. Book/CD.

McCormick, Bill, *Rhythm Changes Guitar Accompaniment*, JA Jazz.

McCormick, Bill, *A Walk Through the Blues*, JA Jazz.

McGuire, E. F., *Guitar Fingerboard Harmony*, Mel Bay Publications, Inc., 1976. Intermediate/ Advanced.

Modal Concept for Jazz Guitar Improv, JA Jazz. Book/CD.

Morgen, Howard, *Concepts: Arranging for Fingerstyle Guitar*, Warner Bros. Publications.

Morgen, Howard, *Howard Morgen's Solo Guitar*, Warner Bros. Publications.

Munro, Doug, *Jazz Guitar: Bebop and Beyond*, Warner Bros. Publications. Book/CD.

Munro, Doug, *Jazz Guitar: Swing to Bebop*, Warner Bros. Publications. Book/CD.

Nunes, Warren, *The Jazz Guitar Chord Bible Complete*, Warner Bros. Publications.

Pass, Joe, *Joe Pass Guitar Chords*, Mel Bay Publications, Inc. Advanced.

Pass, Joe, *On Guitar*, Warner Bros. Publications. Book/CD.

Rector, Johnny, *Deluxe Encyclopedia of Jazz Guitar Runs, Fills, Licks & Lines,* Mel Bay Publications, Inc., 1984. Intermediate/Advanced.

Rector, Johnny, *Encyclopedia of Guitar Chord Progressions,* Mel Bay Publications, Inc. Book/CD.

Rector, Johnny, *Guitar Chord Progressions,* Mel Bay Publications, Inc., 1977. Intermediate/Advanced.

Rochinski, Steve, *Jazz Guitar Improv: The Motivic Basis,* Hal Leonard Publications. Book/CD.

Rochinski, Steve, *Tal Farlow: The Elements of Bebop Guitar,* Hal Leonard Publications.

Sanchez, Rey, *Basic Guitar Chords,* Warner Bros. Publications, 1984. Beginner.

Scofield, John, *Jazz-Funk Guitar I,* Warner Bros. Publications. Book/CD.

Scofield, John, *Jazz-Funk Guitar II,* Warner Bros. Publications. Book and cassette.

Smith, Dave, *Method of Jazz Improvisation With the Theoretical Explanation for Guitar,* Warner Bros. Publications.

Smith, Stan, *Jazz Harmony on the Guitar: A Linear/Structural Approach,* Houston Publishing, Inc. Book/CD.

Sokolow, Fred, *The Complete Jazz Guitar,* Warner Bros. Publications. Book/CD.

Stebal, John P., *Guitar Chords for Stage Band & Combo.* Intermediate.

Stern, Leni, *Leni Stern: Composing and Compositions,* Warner Bros. Publications. Book/CD.

Stern, Mike, *Ultimate Play-Along for Guitar,* Warner Bros. Publications. Book/2 CDs.

Theroit, Shane, *New Orleans Funk Guitar,* Warner Bros. Publications. Book/CD.

Umble, Jay, *The Jazz Guitarist's Thesaurus.* Book/CD.

White, Leon, *Chord Systems: Structure and Application,* Professional Music Products, 1979. Beginner/Intermediate/Advanced.

Willmott, Bret, *Complete Book of Harmony, Theory & Voicing,* Mel Bay Publications, Inc.

Wyatt, Keith, *Jump, Jive 'n' Swing Guitar,* Warner Bros. Publications. Book/CD.

Guitar Reading Materials

Leavitt, William G., *Advanced Reading Studies for Guitar,* Hal Leonard Publications. Advanced.

Leavitt, William G., *Classical Studies for Pick-Style Guitar,* Hal Leonard Publications, 1968. Intermediate.

Leavitt, William G., *Melodic Rhythms for Guitar,* Hal Leonard Publications.

Leavitt, William G., *Reading Studies for Guitar,* Hal Leonard Publications.

White, Leon, *Sight to Sound,* Dale Zdenek Publications, 1976. Beginner.

Guitar Solos/Transcriptions

Bill Evans Collection for Guitar, Warner Bros. Publications. Book/CD.

Brown, Steve, *Jazz Solos for Guitar,* Vol. 1, Kendor Music, Inc.

DeMause, Alan, *Joe Pass Virtuoso #3,* Mel Bay Publications, Inc.

Ellington, Duke, *Duke Ellington for Jazz Guitar,* Hal Leonard Publications.

Erquiaga, Steve, *Guitar Duets,* Advance Music. Book/CD.

Faria, Nelson, *The Brazilian Guitar Book,* Sher Music. Book/CD.

Ferguson, Jim, *All Blues for Jazz Guitar,* Mel Bay Publications, Inc. Book/CD.

Galbraith, Barry, *CD Play-A-Long,* JA Jazz.

Galbraith, Barry, *Guitar Improvisation*, JA Jazz.

Galbraith, Barry, *Guitar Comping*, JA Jazz.

Goodrick, Mick, *The Advancing Guitarist*, Hal Leonard Publications.

Greene, Ted, *Chord Chemistry*, Warner Bros. Publications.

Greene, Ted, *Jazz Guitar Single Note Soloing*, Vol. 1, Warner Bros. Publications.

Hall, Jim, *Jazz Guitar Environments*, Hal Leonard Publications. Book/cassette.

Hart, Bill, *Billy Hart Solo Jazz*, JA Jazz.

Henderson, Scott, *Scott Henderson Guitar Book*, Hal Leonard Publications.

Hodel, Brian, *The Brazilian Masters*, JA Jazz.

Khan, Steve, *Wes Montgomery Guitar Folio*, Plymouth Music.

Leavitt, William, *Melodic Rhythms for Guitar*, Hal Leonard Publications.

Leon, Roland, *Joe Pass Live*, Mel Bay Publications, Inc. Book/CD.

Marshall, Wolf, *The Best of Jazz Guitar*, Hal Leonard Publications.

Martino, Pat, *The Early Years*, Warner Bros. Publications.

Martino, Pat, *Creative Force, Part 1*, Warner Bros. Publications.

Metheny, Pat, *Pat Metheny Songbook*, Hal Leonard Publications.

Montgomery, Wes, *The Early Years*, Mel Bay Publishing, Inc.

Montgomery, Wes, *The Best of Wes Montgomery*, JA Jazz. Book/CD.

Montgomery, Wes, *The Boss Guitar of Wes Montgomery*, two volumes, JA Jazz.

Montgomery, Wes, *Wes Montgomery Artist Transcriptions*, Hal Leonard Publications.

Morgen, Howard, *Morgen Gershwin Collection for Guitar*, Warner Bros. Publications.

Pass, Joe, *Jazz Guitar Cassette/Guide*, Alfred Publishing. Intermediate.

Pass, Joe, *Joe Pass Chord Solos*, Alfred Publishing. Advanced.

Pass, Joe, *The Joe Pass Collection*, Hal Leonard Publications.

Pass, Joe, *Joe Pass Guitar Chords*, Alfred Publishing.

Pass, Joe, *Joe Pass Guitar Style*, Alfred Publishing.

Pass, Joe, *Virtuoso Standards: Songbook Collection*, Warner Bros. Publications.

Pass, Joe and, Herb Ellis, *Jazz Duets*, Alfred Publishing.

Raney, Jimmy, *Jimmy Raney Solos*, Volume 29, JA Jazz. Book/CD.

Raney, Jimmy, *Play Duets With Jimmy Raney*, JA Jazz. Book/CD.

Scofield, John, *John Scofield: Guitar Transcriptions*, Hal Leonard Publications.

Sokolow, Fred, *Jazz Chord Solos for Guitar*, Sokolow Music.

Stern, Mike, *Mike Stern Guitar Solos*, JA Jazz.

Towey, Dan, *Chord Melody Standards*, Hal Leonard Publications.

Variotta, Greg, *Mike Stern: Standards*, JA Jazz.

Various authors, *50 Essential Bebop Heads*, Hal Leonard Publications.

Various authors, *Great Horn Solos for Jazz Guitar*, JA Jazz.

Various authors, *Jazz Guitar 2000*, Mel Bay Publications, Inc. Book/3 CDs.

Various authors, *Modern Jazz Greats*, Hal Leonard Publications.

Voelpel, Mark, *Charlie Parker for Guitar*, JA Jazz.

Wittner, Gary, *Thelonious Monk for Guitar*, Hal Leonard Publications.

Guitar Jazz Ensemble Materials

Anderson, Tom, *Playing Guitar in a Jazz/Big Band,* Hal Leonard Publications.

Bruner, Tom, *The Arranger/Composer's Complete Guide to the Guitar,* Mel Bay Publications, Inc., 1980.

Grassel, Jack, *Guitar Seeds,* Warner Bros. Publications.

Grassel, Jack, *Jazz Rhythm Guitar,* Hal Leonard Publications.

Bass

Bass Methods

Bacon, Tony, *Bass Book: A Complete Illustrated History of Bass Guitars,* Miller Freeman, Inc.

Berryman, Lew, *Intonation Plus,* JA Jazz. Book/CD.

Bredice, Vincent, *Mel Bay's Deluxe Jazz/Rock Bass Method,* Mel Bay Publications, Inc.

Brown, Ray, *Ray Brown's Bass Method,* JA Jazz.

Cacibauda, J., *No Nonsense Electric Bass,* Warner Bros. Publications. Beginner.

Carter, Ron, *Comprehensive Bass Method,* Hansen House.

Clayton, John, *Big Band Bass,* Warner Bros. Publications, 1978.

Coolman, Todd, *The Bottom Line,* JA Jazz, 1992.

Davis, Arthur, *System for Double Bass,* JA Jazz.

Dean, Dan, *Hal Leonard Electric Bass Method,* Vols. 1–6, Hal Leonard Publications.

Del Puerto, Carlos, and Silvio Vegara, *The True Cuban Bass,* Sher Music.

Dowd, Charles, *Jazz, Rock and Latin Sourcebook,* Warner Bros. Publications. Book/CD.

Drums, Warner Bros. Publications. Book/CD.

Friedland, Ed, *Building Walking Bass Lines,* Hal Leonard Publications.

Goines, Lincoln, and Robby Ameen, *Funkifying the Clave: Afro-Cuban Grooves for Bass and Drums.* Book/CD.

Houghton, Steve, and Tom Warrington, *Essential Styles for The Drummer and Bassist,* Alfred Publishing.

Leibman, Jon, *Funk Bass,* Hal Leonard Publications.

Leibman, Jon, *Funk/Fusion Bass,* Hal Leonard Publications.

Patino, Manny, and Jorge Moreno, *Afro-Cuban Bass Grooves,* Warner Bros. Publications. Book/CD.

Pastorius, Jaco, and Jerry Jemmott, *Modern Electric Bass,* Manhattan Music/DCI. Book/CD.

Patitucci, John, *Electric Bass,* Warner Bros. Publications. Book/CD.

Patitucci, John, *Electric Bass 2,* Warner Bros. Publications. Book/CD.

Patitucci, John, *John Patitucci: Electric Bass,* JA Jazz. Book/CD.

Patitucci, John, *Ultimate Play-Along for Bass,* Level 1, Vol. 2, Warner Bros. Publications. Book/CDs.

Raney, Chuck, *The Complete Electric Bass Player,* JA Jazz. 5 books.

Raney, Chuck, *Time Signatures for Bass,* Mel Bay Publications, Inc.

Reid, Rufus, *The Evolving Bassist,* Myriad Publications, 1974. Intermediate.

Reid, Rufus, *The Evolving Bassist: Millennium Edition*, JA Jazz. All levels.

Reid, Rufus, *Evolving Upward*, Myriad Limited, 1977. Advanced.

Roberts, Jim, *How the Fender Bass Changed the World*, BackBeat Books.

Sher, Chuck, *The Improviser's Bass Method*, JA Jazz.

Sher and Johnson, *Concepts for Bass Soloing*, JA Jazz.

Snidero, Jim, *Jazz Conception for Bass*, JA Jazz. Book/CD.

Warrington, Tom, *Bass in the Rhythm Section*, Warner Bros. Publications. Book/CD.

Weigert, Dave, *Jazz Workshop for Bass and Drums*, JA Jazz. Book/CD.

Bass Chord/Scale/Improvistion

Anderson, Tom, *I Walk the Line*, Hal Leonard Publications.

Berg, Kris, *Bass Lines in Minutes*, JA Jazz.

Brown, Ray, *Essential Scales, Patterns and Exercises*, Hal Leonard Publications.

Carroll, Frank, *Easy Electric Bass*, Alfred Publishing.

Carter, Ron, *Building Jazz Bass Lines*, Hal Leonard Publications. Book/CD.

Carter, Ron, *Ron Carter: The Collection*, Hal Leonard Publications.

Drew, Lucas, *Basic Electric Bass*, Vol. 2, Sam Fox Publishing.

Friedland, Ed, *Building Walking Bass Lines*, Hal Leonard Publications. Book/CD.

Friedland, Ed, *Expanding Walking Bass Lines*, Hal Leonard Publications. Book/CD.

Gertz, Bruce, *22 Contemporary Melodic Studies for Electric Bass*, Bruce Gertz Music.

Gertz, Bruce, *Walkin'*, Berklee Press, Hal Leonard Publications.

Hilliker, T., and J. Goldsby, *Ron Carter Bass Lines*, Jamey Abersold.

Kaye, Carol, *Electric Bass Lines*, Books 1, 2, 4, and 5, Alfred Publishing.

Kaye, Carol, *How to Play Electric Bass Chords*, Alfred Publishing.

Leonhart, D., and Ken Slone, *Rufus Reid Bass Lines*, JA Jazz.

Martinez, Fernando, *Funk Grooves for Bass*, JA Jazz. Book/CD.

Mauleon, Rebecca, *Salsa Guidebook*, Sher Music.

Patino, Manny, and Jorge Moreno, *Afro-Cuban Bass Grooves*, Warner Bros. Publications.

Pliskow, Dan, *Jazz Bass Lines*, Dan Pliskow, 1975.

Progris, James, *Basic Electric Bass*, Vol. 3, Sam Fox Publishing.

Raney, Chuck, *Time Signature Studies for Bass*, Mel Bay Publications, Inc.

Reid, Rufus, *The Evolving Bassist: Millennium Edition*, Warner Bros. Publications.

Richmond, Mike, *Modern Walking Bass Technique*, Ped Xing Music.

Sher, Chuck, *The Improviser's Bass Method*, Sher Music Co.

Stagnaro, Oscar, and Chuck Sher, *The Latin Bass Book: A Practical Guide*, Sher Music Co.

Stinnett, Jim, *Creating Jazz Bass Lines*, JA Jazz.

Bass Reading Materials

Kaye, Carol, *Bass I: Music Reading Practice*, Alfred Publishing.

Kaye, Carol, *Bass I: Music Reading Practice Plus Theory,* Alfred Publishing.

Stinnett, Jim, *Reading in Bass Clef,* JA Jazz.

Bass Bowing Materials

Goldsby, John, *Bowing Techniques for the Improvising Bassist,* JA Jazz.

Bass Solos/Transcriptions

Carter, Ron, *Volume 6, 15, 36,* JA Jazz.

Coolman, Todd, *The Bass Tradition,* JA Jazz, 1985. Intermediate/Advanced.

Coolman, Todd, *The Bottom Line,* JA Jazz.

Coolman, Todd, *Vol. 37,* JA Jazz.

Cranshaw, Bob, *Vol. 42,* JA Jazz.

Gilmore, Steve, *Vol. 25, 34,* JA Jazz.

Goldsby, John, *Bass Notes,* JA Jazz. Book/CD.

Houghton, Steve, and Tom Warrington, *Blues Master Tracks,* Alfred Publishing.

Kaye, Carol, *Electric Bass Lines,* Book 4, Alfred Publishing. Intermediate.

Laird, Rick, *Jazz Riffs for Bass,* Hal Leonard Publications. Intermediate/Advanced.

Nahmann, Volker, *The Music of Oscar Pettiford,* Volker Manrmann. Intermediate/Advanced.

Parker, Charlie, *Charlie Parker Omnibook—Bass Clef,* Warner Bros. Publications.

Reid, Rufus, *Vol. 1 and Vol. 3,* JA Jazz.

Seaton, Lynn, *Jazz Solos for Bass,* Vol. 1, Kendor Music, Inc.

Sher, Chuck, *The Improviser's Bass Method,* Sher Music, 1979. All levels.

Stinnet, Jim, *Arcology = Paul Chambers Solos II,* JA Jazz.

Stinnet, Jim, *Paul Chambers,* JA Jazz. Intermediate.

Wheeler, Tyrone, *Vol. 54 and 70,* JA Jazz.

Vibraphone

Vibraphone Method/Technique/Chords

Brown, Tom, *Mallets in Mind,* Kendor Music, Inc., 1972.

Delp, R., *Vibraphone Technique,* Hal Leonard Publications, 1973.

Feldman, Victor, *All Alone by the Vibraphone,* Alfred Publishing, 1971.

Friedman, D., *Vibraphone Technique,* Hal Leonard Publications, 1973.

Metzger, Jon, *Jazz Vibes: The Art and Language,* JA Jazz.

Samuels, David, *A Musical Approach to Four Mallet Technique for Vibraphone,* Excelsior Music Publishing Co.

Viola, Joseph, and R. Delp, *Chord Studies for Mallet Instruments,* Hal Leonard Publications, 1973.

Saxophone

Saxophone Technique

Allard, Joe, *Three Octave Scales and Chords,* Charles Colin Music Publications.

Bergonzi, Jerry, *The Inside Improvisation Series,* Advance Music.

Butler, Hunt, *20 Solos of Cannonball Adderley,* Brett Music.

Cooper, Bob, *Jazz Development for the Saxophonist,* Mel Bay Publications, Inc.

DeFranco, Buddy, *Hand in Hand with Hanon,* Buddy DeFranco Enterprises.

DeVille, Paul, *Universal Method for Saxophone,* Carl Fisher.

Dolphy, Eric, *Collection,* JA Jazz.

Higgins, Dan, *Jazz Duos,* JA Jazz.

Lateef, Yusef, *123 Duets,* Fana Music.

Leonard, J. Michael, *Extended Technique for the Saxophone,* J. Michael Leonard Press.

Liebman, David, *Developing a Personal Saxophone Sound,* Dorn Publishers.

Miedema, Harry, *Jazz Styles and Analysis,* DB Music Workshop Publishers.

Mintzer, Bob, *Playing the Saxophone,* Kendor Music, Inc.

Mishkit, Bruce, *Lessons With the Greats for Sax/Flute,* Warner Bros. Publications.

Nelson, Oliver, *Patterns for Improvisation,* Nolsen Music, JA Jazz.

Niehaus, Lennie, *Basic Jazz Conception for Saxophone,* 2 Volumes, Professional Drum Shop, 1966. Beginner.

Niehaus, Lennie, *Developing Jazz Concepts for Saxophone,* JA Jazz.

Niehaus, Lennie, *Intermediate Jazz Conception for Saxophone,* Professional Drum Shop, 1964. Intermediate.

Northway, Ernie, *Guide to the Saxophone,* NC & A Press, 1979. Beginner/Intermediate.

O'Neill, John, *The Jazz Method for Sax,* JA Jazz. Book/CD.

Parker, Charlie, *The Omnibook,* Warner Bros. Publications.

Pauer, Fritz, *Saxophone Duets,* JA Jazz.

Seckler, Stan, *Developing the Jazz Sax Section,* JA Jazz.

Seckler, Stan, *Take the Lead,* Houston Publishing, Inc.,1977.

Snidero, Jim, *Jazz Conception for Saxophone,* Advance Music. Book/CD.

Teal, Larry, *The Art of Saxophone Playing,* Summy Birchard.

Vadala, Chris, *Improve Your Doubling,* Dorn Publishing.

Viola, Joe, *Technique of the Saxophone,* Berklee Press.

Wilenski, Danny, *Advanced Sax,* Mel Bay Publications, Inc.

Yasinitsky, Greg, *For Saxes Only: 10 Jazz Duets,* Warner Bros. Publications.

Yellin, Peter, *Jazz Saxophone,* Vols. 1, 2, 3, Charles Colin Music Publications.

Saxophone Chord/Scale/Improvisation

Allard, Joe, *Three Octave Scales and Chords,* Charles Colin Music Publications.

Bergonzi, Jerry, *The Inside Improvisation Series,* Advance Music.

Berle, Arnie, *How to Create and Develop a Jazz Sax Solo,* Mel Bay Publications, Inc.

Berle, Arnie, *Jazz Saxophone Licks and Patterns,* Mel Bay Publications, Inc.

Campbell, Gary, *Triad Pairs for Jazz,* Warner Bros. Publications.

Gross, John, *Multiphonics for Saxophone,* JA Jazz.

Harris, Eddie, *Intervallistic Concept,* JA Jazz.

Herman, Woody, *Sax Scales, Chords and Solos* (original 1946 edition), JA Jazz.

Klose, H., *25 Daily Exercises for Sax,* Astor Books.

Klose, H., *Daily Exercises for Saxophone,* JA Jazz.

Kynaston, Trent, *Daily Studies for all Saxophones,* JA Jazz.

Lateef, Yusef, *123 Duets,* Fana Music.

Lateef, Yusef, *Repository of Scales & Melodic Patterns,* Fana Music.

Leonard, J. Michael, *Extended Technique for the Saxophone,* J. Michael Leonard Press/
  Mel Bay Publications, Inc.

Liebman, David, *Chromaticism/Non-Diatonic Scales,* JA Jazz.

Marienthal, Eric, *Comprehensive Jazz Studies and Exercises,* Warner Bros. Publications.

McLean, Jackie, *Daily Warm-up Exercises for Saxophone,* JA Jazz.

Neely, Blake, *Saxophone 1,* JA Jazz. Book/CD.

Nelson, Oliver, *Patterns for Improvisation,* JA Jazz.

Niehaus, Lennie, *Jazz Duets*, Vols. 1 and 2, JA Jazz.

Niehaus, Lennie, *Jazz Improvisation for Saxophone,* JA Jazz.

Niehaus, Lennie, *Lennie Niehaus Plays the Blues in All 12 Keys,* JA Jazz. Book/CD.

Osland, Miles, *Sax Scale Anthology,* Vols. 1 and 2, JA Jazz.

Parker, Charlie, *The Omnibook,* Warner Bros. Publications.

Rascher, Sigurd, *158 Saxophone Exercises,* Hal Leonard Publications.

Viola, Joseph, *Creative Reading Studies,* JA Jazz.

Viola, Joseph, *The Technique of the Saxophone*, Vol. 2 (Chord Studies), Hal Leonard Publications,
  1963. Advanced.

Viola, Joseph, *The Technique of the Saxophone*, Vol. 3 (Rhythm Studies), Hal Leonard Publications.
  Advanced.

Saxophone Altissimo Register Materials

Allard, Joe, *Three Octave Scales and Chords,* JA Jazz.

Gross, John, *Multiphonics for Saxophone,* JA Jazz.

Leonard, J. Michael, *Extended Technique for the Saxophone,* Michael J. Leonard Press.

Lang, Rosemary, *Beginning Studies in the Altissimo Register,* Lang Music, 1971. All levels.

Luckey, Robert A., *Saxophone Altissimo,* Olympia Music Publishing.

Nash, Ted, *Studies in High Harmonics,* Warner Bros. Publications, 1956. Intermediate/Advanced.

Rascher, Sigurd M., *Top-Tones for the Saxophone,* Carl Fischer, 1942. Intermediate/Advanced.

Saxophone Solos/Transcriptions

15 Alto Saxophone Transcribed Solos, JA Jazz.

15 Tenor Saxophone Transcribed Solos, JA Jazz.

Baker, David N., *The Jazz Style of Cannonball Adderley*, Warner Bros. Publications. Intermediate/ Advanced.

Baker, David N., *The Jazz Style of Charlie Parker*, Warner Bros. Publications. Intermediate/Advanced.

Baker, David N., *The Jazz Style of John Coltrane*, Warner Bros. Publications. Intermediate/Advanced.

Berg, Bob, *More Tenor Solos*, JA Jazz.

Bergonzi, Jerry, *Jerry Bergonzi Solos*, JA Jazz.

The Brecker Brothers, Hal Leonard Publications.

Brecker, Michael, *Michael Brecker Collection*, Hal Leonard Publications.

Brignola, Nick, *Nick Brignola Bari Sax Solos*, JA Jazz.

Butler, Hunt, *20 Solos of Cannonball Adderley*, Brett Publishing.

Campbell, Gary, *Hank Mobley Solos*, Houston Publishing, Inc.

Carter, Benny, *Benny Carter Collection*, Hal Leonard Publications.

Carter, Benny, *Benny Carter Plays Standards*, Hal Leonard Publications.

Coan, Carl, *Michael Brecker Artist Transcriptions*, Hal Leonard Publications.

Coan, Carl, *John Coltrane Transcriptions*, Hal Leonard Publications.

Coltrane, John, *John Coltrane Artist Transcriptions*, Hal Leonard Publications.

Coltrane, John, *John Coltrane Plays Giant Steps*, Hal Leonard Publications.

Coltrane, John, *The Music of John Coltrane*, Hal Leonard Publications.

Coltrane Plays Standards, Hal Leonard Publications.

Desmond, Paul, *Paul Desmond Solos: The Collection*, Hal Leonard Publications.

Dolphy, Eric, *Eric Dolphy Collection*, JA Jazz.

Fishman, Greg, *Stan Getz Tenor Solos*, Hal Leonard Publications.

Fishman, Greg, *Tenor Saxophone Standards*, Hal Leonard Publications.

Gordon, Dexter, *Dexter Gordon*, Hal Leonard Publications.

Grossman, Steve, *Steve Grossman: Nine Tenor Solos*, JA Jazz.

Henderson, Joe, *The Best of Joe Henderson*, Hal Leonard Publications.

Henderson, Joe, *Joe Henderson Solos*, Warner Bros. Publications.

Keller, Gary, *Alto Sax Solos for the Performing Artist*, JA Jazz.

Keller, Gary, *Sonny Stitt: Greatest Alto Solos*, Houston Publishing, Inc.

Keller, Gary, *Sonny Stitt: Tenor Solos*, Houston Publishing, Inc.

Koz, Dave, *Off the Beaten Path*, Warner Bros. Publications.

Kynaston, Trent, *Alto Sax Blues Solos*, JA Jazz.

Kynaston, Trent, *Bob Berg: Jazz Tenor Solos*, Corybant Productions.

Kynaston, Trent, *Blues Solos Jazz Tenor Sax*, JA Jazz.

Kynaston, Trent, *The Music of Joshua Redman*, Warner Bros. Publications.

Kynaston, Trent, *Rhythm Solos: Jazz Tenor Sax*, Corybant Productions.

Liebman, David, *David Liebman Tenor Solos*, JA Jazz.

Liebman, David, *Scale Syllabus Solos,* JA Jazz.

Liebman, David, and Michael Gerber, *Souls and Masters,* JA Jazz.

Lovano, Joe, *Joe Lovano Artist Transcriptions,* Hal Leonard Publications.

Luckey, Robert, *West Coast Jazz Sax Solos,* Olympia Music.

Margitza, Rick, *Rick Margitza Jazz Tenor Solos,* JA Jazz.

Miedema, Harry, *Jazz Styles and Analysis,* DB Music Workshop Publications.

Mintzer, Bob, *Jazz Solos for Alto Sax,* Vol. 1., Kendor Music, Inc.

Mintzer, Bob, *Jazz Solos for Baritone Sax,* Vol. 1., Kendor Music, Inc.

Mintzer, Bob, *Jazz Solos for Tenor Sax,* Vol. 1., Kendor Music, Inc.

Moody, James, *James Moody Collection,* Hal Leonard Publications.

Morgan, Frank, *Frank Morgan Collection,* JA Jazz.

Niehaus, Lennie, *Developing Jazz Concepts for Saxophone,* JA Jazz.

Niehaus, Lennie, *Dexter Gordon Solos,* JA Jazz.

Niehaus, Lennie, *Jazz Conception for the Saxophone,* JA Jazz.

Niehaus, Lennie, *Lennie Niehaus Plays the Blues in All 12 Keys,* JA Jazz.

Nystrom, Todd, *David Sanborn Collection,* Warner Bros. Publications.

Osland, Miles, *The Music of Bob Mintzer,* Warner Bros. Publications.

Parker, Charlie, *Charlie Parker: A Jazz Master,* Warner Bros. Publications.

Parker, Charlie, *Charlie Parker Omnibook,* Warner Bros. Publications.

Pepper, Art, *The Art Pepper Collection,* Warner Bros. Publications.

Pepper, Art, *The Genius of Art Pepper,* Warner Bros. Publications.

Price, Tim, *The Cannonball Adderley Collection,* Hal Leonard Publications.

Price, Tim, *Great Tenor Sax Solos,* JA Jazz.

Rollins, Sonny, *Sonny Rollins Collection,* Hal Leonard Publications.

Sanborn, David, *Solo Collection,* Warner Bros. Publications.

Seckler, Stan, *Take the Lead,* Houston Publishing, Inc.

Shorter, Wayne, *Wayne Shorter Artist Transcriptions,* Hal Leonard Publications.

Stitt, Sonny, *Sonny Stitt: Tenor Solos,* JA Jazz.

Tabackin, Lew, *The Lew Tabackin Collection,* Hal Leonard Publications.

Turrentine, Stanley, *Stanley Turrentine Artist Transcriptions,* Hal Leonard Publications.

Watts, Ernie, *Ernie Watts Saxophone Collection,* Hal Leonard Publications.

Young, Lester, *Lester Young Tenor Sax Solos,* JA Jazz.

Trumpet

Trumpet Technique

Caruso, Carmine, *Musical Calisthenics for Brass,* JA Jazz.

Colin, Allan, *Extensions for the Trumpet Player,* JA Jazz.

Colin, Charles, *Trumpet Lip Flexibilities,* three volumes, Charles Colin Music Publications.

D'Aveni, Toni, *Jazz Trumpet Tech #1*, Vols. 1 and 2, Hal Leonard Publications.

Harbison, Pat, *Technical Studies for the Modern Trumpet Player*, JA Jazz.

Kotwica, Raymond S., and Joseph Viola, *Chord Studies for Trumpet*, Hal Leonard Publications. Intermediate.

Lipsius, Fred, *Reading Key Jazz Rhythms*, JA Jazz.

McNeil, John, *Jazz Trumpet Techniques*, Warner Bros. Publications.

McNeil, John, *The Art of Jazz Trumpet*, Vols. 1 and 2, Gerard & Sarzin Publishing Co.

Pauer, Fritz, *Jazz and Latin Duets*, JA Jazz.

Reyman, Randall, *Technical Drills for the Jazz/Commercial Trumpet Player*, Kendor Music, Inc.

Sandoval, Arturo, *Playing Technique & Performance Studies for Trumpet (Basic)*, Vol. 2, Hal Leonard Publications.

Sandoval, Arturo, *Playing Technique & Performance Studies for Trumpet (Advanced)*, Vol. 3, Hal Leonard Publications.

Shew, Bobby, *Exercises and Etudes for Jazz and Classical Players*, JA Jazz.

Snidero, Jim, *Jazz Conception for Trumpet*, Advance Music.

Wiskirchen, Rev. George, *A Manual for the Stage or Dance Band Trumpet Player*, Hal Leonard Publications. Beginner/Intermediate.

Trumpet Upper Range Materials

Lynch, John, *Altissimo Trumpet Playing*, JA Jazz.

Maggio, Louis, *Pedal Tone Approach to High Notes*.

Spera, Dominic, *Take the Lead*, JA Jazz.

Stuart, Glenn, *The Art of Playing Lead Trumpet*, Glenn Stuart, 1974.

Zorn, Jay D., *Exploring The Trumpet's Upper Register*, Kendor Music, Inc., 1975.

Trumpet Solos/Transcriptions

15 Transcribed Trumpet Solos, JA Jazz.

Armstrong, Louis, *A Jazz Master*, Warner Bros. Publications.

Baker, Chet, *Solos*, 11 Transcribed Solos, JA Jazz.

Baker, Chet, *Solos*, 13 Transcribed Solos, JA Jazz.

Baker, David N., *Clifford Brown Styles and Analysis*, JA Jazz.

Baker, David N., *The Jazz Style of Fats Navarro*, Warner Bros. Publications. Intermediate/Advanced.

Baker, David N., *The Jazz Style of Miles Davis*, Warner Bros. Publications. Intermediate/Advanced.

Bastion, Jim, *Chet Baker: Trumpet Artistry*, JA Jazz.

Bastion, Jim, *Chet Baker's Greatest Scat Solos*, JA Jazz.

Brown, John Robert, *Jazz Trumpet 2*, International Music Publications, 1987. Intermediate/Advanced.

Bunnell, Jeff, *Blue Mitchell Solos*, Hal Leonard Publications.

Cervantes and Ruiz, *Clifford Brown: Solo Patterns Study*, Charles Colin Music Publications.

Davis, Miles, *Kinda Blue Complete Transcriptions*, Hal Leonard Publications.

Davis, Miles, *Kind of Blue*, Hal Leonard Publications.

Davis, Miles, *Originals,* Hal Leonard Publications.

Davis, Miles, *Standards,* Hal Leonard Publications.

Davison, Mike, *Randy Brecker Artist Transcriptions,* Hal Leonard Publications.

Ecklund, Peter, *Bix Beiderbecke Great Cornet Solos,* JA Jazz.

Ecklund, Peter, *Great Trumpet Solos of Louis Armstrong,* Hal Leonard Publications.

Harbison, Pat, *20 Authentic Bebop Solos,* JA Jazz. Book/CD.

Harrell, Tom, *Jazz Trumpet Transcriptions,* Hal Leonard Publications.

Hubbard, Freddie, *Artist Transcriptions,* Hal Leonard Publications.

Jarvis, Jeff, *Jazz Solos for Trumpet,* Vol. 1, Kendor Music, Inc.

Jazz and Latin Duets for Trumpet, JA Jazz.

Lewis, Marc, *Clifford Brown Complete Transcriptions,* Hal Leonard Publications.

Marsalis, Wynton, *Ballads,* Warner Bros. Publications.

Marsalis, Wynton, *Standards,* Warner Bros. Publications.

Martin, Bob, *Duets for Trumpet,* Hal Leonard Publications.

Miles Davis Standards, Vol. 1, JA Jazz.

Paperelli, Frank, *Dizzy Gillespie: A Jazz Master,* Hal Leonard Publications.

Redd, Robert, *Lee Morgan Solos,* JA Jazz.

Rodney, Red, *Then and Now,* Charles Colin Music Publications.

Shaw, Woody, *Greatest Hits of Woody Shaw,* Warner Bros. Publications.

Shew, Bobby, *Bobby Shew Solos,* JA Jazz.

Slone, Ken, *28 Modern Jazz Trumpet Solos,* Books 1 and 2, Warner Bros. Publications.

Slone, Ken, *Clifford Brown Trumpet Solos,* Warner Bros. Publications, 1982.

Stewart, Thomas, *The Artistry of Roy Eldridge,* JA Jazz.

Vizzutti, Allen, and M. Garson, *Trumpet Solos for the Performing Artist,* JA Jazz. Book/CD.

Vizzutti, Allen, *Allen Vizzutti: Play-Along Solos,* Hal Leonard Publications. Books/CDs.

Trumpet Links

The Art of Jazz Trumpet - http://www.changingtones.com/trmpt00.html

International Trumpet Guild - http://www.trumpetguild.org

The Ralph Jones trumpet page - http://www.whc.net/rjones

Raw Brass - trumpet players, info gateway - http://rawbrass.com

Stanton's Trumpet Page - http://www.stantondesign.com/trumpet

The Trumpet Gearhead - http://www.dallasmusic.org/gearhead

Trumpet Geeks International - http://www.trumpetgeek.com

Trumpet Herald - http://www.trumpetherald.com

Trumpet Lessons Online - http://www.trumpetlessons.com/welcome.html

Trumpet Links - http://www.s-hamilton.k12.ia.us/iba/lnktpt.html

Trumpet Studio - http://www.trumpetstudio.com

Trumpet Topics - http://gopher.fsu.edu/~bgoff/tpt-tips/tips.html

Trumpet World - http://www.angelfire.com/in/TrumpetWorld

Trumpetjazz.com - http://www.trumpetjazz.com

Trombone

Trombone Technique

Baker, Buddy, *Tenor Trombone Method*, Warner Bros. Publications.

Baker, David N., *Contemporary Techniques for the Trombone*, Vols. 1 and 2, Charles Colin Music, 1974.

Baker, David N., *The Jazz Style of J.J. Johnson*, Hansen House. Intermediate/Advanced.

Bert, Eddie, *Trombone Method*, Charles Colin Music Publications.

Charlie Parker Omni Book, bass clef book, Warner Bros. Publications.

Colin, Charles, *Trombone/Bass Clef: Lip Flexibilities*, Charles Colin Music Publications.

Dietrich, Kurt, *Duke's Bones: Ellington's Greatest Trombonists*, JA Jazz.

Ervin, Thomas, *Range Building on the Trombone*, JA Jazz.

Fox, *The Art of Doodle Tonguing for Trombone*, Warner Bros. Publications, 1991. Intermediate/Advanced.

Grey, Al, *Plunger Techniques*, Second Floor Music. All levels.

Hunsberger, Donald, *Remington Warm-Up Studies*, Accura Music.

Kleinhammer and Yeo, *Mastering the Trombone*.

Malone, Tom, *Alternate Position System for Trombone*, JA Jazz.

Martin, Bob, *Jazz Duets for Trombone*, 20 duets, Vol. 1, Hal Leonard Publications.

McChesney, Bob, *Doodle Studies and Etudes*, Chesapeake Music.

Rochut and Bordogni, *Melodious Etudes for Trombone*, three volumes.

Snidero, Jim, *Easy Jazz Conception for Trombone*, Advance Music. Book/CD.

Snidero, Jim, *Jazz Conception for Trombone*, Advance Music. Book/CD.

Van Lier, Bart, *Coordination Training Program for Trombone Playing*, JA Jazz.

Waits, Greg, *Advanced Flexibility Studies for the Jazz Trombonist*, JA Jazz.

Watrous, Bill, and Alan Ralph, *Trombonisms*, JA Jazz.

Watts, Greg, *Advanced Flexibility Studies for the Jazz Trombonist*, JA Jazz. Book/CD.

Weist, Steve, *Trombone Take the Lead*, JA Jazz.

Wilson, Phil, and Joseph Viola, *Chord Studies for Trombone*, Hal Leonard Publications.

Winding, Kai, *Mr. Trombone*, Mel Bay Publications, Inc. All levels.

Trombone Solos/Transcriptions

Fedchock, John, *Jazz Solos for Trombone*, Kendor Music, Inc.

Johnson, J. J., *The J. J. Johnson Collection*, Hal Leonard Publications.

Johnson, J. J., *J. J. Johnson Solos*, JA Jazz.

Leisenring, John, and Hunt Butler, *J. J. Johnson Trombone Solos*, JA Jazz. Intermediate/Advanced.

Parker, Charlie, *Omnibook: Bass Clef*, Warner Bros. Publications.

Rosolino, Frank, *Frank Rosolino: Fond Memories Of*, JA Jazz.

Whigham, Jiggs, *Jazz Solos*, JA Jazz.

Trombone Quartets and Quintets

Hampton, Slide, *Slide Hampton's World of Trombones,* four bones and rhythm, JA Jazz.

McDonald, Barry, *Barry McDonald Arrangements for 5 Bones and Rhythm,* JA Jazz.

Reeves, Scott, *Scott Reeves Jazz Bone Quartet Arrangements with Rhythm Section Parts,* JA Jazz.

Bass Trombone Materials

Aharoni's Method for Bass Trombone, Robert King Music.

Blazevich, V., *70 Studies for Tuba,* Robert King Music.

Faulise, Paul, *The F and D Double Valve Bass Trombone,* PF Music Company.

Clarinet and Flute

Bay, Bill, *Flute Improvising Workbook,* Mel Bay Publications, Inc., 1980.

Bay, Bill, *Jazz Flute Studies,* Mel Bay Publications, Inc.

Bolling, Claude, *Suite for Flute and Jazz Piano Trio,* Hal Leonard Publications.

Brilhart, Arnold, and Artie Shaw, *Artie Shaw's Jazz Technic,* Vols. 1 and 2, JA Jazz.

DeFranco, Buddy, *Hand in Hand with Hanon,* Hal Leonard Publications.

Garson, Michael, and Eddie Daniels, *Clarinet Solos for the Performing Artist,* Alfred Publishing. Book/CD.

Garson, Michael, and Jim Walker, *Flute Solos for the Performing Artist,* Alfred Publishing. Book/CD.

Garson, Michael, and Jim Walker, *The Music of Free Flight,* Warner Bros. Publications. Book/CD.

Goodman, Benny, *Benny Goodman Swing Classics,* Hal Leonard Publications.

Goodman, Benny, *Benny Goodman's Clarinet Method,* (original 1941 version), JA Jazz.

Higgins, Dan, *Flute Jazz,* JA Jazz.

Lateef, Yusef, *Flute Book of the Blues,* Fana Music.

McGee, Andy, *Improvisation for Flute,* Hal Leonard Publications. Intermediate.

Most, Sam, *Jazz Flute Conceptions,* Alfred Publishing, 1974. Intermediate.

Newton, James, *The Improvising Flute,* Hal Leonard Publications.

Newton, James, *The Improvising Flute,* JA Jazz.

O'Neill, John, *Jazz Method for Clarinet,* JA Jazz. Book/CD.

O'Neill, John, *Jazz Method for Flute,* JA Jazz. Book/CD.

Osland, Miles, *The Music of Nestor Torres,* Warner Bros. Publications.

Schiff, Ronnie, *Solos for Jazz Flute,* Carl Fisher.

Shaw, Artie, *Jazz Technique,* Book 1, Warner Bros. Publications.

Shaw, Artie, *Jazz Technique,* Books 2–14 Clarinet Etudes, Warner Bros. Publications.

Snidero, Jim, *Jazz Conception for Clarinet,* Advance Music. Book/CD.

Snidero, Jim, *Jazz Conception for Flute,* Advance Music. Book/CD.

Vadala, Chris, *Improve Your Doubling,* Dorn Publishing.

Strings

Abell, Usher, *Jazz Violin Studies,* Mel Bay Publications, Inc. Intermediate/Advanced.

Baker, David N., *Jazz Bass Clef Explorations,* JA Jazz.

Baker, David N., *Jazz Expressions and Explorations,* JA Jazz.

Baker, David N., *A New and Innovative System for Learning to Improvise for Strings,* JA Jazz..

Baker, David N., *String Instruments Improvisation,* Vol. 1 Violin and Viola, Alfred Publishing. All levels.

Baker, David N., *String Instruments Improvisation,* Vol. 2, Cello and Bass, Alfred Publishing. All levels.

Blake, John, *Jazz Improvisation Made Easy for Strings,* Vol. 1, P.O. Box 186, Westford, MA 01886. Book/CD.

Friedlander, Erik, *Olympic Cello Workout,* www.erikfriedlander.com.

Glaser, Matt, *Chord Studies for Violin,* Berklee Press.

Glaser, Matt, and Stephane Grappelli, *Jazz Violin.* Intermediate/Advanced.

Lieberman, Julie, *Improvising Violin,* Huiksi Music, Hal Leonard Publications.

Lieberman, Julie Lyonn, *The Contemporary Violinist,* Huiksi Music, Hal Leonard Publications.

Lieberman, Julie Lyonn, *Planet Musician,* Huiksi Music, Hal Leonard Publications.

Lowinger, Gene, *Jazz Violin,* G. Schirmer, Inc. Intermediate/Advanced.

Norgaard, Martin, *The Jazz Fiddle Wizard,* Mel Bay Publications, Inc.

Nunes, Warren, and Cathye Lynne Smithwick, *Solo Jazz Violin,* Charles Hansen. Intermediate.

Sabien, Randy, and Bob Phillips, *Jazz Philharmonic,* Alfred Publishing.

White, Chris, *Jazz Cello, Viola, or Violin,* Cello Works.

String Web Sites

www.StringsCentral.com

www.JulieLyonn.com

www.groups.yahoo.com/group/IAJEStrings

www.shoko.calarts.edu/-chung/JazzViolin.html

Jazz Vocal

Vocal Technique/Scat Materials

Baker, Chet, *Chet Baker's Greatest Scat Solos,* JA Jazz.

Campbell and Lewis, *Harmony Vocals,* JA Jazz. Book/CD.

Chromatic Pitch Pipe, JA Jazz.

Clayton, Jay, *Sing Your Song,* JA Jazz. Book/CD.

Coker, Patty, and David N. Baker, *Vocal Improvisation: An Instrumental Approach,* Warner Bros. Publications. Intermediate/Advanced.

Coker, Patty, *The Singer's Jazz Session*, Warner Bros. Publications.

DiBlasio, Denis, *Guide for Jazz and Scat Vocalists,* JA Jazz.

Fredrickson, Scott, *Scat Singing Method,* Scott Fredrickson. Beginner/Intermediate.

Jhaveri, Niranjan, *New Vocal Techniques for Jazz,* Book/CD.

Jobim, Antonio Carlos, voice and piano, JA Jazz.

McCurdy, Ron, and Willie Hill, Jr., *Approaching the Standards for Jazz Vocalists,* Warner Bros. Publications, 2000.

Metcalf, Joni and Jan Stentz, *Learn How to Sing Jazz Scat*, Mitchell Madison.

Nakasian, Stephanie, *It's Not on the Page,* Stephanie Nakasian.

Snidero, Jim, *Jazz Conception for Scat Vocals,* Advance Music.

Stoloff, Bob, *Scat! Vocal Improv Techs,* JA Jazz.

Swain, Alan, *Scat,* Jasmine Music Publishers. Beginner/Intermediate.

Swain, Alan, *Scat II,* Jasmine Music Publishers. Intermediate/Advanced.

Weir, Michele, *Vocal Improvisation,* Advance Music.

Jazz Camps

Bud Shank Jazz Workshop

Interlochen Arts Camp

Jamey Aebersold Summer Workshops (contact his Web site: www.jazzbooks.com)

Manhattan School of Music Summer Workshop

Stanford Jazz Workshop

The University of Colorado Mile High Jazz Camp

The University of Kansas at Lawrence Jazz Camp

The University of Massachusetts at Amherst, Jazz in July

SECTION III:
SOFTWARE AND INSTRUCTIONAL VIDEOS

Software

New software programs are being produced at a rapid rate. Some that are available as of this printing include:

MIDI Sequencing and Notation Software

Allegroassai - Amadeus Opus Lite: Music notation software that allows the creation of a new score from scratch or the modification of an Opus Digital Score.

Autoscore Deluxe: Technologically advanced real-time audio-to-MIDI software that can convert your singing or playing into written music and greatly expand your current MIDI setup.

Autoscore Pro: Same as above, with additional features.

Cakewalk Express MIDI Pack: Integrated multitrack MIDI sequencing and digital audio recording; ten-foot MIDI adapter cable included.

Cakewalk Home Studio 2002: Integrated multitrack MIDI and digital audio sequencing, with lots of advanced features from Sonar.

Cakewalk Home Studio 9: Integrated multitrack MIDI and digital audio sequencing, with support for RealMedia, Crescendo, and ActiveX plug-ins.

Cakewalk SONAR: Professional digital multitrack recording system.

Cubase VST 5: MIDI sequencer with audio recording.

Cubase VST Score: Professional sequencer with audio recording and score printing.

Desktop Sheet Music: Notation and score printing software.

Finale: Notation and score printing software. All levels.

Logic Audio Gold: Professional Digital Audio, MIDI, and scoring system.

Logic Audio Platinum: Professional digital audio, MIDI, and scoring system.

Logic Audio Silver: Professional digital audio, MIDI, and scoring system.

MicroLogic A/V: Inexpensive multifunctional entry-level sequencing software.

MIDISCAN 3: Converts printed sheet music into multitrack MIDI files.

Muro, Don, *The Art of Sequencing: A Step by Step Approach*, JA Jazz.

PianoScan: Converts piano sheet music into MIDI files.

Sequencer Plus Gold: Comprehensive sequencing program.

Sibelius: Professional music notation, score printing, and publishing software.

SmartSCore: Fully integrated music scoring, MIDI sequencing, and music scanning with advanced recognition technology.

Transcribing Software

Bias – Deck: Multitrack recording and editing. Record, edit, and play back up to 64 tracks of audio, with 999 virtual tracks.

Listen and Learn Transcriber Software, JA Jazz: Record and play back at 1/2, 1/3, 1/4, and 1 1/2 of original speed without changing the pitch.

Performer: Mark of the Unicorn. Macintosh.

TR-400 Digital Transcribing Box, JA Jazz.

Transcribing Software – Slow Gold, JA Jazz. CD-ROM for Windows 95.

Improvisation/Play-Along Software

ACID Latin 2.0 by Sonic Foundry: Create music with professionally recorded royalty-free loops.

Band-in-A Box Mega Pak: The latest version of Band-in-a-Box on CD with all the add-ons.

Fruityloops 3: Electronic music creation software.

Groove Maker Max: DJ software for the electronic age. Play, mix, edit, and randomize grooves on the fly.

Guitar Interactive SongBook—B. B. King: Play along with the King of Blues.

Jammer Hit Session: Create full arrangements of music on your PC in just minutes.

Jammer Pro: JAMMER Professional v3.0 - Songwriting and music composition on your PC. Version 3.0 introduces many new features that are designed to increase flexibility and enhance the creative process.

Jazz Instruction Software

Baker, Malcolm Lynne, and John Ellinger, *MiBAC Music Lessons*, MiBAC. All levels.

Band-in-A-Box: The latest version of Band-in-a-Box on CD with all the add-ons. All levels.

Brownlee, Joe, *Keyboard Extended Jazz Harmonies*, Electronic Courseware Systems.

Brownlee, Joe, *Keyboard Jazz Harmonies*, Electronic Courseware Systems.

Carter, Allen, *Developing the Instrumental Jazz Ensemble*, AC Muzik. CD-ROM.

Carter, Allen, *Interactive Arranging*, AC Muzik. CD-ROM.

Evans, Jeffery, *Práctica Música*, Ars Nova. Beginner/Intermediate.

Music Ace: Interactive music teaching program for kids.

Music Ace 2: The second title in the Music Ace series from Harmonic Vision. Beginner/Intermediate.

Music Lessons: ML teaches general music theory concepts that apply to all instruments.

Musition: Educational music theory package.

Piano Suite Basic: Interactive piano teaching software. Beginners.

Piano Suite Bundle: Piano teaching software with keyboard and MIDI interface.

Piano Suite Premiere: For all ages.

Web Sites
Music Software

www.ars-nova.com/practica
www.cakewalk.com
www.cdromshop.com
www.childrenseducationalsoftware.com
www.codamusic.com
www.halycom.com
www.jumpmusic.com
www.jwpepper.com
www.mcc.ac.uk
www.mccormicksnet.com/smartscr

www.midisoft.com

www.motu.com

www.musicalsoftware.com

www.musicians.about.com

www.musitek.com

www.noteworthy.com

www.opcode.com

www.pendersmusic.com

www.pgmusic.com/

www.playjazz.com

www.pyware.com

www.rising.com.au/auralia/

www.sfoundry.com

www.sibelius.com

www.soundquest.com

www.soundtree.com

www.soundtrek.com

www.sseyo.com

www.voicecrystal.com

www.votetra.com

www.wildcat.com

www.windmusicplus.com

www.wwandbw.com

Music Publishers/Distributors

www.advancemusic.com

www.alfred.com

www.arts.unco.edu/UNCJazz

www.barnhouse.com

www.fjhmusic.com

www.halleonard.com

www.jazzatlincolncenter.org

www.jazzbooks.com

www.jfraser.com

www.jwpepper.com

www.kendormusic.com

www.kjos.com

www.marinamusic.com

www.melbay.com

www.otterdist.com

www.ottermusicsales.com

www.oup.co.uk.com

www.pendersmusic.com
www.scarecrowpress.com
www.seabreezejazz.com
www.secondfloormusic.com
www.shermusic.com
www.sierramusic.com
www.walrusmusic.com
www.warnerbrospublications.com
www.wwandbw.com
www.yahama.com

Musical Instrument Manufacturers

www.boosey.com
www.calicchio.com
www.daddario.com
www.edwards-instruments.com
www.gleblanc.com
www.guildguitars.com
www.jupitermusic.com
www.kanstul.com
www.kyddbass.com
www.ludwig-drums.com
www.pearldrum.com
www.rayburn.com
www.remodrums.com
www.ricoreeds.com
www.rolandUS.com
www.sabianltd.com
www.samashmusic.com
www.selmer.com
www.steinway.com
www.thomastik-infeld.com
www.unitedmusical.com
www.usahorn.com
www.vandoren.com
www.vicfirth.com
www.wwandbw.com
www.yahama.com
www.yahama.com/band
www.yahamadrums.com
www.zildjian.com

SECTION IV: INSTRUCTIONAL VIDEOS

Drums Set Videos

Bellson, Louie, *The Musical Drummer,* Warner Bros. Publications. VHS.

Bissonette, Gregg, *Playing, Reading and Soloing With a Band,* Warner Bros. Publications.

Cameron, Clayton, *Live at PAS,* Warner Bros. Publications.

Cameron, Clayton, *The Living Art of Brushes,* Warner Bros. Publications.

Carter, Allen, *The Developing Drummer,* AC Muzik. CD.

Chambers, Dennis, *In the Pocket,* Warner Bros. Publications.

Chambers, Dennis, *Serious Moves,* Warner Bros. Publications.

Cobham, Billy, *Drums by Design,* Warner Bros. Publications.

Erskine, Peter, *Everything Is Timekeeping and Timekeeping 2,* Warner Bros. Publications.

Gadd, Steve, *In Session,* Warner Bros. Publications.

Gadd, Steve, *Live at PAS,* Warner Bros. Publications.

Gadd, Steve, *Up Close,* Warner Bros. Publications.

Gadd, Steve, and Giovanni Hidalgo, *Modern Drummer Festival,* Warner Bros. Publications.

Gatzen, Bob, *Drum Tuning,* Warner Bros. Publications.

Hakim, Omar, *Express Yourself,* Warner Bros. Publications.

Hakim, Omar, *Let It Flow,* Warner Bros. Publications.

Houghton, Steve, *The Complete Rhythm Section,* Warner Bros. Publications.

Houghton, Steve, *The Drummer's Guide to Reading Drum Charts,* Warner Bros. Publications.

Houghton, Steve, *Drum Set Masterclass,* Warner Bros. Publications.

Houghton, Steve, *Drums in the Rhythm Section,* Warner Bros. Publications.

Jones, Elvin, *Different Drummer,* Warner Bros. Publications. VHS.

Kennedy, Will, *Be a Drumhead,* Warner Bros. Publications.

Krupa, Gene, *Jazz Legend,* Warner Bros. Publications.

Legends of Jazz Drumming, Part 1, 1920–1950, Warner Bros. Publications.

Legends of Jazz Drumming, Part 2, 1950–1970, Warner Bros. Publications.

Miller, Russ, *The Drum Set Crash Course,* Warner Bros. Publications.

New Orleans Drumming, Boxed Set, Warner Bros. Publications.

Rich, Buddy, *Jazz Legend,* Part 1 and 2, Warner Bros. Publications.

Rich, Buddy, *Memorial Concert,* 1, 2, 3, and 4, Warner Bros. Publications.

Roach, Max, *In Concert and in Session,* Warner Bros. Publications.

Smith, Steve, *Steve Smith Video,* Warner Bros. Publications.

Soph, Ed, *The Drum Set—Ed Soph,* JA Jazz.

Soph, Ed, and Harold Arnold, *The Drumset: A Musical Approach,* Warner Bros. Publications.

Thigpen, Ed, *The Essence of Brushes,* Warner Bros. Publications.

Various artists, *Developing a Groove,* Warner Bros. Publications.

Weckl, Dave, *Back to Basics,* Warner Bros. Publications.

Zoro, *The Commandments of R&B Drumming,* Warner Bros. Publications. 3-video set.

Latin Percussion Videos

Acuna, Alex, *Live at PAS,* Warner Bros. Publications.

Acuna, Alex, *Drums and Percussion,* Warner Bros. Publications.

Acuna, Alex, *South American, Caribbean, African and American Jazz,* Warner Bros. Publications.

Adolfo, Antonio, *Secrets of Brazilian Music.* Instruction on rhythm section roles in Brazilian music. Advanced for drums, timbales, congas.

Berroa, Ignacio, *Mastering the Art of Afro-Cuban Drumming,* Warner Bros. Publications.

Changuito (Jose Luis Quintana), *Evolution of the Tumbadoras,* History and techniques of playing congas (in English and Spanish), Warner Bros. Publications.

Changuito (Jose Luis Quintana), *The History of Songo,* Instruction on drum set, congas, and timbales (in English and Spanish), Warner Bros. Publications.

Conte, Luis, *Live at PAS,* Afro, Warner Bros. Publications.

Hernandez, Horacio "El Negro," *Festival: Horacio "El Negro" Hernandez,* Warner Bros. Publications.

Hidalgo, Giovanni, *Conga Virtuoso,* Advanced techniques on congas and rhythms of Puerto Rico in English and Spanish, Warner Bros. Publications.

Hidalgo, Giovanni, *In the Tradition,* Basic sounds, tuning and techniques, and patterns - (in English and Spanish), Warner Bros. Publications.

Hidalgo, Giovanni, *Mano a Mano (One on One),* Conga technique master class (in English and Spanish), Warner Bros. Publications.

Moreira, Airto, *Brazilian Percussion,* Warner Bros. Publications.

Moreira, Airto, *Listen and Play,* Warner Bros. Publications.

Sanabria, Bobby, *Getting Started on Congas: Basics,* Warner Bros. Publications.

Sanabria, Bobby, *Getting Started on Congas: Technique for One and Two Drums, Fundamento 1,* Warner Bros. Publications.

Sanabria, Bobby, *Getting Started on Congas: Technique for Two and Three Drums, Fundamento 2,* Advanced-level instruction on congas, Warner Bros. Publications.

Vibraphone Videos

Samuels, Dave, *Mallet Keyboard Musicianship,* Vols. 1 and 2, Masterplan, 1988. All levels.

Keyboard Videos

Bernhardt, Warren; Happy Traum; and Khosravi Cambiz, *You Can Play Jazz Piano! Video One: Getting Started; Video Two: Basic Keyboard Harmony;* and *Video Three: Soloing and Performing,* 90 min., Homespun Video, 1988, 1990.

Corea, Chick, *2-pac: Keyboard Workshop and Electric Workshop,* Warner Bros. Publications.

Corea, Chick, *Chick Corea: Electric Workshop,* 60 min., New York, DCI Music Video, 1988.

Corea, Chick, *Chick Corea: Keyboard Workshop,* 60 min., New York, DCI Music Video, 1987.

Dobbins, Bill, *The Evolution of Solo Jazz Piano, Part 1: Traditional Styles; Part 2: Modern Styles,* 100 min., Advance Music, 1990.

DeJohnette, Jack, *The Keith Jarrett Trio Concert,* 120 min., RCA Victor Video, 1993.

Duke, George, *Keyboard Improvisation,* Vol. 1, 60 min., DCI Music Video, Warner Bros. Publications, 1988. 2-video pack.

Ellington, Duke; Robert Drew; and Mike Jackson, *On the Road With Duke Ellington,* 58 min., Direct Cinema, 1980.

Evans, Bill; Chuck Israels; and Larry Bunker, *Jazz 625: Bill Evans Trio I & II,* 72 min., BBC Enterprise and TCB Releasing, published by VAP Video, 1994.

Fagen, Donald; Bernhardt Warren; and Traum Happy, *Playing, Writing and Arranging: Concepts for Jazz/Rock Piano,* 70 minutes, Homespun Video, 1993.

Hancock, Herbie, *Herbie Hancock Trio: Hurricane!,* 60 min., View Video.

Hines, Earl; Hawkins Coleman; and Genus Karl, *Jazz With Earl Hines & Coleman Hawkins,* 28 min., Rhapsody Films, 1986.

Houghton, Steve; Tom Warrington; Paul Viapiano, and Tom Ranier, *The Contemporary Rhythm Section,* 5 videos, 380 min., Warner Bros. Publications, 1992.

Jarrett, Keith; Gary Peacock; and Andy LaVerne, *Andy LaVerne's Guide to Modern Jazz Piano,* 2 volumes, 180 min., Homespun Video.

LaVerne, Andy, *Jazz Piano Standards*, 90 min., Homespun Video.

LaVerne, Andy; John Abercrombie; Steve LaSpina; and Jeff Hirshfield, *Andy LaVerne's Modern Jazz Piano for Solo or Group Playing,* 2 volumes, 180 min., Homespun Video, 1990.

Peterson, Oscar; Elitha Peterson; Sylvia Sweeney; Michael Allder; and William Cunningham, *Music in the Key of Oscar,* 95 min., National Film Board of Canada, 1992.

Radd, John and Richard Wolf, *Radd on Jazz Piano,* 106 min., University of Wisconsin-Madison, 1986.

Ranier, Tom, *Piano in the Rhythm Section,* Warner Bros. Publications.

Shearing, George, *Lullaby of Birdland,* 60 min., V.I.E.W. Video, 1992.

Tyner, McCoy, *McCoy Tyner,* recorded live at Warsaw Jazz Festival, 58 min., Lyra Productions/America, Inc., 1991, 1993.

Guitar Videos

Beyer, John; Herb Ellis; Charlie Byrd; and Barney Kessel, *Great Guitars,* recorded April 19, 1979, 59 min., Shanachie Entertainment, released 1994.

Beyer, John; Charlie Byrd; Herb Ellis; Barney Kessel; Joe Byrd; and Wayne Phillips, *Great Guitars,* recorded March 27, 1979, 58 min., Rhapsody Films, released 1995.

DiMeola, Al, *Al DiMeola,* 75 min., REH Publications, Inc., 1991.

Diorio, Joe; Martin Mayo; and Don Mock, *Creative Jazz Guitar,* 60 min., REH Video, 1989.

Ellis, Herb; Tal Farlow; and Charlie Byrd, *Tal Farlow, Herb Ellis & Charlie Byrd in Concert,* 80 min., Rounder Records, 1998.

Ellis, Herb; Martin Mayo; Steve Trovato; and Keith Wyatt, *Swing Jazz: Soloing & Comping,* 60 min., REH Video, 1989.

Henderson, Scott; Mayo Martin; and Trovato Steve, *Jazz Fusion Improvisation,* 60 min., REH Video, 1988.

Henderson, Scott, and Don Mock, *Melodic Phrasing,* 75 min., Warner Bros. Publications, 1992.

Houghton, Steve; Tom Warrington; Paul Viapiano; and Tom Ranier, *The Contemporary Rhythm Section,* Warner Bros Publications, 1997, 1992.

Kessel, Barney, *Jazz Guitar Improvisation:* 90 min., Rumark Video, Inc., 1985.

Kessel, Barney, *Jazz Guitar Improvisation: Chord-Melody Style*, 45 min., Rumark Video, 1986.

Kessel, Barney, *Jazz Guitar Improvisation: Progressive Concepts,* 53 min., Rumark Video, 1986.

Kessel, Barney; Wes Montgomery; Joe Pass; Herb Ellis; and Kenny Burrell, *Legends of Jazz Guitar,* Vol. 1, 60 min., Rounder Records, 1995.

Kessel, Barney; Wes Montgomery; Joe Pass; Kenny Burrell; Charlie Byrd; and Grant Green, *Legends of Jazz Guitar,* Vol. 2, 60 min., Rounder Records, 1995.

Kessel, Barney; Jim Hall; Herb Ellis; Tal Farlow; Pat Martino; and Charlie Byrd, *Legends of Jazz Guitar,* Vol. 3, 63 min., Rounder Records, 1995.

Martino, Pat, *Martino/Quantum Guitar/Concepts,* 75 min., Warner Bros. Publications.

Martino, Pat, *Martino/Quantum Guitar/Analysis,* 70 min., Warner Bros. Publications.

Martino, Pat, *Pat Martino/Highlights,* 30 min., Warner Bros. Publications.

Martino, Pat, and Don Mock, *Creative Force,* Parts 1 and 2, 180 min., Warner Bros. Publications, 1993.

Martino, Pat, *Creative Force: Boxed Set,* 180 min., Warner Bros. Publications.

Mock, Don, *Beyond Basics/Jazz Guitar Rhythm Chops,* Warner Bros. Publications.

Pass, Joe, *An Evening With Joe Pass,* 90 min., REH Video, 1994.

Pass, Joe and Don Mock, *Jazz Lines,* 60 min., REH Video, 1989.

Pass, Joe, *Joe Pass* two-pack/boxed set including *An Evening With Joe Pass* and *Jazz Lines,* 150 min., Warner Bros. Publications.

Randall, Elliott, *On Guitar: Part I, Style and Technique,* 65 min., Music Video, Warner Bros. Publications.

Schmid, Will, *Beginning Guitar,* 60 min., Hal Leonard Publications, 1986.

Scofield, John, *Jazz-Funk Guitar I,* 65 min., distributed by Warner Bros. Publications, 1992.

Scofield, John, *Jazz-Funk Guitar II,* 63 min., DCI Music Video, 1992.

Scofield, John, *John Scofield on Improvisation,* 60 min., DCI Music Video, 1983 or 1984.

Strong, Clint, *Mastering Jazz Licks,* 90 min., Warner Bros. Publications.

Viapiano, Paul, *Guitar in the Rhythm Section,* Warner Bros. Publications.

Electric Bass/Acoustic Bass Videos

Bailey, Steve, *Steve Bailey: Fretless Bass,* 90 min., Warner Bros. Publications.

Bailey, Steve; Victor Wooten; Keith Wyatt; and Don Mock, *Bass Extremes Live,* 107 min., CPP Media Group, originally produced by REH Video in 1993, 1994.

Deardorf, Chuck (host); Jaco Pastorius, John Patitucci; Victor Wooten; and Steve Bailey, *Chuck Deardorf: Bass Tips,* 48 min., Warner Bros. Publications.

Egan, Mark, and Danny Gottlieb, *Bass Workshop,* 61 min., New York, DCI Music Video, 1989.

Jackson, Randy, *Mastering the Groove,* 58 min., Warner Bros. Publications.

Kaye, Carol, *Carol Kaye Electric Bass Video,* 150 min., Camelot-Gwyn Pub., 1986.

Pastorius, Jaco, and Jerry Jemmott, *Jaco Pastorius: Modern Electric Bass,* 90 min., DCI Music Video, distributed by Warner Bros. Publications, 1989.

Patitucci, John, *Bass Day New York 97,* 66 min., DCI Music Video Productions, Inc.

Patitucci, John, *Electric Bass: A Dictionary of Grooves and Techniques,* 85 min., Warner Bros. Publications.

Patitucci, John, *Electric Bass 2: Soloing, Ear-Training and Six-String Technique,* 70 min., Warner Bros. Publications, 2-pack.

Patitucci, John, *Patitucci/Electric Bass 1 Spanish (Bajo Eléctrico – Diccionario de "Grooves" y Técnica Video),* with Spanish subtitles, 85 min., Warner Bros. Publications.

Patitucci, John, and Dave Weckl, *John Patitucci: Electric Bass 1 (Intermediate) & 2 (Advanced),* 155 min., DCI Music Video Productions, Inc., 1989, 1990.

Rainey, Chuck, *Chuck Rainey: Fusion Bass,* 70 min., Warner Bros. Publications, 1993.

Reid, Rufus, and Michael Moore, *Bass Day 97: Featuring Rufus Reid & Michael Moore,* Warner Bros. Publications.

Swan, Paul, *Electric Bass Fingerings,* SWAN Software, Apple II+, IBM.

Warrington, Tom, *Tom Warrington: Bass in the Rhythm,* Warner Bros. Publications.

Willis, Gary, *Progressive Bassics,* 60 min., Warner Bros. Publications.

Wooten, Victor, *Super Bass Solo Technique,* 70 min., Warner Bros. Publications.

Saxophone Videos

Allard, Joe, and Jay Weinstein, *The Master Speaks: Joe Allard's Saxophone and Clarinet Principles,* 35 min., American Production Services, 1988.

Eastwood, Clint; Forest Whitaker; Diane Venora; Michael Zelniker; Samuel Wright; and Keith David, *Bird,* 161 min., Warner Home Video, originally released as a motion picture in 1988, 2001.

Getz, Stan, *Vintage Getz,* two cassettes 108 min., A*Vision Entertainment, filmed in California in 1983, 1990.

Gregory, Dick; Don Murray; Diane Varsi; and Robert Hooks, *Sweet Love, Bitter,* 1966 film based on the life of Charlie "Bird" Parker, Rhapsody Films, 1992.

Jacquet, Illinois; Arthur Elgort; and Ronit Avneri, *Texas Tenor: The Illinois Jacquet Story,* 81 min., Rhapsody Films, 1991, 2000.

Liebman, Dave, and Gene Perla, *The Complete Guide to Saxophone Sound Production,* 143 min., Caris Music Services, 1989.

Marienthal, Eric, *Modern Sax,* 74 min., DCI Music Video, 1991.

Marienthal, Eric, *Play Sax From Day One,* 61 min., DCI Music Video, 1991.

Marienthal, Eric, *Tricks of the Trade,* 70 min., Warner Bros. Publications.

Marsalis, Branford; Burrill Crohn; and Michael Chertok, *Reed Royalty,* 58 min., Video Artists International, 1992.

Monk, Thelonious, and Charlotte Zwerin, *Thelonious Monk: Straight No Chaser,* 90 min., Warner Home Video, 1988, 1992.

Mulligan, Gerry, *Gerry Mulligan: A Master Class on Jazz and Its Legendary Players,* 68 min., Hal Leonard, 1995.

Tavernier, Bertrand; David Rayfiel; Herbie Hancock; Dexter Gordon; François Cluzet; Haker, Gabrielle; Bobby Hutcherson; Lonette McKee; and Martin Scorsese, *'Round Midnight,* 132 min., Warner Home Video, 2001.

Trumpet Videos

Armstrong, Louis, Gary Giddins; Hattie Winston; and Melvin Van Peebles, *Satchmo: Louis Armstrong,* 86 min., CMV Enterprises.

Baker, Chet; Bruce Weber; and Nan Bush, *Let's Get Lost,* Columbia Video.

Beiderbecke, Bix; Richard Basehart; and Brigitte Berman, *Bix: Ain't None of Them Play Like Him Yet*, 116 min., Playboy Home Video.

Davis, Miles, *Miles Ahead: The Music of Miles Davis*, 60 min., produced by WNET/Thirteen in association with Obenhaus Films, Inc., Toby Byron/Multiprises.

Gillespie, Dizzy; Bryan Elsom; and Leonard G. Feather, *A Night in Tunisia: A Musical Portrait of Dizzy Gillespie*, 28 min., View Video, Educational Video Network, 1990.

Gillespie, Dizzy, and Billy Eckstine, *Things to Come*, 55 min., Vintage Jazz Classics, 1993.

Hirt, Al, *Jazz Then—Dixieland, 1 & 2*, 60 min., Century Home Video, 1983.

Marsalis, Wynton, *Blues and Swing*, 79 min., distributed by Clearvue/eav, 1988.

Marsalis, Wynton; Yo-Yo Ma; Daniel Anker; Laura Mitgang; and Michael Lindsay-Hogg, *Tackling the Monster: Marsalis on Practice*, 53 min., Sony Classical Film and Video, 1995.

Marsalis, Wynton; Seiji Ozawa; Daniel Anker; Laura Mitgang; and Gary Bradley, *Listening for Clues: Marsalis on Form*, 53 min., Sony Classical Film & Video, 1995.

Marsalis, Wynton; Eric Reed; Mark Inouye; Seiji Ozawa; Daniel Anker; Laura Mitgang; Michael Lindsay-Hogg; John Philipp Sousa; Scott Joplin; Louis Armstrong, *Sousa to Satchmo: Marsalis on the Jazz Band*, 54 min., Sony Classical Film & Video, 1995.

Marsalis, Wynton; Seiji Ozawa, *Marsalis on Music: Marsalis on Rhythm/Why Toes Tap*, 54 min., Sony Classical Film & Video, 1995.

McNeil, John; Ron Vincent; Dean Johnson; Bill McHenry; and Carlton Holmes, *A Unique Approach to Improvising on Chords and Scales*, 53 min., International Production Group, Inc., 2000.

McNeil, John; Ron Vincent; Rufus Reid; Bill McHenry; and Carlton Holmes, *Becoming an Improviser: Creative Practice With Chords and Scales*, 56 min., International Production Group, Inc., 2001.

Spera, Dominic; Richard Wolf; James Madison; and William Endle, *Spera on Jazz*, 160 min., University of Wisconsin at Madison, 1986.

Terry, Clark, and Major Holley, *Trumpet Course: Beginner-Intermediate With Clark Terry*, 50 min., Kultur International Films, 1981, 1990.

Vizzutti, Allen, *Steps to Excellence: A Trumpet Clinic*, 60 min., Yamaha Musical Products, 1984.

Trombone Videos

Johnson, J. J.; Jamey Aebersold; Phil DeGreg; Tyrone Wheeler; and Art Gore, *J. J. Johnson in Concert*, 120 min., JA Jazz, Inc., recorded live February 1, 1991.

Rosolino, Frank, and Shelly Manne, *Frank Rosolino/Shelly Manne: Trombone and Drums*, 45 min., Green Line Video (1958–1963), 1991.

Transcribing Videos

Liebman, Dave; Gene Perla; Caris Visentin Liebman; and Gunnar Mossblad, *The Improviser's Guide to Transcription*, Caris Music Services.

Improvisation Videos

Argersinger, Charles, *Master Class Series: Approaches to Improvisation*, Master Class Productions. Intermediate.

Spera, Dominic, *Spera on Jazz*, University of Wisconsin at Madison. Beginner/Intermediate.

Taylor, Billy, *Billy Taylor on Improvisation on Piano*, Music Education Video. Intermediate.

MIDI Videos

Muro, Don, *An Overview of Electronic Musical Instruments*, J. D. Wall Publishing.

Untangling MIDI, Part One, Hal Leonard Publications. All levels.

Rock Ensemble Technique Videos

Hancock, Herbie, *RockSchool*, Vols. 1–6, Warner Home Video.

Non-Instructional DVDs

Many jazz DVDs are available. This list is a sampling.

Abercrombie/Erskine/Mintzer/Patitucci Band, Hal Leonard.

Baker, Chet, *Live at Ronnie Scott's*, JA Jazz. Video/DVD.

Basie, Gillespie, Coltrane, JA Jazz.

Bird, JA Jazz.

Bix, JA Jazz.

Burns, Ken, *Jazz: A Film by Ken Burns*, PBS Home Video.

Casino Lights '99, JA Jazz.

Davis, Miles, *Live in Montreal*, JA Jazz.

Dizzy's Dream Band, JA Jazz.

Frank, Dave, *Breakthrough to Improv*, JA Jazz.

Gillespie, Dizzy, *A Night in Chicago*, JA Jazz.

Gordon, Dexter, *'Round Midnight*, JA Jazz.

A Great Day in Harlem, JA Jazz.

Jarrett, Keith, *The Open Theatre East, 1993*, JA Jazz.

Jazz Casual—Basie, Gillespie, Coltrane, JA Jazz.

Jazz Casual—McRea, Torme, Rushing, JA Jazz.

Jazz Scene U.S.A., JA Jazz.

Lady Day: The Many Faces of Billie Holiday, JA Jazz.

Legends of Jazz Guitar, Vol. 1, JA Jazz.

Leibman, David, *Understanding Jazz Rhythm: The Concept of Swing*, JA Jazz.

Liebman, David, *Improviser's Transcription Guide*, JA Jazz.

Marsalis, Wynton, *Marsalis on Music: Listening for Clues*, JA Jazz.

Metheny, Herbie Hancock, Jack DeJohnette, Dave Holland in Concert, JA Jazz.

Metheny, Pat, *Group—We Live Here*, JA Jazz.

Metheny, Pat, *Secret Story*, JA Jazz.

Mingus, Charles, *Triumph of the Underdog*, JA Jazz.

Modern Drummer Festival 2000, JA Jazz.

Monk, Thelonious, *Straight, No Chaser*, JA Jazz.

Mulligan, Gerry, *Workshop Video*, Hal Leonard.

Nancy Wilson at Carnegie Hall, JA Jazz.

Pass, Joe, *The Genius Of*, JA Jazz.

Rollins, Sonny, *Saxophone Colossus*, JA Jazz.

Steps Ahead—Tokyo Live, JA Jazz.

Swing, Swing, Swing, Hal Leonard Publications.

The Genius of Joe Pass, JA Jazz.

The Singer's Toolbox, JA Jazz.

Torme, Rushing, McRae, JA Jazz.

Grover Washington, Jr., *In Concert*, JA Jazz.

Grover Washington, Jr., *Standing Room Only*, JA Jazz.

Non-Instructional Videos

Thousands of jazz videos are available today. This list is a sampling.

Airto and Flora Purim: Latin Jazz All-Stars, Hal Leonard Publications.

Akiyoshi, Toshiko, *Toshiko Akiyoshi Orchestra: Strive for Jive*, JA Jazz.

Brubeck, Dave, *Jazz Casual*, Rhino Records.

Buddy Rich: Live at Montreal Jazz Festival, Hal Leonard.

Classic Drum Solos and Battles, JA Jazz.

Davis, Miles, *Live in Montreal*, JA Jazz.

Dexter Gordon Quartet, Hal Leonard Publications.

Dizzy Gillespie: A Night in Tunisia, Hal Leonard Publications.

Evans, Gil, *Gil Evans and His Orchestra*, JA Jazz.

Gillespie and Eckstine, *Things to Come*, JA Jazz.

Hampton, Lionel, *Lionel Hampton's Jazz Circle*, JA Jazz.

Hampton, Lionel, *Lionel Hampton: One Night Stand*, The Jazz Store.

Harris, Barry, *Spirit of Bebop*, JA Jazz.

In Concert: Pat Metheny/Herbie Hancock/Jack DeJohnette/Dave Holland, JA Jazz.

Kirk, Rahsann, *Roland Kirk: The One Man Twins*, JA Jazz.

Latino Session, JA Jazz.

Lewis, Mel, *Mel Lewis and His Big Band*, JA Jazz.

McCann, Les, and Eddie Harris, *Swiss Movement*, JA Jazz.

New Orleans: Louis Armstrong and Billie Holiday, JA Jazz.

Oscar Peterson: Music in the Key of Oscar, Hal Leonard Publications.

Rich, Buddy – At the Top, JA Jazz.

Rollins, Sonny – Jazz Casual, JA Jazz.

Rushing, Jimmy, *Jazz Casual*, JA Jazz.

Tony Bennett's New York, JA Jazz.

Torme, Mel, *Jazz Casual*, JA Jazz.

Witherspoon, Jimmy, and Ben Webster, *Jazz Casual*, JA Jazz.

Zoot Sims Quartet and Shelly Manne Quartet, JA Jazz.

APPENDIX B
CONTRIBUTING AUTHORS

Jennifer Shelton Barnes is a highly sought-after jazz vocalist, educator, clinician, and arranger throughout the United States and Canada. She has taught privately and directed *DownBeat* magazine award-winning vocal jazz ensembles at universities for more than ten years, including Western Michigan University, the University of Miami, Northern Illinois University, and Chicago College of the Performing Arts at Roosevelt University. She has served as a guest conductor for district and all-state music festivals (including Illinois, Wisconsin, Arizona, Washington, and Oregon) and has taught jazz vocals at the Jamey Aebersold Jazz Camps for four years. Her vocal arrangements are published by UNC Jazz Press. In addition to her teaching activities, Jennifer is an active performer having recently released her debut CD recording, *You Taught My Heart* (available on her own label through Amazon.com), comprised of jazz standards from both the instrumental and vocal traditions. She has extensive experience in commercial studio work as well as live performances with big bands and small groups at jazz clubs in Chicago and throughout the Midwest. Jennifer earned a master of music degree in studio music and jazz performance from the University of Miami, Florida, and a bachelor of music degree from Western Michigan University.

Lindsey Blair is a guitarist highly in demand. He has performed with Maynard Ferguson, David Liebman, Dizzy Gillespie, John Secada, Bob Mintzer, and Arturo Sandoval, among others. He has taught at prestigious guitar schools including the Dick Grove School of Music and the Guitar Institute. Currently he teaches guitar and electric guitar at Florida International University in Miami.

Arthur Dawkins is professor of music and director of jazz studies at Howard University. As saxophonist and woodwind doubler, his performance credits include the Smithsonian Jazz Masterworks Orchestra, the National Symphony Orchestra, and theater pit orchestras. He is a member of the International Association of Jazz Educators (IAJE) Resource Team.

Marcia Dunscomb is a composer, author, educator, and pianist. Her works in print include *Melody Maker*, *Evolution of Jazz* and *Anatomy of Music* (McGraw-Hill). She is a contributing author for *Jazz Pedagogy: The Jazz Educator's Handbook and Resource Guide*, (J. Richard Dunscomb and Dr. Willie Hill, Jr., Warner Bros. Publications); *Teaching Jazz - A Course of Study* (MENC/IAJE), *Jazz Studies Guide* (MTNA/IAJE); and numerous other publications. Frequently called upon as a clinician and adjudicator, Mrs. Dunscomb has been one of the foremost pioneers in the field of teaching jazz and improvisation to young children. She has presented for many organizations, including the IAJE; the National Piano Foundation, and the Stan Kenton Summer Jazz Camps. She is a member of the Resource Team and Curriculum Committee for the International Association of Jazz Educators, and has served as a faculty member of the Teacher Training Institute sponsored by the IAJE and MENC.

Allan R. Kaplan is director of jazz studies and trombone professor at New Mexico State University. Dr. Kaplan's education includes bachelor and master of music degrees from the Manhattan School of Music and a Ph.D. in music education from New York University/Manhattan School of Music. From 1975 to 1989 he was principal trombone of the Oklahoma Symphony Orchestra. Previous to that position, he performed in Broadway musicals, as solo trombone of the Goldman Band and at Lincoln Center and was a member of the New York Brass Choir. In addition, Dr. Kaplan has a strong background as a public school music educator. Dr. Kaplan has recorded on the Angel label with Maestro Herrera de la Fuente, on the MENC video series *The World's Greatest Music,* on various labels with the Goldman Band, with the Light Fantastic Players, and with Richie Havens. In the commercial music field, he has performed with artists such as Lena Horne, Burt Bacharach, Sammy Davis Jr., Henry Mancini, Mel Torme, Cher, The Oak Ridge Boys, Peggy Lee, and Sarah Vaughan. He is a member of the Quintessential Brass Quintet and an Edwards/Getzen clinician.

Kimberly McCord is assistant professor of music at Illinois State University. She received her doctorate in music education with a secondary emphasis in music technology from the University of Northern Colorado. Previous to going to ISU, she taught at Western Connecticut State University and the Denver Public Schools. McCord is a frequent presenter on jazz improvisation in the general classroom, music technology in K–12 music, and special needs children and music. She is co-authoring a soon-to-be published jazz improvisation method for elementary general music. Her articles are included in *Music Educators Journal, The New Grove Dictionary of Jazz, The Jazz Educators Journal, The Jazz Educators Research Journal, Journal of Technology in Music Learning,* and *Technological Directions in Music Education.* In collaboration with Margaret Fitzgerald, a chapter on their collaborative research project appeared in the MENC publication; *Music Makes the Difference.* McCord is a co-author of *Strategies for Teaching: Technology by MENC.* She has been a member of the IAJE Teacher Training Institute faculty for four years and serves IAJE as coordinator for general music and as a member of the general music resource team.

Bill McFarlin has been associated with the administration of the IAJE since 1984. He served as IAJE executive administrator until 1986 and as executive director from 1986 to 1993. From 1993 to 1995, he was director of administration and education for Learning Resources Network (LERN), the world's largest association in the field of lifelong learning, and then returned to IAJE in 1996. As chief executive officer, Bill is responsible for the association's management and serves as a member of the IAJE Executive Board. Prior to joining IAJE in 1984, Bill served on the administration of Blue Lake Fine Arts Camp, a non profit arts organization based in Western Michigan. Among his responsibilities was management of Blue Lake's 100,000-watt National Public Radio station (WBLV-FM), coordination of the summer camp's jazz instruction program, and direction of their 6,000-seat performing arts facility. A graduate of Boston's Berklee College of Music, Bill has performed or recorded with numerous artists and entertainers including Dizzy Gillespie, Mel Torme, Pearl Bailey, Lena Horne, Bob Hope, and Red Skelton. Bill has served as a member of the National Endowment for the Arts Jazz and Music Overview Panels, has presented and moderated panels at numerous industry conferences, and has served as an adjudicator at educational jazz festivals throughout North America. He is a recipient of the IAJE Lawrence Berk Leadership Award, the IAJE Presidents Award, and the Berklee College of Music Distinguished Alumni Award. Bill is an active member of the American Society of Association Executives, Phi Mu Alpha Sinfonia, the MENC, and the American Federation of Musicians.

Bob Montgomery is an internationally recognized performing artist, having appeared throughout Europe, Scandinavia, Australia, Canada, China, Mexico, Japan, and the United States. Bob has toured Europe with Clark Terry's Big Bad Band; served as artist-in-residence in Adelaide, South Australia; appeared as featured soloist with the Albuquerque Jazz Orchestra for the International Trumpet Guild; and appeared at Town Hall in New York City with Clark Terry for the New York JVC Jazz Festival's tribute to Clark Terry. Bob's reputation as an educator has earned him many awards, including Teacher of the Year, Jazz Educator and Performer of the Year, and Colorado Jazz Educator of the Year. Bob has served both Kansas and Colorado as state IAJE president, and he has directed all-state jazz ensembles in Colorado, Kansas, Arizona, Iowa, and Oklahoma. Bob was founder and director of Clark Terry's All American Jazz Camp and Rich Mattison's Mile High Jazz Camp; executive director of Colorado Jazz Workshops, Inc.; and a member of the board of trustees for the International Foundation for Jazz. Bob is a national artist/clinician for the Yamaha Musical Instrument Company.

Peter Olstad has toured playing lead and jazz trumpet with the bands of Buddy Rich, Maynard Ferguson, Woody Herman, Tommy Dorsey, and Mel Torme. He has more than 20 years of experience as a freelance trumpet player both in Los Angeles and New York, playing in almost every kind of musical situation possible—from Broadway shows to avant-garde jazz. He is currently playing lead trumpet for Tom Jones on his world tour and is a clinician and performing artist for Yamaha.

Michael Orta, jazz pianist, has been very active on the jazz scene. He recorded two albums with his jazz/fusion group The Wave on the Atlantic Jazz record label. This outfit also displayed his compositional abilities. In 1991, Michael toured as pianist for the Arturo Sandoval group as well as recording on Sandoval's American debut album on GRP, *Flight to Freedom*. In 1993, Michael was chosen as one of five finalists in the prestigious Great American Jazz Piano Competition. In 1994, Michael spent the year touring and recording with the Paquito D'Rivera group. He played concerts and clubs in Trinidad, Curaçao, Mexico, Puerto Rico, Paris, Germany, Switzerland, Poland, Romania, Greece, Holland, and Slovenia. Michael has also been an active clinician, sharing his musical knowledge and philosophies with music students in the U.S., Europe, Africa, and South America. Michael is assistant professor of jazz studies/piano at Florida International University, teaching jazz piano, jazz improvisation, and directing both jazz and salsa ensembles. Michael has released his debut album, *Freedom Tower,* on the Fantasy/Contemporary label.

Nicky Orta has performed/recorded with some of the top names in jazz, such as Randy Brecker, James Moody, Bob Mintzer, Arturo Sandoval, Paquito D'Rivera, Dave Weckl, Othello Molineaux, and many others. In the Latin genre he has performed/recorded with the likes of Julio Iglesias, Gloria Estefan, Alejandro Fernandez, Carlos Ponce, and others. As an active participant in the field of jazz education, he has given clinics in the United States, Central and South America, Europe, and Africa. From 1992 to 1994 he co-organized three successful Jazz Bass Conferences in Miami, Florida. He was interviewed by *Bass Player* magazine (*Bull Ring Bass With Julio Iglesias* and *Bass Notes* in July 1996). He also appeared in *Jazz Player* magazine (Nov./Dec. 1994) and *BD Guide* (*Latin Jazz: It's Not What You May Think.* Nov./Dec. 1993) as a contributing author. He is currently an adjunct faculty member at Florida International University where he teaches jazz bass and jazz improvisation.

Remy Taveras is a much sought-after jazz drummer. One of the young jazz lions, he began his musical career as a classical percussionist in his native Dominican Republic where he became a member of the professional Dominican Symphony. He studied jazz drums at the Musicians Institute in Los Angeles, California and Florida International University in Miami, Florida. He has performed with Arturo Sandoval, Paquito D'Rivera, David Sanborn, John Fedchock, Nestor Torres, and Tito Puente, to name just a few.

Jerry Tolson teaches music education and jazz studies at the University of Louisville where he directs instrumental and vocal jazz ensembles and teaches jazz pedagogy classes. A graduate of Drake University and the University of North Texas, Tolson is active nationally as a clinician, adjudicator, guest conductor, and jazz camp instructor. He is also active as a jazz composer/arranger. His vocal jazz charts are published by UNC Jazz Press. Performing on flute, saxophone, keyboards, and vocals, Tolson leads three jazz/popular music groups and has done freelance work with many top names in the entertainment business. Tolson has been named to *Who's Who Among America's Teachers* and has been the recipient of the Kentucky Music Educators College Teacher of the Year award.

Chris Vadala is one of this country's foremost woodwind artists and is in demand as a jazz/classical performer and educator. Professor Vadala is currently director of jazz studies and professor of saxophone at the University of Maryland. He has appeared on more than 100 recordings to date, including five Gold and two Platinum, as well as for innumerable jingle sessions and film and TV scores. A graduate of the Eastman School of Music, he earned the performer's certificate in saxophone as well as a B.M. in music education. He received an M.A. in clarinet from Connecticut College in addition to post-graduate study at Eastman School of Music.

GLOSSARY

by Marcia F. Dunscomb

A cappella - Without instrumental accompaniment.

AABA form - A musical form (usually 32 bars) form in which the melody A is stated twice, followed by a contrasting melody B referred to as the bridge, followed by a restatement of the first melody A.

Acoustic - Without any artificial amplification.

Afro-Cuban jazz - A style of jazz that is a blend of Afro-Cuban folk music and bebop. Usually the Afro-Cuban elements are in the rhythm section and the bebop elements are played by the horns.

Angular melodies - Melodies with wide leaps and sudden changes of direction. Typical of bebop improvisations.

Articulation - See *jazz articulation*.

Back line - The rhythm section of a jazz ensemble.

Backbeat - Strong accents on the second and fourth beats of the measure.

Backgrounds - Patterns or supporting music played behind a soloist by sections of the band.

Balance - To bring into proportion melody, harmony, and rhythm.

Ballad - A slow, usually lyrical composition.

Bebop (bop) - A style of jazz originated by jazz musicians Charlie Parker and Dizzy Gillespie. Identifiable by rapid tempos; complex harmonies; angular, highly syncopated, dissonant melodies; and improvisations based on the chord changes rather than the melody.

Basie style - Refers to the unique characteristic, sound, and relaxed feel of the Count Basie Band. The Basie Band was a popular big band during the 1940s through the 1970s.

Big band - A jazz ensemble that traditionally includes five saxes, four trumpets, four trombones, and a rhythm section of piano, bass, drums, and sometimes guitar.

Blues - A type of vocal or instrumental music, usually constructed in a 12-bar, three-phrase form.

Blues scale - A six-note scale used extensively in jazz and blues styles. It is constructed from the following scale degrees from the major scale: 1-♭3-4-♭5-5-♭7.

Bombs - Accents played by the drummers that do not necessarily coincide with those played by the soloist or ensemble. Typically used in bebop-style improvisation.

Boogie woogie - Piano style with a repeating left-hand pattern that was copied from the early blues guitarists. Sometimes called eight-to-the-bar style or barrelhouse style.

Bossa nova - Dance music of Brazil that combines the samba with jazz.

Brazilian jazz - A blend of bebop with Brazilian folk music.

Break - Solo spot (usually about two measures) at the end of a chorus, usually the first chorus, where the ensemble stops playing and the soloist improvises.

Bridge - (1) The third eight-measure phrase in a 32-bar form. The bridge has different melody and different chord changes from the other three sections of this form. (2) The B section in a composition with AABA form.

Call-and-response - A simple musical idea that is played (call) and then in turn responded to with a similar musical idea (response).

Cha-cha-cha - A medium-slow dance that evolved from the Cuban *danzon* mambo.

Changes - The chord progression or harmony of a composition.

Chart - For jazz ensemble, the written composition or arrangement.

Choking - Muted playing on guitar.

Chops - Technical facility. A musician with chops has the ability to play with command on his or her instrument.

Chord alteration - The process of lowering or raising one or more notes in a chord.

Chord changes - A series of successive chords or harmony notes that accompany the melody of a tune.

Chord substitution - Reharmonizing a composition by replacing one chord with another.

Chord symbols - A shorthand notation that indicates the chord tones to be played. For example: Cmaj7 is spelled C E G B.

Chord voicing - Arrangement of chord tones as played by keyboardists and guitarists

Chorus - One time through the form of a composition.

Chromatic scale - A scale built with half steps.

Classic blues - Blues sung by a vocalist and accompanied by an ensemble, either a combo or a big band.

Clave - (1) A pair of round wooden sticks that are struck together as a rhythmic accompaniment in Latin-American music. (2) A rhythmic pattern. Literally means "key."

Collective improvisation - Two or more musicians improvising at the same time.

Combo - Small performing ensemble, usually consisting of a rhythm section and one or more horns.

Comp (comping) - A piano, vibraphone, or guitar style of playing the chord changes to accompany a soloist or sections of the ensemble.

Comping patterns - Rhythmic and harmonic patterns typically played by the piano and/or guitar.

Consonance/consonant - A group of two or more notes that are related harmonically and sound as if they fit together.

Cool jazz - A style of jazz with relaxed tempos and lots of open space in the melodies. The mood of cool music is more intellectual than emotional.

Cross-section voicing - An arranging technique for big band in which instruments from several sections play a harmonized line together to create different tone colors.

CuBop - Another name of Afro-Cuban jazz.

Cutting contest - A musical game of one-upmanship where the performers attempt to outdo each other.

Dance band - Another name for a swing band.

Diatonic improvisation - Improvisation that uses only notes that are in the diatonic scale.

Diatonic scale - An unaltered major or minor scale.

Dissonance/dissonant - A group of two or more notes that are not related harmonically and sound harsh. In jazz, the dissonance is used effectively to create tension, which is released when the dissonance is resolved.

Distortion - Inaccurate reproduction of sound. A technique used by electric guitarists and bassists as a special effect.

Dixieland - Early instrumental jazz usually indicating the Chicago style of traditional jazz.

Doo-wah - The sound produced by a brass player by passing either a hat or a plunger over the bell of the instrument creating an open or closed sound. Doo is notated with a "+" is the closed sound and wah notated with an "o" is the open sound.

Dorian mode - (1) A scale built on the second scale degree of a major scale (2) The Dorian scale can be realized by playing a major scale with lowered 3rd and 7th scale degrees.

Double - The ability to play more than one instrument. Usually the saxophonists will double on flute and/or clarinet.

Double time - When the music changes to a tempo exactly twice as fast as the original tempo. Double time is often used for the improvisation section of a ballad. Usually the chord progression continues at the original tempo.

Duo - A performance by two musicians.

Effects - Electronic devices that distort the natural sound of an instrument.

Embellishments - Common devices that are used in jazz improvisation, also called ornamentation.

Even eighth notes - A way of playing the eighth notes so they evenly divide the beat in half. Ragtime, jazz/rock fusion, and Latin jazz are played with even eighth notes.

EWI - Electronic wind instrument. A synthesizer that is played with a mouthpiece similar to a saxophone or clarinet that can reproduce the sound of many other instruments. EVI (Electronic Valve Instrument) is the version for a brass player.

Fakebook - Book containing a collection of lead sheets.

Fall - A special musical effect of falling or dropping off at the end of a note. Falls can be long or short.

Falsetto - Male vocalist singing in a very high range. Falsetto singing was an African tradition.

Field holler - A style of singing by plantation workers.

52nd Street - The street in Manhattan, New York, that was the center for the development of the bop style of jazz.

Fill - Improvised melodies or drum figures that are played in the open spaces of a musical arrangement.

Flamenco - A style of Spanish gypsy dance.

Flugelhorn - A brass wind instrument similar to the trumpet or cornet but larger. The flugelhorn has a conical bore and therefore a more mellow sound than a trumpet.

Form - The design pattern of a musical composition. Some common forms of jazz are 12-bar blues and 32-bar song form.

Freddie Green guitar style - Playing downstrokes on each of the four beats in a swing chart. The voicings he used were generally root, third, and seventh.

Free jazz - A style of playing jazz that is totally improvised. It is free from the constraints of form, chord changes, meter, melody, and so on.

Front line - The horn section of an early jazz instrumental ensemble. Instruments were usually cornet (or trumpet), clarinet, and trombone.

Fugue - A musical composition in which a theme is played by more than one voice. The theme is presented by each voice, one after the other, resulting in counterpoint.

Funky - A style of jazz with strong blues and gospel feel.

Fusion - Blending of two musical styles into a new style.

Ghost band - A band whose leader has died but which continues to perform using the leader's name.

Ghosted note - An unaccented note whereby the pitch and articulation are suggested or implied rather than played full.

Gig - Musician's term for a performing job.

Gospel - A type of music typical of Southern religious services.

Growl - A technique of humming while playing, used by horn players, to create a specific sound.

Guaguanco - One of the three styles of Cuban rumba, featuring a heightened polyrhythmic structure.

Hard bop - Modified form of bebop. Also known as mainstream or straight-ahead style.

Harmonic rhythm - The frequency of chord changes. In a basic blues, the harmonic rhythm is quite slow, often remaining on the same chord for several measures. In bebop, the harmonic rhythm is much faster, often with two or more chords per measure.

Harmony - The chord structure of a composition.

Head - The original melody and harmony of a composition.

Head arrangement - An arrangement for performance that is not written down. A typical head arrangement for a combo includes the introduction, head, two choruses sax solo, two choruses trumpet solo, head, and the ending.

Hi-hat cymbal (sock cymbal) - A pair of cymbals that are installed on a stand and operated by a foot pedal.

Hold back - To play on the backside of the beat, producing a relaxed feel.

Horn section - A group of the same instrument as the trumpet section (2–5 trumpets), sax sections (2–5 saxophones) and the trombone section (2–5 trombones).

Improvisation - The process of spontaneously creating new melody over the chord changes of a tune. Scales, chords, and melodies are guides.

Improvise/improvisation - To create a new melody while performing. Spontaneous composition.

Inside - Playing inside implies improvisation that uses many chord tones and has a consonant sound.

Instrumental solo - A performance by one instrument usually accompanied by the rhythm section.

Jam session - Musicians performing together without rehearsal.

Jazz - Music rooted in improvisation and characterized by syncopated rhythms, a steady beat, and distinctive tone colors and performance techniques. Developed in the United States from the musical and rhythmical roots of Africa, jazz blended with American and western European influences at the start of the twentieth century in New Orleans.

Jazz articulation - The attack or beginning of a note. For wind instruments, the jazz articulation usually begins with a D tongue syllable.

Jazz orchestra - A big band.

Jazz standard - A composition that that has endured the test of time and considered one that a jazz musician is expected to have memorized.

Jazz syllables - Phonetic sounds that imitate those made by wind players in the jazz idiom. Also known as scat syllables.

Kansas City swing - A swing style that emphasizes medium tempos and riff-like melodies.

Kicks - Accents played by the drummer that coincide with those played by the soloist or ensemble.

Lay back (laidback) - The relaxed feeling attained when a performer plays slightly behind the beat. The tempo does not slow down.

Latin jazz - A broad term used to describe the blend of Afro-Cuban, Brazil, and other Latin American music with jazz. A blend of jazz elements (usually bop) with elements from Latin-American folk music

Lay out - To rest or to stop playing for a portion of a piece.

Lead player - The musician in the section that other section members follow for style, dynamics, attack, and so on.

Lead sheet - The melody, chord changes, and sometime lyrics of a composition.

Lick - A riff or short musical idea.

Lyrical - A melody that is smooth and singable.

Lyrics - The words of a song.

Mainstream - Hard-bop or straight-ahead style jazz. Bop-flavored jazz.

Mambo - A typical Cuban dance rhythm played in an alla-breve feel. A dance of the Caribbean similar to the rumba.

Melodic extensions - Melodies using the upper extensions of the chord tones such as the ninth, eleventh, and thirteenth.

Melodic improvisation - An improvisational technique that uses various embellishments and rhythmic variation of an established melody.

Melodic sequence - Transposing a motive to different notes in the scale.

Melody - The arrangement of pitches that when combined with rhythm make the recognizable part of a tune.

Merengue - A Haitian and Dominican dance.

MIDI (Music Instrument Digital Interface) - A digital interface developed by keyboard instrument manufacturers to enable all brands to communicate with each other, as well as computers.

Mixolydian mode - (1) A scale built on the 5th scale degree of a major scale. (2) A major scale with the 7th degree lowered one half step.

Modal jazz - A compositional style where the music is based on one scale or mode rather than chord changes.

Mode - A musical scale built from the major scale with the tone center shifted to a different scale degree. The Dorian mode is built on scale degree two. The Mixolydian scale is built on scale degree five.

Monitor - A speaker used to project the amplified or reinforced sound back to the stage.

Montuno - A repeated, syncopated phrase played on the piano, usually two bars in length, played during improvisation sections in Latin jazz.

Musical Popular Brasileira - A name given to both Brazilian folk music and popular music.

Mute - Any device that is put over or in the bell of an instrument to change the sound. Various types of mutes are used, including: straight, cup, plunger, Harmon, bucket, and practice.

Ostinato - A repeating pattern.

Outside - Playing outside implies improvisation that uses many non-chord tones to create dissonance and increase tension.

Overdubbing - A process of recording in which several tracks are recorded one over the over. One performer can sing or play several parts on a recording by means of overdubbing.

Pentatonic scale - A five-note scale comprised of notes 1, 2, 3, 5, and 6 of a major scale.

Play in two - In a typical 4/4 meter, the rhythm section (the bass player plays two half notes per measure) will play only two beats per measure, producing a relaxed feel with less drive.

Polychord - More that two chords played at once or one chord stacked on top of another.

Polyrhythm - Two or more rhythm patterns being performed simultaneously.

Pops - Brass punches. Short, accented notes played by the trumpet and trombone section.

Pre-jazz - Any of the types of music that pre-dated jazz and eventually evolved into jazz styles.

Progressive jazz - Big bands playing modern jazz, frequently with additional instruments such as strings, French horns, and so on.

Pulse - A steady beat.

Quartet - A performing ensemble consisting of four musicians.

Quote - Use of a familiar melody during an improvised solo.

Ragtime - Piano style with stride left hand and highly syncopated right hand.

Re-harmonize - Substituting different chords for the original harmony of a composition. The result is usually a richer, more interesting sound.

Resolve - The movement of one chord to another usually from dissonance to consonance.

Rhythm - The duration of the pitches that, when combined with melody, gives us a recognizable tune.

Rhythm changes - The chord progression for Gershwin's "I Got Rhythm." Many tunes are based on these chord changes.

Rhythm section - The section of a jazz ensemble responsible for the harmony and tempo or time. Today's rhythm section usually consists of piano, bass, and drum set. It can also include guitar and Latin percussion.

Rhythmic displacement - Moving a rhythmic pattern to begin on a different beat of the measure.

Rhythmic improvisation - Using rhythm to improvise in the style of the selection.

Rhythmic punctuation - A comping style with short interjections by the piano or guitar player, which will add to the overall rhythmic energy.

Ride cymbal - A medium-sized cymbal usually suspended on a cymbal stand played with a stick. Used for playing ride patterns, particularly in swing-style jazz.

Ride patterns - The time-keeping patterns played on the ride cymbal by the drummer.

Riff - A short fragment of melody.

Rumba - A ballroom dance that originated in Cuba.

Rural blues/country blues - Usually sung by a male singer either unaccompanied or self-accompanied on banjo or guitar.

Salsa - A Caribbean music similar to the mambo. A term used in the late sixties and seventies to describe New York City's version of Afro-Cuban music.

Samba - An African dance that was modified into a ballroom dance in Brazil with a definite alla-breve or two feel.

Scat singing - To vocalize using jazz articulation syllables.

Shout chorus - The final tutti chorus, usually at a high level of volume and with much energy and excitement.

Shuffle rhythm - A way of playing swing eighths with a dotted-eighth feel. This rhythm is typical of Kansas City jazz styles.

Sideman - Any member of a performing ensemble who is not the leader or featured soloist.

Sit in - When a musician spontaneously joins a group to perform.

Slow swing style - A slow tempo style of swing with a triplet beat subdivision.

Sock cymbal - See *hi-hat cymbal*.

Soli - Unison or harmonized playing by a group of instruments.

Solo - (1) Performance by a single musician. (2) Featured performance by a single musician, usually accompanied by the rhythm section.

Son - A style of popular dance music combining Spanish and African elements.

Son montuno - One of the old traditional rhythms of Cuba. The tempo is medium to medium fast with either an alla-breve (two feel) or a 4/4 feel.

Songo - A contemporary Cuban style that blends elements of son, rumba, American jazz, and funk.

Sound reinforcement - Artificially increasing the volume.

Soundie - A low-budget short film featuring popular music of the 1940s. Soundies could be viewed on coin-operated machines called panorams that were found in public places.

Speakeasy - A nightclub that operated illegally during Prohibition. Many musicians found employment in speakeasies.

Stage band/jazz band - A jazz ensemble.

Steady beat - The pulse of the music.

Stomp - Repetition of a rhythmic figure within melodic figures.

Stop time - An effect where the rhythm section plays only on the downbeat of each measure or every other measure.

Straight-ahead - Hard bop, mainstream jazz style.

Straight-eighths - Even eighth notes.

Stride/stride-style piano - Piano style where the left hand plays with an "oom-pah" left hand (i.e., root-chord-root-chord) while the right hand is highly syncopated and improvisational.

Subdivide - Division of the pulse into smaller units.

Substitute chords - Chords that replace the original chords of a composition or are added to the original chords. The result is a more complex and more interesting harmonic structure.

Swing eighth notes - A concept of playing a group of two eighth notes so that the first is longer than the second (long-short). The second eighth note is actually played like the last third of a triplet and is slightly accented.

Swing-style - A style of jazz characterized by big band arrangements, sectional call-and-response, swing eighth notes, lyrical melodies, and dance-like tempos.

Syncopation - Displacing expected beats by either anticipating or delaying. An emphasis of rhythm that occurs by accenting beats that is normally weak.

Synthesizer - An instrument, usually a keyboard, that can electronically reproduce the sound of many other instruments.

Tailgate trombone - In parades, when the band played while riding on a wagon or a truck, the trombone player sat at the rear in order to have room to operate the slide. The early jazz style of trombone playing is referred to as tailgate trombone.

Third-stream jazz - A style of music that blends elements from European classical music with elements of jazz.

Timbre - The distinctive tone color or individual sound of an instrument or voice.

Time/time keeping - A solid tempo or pulse and rhythmic groove.

Time charts - Compositions written in unusual meters or in mixed meters.

Trading fours - A style of improvisation where four-measure solos alternate between two soloists or between one soloist and the ensemble. Typically a soloist will alternate four-measure solos with the drummer. Trading twos and trading eights is also common.

Traditional jazz - Early instrumental jazz. Sometimes called Dixieland.

Transcribe - The process of notating an improvised solo.

Trio - A performing ensemble consisting of three musicians.

Triplet feel - Subdividing a quarter note and implying a triplet.

Tritone substitution - Using the chord based on the raised fourth.

Turnaround - The chord progression at the end of a chorus that takes you back harmonically to the beginning of the next chorus. A turnaround is usually two measures long.

Tutti - All instruments playing together.

Twelve-bar blues form - A twelve-measure form consisting of three four-measure phrases.

Two-beat bass - A bass pattern that emphasizes two strong beats in each measure. Ragtime and some early instrumental jazz had a two-beat bass. Latin jazz often has a two-beat bass pattern.

Two feel - A relaxed style for rhythm section that emphasizes two strong beats per measure.

Unison lines - Two or more instruments (or voices) playing the same notes.

Unusual meters - Non-typical beat-groups for a composition. The most typical ones are 2, 3, or 4.

Upper extensions - Chords that go beyond the seventh scale tone. Upper extensions are the ninth, eleventh, and thirteenth of a chord.

Uptempo - fast.

Urban blues/city blues - Blues sung by a female singer, usually accompanied by a piano or a small combo.

Vamp - A repeated section of a song or arrangement.

Vibrato - Even and rapid fluctuation in pitch.

Vocalese - Lyrics written to fit the melody of a jazz improvisation.

Voicings - Arranging the notes in a piano or guitar chord.

Walking bass - A four-beat bass pattern that outlines the harmony.

Waltz - Originally a European dance. Jazz waltzes add syncopation.

Woodshed - To practice diligently.

INDEX

A

B

Vocal quartet, 181
Vocal with big band, 180, 181
Voicings, 105, 107, 154, 188, 189, 190, 193,
    194, 195, 197, 198, 201, 202, 228, 230, 232,
    235, 286, 300, 301, 311, 318, 331, 336, 337,
    338, 378, 385

W

Wackerman, Chuck, 32, 40
Walking bass, 385
Walking bass lines, 205, 206, 207, 209, 212,
    344, 345
Warrington, Tom, 345, 366
Washboard Rhythm Kings, 127
Washington Middle School, Seattle, WA, 31, 37
Watrous, Bill, 353
Weather Report, 23, 28, 93, 127, 128, 212,
    214, 232
West Ottawa High School, Holland, MI, 48
Wheaton, Dr. Jack, 296, 322
Whiteman, Paul, 19, 138, 141, 239
Williams, Patrick, 23, 147, 155, 214
Wilson, Gerald, 146
Wong, Dr. Herb, 296